UNIBANCO GUIDES

RIO DE JANEIRO

About This Guidebook

A team of professional researchers scoured Rio de Janeiro before selecting the hotels, restaurants, attractions, agencies, guides and other services listed in this *Rio de Janeiro Guide*. No compensation of any kind was accepted from the establishments mentioned, and the guidebook's sponsor exercised no editorial input or influence.
We categorize restaurants by price according to the cost of the most popular item on each eatery's menu plus a 10% service fee, which is the standard tipping rate in Brazil. Hotel price categories are based on the daily rate for a double-occupancy room. Addresses, phone numbers, business hours and prices came from the establishments themselves, and the Guide's researchers verified these data. The publisher is not responsible for any inaccuracies or changes that occur after the publication date. Business hours and service prices often change between high and low tourism seasons and should be confirmed in advance whenever possible.

Collaborator

Fernando Gabeira

Sponsor

UNIBANCO

2007

BEÏ
Rua Dr. Renato Paes de Barros, 717, 4º andar
CEP 04530-001 Itaim-Bibi São Paulo SP
Tel.: (11) 3089-8855 Fax: (11) 3089-8899
www.bei.com.br bei@bei.com.br

UNIBANCO GUIDES
RIO DE JANEIRO

BEĨ

All rights reserved by BEĨ

Concept, editing, cover,
graphic design and layout
BEĨ

Editing
BEĨ

Desktop Publishing
BEĨ

Project Consultant and Editor
Ben Harder

Associate Editors
Ankur Ghosh, Dan Epstein, Jenny Pegg,
Laura Martin, and Matt Kinsey

Translation
Alison Entrekin and Lynne Reay Pereira

Proofreading
Ben Harder

Maps and Illustrations
Alex Silva and Luiz Fernando Martini

Photography Coordination
Solange A. Barreira

BEĨ Team:
SENIOR EDITORS: Ana Luisa Martins,
Fabiana Pereira, Laura Aguiar,
Marcelo Pen, and Solange A. Barreira
EDITORIAL ASSISTANTS: Andressa Paiva,
Fernanda Quinta, and Laura Folgueira
DESIGN AND LAYOUT: Alexandre Costa,
Américo Freiria, and Yumi Saneshigue
DESIGN AND LAYOUT ASSISTANTS:
Paulo Albergaria and Rosilene de Andrade
GRAPHIC PRODUCTION: Luis Alvim
ADMINISTRATIVE STAFF: Ana Paula Guerra,
Gabriella Guimarães, and Gercílio Correa
SALES: Ana Maria Capuano and
Fernanda Gomensoro
PRESS AND PUBLIC RELATIONS:
Paula Poleto

Image Digitalization
and Processing
Pancrom

Printing
Pancrom

Dados Internacionais de Catalogação na Publicação (CIP)
(Câmara Brasileira do Livro, SP, Brasil)

Unibanco Guides Rio de Janeiro / concept, editing, cover, graphic design and layout BEĨ; translation Alison Entrekin; maps and illustrations Alex Silva and Luiz Fernando Martini. – São Paulo: BEĨ Comunicação, 2007.

Título original: Guia Unibanco Rio de Janeiro
ISBN 978-85-86518-76-8

1. Rio de Janeiro (Estado) – Guias 2. Turismo – Rio de Janeiro (Estado) 3. Viagens – Guias I. Silva, Alex. II. Martini, Luiz Fernando.

07-3633   CDD-918.168153

Índices para catálogo sistemático:

1. Guias : Rio de Janeiro : Estado : Descrição   918.168153
2. Rio de Janeiro : Descrição : Guias   918.168153

Table of Contents

How to Use This Guidebook Portuguese Glossary and Phrasebook	6
Why Go to Rio de Janeiro	7
I see Rio de Janeiro, by Fernando Gabeira	12

Destinations

Castelo and Environs	17
Praça Quinze de Novembro and Environs	27
Praça Tiradentes and Environs	37
Saúde and Gamboa	45
São Cristóvão and Environs	49
Lapa	53
Santa Teresa	61
Glória and Catete	69
Laranjeiras and Cosme Velho	75
Flamengo	81
Botafogo and Humaitá	89
Urca	97
Leme and Copacabana	101
Ipanema	119
Leblon	139
Lagoa Rodrigo de Freitas	151
Jardim Botânico	155
Gávea	163
Parque Nacional da Tijuca	169
São Conrado	175
Rocinha	178
Barra da Tijuca	179
Recreio and Environs	191
Niterói	197

Getting around Rio de Janeiro
Highways, Main Roads, Taxis, Metro, Buses, and Vans   201

Services   204
Hotels
Restaurants
Show Venues
Nightclubs
Shopping
Shopping Centers
Services

Useful Information   242

Consulates in Rio de Janeiro and Embassies in Brasília   246

Acknowledgments and Photo Credits   248

How to Use This Guide

The *Rio de Janeiro Guide* offers readers suggestions for touring the city and provides essential information for understanding the local culture. The guide is divided into two sections.

The **Destinations** section has **24 chapters** that cover the city's main neighborhoods and attractions.

Throughout the guidebook there are **boxes containing additional information** on many sights and attractions. Particularly pleasant eateries, bars, hotels and guesthouses are highlighted in boxes labeled **Our Recommendation**.

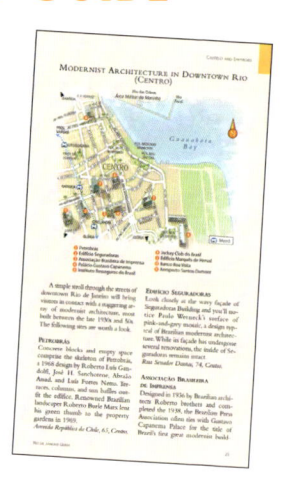

The **Services** section lists establishments – including hotels, restaurants, show venues, nightclubs, shopping centers, and more – that will appeal to foreign visitors. The chapter "Getting Around Rio de Janeiro" provides useful information, such as the location of airports, tips on how to get around, safety, health, and events. Practical and organized, the *Rio de Janeiro Guide* selects, explains and provides tips on the best the "marvelous city" has to offer.

The *Rio de Janeiro Guide* also has a useful **Portuguese Glossary**, with pronunciation tips, and a list of consulates in the city and embassies in Brasília, the capital of Brazil.

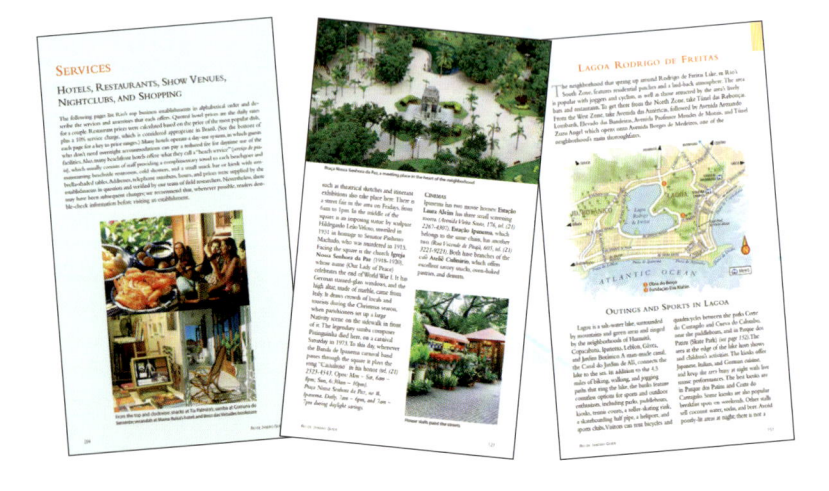

Why Go to Rio de Janeiro

Rio de Janeiro is called the '*cidade maravilhosa*' (marvelous city) for a good reason. The expression, originally from a 1935 carnival song, became the city's official soubriquet in the 1960s. It may be hackneyed, but it's irresistible: 'marvelous' is the first adjective to spring to mind when one gazes out over Rio, with its incredible topology of mountains and sea, forests and enormous rock formations.

Rio's unique geography makes it an active, outward-looking city. Visitors can enjoy large, open spaces in numerous ways: hang gliding and paragliding, rock-climbing, surfing, hiking through the forest, bike riding, strolling along the beaches and beachside promenades, or just wandering around and sampling the refreshments sold right on the street. Roaming the streets gives one a chance to discover that this sunny, easy-going, sports-loving city is also steeped, by pure good fortune, in history and culture.

In the early sixteenth century, Rio's beautiful Guanabara Bay dazzled the first Portuguese sailors to arrive there. It wasn't long before the region attracted other Europeans – mainly the French, who saw these lush lands as a perfect location for their long dreamed-of France

View of Sugarloaf Mountain, from Corcovado

Why Go to Rio de Janeiro

Statue of Christ the Redeemer

Antarctique. The French formed alliances with local indigenous groups, taking advantage of the tensions between these populations and the Portuguese invaders, and decades of violent struggle ensued. While assembling an attack force in 1565, the Portuguese military officer Estácio de Sá founded the hamlet of São Sebastião do Rio de Janeiro. Two years later, the Portuguese drove the French out of the region for good.

Built on a hilltop, the hamlet expanded out toward the plains. It grew in size and importance in the seventeenth century, as gold prospecting blossomed in the interior region called Minas Gerais. During this period, the port of Rio received slave ships from Africa and sent Brazilian gold to Portugal. In 1763, Rio became capital of the colony, and in 1808, during the Napoleonic Wars, the Portuguese court fled there for safety. Rio thus became the capital of the United Kingdom of Portugal, Brazil and the Algarve. It remained the capital of Brazil until the current capital, the built-for-the-purpose city of Brasília, opened for business in 1960.

Rio is eternally fascinating to Brazilians and foreigners alike. It preserves vestiges of its various pasts, including the eras in which it was the seat of colonial government, then the center of an empire, and even the head of the early Brazilian republic. In keeping with that historical mélange, it wears many architectural styles. The iconic stone arches of the Lapa Aqueduct were built in 1757, for example, while the art deco buildings in neighborhoods such as Urca, Glória and Copacabana are reminiscent of the 1930s. Baroque churches abound and include Mosteiro de São Bento (built 1633-1690), Convento de Santo Antônio (1608-1620), Ordem Terceira de São Francisco da Penitência (1657-1747) and Ordem Primeira de Nossa Senhora do Carmo (1761). But neoclassical buildings, such as the Real Gabinete Português de Leitura (1837), dominate downtown Rio. And modernist influences are evident in such buildings as the Palácio Gustavo Capanema (1937-43). Bronze statues made in France speckle the city's public squares. (Rio has the highest number of French-made statues outside of Paris.) Also among the buildings, as well as in them, is a plethora of museums, cultural centers, art galleries, theatres, cinemas, and bookshops. Take, for example, the Brazilian Academy of Letters, founded by legendary Brazilian writer Machado de Assis in 1897, which now occupies a house built in 1922 for the centenary celebrations of Brazil's independence. Or consider the beautiful building occupied by the Banco do Brasil Cultural Center (1880-1906). The city also has a virtual infinity of bars and taverns, some of which are institutions among *cariocas* (Rio natives). These popular hangouts live in harmony with more upscale restaurants, nightclubs, show venues, stores, and shopping centers. Additionally, there is the ubiquitous presence of music: not just samba, but *choro*, *jongo*, bossa nova, funk, jazz, MPB (Brazilian popular music) and electronic music. There is room for everything – and everyone.

Rio de Janeiro's seductiveness arises from this blend of culture and landscape. A little bit of its ability to charm resides each facet of its complex personality. Those facets – the busy beaches, the athleticism, the carnival parades, and the cable cars that climb Sugarloaf Mountain – may be nothing new. But, as the old carnival song says, they are indeed irresistible. And marvelous.

The distinctive sidewalks of the world-famous Copacabana beach

UNIBANCO GUIDES
RIO DE JANEIRO

- Major highways
- Major city thoroughfares
- Metropolitan area limits
- River
- Municipal airport
- Domestic and international airport
- Federal highway
- State highway
- Town with population of over 150,000
- Car racing circuit

Nova Iguaçu

Cabuçu

Mendanha

Angra dos Reis
Paraty
Ubatuba
Santos

AV. JOÃO XXIII
AV. BRASIL

BR 465
BR 101

Santissimo

ZONA OESTE

Bangu

Paciência

ESTR. DAS PEDRAS
ESTR. CAMPO GRANDE

Campo Grande

Rio Cabuçu

RIO DE

Santa Cuz

Engenho Novo

Sepetiba

Guaratiba

Baía de Sepetiba

Pedra de Guaratiba

AV. DAS AMÉRICAS

RJ 071

Recreio dos Bandeirantes

Restinga de Marambaia

Grumari

Pontal de Semambetiba

Barra de Guaraiba

Ilha das Palmas

Ponta do Picão

ATLANTIC

N
1 cm = 5 km
1 inch = 7.9 mi.

São Paulo
Belo Horizonte
Petrópolis

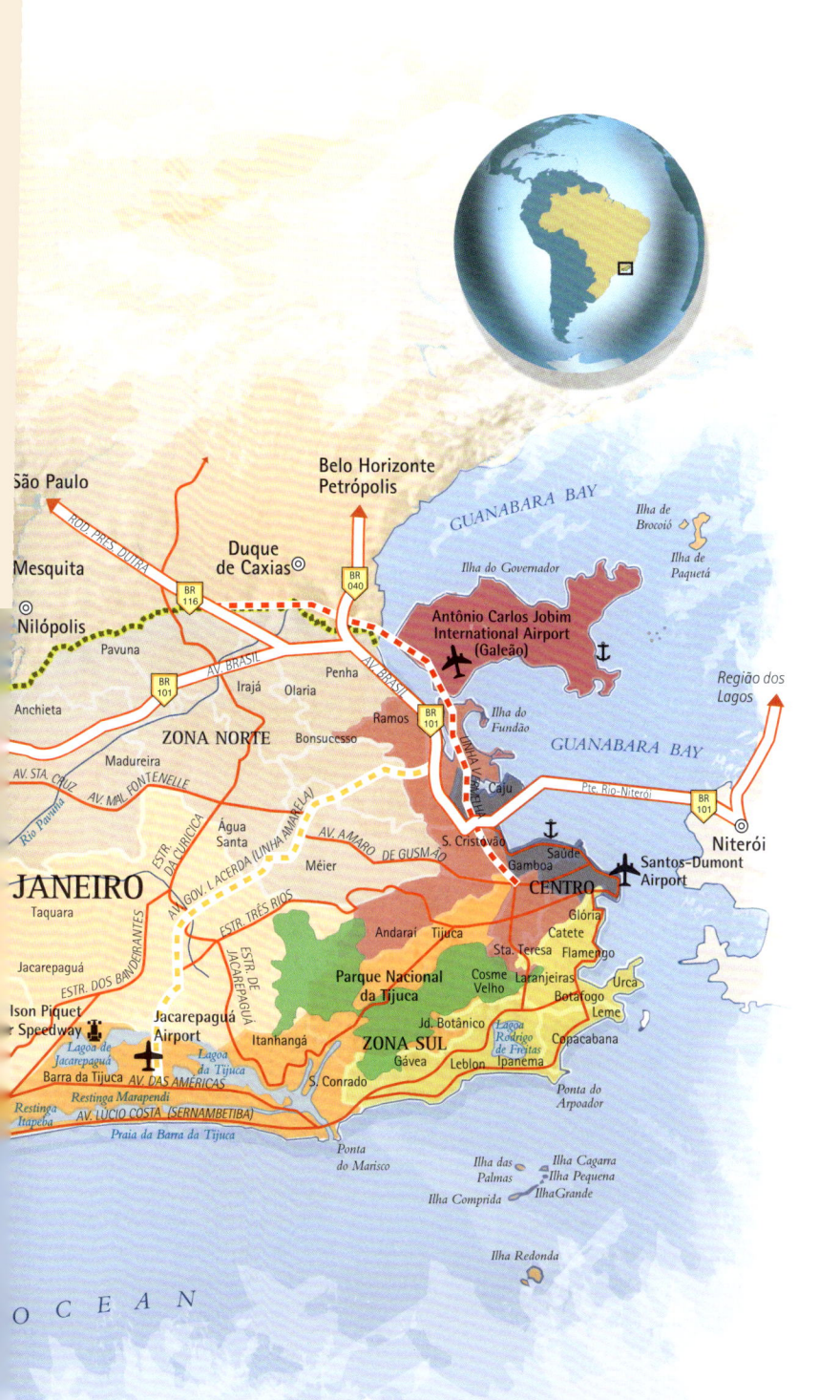

ROD. PRES. DUTRA
BR 116
BR 040

Mesquita
Duque de Caxias
Nilópolis
Pavuna
Anchieta

GUANABARA BAY
Ilha de Brocoió
Ilha de Paquetá
Ilha do Governador

Antônio Carlos Jobim International Airport (Galeão)

AV. BRASIL
BR 101
Irajá
Olaria
Penha
ZONA NORTE
Madureira
Bonsucesso
Ramos
Ilha do Fundão

GUANABARA BAY
Região dos Lagos
BR 101

AV. STA. CRUZ
AV. MAL. FONTENELLE
Rio Pavuna
ESTR. DA CURICICA
Água Santa
AV. AMARO DE GUSMÃO
Caju
LINHA VERMELHA
Pte. Rio-Niterói

Niterói

JANEIRO
AN. GOV. L. ACERDA (LINHA AMARELA)
Méier
S. Cristovão
Saúde
Santos-Dumont Airport

Taquara
ESTR. TRÊS RIOS
Andaraí
Tijuca
Gamboa
CENTRO
Glória

Jacarepaguá
ESTR. DOS BANDEIRANTES
ESTR. DE JACAREPAGUÁ
Parque Nacional da Tijuca
Cosme Velho
Sta. Teresa
Catete
Flamengo
Laranjeiras
Botafogo
Urca
Leme

Ison Piquet Speedway
Jacarepaguá Airport
Itanhangá
Jd. Botânico
ZONA SUL
Gávea
Lagoa Rodrigo de Freitas
Ipanema
Copacabana

Lagoa de Jacarepaguá
Lagoa da Tijuca
Barra da Tijuca
AV. DAS AMÉRICAS
Leblon
Restinga Marapendi
Restinga Itapeba
AV. LUCIO COSTA (SERNAMBETIBA)
S. Conrado
Ponta do Arpoador
Praia da Barra da Tijuca

Ponta do Marisco
Ilha das Palmas
Ilha Cagarra
Ilha Pequena
Ilha Comprida
Ilha Grande

OCEAN

Ilha Redonda

I See Rio de Janeiro

Minha alma canta / vejo o Rio de Janeiro.
My soul sings / I see Rio de Janeiro.

These lines, composed by musical maestro Tom Jobim, describe a return home from a trip overseas. The musician's view of Rio de Janeiro as he approached it from the air gave rise to a beautiful song, and the city's international airport is now named after him.

When I was a boy, I loved to gaze at the lights of Rio. We used to take excursions from our town in the country to the city of Petrópolis, which lies near Rio, in the mountains. From there we would head up the mountain highway to view the city of our dreams below. The experience was not unlike that of the protagonist in Thomas Hardy's *Jude the Obscure*. He, too, was fascinated by city lights.

As time passed I discovered other ways to see Rio de Janeiro from above. A number of local airlines fly from São Paulo to Rio and approach the latter city's airport from the sea, flying directly over its main beaches and the residential towers that line some of those strips of sand.

Another excellent way to see Rio is from a hang glider or paraglider. Gliders take off from an enormous rock in the district of São Conrado and fly over luxurious penthouses, sharing, if only momentarily, the apartments' breathtaking view of the Atlantic.

But the best way to experience Rio's aerial magic – its unique combination of tropical forest greens and blue sea – is by helicopter. Most tours cover the entire city as well as some areas of relatively untouched greenery. On these flights I find it easy to imagine how arriving colonial explorers must have felt when they first sailed into Guanabara Bay.

This introduction barely scratches the surface. Those who truly want to explore the forest and trails of Rio now have this guide to describe the safest and most popular routes. Similarly, Rio's beaches, with their colorful array of humanity, are also worthy of a long visit.

Surfing enthusiasts tend to head for Prainha, an environmental protection area. Since surfers must move around in search of the best waves, most also consult surf websites on a daily basis. Visitors who know a bit of Portuguese can log onto www.waves.com.br to find the wave heights and best surf spots in Rio on any given day.

Coming from the city center, the first beach on Rio's Ipanema shoreline is Arpoador. From here one can see the neighborhood of Gávea and its iconic rock, Pedra da Gávea, at the other end of the beach. For a different perspective, try climbing Pedra da Gávea to look out over the ocean from up high. The climb, while worth the effort, must be done with the help of a local guide. There are dangerous spots for those who don't know the area.

Both Ipanema and Copacabana are home to particularly gay-friendly stretches of beach. People often imagine Rio as a sexually liberal city. An American priest was even recently quoted as saying that Brazil, where people swim nude in the sea, stimulated his sensuality.

This might actually be truer of Germany than Brazil. Although carnival photographs show people dancing around naked or half-naked, don't use these images as an isolated frame of reference. Carnival in Brazil is indeed a time when anything can happen, but what is tolerated during carnival is often repressed the rest of the year. Body culture is widespread in Rio, but radical social liberalism isn't always embraced: When the first attempt at topless sunbathing on a Rio beach took place in 1979, other beachgoers protested.

Although things in Rio aren't as the American priest described them, the social atmosphere is lighter in spirit here than in other Brazilian cities. That's partly why Rio is an attractive destination for other Brazil. In his memoirs, writer Pedro Nava notes that wealthy members of his inland city used to return from Rio de Janeiro more relaxed because they were able to live their romances there. There are no statistics to prove it, but observation suggests that Rio de Janeiro is definitely a city in which lovers kiss more often in public.

The growth of a more intellectual kind of tourism has brought with it the possibility of seeing the city from the hilltop *favelas*, or shantytowns. From there, as from all bird's-eye views, it is evident that Rio's future depends on the conservation of two of its most valuable assets: golden beaches and tropical forest.

Local folk culture is also fueling the growth of tourism. There is no shortage of percussionists playing Brazilian samba throughout Europe and elsewhere in the world. Over the past few years, some foreigners have come to the city to learn to play and dance samba. Upon returning to their homelands they set up small samba schools, often enriched by the participation of Brazilian immigrants.

Lastly, Rio's new athletic venues will certainly help transform the city into an even more international destination. Headquarters for the 2007 Pan American Games, Rio plans to use the new spaces created to gain an edge as it seeks to attract future international sporting events, including the FIFA World Cup.

Three elements – the city's natural beauty, its culture, and its modern athletic facilities – have the potential to make Rio a metropolis that will significantly enhance the Brazil's image in the eyes of the world.

One additional element of this unique image deserves mention: Brazil's cultural diversity and tolerance. In every city across the country, Arabic and Jewish colonies co-exist peacefully. But in Rio, they even share a commercial district. And whenever a new war breaks out in the Middle East, it is there, to the so-called Saara commercial area, that we all run to send out messages of peace.

It would seem that Vinicius de Moraes, poet and exquisite lyricist, had Rio de Janeiro's spirit in mind when he wrote: *É melhor ser alegre que ser triste / A alegria é a melhor coisa que existe (It's better to be happy than sad / Joy is the best thing to be had).*

It isn't always possible, but this simple philosophy is nonetheless the most popular in town.

Fernando Gabeira,
Brazilian writer and politician

Portuguese Glossary and Phrasebook

Pronunciation

Brazilian Portuguese may use familiar characters, but that fact belies its foreignness. A little practice with the language will help you request directions and will ease other attempt to communicate. Many letters are pronounced in ways that seem strange or counterintuitive to native English speakers. For example, double *r*'s and *r*'s that begin words sound like an *h*. In addition, vowels crowned like *(ã)* or followed by an *n* or *m* are nasal, a sound difficult for many foreigners to make. (To say "são", sound out the first three-and-a-half letters of *sound*.) When not nasal, vowels sound like:

a: "ah" or "uh"
e: "e" as in *Meg*, or almost silent
i: "ee"
o: "au" as in *caught*, "o" as in *or*, or "ou" as in *you*
u: by itself, "ou," but "w" when followed by another vowel

Directions

Direita [jee-RAY-ta] – Right
Esquerda [esh-CARE-dah] – Left
Reto [REH-to] – Straight
Vire [VEER-ee] – Turn
Norte [NOR-chee] – North
Sul [SOOL] – South
Leste [LES-chee] – East
Oeste [oo-ES-chee] – West
Aberto [ah-BEAR-too] – Open
Fechado [feh-SHA-doo] – Closed

Transportation

Aeroporto [er-oo-POUR-too] – Airport
Barco [BAHR-koo] – Boat
Bilhete [bil-YEH-chee] – Ticket (for transportation)
Carro [CA-hoo] – Car
Estação [es-ta-SAOW] – Station
Horário [oh-RA-ree-oo] – Schedule
Ônibus [OH-knee-boos] – Bus
Rodoviária (Rod.) [ho-do-vee-AH-ri-a] – Bus station
Trem [TRAYM] – Train

Practicalities

Banco [BAHN-koo] – Bank
Caixa automático [KAI-sha oh-toe-MA-chee-ko] – ATM
Câmbio [KAHM-bee-oo] – Currency exchange
Correio [koh-HAY-oh] – Post office
Drogaria [droh-gah-REE-ah], Farmácia [far-MAH-see-ah] – Pharmacy
Hospital [os-pee-TAW] – Hospital
Livraria [leev-rah-REE-ah] – Bookstore
Loja [LOH-zha] – Store
Médico [MEH-dee-koo] – Doctor
Polícia [poh-LEE-see-ah] – Police
Real [hay-OW] – The Brazilian currency (plural: reais [hay-EYES])
Troco [TROH-koo] – Change

Around Town

Avenida (Av.) [ah-veh-KNEE-da] – Avenue
Bairro [BYE-hoe] – District/suburb
Capela [ca-PEH-la] – Chapel

Casa [KAH-za] – House
Catedral [cah-teh-DROW] – Cathedral
Centro [SEN-chroo] – Center; downtown
Edificio [eh-dee-FEE-see-oo] – Building
Feira [FAY-ra] – Fair
Igreja (Ig.) [ee-GRAY-jah] – Church
Jardim (Jd.) [zhar-DEEM] – Garden
Largo (Lgo.) [LAR-goo] – Plaza
Mercado [mer-KAH-doo] – Market
Museu [moo-SEH-OO] – Museum
Parque [PAR-key] – Park
Ponte [PAHN-chee] – Bridge
Praça (Pça.) [PRAH-shah] – Square
Praia [PRY-ah] – Beach
Rua (R.) [HOO-ah] – Street

IN NATURE

Cachoeira [ka-show-AY-rah] – Waterfall
Caverna [kah-VARE-nah] – Cave
Estrada [ess-TRA-dah] – Road
Fazenda [fa-ZEN-dah] – Farm
Floresta [flo-RES-tah] – Forest
Garganta [gar-GAHN-ta] – Gorge
Gruta [GREW-ta] – Cave
Ilha [EEL-ya] – Island
Lagoa [lah-GO-ah] – Lake
Lago [LAH-goo] – Lake
Mata [MAH-ta] – Forest
Mirante [me-RAHN-chee] – Lookout
Morro [MOE-hoo] – Hill
Parque – Park (Pq. Est. denotes an estadual or state park; Pq. Fl. a florestal or forest park)
Pico [PEE-koo] – Peak
Ribeirão [hee-bay-RAOW] – Brook
Rio [HEE-oo] – River
Rodovia (Rod.) [hoe-doe-VEE-ah] – Highway
Serra [SEH-ha] – Mountain range or continuous hills
Trilha [TREAL-ya] – Trail
Vale [VAH-leh] – Valley
Via [VEE-ah] – Highway

ACCOMMODATIONS

Albergue [all-BEAR-ge] – Hostel
Banheiro [bahn-YAY-roo] – Bathroom
Cama [KAH-ma] – Bed
Hotel [oh-TELL] – Hotel
Pousada [poo-ZAH-da] – Guesthouse
Quarto [KWAR-too] – Room

FOOD AND DRINK

Água [AH-gwa] – Water
Bebida [beh-BEE-dah] – Drink
Bife [BEE-fee] – Steak
Cachaça [ka-SHAH-sah] – Traditional Brazilian white rum, made from sugarcane
Café-da-manhã [kah-FAY da mon-YA] – Breakfast
Caipirinha [kay-pee-REEN-ya] – The most famous Brazilian cocktail, made of cachaça, lime, sugar and ice. Try one with "cachaça envelhecida" (aged cachaça).
Camarão [kah-ma-RAOW] – Shrimp
Cardápio [car-DAH-pee-oo] – Menu
Carne [CAR-knee] – Meat
Carne de porco [CAR-knee jee POUR-koo] – Pork
Cerveja [sare-VAY-ja], chopp [SHOP] – Beer
Churrascaria [chew-hoss-ka-REE-ah] – All-you-can-eat barbeque restaurant
Comida [koo-MEE-dah] – Food
Conta [CONE-tah] – Bill
Frango [FRAN-goo] – Chicken
Lanchonete [lawn-choh-NEH-chee] – Lunch counter, snack bar
Massas [MAH-sauce] – Pasta
Pão [POW] – Bread
Peixe [PAY-shee] – Fish
Prato [PRAH-too] – Plate
Queijo [KAY-jew] – Cheese
Refrigerante [he-free-jer-ON-chee] – Soft drink

Restaurante [hess-tow-RAHN-chee] – Restaurant
Sobremesa [soh-bray-MAY-za] – Dessert
Sorvete [sore-VEH-chee] – Ice cream
Suco [SOO-koo] – Juice

NIGHTLIFE
Bar – Bar
Barraca [ba-HA-ka] – Beach snack bar
Boate [BWA-chee] – Nightclub
Cinema [SEE-nay-ma] – Cinema
Teatro [tay-AHT-roo] – Theatre

KEY WORDS AND PHRASES

Hello – Oi, Olá (informal) [OY, oh-LAH]
Good morning – Bom dia [bome JEE-ah]
Good afternoon – Boa tarde [bwa TAR-jee]
Good evening – Boa noite [bwa NOY-chee]
Goodbye – Tchau [CHOW]
Please – Por favor [pour fah-VOAR]
Thank you (very much) – (Muito) obrigado [MOO-EE-toh oh-bree-GAH-doe] is what men say. Women say: (Muito) obrigada
Yes – Sim [SEEM]
No – Não [NOW]
Today – Hoje [OH-jee]
Tomorrow – Amanhã [ah-mahn-YA]
My name is… – Meu nome é… [may-oo KNOW-me EH]
What's your name? – Qual é seu nome? [k-wow EH say-oo KNOW-me]
I'm sick/hurt – Estou doente/com dor [ess-TOH doe-EN-chee/comb DOOR]
Where is….? – Onde fica….? [OWN-jee FEE-ka]
I need help – Preciso de ajuda [preh-SEE-zoo jee ah-JEW-dah]
I don't speak Portuguese – Não falo português. [NOW FAH-loo pour-chew-GAYss]
How much (is this)? – Quanto custa? [KWAN-too KOOS-tah]
I'd like… – Gostaria… [goes-ta-REE-ia]
Help – Ajuda [ah-JEW-dah]

NUMBERS
0: zero [say-roo]
1: um [OOM]
2: dois [DOYCE]
3: três [TRACE]
4: quatro [KWAH-troo]
5: cinco [SEEN-koo]
6: seis [SAYS]
7: sete [SHE-chee]
8: oito [OY-two]
9: nove [NOH-vee]
10: dez [DAYS]
20: vinte [VEEN-chee]
30: trinta [TREEN-ta]
40: quarenta [kwah-REN-ta]
50: cinqüenta [seen-KWAIN-ta]
100: cem [SAME]
200: duzentos [du-ZEN-toos]
500: quinhentos [keen-YAYN-toos]
1000: mil [MEW]

DAYS
Monday – Segunda-feira (Seg.) [seh-GOON-dah FAY-rah]
Tuesday – Terça-feira (Ter.) [TARE-sah]
Wednesday – Quarta-feira (Qua.) [KWAR-tah]
Thursday – Quinta-feira (Qui.) [KEEN-tah]
Friday – Sexta-feira (Sex.) [SAYSH-tah]
Saturday – Sábado (Sáb.) [SAH-ba-doo]
Sunday – Domingo (Dom.) [doh-MEAN-goo]

Castelo and Environs

The district of Castelo dates back to the 16th century, with origins atop Morro do Castelo (Castle Hill). Though the village eventually expanded to the coastal plain, the hill was razed during the 1920s to improve air circulation, reduce problems caused by rainwater runoff, and demolish unsanitary dwellings. During Rio's rapid 20th century modernization, Castelo and the surrounding areas have had their share of buildings, stores, offices, and movie theaters spring. But even when visiting Castelo today, you're likely to stumble across a handful of old churches tucked among museums and other marvels of 20th-century architecture. Drop in between Tuesday and Sunday, when most attractions are open to the public, and arrive early to beat the crowds. Cinelândia and Carioca are the closest metro stations. Visitors arriving by car can come in by way of Avenida Presidente Antônio Carlos, Avenida Rio Branco, Avenida Marechal Câmara, Avenida Presidente Wilson, Avenida Nilo Peçanha, Avenida Almirante Barroso, or Avenida República do Chile.

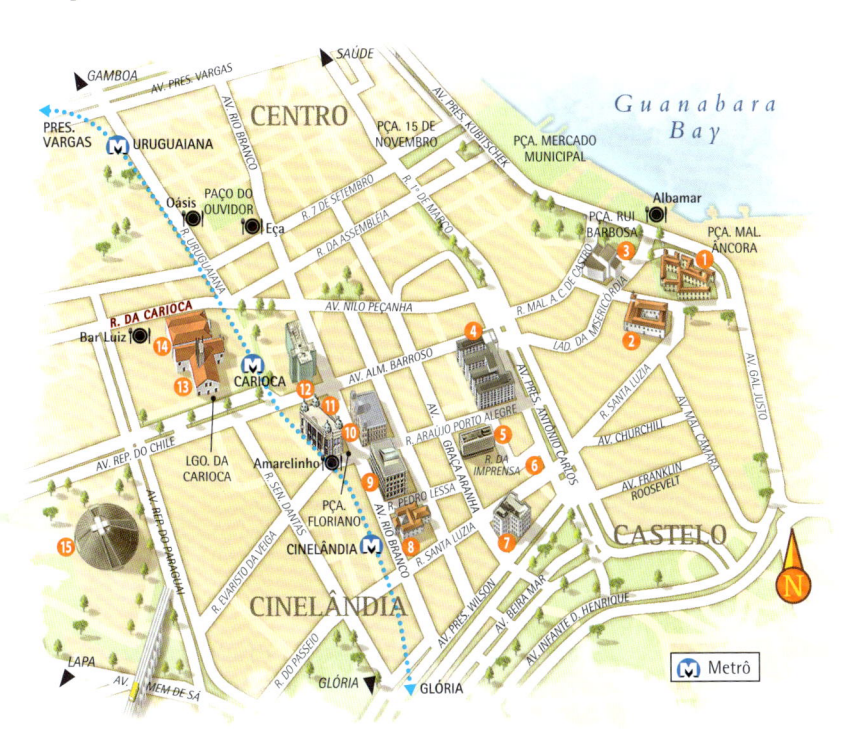

1. Museu Histórico Nacional
2. Igreja Nossa Senhora do Bonsucesso
3. Museu da Imagem e do Som (MIS)
4. Antigo Ministério da Fazenda
5. Palácio Gustavo Capanema
6. Igreja de Santa Luzia
7. Academia Brasileira de Letras
8. Centro Cultural da Justiça Federal
9. Biblioteca Nacional
10. Museu Nacional de Belas-Artes
11. Teatro Municipal
12. Caixa Cultural
13. Igreja e Convento de Santo Antônio
14. Igreja da Ordem Terceira de São Francisco da Penitência
15. Catedral de São Sebastião do Rio de Janeiro

The National History Museum houses one of Brazil's largest collections of native artifacts

❶ Museu Histórico Nacional

The National History Museum houses nearly 300,000 historical items, only some of which are on display at any given time. Permanent exhibitions showcase photographs, artifacts from indigenous archeological sites, carts and carriages, furniture, medical paraphernalia from Imperial Pharmácia pharmacy dating back to 1847, and the largest collection of coins and medals in Latin America. Also of interest are the Imperial Senate throne, where Pedro II sat during legislative assemblies, and paintings of important moments in Brazilian history, such as *Batalha naval do Riachuelo* (*Naval Battle of Riachuelo*, 1883), by Vítor Meireles. There is also a collection of old toys that includes a game of checkers and a wind-up toy that belonged to then-Prince Pedro I. Following recent renovation, the MHN now has five galleries for temporary exhibitions.
Praça Marechal Âncora, no #, Centro, tel. (21) 2550-9260. Tue – Fri, 10am – 5:30pm; Sat, Sun, and holidays, 2pm – 6pm.

❷ Igreja Nossa Senhora do Bonsucesso

This 16th-century wattle-and-daub chapel underwent several renovations in the 17th and 18th centuries, when it was given its current name. The façade was updated in 1818, and a dome built over the main altar. The three 17th-century mannerist panels – the oldest in Rio – and pulpit were taken from Igreja de Santo Inácio, an old church on Morro do Castelo that was part of a complex of Jesuit buildings dismantled in 1922.
Largo da Misericórdia, no #, Centro, tel. (21) 2220-3001. Mon – Fri, 7am – 3:30pm.

❸ Museu da Imagem e do Som (MIS)

Governor Carlos Lacerda opened this Image and Sound Museum in 1965 in commemoration of Rio's fourth centennial. The museum houses an extensive collection of photographs, rare recordings, musical scores, and videos. The museum occupies two buildings. Silvio and Rafael Rebecchi designed the downtown site, which

was built to house an administrative pavilion for a 1922 exhibition and is now listed as a heritage site. Period instruments, some belonging to famous Brazilian musicians, adorn the lobby. The Lapa building houses the museum's administrative headquarters and the National Radio collection, an archive of more than 20,000 digitalized scores *(see page 56)*. Appointments for research and consultation should be made in advance.
Praça Rui Barbosa, 1, Centro, tel. (21) 2220-3481, 2262-0309. Mon – Fri, 11am – 5pm.

❹ ANTIGO MINISTÉRIO DA FAZENDA
The neoclassical former Ministry of Finance was built in 1943 and is entirely of native materials, from the marble in the main portico to the bronze candleholders inside. On the tenth floor, the Museu da Fazenda Federal (Federal Finance Museum) displays old photographs and rare documents from Brazil's economic and financial history, including records of the country's first loan. The adjacent Louis XVI-style Salão Nobre room boasts a majestic silver-and-crystal chandelier. Look to the balcony for two indigenous statues and five mosaic panels depicting different regions of Brazil. From here check out excellent views of downtown Rio and Guanabara Bay. Visits are monitored and by appointment only.
Avenida Presidente Antônio Carlos, 375-A, Centro, tel. (21) 3805-2000. Mon – Fri, 10am – 4pm.

❺ PALÁCIO GUSTAVO CAPANEMA
Gustavo Capanema Palace, an icon of modern architecture, was constructed between 1937 and 1943 with Le Corbusier as project consultant. An impressive roster of designers, including Lúcio Costa, Oscar Niemeyer, Carlos Leão, Ernani Vasconcelos, Jorge Moreira, and Affonso Eduardo Reidy, had a hand in construction. Pillars elevated the building 10 meters above the ground, allowing circulation underneath and open access to the street. The former

---

PEREIRA PASSOS' RIO

Born in São João Marcos, in the Paraíba Valley, in the state of Rio de Janeiro, engineer Francisco Pereira Passos (1836-1913) is known best for his reshaping of downtown Rio in the early 20th century. President Rodrigues Alves named Passos mayor of the Federal District in 1903. Passos took office with the mission of sanitizing and remodeling Rio, which was then the capital of the young republic and had recently suffered recurring epidemics of smallpox, yellow fever, bubonic plague, and tuberculosis. Inspired by Haussmann's modernization of Paris in the 1850s and 60s under Napoleon III, Passos transformed downtown Rio into a construction site: To lay ground for Avenida Central (now Rio Branco) from Praça Mauá (Mauá Square) to Praia de Santa Luzia (Santa Luzia Beach), he had more than six hundred buildings demolished. The avenue opened in November 1905, dotted with neoclassical architecture where colonial dwellings once stood. The new Teatro Municipal (Municipal Theatre), Escola Nacional de Belas-Artes (National School of Fine arts), Supremo Tribunal Federal (Federal Supreme Court), and Biblioteca Nacional (National Library) helped the region quickly gain status as an economic and cultural hub. However, hundreds of former residents of the area found themselves homeless and fled to the hillsides, giving rise to the city's first – and now numerous – shantytowns.

Interior of Gustavo Capanema Palace, a landmark of modern architecture

headquarters of the Ministry of Education and Health, the palace remains a public administration building and permits visitors inside only by appointment. However, exterior tours do grant a peek at the house gardens, designed by legendary landscape artist Burle Marx, panels of painted tiles by Cândido Portinari, and sculptures by Bruno Giorgi. Second-floor offices, furniture, and tapestries are well-preserved. The palace also features galleries for rotating art exhibitions, an auditorium, and, on the ground floor, the well-stocked **Livraria Mário de Andrade** bookshop. *(tel. (21) 2279-8071; Mon – Fri, 10am – 6pm). Rua da Imprensa, 16, Centro, tel. (21) 2220-1490. Mon – Fri, 9am – 5pm.*

CINELÂNDIA

The area surrounding Praça Floriano (Floriano Square) in downtown Rio is home to the Municipal Theatre, the National Museum of Fine Arts, and the National Library. It's known to Cariocas – as the locals are called – as Cinelândia ("Cinemaland"). The nickname dates back to the early 1920s, when Spanish entrepreneur Francisco Serrador opened an entire city block of boutiques, offices, and four movie theaters. One of these, the Odeon, still operates to this day. Renovated in 1999, **Cine Odeon BR** screens popular art and festival films, as well as literary readings and exhibitions. Don't miss Wednesday's Cachaça Cinema Clube, an event that pairs short-film screenings with *cachaça* (Brazilian white rum) tastings. Every first Friday of the month the theater hosts Maratona Odeon, an all-night movie marathon that features live DJs between screenings. New and second-hand bookshops and a café are also on site *(Praça Floriano, 7, Centro; tel. (21) 2240-1093; Daily, 12:45pm – 11:15pm).* Also near Praça Floriano is the **Amarelinho**, one of Rio de Janeiro's oldest bars. This relaxed 1920s haunt, adjacent to the Biblioteca Nacional (National Library), serves *feijoada* (Brazilian black-bean stew) and a variety of other dishes *(Praça Floriano, 55; tel. (21) 2240-8434; daily, 10am – 2am).*

CASTELO AND ENVIRONS

❻ IGREJA DE SANTA LUZIA
One of the city's oldest churches, Igreja de Santa Luzia church is built on the site of Portuguese explorer Ferdinand Magellan's marriage in 1559 to a local woman by the name of Luzia – the chapel's namesake. The current building dates back to 1752, and, despite renovations in 1872, it still maintains its original 18th-century structure. *Rua Santa Luzia, 490, Centro, tel. (21) 2220-4367. Mon – Fri, 8am – 5pm; Sat, 8am – 11am.*

❼ ACADEMIA BRASILEIRA DE LETRAS
A replica of the Petit Trianon at Versailles, the Brazilian Academy of Letters also housed the French Pavilion during Brazil's centennial celebrations. Visits made by appointment allow access to the main hall and the room where academy members meet for a traditional tea on Thursdays. Cândido Portinari and Bruno Giorgi are among the artists represented in the academy's collection of paintings and sculptures. Students and researchers can take advantage of the second floor's extensive Biblioteca Acadêmica Lúcio de Mendonça academic library *(Mon – Fri, 9am – 6pm)*. The neighboring Palácio Austregésilo de Athayde contains several rooms of permanent and temporary art exhibitions. Espaço Machado de Assis offers a look into the life and times (and furniture) of the eponymous legendary Brazilian writer, while Biblioteca Rodolfo Garcia holds the occasional exhibition of rare books *(tel. (21) 3974-2510; Mon – Fri, 9am – noon and 1pm – 6pm)*. Stop off at **Café Academia** for lunch, a quick snack, or an enjoyable afternoon tea *(tel. (21) 2282-5217; Mon – Fri, 9am – 6pm)*. Guided historical tours of the academy are available from April through June and August through September on Mondays, Wednesdays, and Fridays at 2pm and 4pm. Tours must be booked in advance *(tel. (21) 3974-2526; Mon – Fri, 9am – 6pm)*. *Avenida Presidente Wilson, 203, Centro, tel. (21) 3974-2500. Mon – Fri, 9am – 6pm.*

❽ CENTRO CULTURAL DA JUSTIÇA FEDERAL
The Federal Department of Justice Cultural Center, designed by Spanish architect Adolfo Morales de los Rios in 1905, housed the Federal Supreme Court until 1960, when it became headquarters for the Federal Department of Justice. Highlights include an art nouveau marble-and-iron staircase, two panels painted by Rodolfo Amoedo, and exquisite stained-glass windows facing the Sala de Sessões. The center hosts photography exhibitions, classical music concerts, talks, and conferences, and maintains a library well-stocked with art and photography books *(Mon – Fri, noon – 5pm)*. The house theatre seats 144; an on-site cafeteria feeds just as

Federal Department of Justice headquarters

RIO DE JANEIRO GUIDE   21

many *(tel. (21) 3212-2589, 2532-3605; Tue – Wed, noon – 7pm; Thu – Fri, noon – 8pm; Sat, 12:45pm – 8pm; Sun, 1:45pm – 8pm)*. Guided tours must be scheduled at least four days in advance *(tel. (21) 3212-2552)*. A program in Portuguese is available at ccjf.trf2.gov.br.
Avenida Rio Branco, 241, Centro, tel. (21) 3212-2550. Tue – Sun, noon – 7pm.

9 BIBLIOTECA NACIONAL
The National Library's valuable collection of more than 3 million titles includes rare documents on display as special exhibitions, including letters from the Brazilian imperial family, two copies of the 1572 first edition of Camoens' *Os lusíadas* (*The Lusiads*), two copies of the Mainz Bible, printed on parchment in 1462, and an 11th-century Greek gospel. French architect Hector Pepin inaugurated the building in 1910. Bronze sculptures by artists Correia Lima and Rodolfo Bernardelli rest atop the entrance stairs, representing intelligence and study. Forty-minute guided tours lead visitors through the reading and research rooms on the first and second floors, and to the third floor, where panels painted by Rodolfo Amoedo are on display. Tours begin Monday through Friday, at 11am and 3pm. Large groups must book in advance *(tel. (21) 2220-9484)*.
Avenida Rio Branco, 219, Centro, tel. (21) 2220-9608. Mon – Fri, 9am – 8pm; Sat, 9am – 3pm.

10 MUSEU NACIONAL DE BELAS-ARTES
Founded in 1937 by President Getúlio Vargas, the National Museum of Fine Arts maintains a collection of more than 14,000 pieces, more than a third of them by 19th-century Brazilian artists. Spanish architect Morales de los Rios designed the building in 1908 for the Escola Nacional de Belas-Artes (National School of Fine Arts). Museum highlights include *A primeira missa no Brasil* (1860) by Vítor Meireles, *Batalha do Avaí* (1872-77) by Pedro Américo, and *São Tomé das Letras* (1876) by Nicolau Facchinetti. The collection also features works by Frans Post, Cândido Portinari, Anita Malfatti, Lasar Segall, Alfredo Volpi, and Auguste Rodin.
Avenida Rio Branco, 199, Centro, tel. (21) 2240-0068. Tue – Fri, 10am – 6pm; Sat and Sun, 2pm – 6pm.

11 TEATRO MUNICIPAL
Inspired by the Paris Opera House, the Municipal Theater reflects the eclectic early 20th-century architectural style of designer Francisco de Oliveira Passos, son of then-mayor Francisco Pereira Passos. Collaborating with Albert Guilbert, Passos chose to build the theater with its side facing Avenida Rio Branco in order to take advantage of the view of

---

CASA VILLARINO

A large photograph featuring several popular Brazilian musicians from the 1960s denotes the cultural importance of this whisky bar, frequented in decades past by musical icons such as Tom Jobim and Vinicius de Moraes. It was here in 1956, at one of the bar's marble tables, that Jobim and Moraes forged the two-man partnership that would later compose songs for the musical *Orfeu da Conceição*. Popular among all walks of life, Casa Villarino is a great choice for a buffet-style lunch or an after-hours drink accompanied by a treat from the snack menu. Catch a live bossa nova performance on Thursdays from 7pm – 10pm. *Avenida Calógeras, 6-B, Centro, tel. (21) 2240-1627, 2240-9634. Mon – Fri, noon – 10pm.*

CASTELO AND ENVIRONS

Guanabara Bay. World-renowned performance artists such as Isadora Duncan, Nijinsky, Maria Callas, Caruso, and Stravinsky have performed here. Marble staircases with onyx handrails, sculptures by Rodolfo Bernardelli, and paintings by Italian artist Eliseu Visconti complement the grand space, which has a seating capacity of 2,400. The foyer panels are by Rodolfo Amoedo. The Assírio Restaurant, designed by Adolfo Morales de los Rios and unfortunately no longer serving patrons, is still worth a visit for its beautiful decorations. Theater performances run March through December. The Domingo no Municipal program offers concerts and ballets at discount prices every last Sunday of the month *(tickets on sale from 9am)*. Guided tours of the theater are available Monday through Friday, from 1pm to 5pm. Advance booking is advised *(tel. (21) 2299-1667)*.
Praça Floriano, no #, Centro, tel. (21) 2262-3935. Mon – Fri, 10am – 8pm.

⓬ CAIXA CULTURAL
Housed within the Caixa Econômica Federal bank headquarters, next to the busy Largo da Carioca square, the 2006 Caixa Cultural Center is a relative newcomer among Rio's gallery spaces. Four exhibition spaces host temporary shows, which tend to change about every two months. Venue highlights include an arena theatre, two cinemas, a mini-auditorium, and five multi-use rooms used for educational events. Two enormous painted panels by Lídio Bandeira de Melo greet visitors. Caixa owns another cultural space on Avenida República do Chile, also in downtown Rio.
Avenida Almirante Barroso, 25, Centro, tel. (21) 2240-7055. Tue – Sun, 10am – 10pm.

⓭ IGREJA E CONVENTO DE SANTO ANTÔNIO
Listed as a national heritage site in 1938, the Santo Antônio Church and Convent sits nestled atop the last remaining fragment of Santo Antônio

Santo Antônio Church (left) and São Francisco da Penitência Church

Castelo and Environs

Hill, the rest of which was razed during the 1950s. Though the Franciscan convent has undergone several renovations, many of its original paintings, sculptures, and tiles remain intact. The sacristy, fresh off a 2006 restoration, features delightful ceiling paintings and a panel of tiles depicting scenes from the life of Saint Anthony. A majestic chest built by Manuel Setúbal rests inside, preserved in its 1749 state. Restorations should wrap up in 2007. Convent visits must be booked a week in advance, but the church is open to the public seven days a week.
Largo da Carioca, no #, Centro, tel. (21) 2262-0129. Mon – Fri, 8am – 6:30pm; Sat, 8am – 11am and 2pm – 4pm; Sun, 9am – 11am.

⓮ Igreja da Ordem Terceira de São Francisco da Penitência
Construction on the Ordem Terceira de São Francisco da Penitência church began in 1657 and lasted a toilsome 115 years. The last thirty years alone were dedicated to gilding its carved surfaces, a delicate process painstakingly carried out by Portuguese sculptors Manuel de Brito and Francisco Xavier de Brito. The church reopened in 2000, after 12 years of renovations, and now boasts an extensive collection of religious art. A depiction of the glorification of Saint Francis by Caetano da Costa Coelho adorns the main altar ceiling. Also worth a look is the winged statue of Christ set in the high altar. Caretaker Dona Maria Desidéria will happily share tales of the church's history with those who inquire.
Largo da Carioca, 5, Centro, tel. (21) 2262-0197. Tue – Fri, 9am – noon and 1pm – 4pm.

⓯ Catedral de São Sebastião do Rio de Janeiro
This cone-shaped cathedral stands 96 meters tall at its peak and is currently the seat of the Archdiocese of Rio de Janeiro. Architect Edgar Fonceca and engineer Newton Sotto Maior cast their creation in white marble, adding four stained-glass windows and a large cross in ceiling's center. Check out the basement for the **Arquivo Arquidiocesano**, an archive of religious documents dating back to the 12th century *(Tue – Thu, 2pm – 5:30pm)*, and the **Museu de Arte Sacra**, a religious art museum that holds about 5,000 artifacts, including paintings, sculptures, clothing, books, and furniture *(Sat – Sun, 9am – 11am and 1pm – 4pm)*.
Avenida República do Chile, 245, Centro, tel. (21) 2240-2669, 2240-2869, 2240-1797. Mon – Sun, 7:30am – 5:30pm.

Rua da Carioca

Not far from the bustling Largo da Carioca, the Carioca Street holds its own 'scene.' Patrons say **Bar Luiz**, opened in 1887 by the Adolph Rumjaneck, serves some of the best draft beer ("chope" or "chopp") in the city. Formerly called Bar Adolph, the hangout changed names during World War II following anti-Nazi attacks. Nevertheless, a German menu remains. Legendary musicians Ari Barroso and Bezerra da Silva frequented the bar, where wall-mounted photos of Rio lend an Old World ambience *(Rua da Carioca, 39; tel. (21) 2262-6900; Mon – Sat, 11am – 11pm)*. International DJs take the stage at **Cine Íris'** semiannual Loud! rave. These include Germany's Peter Krüder and Brazilian bands such as Los Hermanos, Cachorro Grande, and Bidê ou Balde. The art nouveau building, built in 1909, boasts its original staircase and wooden ticket booth *(information on the rave: tel. (21) 2266-1014)*.

CASTELO AND ENVIRONS

MODERNIST ARCHITECTURE IN DOWNTOWN RIO (CENTRO)

1. Petrobrás
2. Edifício Seguradoras
3. Associação Brasileira de Imprensa
4. Palácio Gustavo Capanema
5. Instituto Resseguros do Brasil
6. Jockey Club do Brasil
7. Edifício Marquês de Herval
8. Banco Boa Vista
9. Aeroporto Santos-Dumont

A simple stroll through the streets of downtown Rio de Janeiro will bring visitors in contact with a staggering array of modernist architecture, most built between the late 1930s and 50s. The following sites are worth a look.

PETROBRÁS
Concrete blocks and empty space comprise the skeleton of Petrobrás, a 1968 design by Roberto Luís Gandolfi, José H. Sanchotene, Abraão Assad, and Luís Fortes Netto. Terraces, columns, and sun baffles outfit the edifice. Renowned Brazilian landscaper Roberto Burle Marx lent his green thumb to the property gardens in 1969.
Avenida República do Chile, 65, Centro.

EDIFÍCIO SEGURADORAS
Look closely at the wavy façade of Seguradoras Building and you'll notice Paulo Werneck's surface of pink-and-grey mosaic, a design typical of Brazilian modernist architecture. While its façade has undergone several renovations, the inside of Seguradoras remains intact.
Rua Senador Dantas, 74, Centro.

ASSOCIAÇÃO BRASILEIRA DE IMPRENSA
Designed in 1936 by Brazilian architects Roberto brothers and completed the 1938, the Brazilian Press Association often ties with Gustavo Capanema Palace for the title of Brazil's first great modernist building.

Pillars support this marvel, which features a granite-lined foyer, a roof garden and vertical concrete Venetians as sun baffles.
Rua Araújo Porto Alegre, 71, Centro.

Gustavo Capanema Palace

Le Corbusier oversaw the construction of Palácio Gustavo Capanema between 1937 and 1943. Former headquarters of the Ministry of Education and Health and an icon of modern architecture, the palace was designed and built by a team of greats: Lúcio Costa, Oscar Niemeyer, Carlos Leão, Ernani Vasconcelos, Jorge Moreira, and Affonso Eduardo Reidy, among others. The building rests on 10-meter high pillars, with dedicated space for art exhibitions and theatrical performances.
See page 19 for more information. Rua da Imprensa, 16, Centro.

Instituto de Resseguros do Brasil

The Resseguros do Brasil Institute sits atop a series of pillars, its loftiness accented by high ceilings and a spiral staircase. The furniture, door handles, and light switches were created specially by the Roberto brothers to complement their design of the building.
Avenida Marechal Câmara, 171, Centro.

Jockey Club Brasileiro

The headquarters of the Jockey Club of Brasil occupies an entire city block. Built in 1956, the building features design by Lúcio Costa and interiors by Jorge Hue. A vertical garage in the structure's center is of particular interest.
Avenida Presidente Antônio Carlos, 501, Centro.

Edifício Marquês de Herval

Designed by the Roberto brothers in 1952, the 36-story Marquês de Herval Building is nicknamed – in typical Carioca whimsy – "Tem Nego Bebo Aí" ("There's a Drunk Over There"). Its modern, tapered surfaces and leaning windowsills lend the façade an illusion of intoxicated movement. Inside is **Livraria Leonardo da Vinci**, a bookshop founded in 1952 by Italian Vanna Piraccini and popular among Rio intellectuals *(store 2, 3, 4 and 9; tel. (21) 2533-2237; Mon – Fri, 9am – 7pm; Sat, 9am – 12:30pm)*. **Sebo Berinjela**, one of Rio's oldest used bookshops specializing in the social sciences, humanities, and literature, is also a tenant. *(store 10; tel. (21) 2215-3528; Mon – Fri, 9am – 7:30pm; Sat, 10am – 1pm)*.
Avenida Rio Branco, 185, Centro.

Banco Boa Vista

The 14-story Boa Vista Bank building, designed by Oscar Niemeyer in 1946, features pillars, glass bricks and sun baffles. A Paulo Werneck mosaic adorns the foyer, and an enormous tempera-painted panel by Cândido Portinari lines the mezzanine.
Praça Pio X, 118, Centro.

Aeroporto Santos-Dumont

Designed by the Roberto brothers in 1937 and built between 1938 and 1944, the terminal of Santos-Dumont Airoport sits atop pillars and features towering ceilings. Burle Marx landscaped the airport's gardens in 1938.
Praça Senador Salgado Filho, no #, Centro.

Praça Quinze de Novembro and Environs

Praça Quinze – as Praça Quinze de Novembro square is known by locals – is home to several notable historic buildings, including the former viceroys' grand residence and a number of gracious churches from Brazil's colonial period. The square sits between Rua Primeiro de Março and Avenida Alfredo Agache and extends down to the quay where boats depart for Rio, Niterói, and Ilha Paquetá (Paquetá Island). A stroll through the area will take you past museums, cultural centers, bookshops, and monuments. Morro de São Bento (São Bento Hill) and the Centro Cultural da Marinha (Navy Cultural Center) are further away and the best way to reach them is by taxi. All other attractions discussed in this section can be reached on foot. There are bistros, cafes and some restaurants for pit stops along the way. The metro is not a good transportation option, as the nearest station, Estação Uruguaiana, is a bit far from Praça Quinze. The nearest main avenues that run through the area around the square are: Avenida Presidente Kubitschek, Avenida Alfredo Agache, Avenida Rio Branco, and Avenida Presidente Vargas.

1. Igreja do Mosteiro de São Bento
2. Sede do Iphan
3. Igreja Nossa Senhora da Candelária
4. Centro Cultural Banco do Brasil
5. Casa França–Brasil
6. Centro Cultural Correios
7. Igreja Nossa Senhora da Lapa dos Mercadores
8. Igreja Santa Cruz dos Militares
9. Igreja da Ordem Terceira de Nossa Senhora do Monte do Carmo
10. Igreja de Nossa Senhora do Monte do Carmo
11. Praça Quinze
12. Paço Imperial
13. Palácio Tiradentes
14. Espaço Cultural da Marinha
15. Confeitaria Colombo

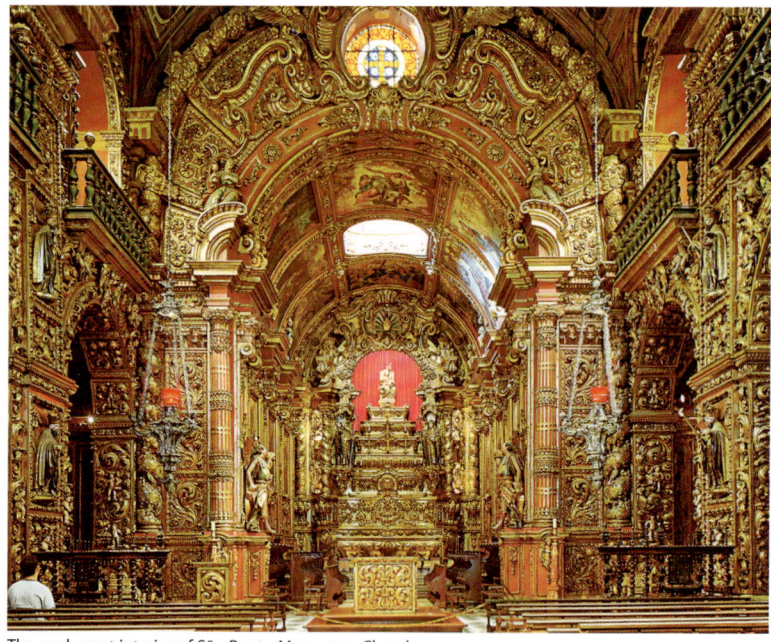

The exuberant interior of São Bento Monastery Church

❶ Igreja do Mosteiro de São Bento
Rio de Janeiro's greatest baroque monument, the São Bento Monastery Church, dates to 1690. During the 20th century the church underwent small-scale renovations, but the building itself has remained largely unchanged for the past three hundred years. The church's austere façade gives no hint of the rich interior and its gilt woodcarvings. Eight magnificent side altars are decorated with 17th- and 18th-century statues, and soft lighting preserves the pieces while creating a timeless atmosphere. Note the delicate angel wood carvings found throughout the church and, in the sacristy, the representation of Christ in the panel *Senhor dos martírios* (*The Lord of Martyrs*), painted by Friar Ricardo do Pilar around 1690. The chancel has carvings by master artist Inácio Ferreira Pinto. The cloister is only opened a few days a year, on Palm Sunday and Corpus Christi. On Sundays at 10am the monks sing Gregorian chants at mass – be sure and get there early if you want to hear them.
Rua Dom Gerardo, 68, Centro, tel. (21) 2291-7122. Daily, 8am – 11am and 2:30pm – 6pm.

❷ Iphan (National Institute for Historical and Artistic Heritage) Headquarters
Designed by architect Ramos de Azevedo and completed in 1908, most of the current Sexta Superintendência Regional do Iphan building is closed to the public. However, visitors are allowed to visit its restaurant and bookstore and view its foyer and Sala do Patrimônio hall. The foyer contains an impressive set of enormous doors with carved maritime images, as well as beautiful fresco paintings and a large chandelier. The Sala do Patrimônio hosts temporary history exhibits and the occasional musical performance

(for program information call (21) 2203-3145). On the ground floor is the charming **Livraria da Travessa**, a bookshop specializing in art, photography, and literature. At the building's pleasant restaurant-cafe, the **Bazzar**, intellectuals and lovers of literature meet behind a glass façade *(tel. (21) 2253-8949; Mon – Fri, 9am – 8pm; Sat, 9am – 1pm).*
Avenida Rio Branco, 46, Centro, tel. (21) 2203-3110. Mon – Fri, 10am – 6pm.

❸ Igreja Nossa Senhora da Candelária

Legend has it that a ship's captain built the original chapel of the Nossa Senhora da Candelária Church at the end of the 16th century as thanks to Our Lady of Candlemas for saving him from becoming shipwrecked. The current church went up in its place (1775-1898) and survived a series of demolitions in the area when Avenida Presidente Vargas was built in 1944. The church's interior is lined with marble, and panels painted by Zeferino da Costa circa 1880 decorate the nave ceiling and tell the story of the church's early days. Take time to admire the beautiful bronze doors by Portuguese sculptor Antônio Teixeira Lopes, which date from 1901. Praça Pio X (Pius X Square), in front of the church, is home to the 1934 sculpture *Mulher com ânfora (Woman with Amphora)* by São Paulo artist Humberto Cozzo. The statue is well worth a look.
Praça Pio X, Centro, tel. (21) 2233-2324. Mon – Fri, 7:30am – 3:50pm; Sat, 9am – noon; Sun, 9am – 1pm.

❹ Centro Cultural Banco do Brasil

The Bank of Brazil Cultural Center building (constructed 1880-1906) was designed by Francisco Joaquim Bethencourt da Silva, a follower of the neoclassical architect Grandjean de Montigny. Built to house the city's third Praça do Comércio (Stock Market), it became the property of the Bank of Brazil in the 1920s, and has been home to the bank-sponsored cultural center since 1989. It hosts

Skylight in the Banco do Brasil Cultural Center Hall

Doric columns at the Casa França-Brasil Foundation

popular place to meet, relax, and enjoy an after-hours drink. First-time visitors may want to take a few minutes to appreciate the building's eclectic yet refined architecture, particularly the skylight in the beautiful central hall. *Rua Primeiro de Março, 66, Centro, tel. (21) 3808-2020. Tue – Sun, 10am – 9pm.*

❺ Casa França-Brasil Foundation

The Casa França-Brasil, Rio's first neoclassical building, was designed by French architect Grandjean de Montigny, who came to Brazil in 1816 with the French Mission. In 1820, the house became the Praça do Comércio (Stock Market). It was the scene of a violent incident the following year when royal troops forced their way into it to break up a protesting crowd that was demanding a liberal constitution. In subsequent incarnations, the space housed the city's customs headquarters, a bank archive, and a court of law. Today it is a cultural center that hosts traveling exhibitions throughout the year (program details are available some of Rio's top events, including art exhibitions, concerts, and plays, and the building also houses a cinema, library, restaurant, and the bookshop **Livraria da Travessa**, with art books, exhibition catalogues, CDs of Brazilian music and gifts *(tel. (21) 3808-2066, Tue – Sun, noon – 8pm)*. Locals have made it a

---

Rua do Ouvidor (Magistrate Street)

"...*the busiest and most popular, the most frivolous, indiscreet, noisy, extravagant, gossipy, polyglot, comprehensive of a street in the city of Rio de Janeiro,*" wrote 19th century writer Joaquim Manuel de Macedo about the historic Rua do Ouvidor (Magistrate Street). The thoroughfare was first constructed in the late 16th century and given the name Desvio do Mar (Detour from the Sea). It came by its current name in the mid-18th century when the Crown magistrates built their houses there. English and French sophisticates, luxury stores, and publishing houses followed not far behind, and by the 19th century the street had become the "busiest and most popular" in Rio de Janeiro. In 1860 it was the first street to be lit by gas, and in 1891 it was also the first to upgrade to electric lighting. However, the opening of the Avenida Central in the early 20th century led to a decline in the popularity of Rua do Ouvidor as the fashion and elegance moved elsewhere. Nowadays it still retains bit of its original charm. Houses with fancy façades and the cobbled streets remain, but the shops are now mostly discount stores. Getting there is difficult, as it is closed to cars. Worth a bit of extra walking is the **Rio Minho** seafood restaurant, a Rua do Ouvidor resident since 1884 and a lunch destination frequented by famous local personalities, including the baron of Rio Branco and the philologist Antônio Houaiss. Try the *peixada com alho e açafrão*, a fish stew with garlic and saffron *(Rua do Ouvidor #10, Centro, tel. (21) 2509-2338; Mon – Fri, 11am – 4pm)*.

only in Portuguese at www.casafrancabrasil.rj.gov.br). Architectural highlights include 24 Doric columns (made of wood, with a style of painting known as *trompe l'oeil* that imitates marble) under the large central dome and skylight. There is a small bookshop that sells exhibition catalogues, a café, and a cinema. At the back of the building the **Arte Temperada Bistrô e Buffet** serves both French and Brazilian dishes. A particularly delicious menu option is the *carne-de-sol* (a kind of jerked meat, in this case made with filet mignon) served with traditional, homemade *manteiga de garrafa* butter, chunks of fried cassava, and pumpkin puree *(tel. (21) 2253-2589; daily, noon – 7pm).*
Rua Visconde de Itaboraí, 78, Centro, tel. (21) 2253-5366. Tue – Sun, noon – 8pm.

❻ POSTAL SERVICE CULTURAL CENTER
Construction of this eclectically designed building began around 1920. It was originally intended to serve as a venue for courses run by Lloyd Brasileiro. Before its inauguration in 1922, however, the building was purchased by the Brazilian Postal Service, which continued to use it through the 1980s. After a series of renovations it became the Centro Cultural Correios (Postal Service Cultural Center) in 1993. It still retains original elements of the 1920s interior, such as its tiny elevator. Free art exhibitions are held here, and the auditorium hosts a program of films, plays, and musical performances. The ground floor has a small gallery for exhibitions, a pleasant restaurant, and, of course, a post office. The adjacent square, **Praça dos Correios**, is sometimes host to open-air events and film screenings, like the Anima Mundi animation festival.
Rua Visconde de Itaboraí, 20, Centro, tel. (21) 2253-1580. Tue – Sun, noon – 7pm.

❼ IGREJA NOSSA SENHORA DA LAPA DOS MERCADORES
The modest Nossa Senhora da Lapa dos Mercadores Church, decorated in the baroque style on the outside and the rococo style on the inside, is considered by many to be the most charming little church in Rio de Janeiro. Its interior is home to many fine woodcarvings, and daylight spills into the sacristy through a skylight. Built by street vendors in 1750, it was first and foremost a public chapel. Extensive renovations in the 19th century were complicated by the Brazilian Naval Revolt of 1893, when cannon fire aimed at Itamaraty Palace hit the church's bell tower, instead, and knocked down a marble statue of the Madonna. The statue, which miraculously survived the ordeal unscathed, and the cannonball now sit in the sacristy.
Rua do Ouvidor, 35, Centro, tel. (21) 2509-2339. Mon – Fri, 8am – 2pm.

❽ IGREJA SANTA CRUZ DOS MILITARES
Constructed under the supervision of Brigadier José Custódio de Sá e Faria,

Nossa Senhora da Lapa dos Mercadores Church

the Santa Cruz dos Militares Church (built between 1780 and 1811) is custodian of the first map of Rio de Janeiro, drawn in 1812. Only researchers can view the artifact, however, and permission is granted on a request-by-request basis. The building's façade is decorated with marble statues of the evangelists Matthew, Mark, Luke, and John. The bones of military personnel of centuries past are buried within its walls. This church, which was listed as a national heritage site in 1938, hosted the wake of the Count of Eu, Princess Isabel's husband. Guided tours are provided.
Rua Primeiro de Março, 36, Centro, tel. (21) 2509-3878. Mon – Fri, 9am – 1pm and 2pm – 4pm; Sat, 9am – 1pm.

⑨ IGREJA ORDEM TERCEIRA DE NOSSA SENHORA DO MONTE DO CARMO
It took 15 years, beginning in 1755, to build Ordem Terceira de Nossa Senhora do Monte do Carmo Church. Known for many years as Capela dos Terceiros (Chapel of the Third Order), it is one of the only churches in Rio whose façade is made completely of stone. The architectural style is a mix of baroque and rococo. Inside are six altars that depict the Passion of Christ. The sacristy is home to a marble basin by master sculptor Valentim. In the high altar is a rare wooden statue of Emerentiana, Christ's great grandmother, portrayed alongside her daughter Saint Anne, and the Virgin Mary, who is holding the baby Jesus.
Rua Primeiro de Março, no #, Centro, tel. (21) 2242-4828. Mon – Fri, 8am – 4pm; Sat, 8am – noon.

⑩ IGREJA NOSSA SENHORA DO MONTE DO CARMO (FORMER CATHEDRAL)
The 18th century church was originally built to serve as a chapel for the royal family, and it subsequently functioned as a cathedral until 1977. The church is noteworthy for its marble basin, majestic ceiling paintings, high altar ornamented with wrought silver, and rococo-style carvings by master sculptor Inácio Ferreira Pinto (who is also responsible

Chapel of the Third Order: six altars illustrate the Passion of Christ

for the chancel in the church at São Bento Monastery). For two centuries, Rio de Janeiro's most important Catholic ceremonies were held here, including Pedro I's coronation mass and the royal family's weddings and baptisms. It was also the residence of Father José Maurício (1767-1830), one of the greatest names in Brazilian colonial music. Unfortunately the outside of the church has been changed, and many of its original architectural and decorative elements were lost. A full restoration, however, is scheduled to be completed by 2008 to commemorate the bicentennial of the Portuguese royal family's arrival in Brazil.
Rua Sete de Setembro, 15, corner of Rua Primeiro de Março, Centro, tel. (21) 2242-7766. Mon – Fri and every first Saturday of the month, 8am – 4 pm.

⓫ Praça Quinze de Novembro
Heading for Quinze de Novembro Square along the narrow alley known as Travessa do Comércio, one must pass under the **Arco do Telles**, a small arched passage built under the home of the Telles de Menezes family in the 18th century. Other historic landmarks sit nearby, including the Paço Imperial (Imperial Palace) and the 18th century pyramid-shaped marble and gneiss

---

Ilha de Paquetá

Boats and catamarans depart for the bucolic sands of Paquetá Island from Praça Quinze. The tiny island is a quiet place, and home to a number of cultural attractions, including the **Casa de Artes de Paquetá** art gallery *(tel. (21) 3397-0517; daily, 10am – 5pm)*, **Capela de São Roque** chapel *(open only for mass: Tue, 6pm; Thu, 3pm; Sun, 8am)* and the **Solar Del Rei** library *(tel. (21) 3397-0388; Tue – Sat, 8:30am – 4:30pm)*. Visitors also enjoy strolling through the island's pleasant green areas.

Fountain by Mestre Valentim

chafariz (fountain) by Master Valentim. In 1990, excavations around the fountain revealed elements of an old quay. This quay, called Pharoux Quay, once served as a gateway to the city. It was built in the 19th century to connect the cities of Rio and Niterói (located on the other side of the bay) by ferry. Today, boats continue to churn the waters between Rio, Niterói, and Ilha Paquetá (Paquetá Island), and they once again stop here, at what's now called **Estação das Barcas**. Timetables in Portuguese are available at www.barcas-sa.com.br.
In the center of the square is a late 19th-century monument to General Osório by the sculptor Rodolfo Bernardelli; the bronze statue was created in Paris and shipped to Brazil.

⓬ Paço Imperial
The colonial-style Imperial Palace, a national heritage site, served as primary residence of the viceroys of Brazil from 1743 to 1808, when it became the seat of the Portuguese Government under

Imperial Palace: from royal residence to cultural center

Dom João and his court. Less than ten years into his tenure, the colony was promoted to the title of United Kingdom of Portugal, Brazil, and the Algarve. Finally, in 1822, the palace was made the official seat of the Imperial Government. It was here that João VI was proclaimed king of Portugal, here that slavery was abolished with the signing of the Lei Áurea in 1888, and here in 1822 that the ruling prince, Pedro I, defied orders to return to Portugal and declared he would remain in Brazil – an event known as the Dia do Fico ("I shall stay" day). After Brazil became a republic the building served as headquarters for the national postal and telegraph service. Restored in 1985, it is currently home to the **Livraria Imperial**, a second-hand book

---

ILHA FISCAL AND ILHA DAS COBRAS

Trips around Rio's islands offer hours of contact with nature and history. Tiny **Fiscal Island** is home to a neo-Gothic castle designed to house a Ministry of Finance inspection post. The castle was built, but the ministry never showed up. Brazil's last imperial ball was held here just days before the country was proclaimed a republic in 1889. Some parts of the castle are open to visitors, including the Torreão, a tower with an ancient four-faced clock, and the Ala do Cerimonial wing, where there is a sitting room and a dining area with original 19th-century furnishings still intact. Note the imperial coat of arms at the main entrance, and take a minute to look at the castle's beautiful English stained-glass windows, which portray Pedro II and Princess Isabel. Visits are guided. Boats leave the mainland for the island from the Espaço Cultural da Marinha (Navy Cultural Center) on Avenida Alfredo Agache, no #, Praça Quinze, Centro *(the boat service is run by the Espaço Cultural da Marinha; tel. (21) 2233-9165)*. Located within historic Fortaleza de São José (São José Fortress), the Museu do Corpo dos Fuzileiros Navais on **Ilha das Cobras** (Snake Island) is a naval museum. The underground museum displays uniforms, naval documents, medals, old weapons, and silverware. Ilha das Cobras is connected to the mainland by a bridge. One can reach the island from Primeiro Distrito Naval, at Praça Barão de Ladário on the mainland *(tel. (21) 2126-5035; Tue – Fri, noon – 4pm; open Sat and Sun on the second weekend of each month)*.

PRAÇA QUINZE DE NOVEMBRO AND ENVIRONS

shop that specializes in the arts and humanities *(tel. (21) 2533-4537; Mon – Fri, 9am – 8pm; Sat, 11am – 5pm)*, as well as the **Arlequim** music store, which sells classical music, jazz, and Brazilian pop *(tel. (21) 2240-9398; Mon – Fri, 9am – 8pm; Sat, 10am – 5pm)*. There is also a movie theatre where festival films are shown. **Bistrô do Paço**, in the courtyard, is a nice place to stop for coffee *(tel. (21) 2262-3613; daily, 11am – 7pm)*. Right next door, the **Atrium** restaurant serves risottos and meat-based meals, among other dishes *(tel. (21) 2220-0193; Mon – Fri, 11:30am – 3:30pm)*.
Praça Quinze de Novembro, 48, Centro, tel. (21) 2533-4491. Tue – Sun, noon – 6pm.

⓭ PALÁCIO TIRADENTES

The dome of the majestic Tiradentes Palace is covered with allegorical statues depicting the Republic of Brazil and its independence. The palace is now home to the legislative assembly; it previously housed the Chamber of Deputies until the 1960s. The palace was built in 1926 to replace an old building that served as the seat of the empire's political power, as well as home to the prison in which Tiradentes, Brazil's independence martyr, was held before his execution. Take a walk through the palace and relive a little of Brazil's history with a guided tour; tours are available in English, French, Spanish, and Portuguese. Also worth noting is a painting by Eliseu Visconti, which illustrates the drafting of the 1891 Brazilian Constitution.
Rua Primeiro de Março, no #, Centro, tel. (21) 2588-1000. Mon – Sat, 10am – 5pm; Sun, noon – 5pm.

⓮ ESPAÇO CULTURAL DA MARINHA

The Navy Cultural Center takes visitors through history of navigation and sailing in Brazil. Near the entrance is a galliot (a small galley) built in 1808 for the Imperial family. Navigational tools such as maps and compasses are on display, as well as vessels from different eras. The center also displays works of

Different types of vessels are on display at the Navy Cultural Center

Art nouveau décor at Confeitaria Colombo

art (religious statues, Chinese porcelain, et cetera) pulled from shipwrecks along the Brazilian coast. Guided tours to Ilha Fiscal leave from here Thursday through Sunday at 1pm, 2:30pm and 4pm, except every second weekend of the month *(for further information see page 34)*. *Avenida Alfredo Agache, no #, Centro, tel. (21) 2104-6025. Ilha Fiscal tour bookings: tel. (21) 2104-6721, 2104-6992. Tue – Sun, noon – 5pm.*

Can of gaufrettes

15 Confeitaria Colombo
A visit to this traditional confectioner's is a step back in time: the Belgian mirrors, jacaranda furniture, Portuguese floors, and Italian marble date back to the day its doors first opened in 1894. It is one of the few places in Rio with art nouveau décor. The menu pays homage to illustrious patrons of old: there is (starlet) Virgínia Lane tea, *file mignon à gaúcha* (gaucho-style *file mignon* whose name is a reference to President Getúlio Vargas), and *sopa creme de palmito* (cream of palm heart soup, which was musician Chiquinha Gonzaga's favorite). The list of other famous clients includes writers Olavo Bilac and Machado de Assis.

Some desserts, like the *pastel de nata* (custard pastry), *trouxinha de ovos*, and *ovos moles* (both sweet, egg-based desserts), are still made according to century-old recipes. Delicious, crunchy *gaufrettes* (waffle cookies) have accompanied Confeitaria Colombo ice cream since 1920. Upstairs, **Restaurante Cristóvão** serves buffet lunch. An adjacent room houses the **Espaço Memória**, a small museum-like hall that displays tableware, crystal, and original menus. Visitors can purchase replica teacups, carafes, ashtrays, and menus. A pianist plays popular and classical music during lunch *(noon – 4pm)* and happy hour *(6pm – 8pm)*.
Rua Gonçalves Dias, 32, Centro, tel. (21) 2232-2300. Mon – Fri, 9:30am – 8pm; Sat, 9:30am – 5pm.

Praça Tiradentes and Environs

In the heart of Rio sits Praça Tiradentes, a square where humanity comes to a boil in a sea of heavy traffic. Yet the modern chaos of commerce and busy lives flows smoothly around numerous historic treasures. Various enduring churches, restaurants, theaters, and other noteworthy buildings have graced the square and surrounding streets for over a century. Though traffic is consistently heavy, you can get there by taxi or private car. Avenida Marechal Floriano, Avenida Presidente Vargas, Avenida Rio Branco, and Rua Senhor dos Passos all converge at the square. Alternatively, visitors can take the metro to any one of the following stations: Estação Central do Brasil, Estação Presidente Vargas, or Estação Uruguaiana.

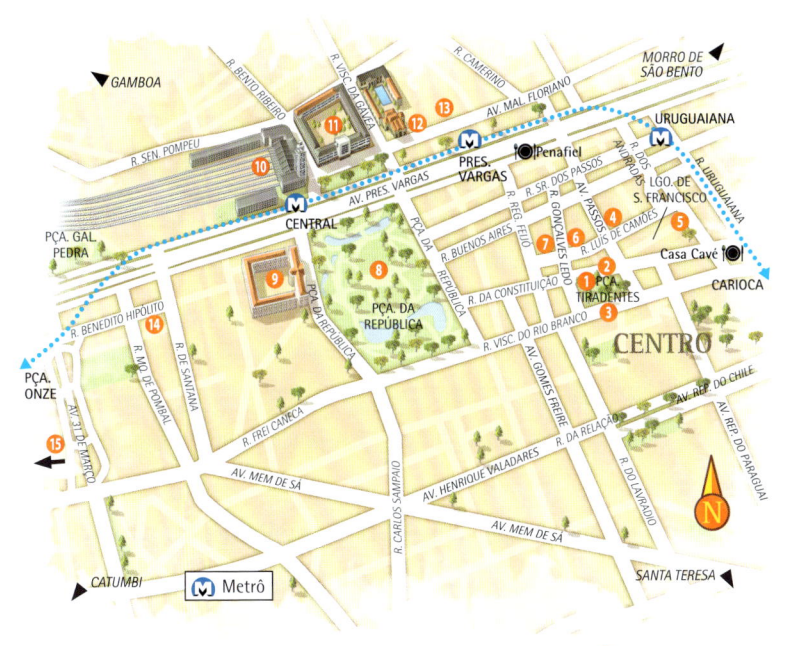

❶ Praça Tiradentes
❷ Teatro João Caetano
❸ Teatro Carlos Gomes
❹ Real Gabinete Português de Leitura
❺ Igreja de São Francisco de Paula
❻ Centro de Arte Hélio Oiticica
❼ A Gentil Carioca
❽ Campo de Santana
❾ Arquivo Nacional
❿ Estação Central do Brasil
⓫ Palácio Duque de Caxias
⓬ Palácio Itamaraty
⓭ Centro Cultural Light
⓮ Centro Cultural Calouste Gulbenkian
⓯ Sambódromo

❶ Praça Tiradentes

Four hundred years ago parts of Praça Tiradentes would have been knee deep in a 16th-century swamp. Damp though it was, at the time the area was already a meeting place for merchants. The area was originally known as Campo dos Ciganos (Gypsy Field), named for the gypsies who moved there when they were banished from Portugal in the early 18th century. The area was later named Campo da Lampadosa (Lampadosa Field), after the Nossa Senhora da Lampadosa Church that was built here

Praça Tiradentes and Environs

Statue of Dom Pedro I, by Louis Rochet, in Tiradentes Square

in 1748. Lampadosa is a saint worshiped by people of Africa *(Avenida Passos, 15, Centro, tel. (21) 2224-0898; Mon – Fri, 7am – 5pm; Sat, 7am – noon)*. The square was given its current name in 1892 in honor of Tiradentes, Brazil's martyr of independence, who attended mass in the square before he was executed. By the end of the 19th century all the remaining swampland had been filled and the area was frequented by Rio's elite. The eclectic, neoclassical buildings of the period are currently being restored to their former glory under the Ministry of Culture's Monumenta program. Nowadays, cultural attractions and historic buildings are crammed between noisy discount stores and bus terminals that cater to Rio's outer neighborhoods.

❷ **Teatro João Caetano and**
❸ **Teatro Carlos Gomes**
Two of Brazil's oldest theaters stand in Praça Tiradentes. Opened in 1810 as the Teatro Real de São João, the theater

---

Downtown Rio's Musical and Culinary Surprises

The dance hall **Gafieira Estudantina** opened its doors 75 years ago and has since become a meeting place for dancers and bohemians. The nowadays modernized facilities offer practice and performance space for a wide variety of musical groups, and the Gafieira's large parties draw a young crowd. The house's offerings change frequently – the best way to find out what's on is to visit www.estudantinamusical.com.br *(Praça Tiradentes, 79-81, Centro, tel. (21) 2232-1149; Thu – Sun, 10pm – 6am)*. **Casa Paladino**, another popular club, is housed in a 20th-century warehouse with a belle époque-style tavern out the back. The old watering hole, famous for its omelets, draws a faithful crowd that's every bit as interested in its history as in its delightful dishes *(Rua Uruguaiana, 224, Centro, tel. (21) 2263-2094; Mon – Fri, 7am – 8:30pm; Sat, 8am – noon)*.

today known as **João Caetano Theater** has seen both real and imagined dramas play out between its walls, including the ratification of the Portuguese Constitution by Dom Pedro in 1821. After sustaining damage from three large fires, the building was demolished, rebuilt, reopened, and renamed in 1923. The theater's 1,222 seats are frequently filled thanks to its busy calendar of shows, plays, and dance performances. On Wednesdays the Sambando e Chorando Project *(12:30pm)* features remarkable samba and *choro* music. Visitors may also want to take in the two carnival-themed panels by Di Cavalcanti on the second floor *(Praça Tiradentes, no #, Centro, tel. (21) 2221-1223. Box office: Tue – Fri, 2pm – 6pm)*. **Carlos Gomes Theater**, opened in 1888, was named in honor of São Paulo composer Carlos Gomes. Some of Brazil's greatest actors have performed here. The theater was twice destroyed by fire and rebuilt before ultimately sitting abandoned for years. In 1993, the city council bought, renovated, and reopened it. It seats 685 and features a wide variety of performances Thursday through Sunday *(Praça Tiradentes, no #, Centro, tel. (21) 2232-8701. Box office: Tue – Sun, 2pm – 6pm)*.

❹ Real Gabinete Português de Leitura

The most spectacular Portuguese-language library outside of Portugal is housed in this Manueline-style building that first opened in 1837. In the magnificent 75-foot-high medieval-looking reading room patrons sit at carved jacaranda tables under stained-glass skylights. The library holds some 350,000 titles, including such rarities as a copy of the 1572 first edition of Camoens's *Os Lusíadas* (a Brazilian classic, published in English as *The Lusiads*), and *Dicionário da língua tupy* (*Dictionary of the Tupi Language*; tupi was a native Brazilian language), by poet Gonçalves Dias. Rare works are only exhibited on special occasions. *Rua Luís de Camões, 30, Centro, tel. (21) 2221-3138. Mon – Fri, 9am – 6pm.*

❺ Igreja de São Francisco de Paula

Built over the course of nearly a hundred years beginning in 1759, the baroque elements of São Francisco de Paula Church's architecture are mixed with more classical features introduced during the church's many renovations. Although the building is in a poor state of repair and surrounded by itinerant street vendors, it is well worth a visit, especially to see the beautifully carved retable in the main altar whose craftsmanship is attributed to Mestre Valentim. *Largo de São Francisco, no #, Centro, tel. (21) 2509-0067. Mon – Fri, 9am – 1pm.*

Interior of the Real Gabinete Português de Leitura

Our Recommendation

🍴 The traditional and atmospheric **Penafiel** restaurant has been serving hearty Portuguese dishes since 1913. We suggest you try the *arroz de lula* (rice with squid) and the delicious *empada de palmito* (pastry filled with palm heart), which comes with sliced potatoes fried in Portuguese olive oil. *Rua Senhor dos Passos, 121, Centro, tel. (21) 2224-6870. Mon – Fri, 11am – 3:30pm)*

More restaurant information can be found on page 210.

❻ Centro de Arte Hélio Oiticica
Originally designed as a home for the Rio de Janeiro Conservatory of Music, the Hélio Oiticica Art Center's imposing 19th century headquarters house part of the collection of 60s and 70s vanguard artist Hélio Oiticica (1937-80). Now only shown on rare occasions, visitors who wish to see his work should call in advance for exhibit schedules. The center also holds exhibitions by famous names like Mira Schendel and Richard Serra. Most exhibits last two months and occupy all three floors. The center also hosts lectures, debates, and conferences. This beautifully restored building is an attraction in and of itself and is worth a visit, even when no exhibition is taking place. *Rua Luís de Camões, 68, Centro, tel. (21) 2232-4213. Tue – Fri, 11am – 7pm; Sat, Sun, and public holidays, 11am – 5pm.*

❼ A Gentil Carioca
Tucked away in the busy Saara commercial district is one of Rio's most important art galleries. Founded in 2003 by artists Ernesto Neto, Laura Lima, Márcio Botner, and Franklin Cassaro, A Gentil Carioca specializes in vanguard art. The gallery

---

Shopping in Saara and environs

The small area bordered by Avenida Presidente Vargas, Praça da República, Rua da Constituição, and Rua dos Andradas is known as the Saara District. Its sidewalks are jammed with stores selling clothes, toys, fabrics, carnival costumes, and all manner of knickknacks at affordable prices. Those who wish to venture into the narrow, cobbled streets should be prepared: The walkways overflow with shoppers and sellers and an incessant clamor issues forth from loudspeakers tapped into the public power lines overhead. Wear lightweight clothes and comfortable shoes. Traditionally a hub of the Arab community, the district is also home to many Portuguese who invested in its fabric, dressmaking, and sewing notions businesses in the early 20th century. Many original establishments have withstood the test of time and are still very successful. Famous, fun **Casa Turuna** was founded in 1915 and sells thousands of carnival items year-round *(Rua Senhor dos Passos, 122-124, Centro, tel. (21) 2509-3908. Mon – Fri, 9am – 6:30pm; Sat, 8:30am – 1:30pm)*. At the **Casa Pinto** fabric shop *(photo)*, opened in 1937, proprietor José helps customers personally *(Rua Buenos Aires, 233-235, Centro, tel. (21) 2224-0085. Mon – Fri, 9am – 6pm; Sat, 9am – 1pm)*. Just beyond the district's border sits the **Casa Cruz** stationery store, the oldest establishment in the area; its doors first opened in 1893. *(Rua Ramalho Ortigão, 26-28, Largo de São Francisco, Centro, tel. (21) 2506-3549. Mon – Fri, 8am – 7pm; Sat, 8:30am – 1:30pm)*.

PRAÇA TIRADENTES AND ENVIRONS

The National Archives holds an important collection of historical documents, photographs, and maps

is a meeting place for contemporary artists and art lovers alike.
Rua Gonçalves Ledo, 17, Centro, tel. (21) 2222-1651. Tue – Fri, noon – 7pm; Sat, noon – 5pm.

❽ Campo de Santana

Campo de Santana (Santana Field) was bestowed with its current name in the mid-18th century, when Nossa Senhora de Santana Chapel was built here. The chapel was demolished in the 19th century to make way for a railway station known today as Central do Brasil (the setting for Walter Salles's 1998 film *Central Station*). The field was used for military training exercises and official celebrations before it was landscaped and turned into a park at the request of Dom Pedro II. Inaugurated in 1880, the 3.5-acre park is dotted by works of art and centuries-old fig trees. The collection of outdoor art includes four fountains by French artists as well as a monument to Brazilian military man and politician Benjamin Constant. The Municipal Parks and Gardens Department headquarters is located in the park.
Praça da República, no #, Centro. Daily, 9am – 5pm.

❾ Arquivo Nacional

The neocolonial National Archives building housed the Brazilian Mint until 1983. It currently stores documents, photographs, maps, and audiovisual materials related to the history of Brazil from the colonial period through the 1980s. Some

Our Recommendation

🍽 Though founded by a Frenchman, **Casa Cavé** is famous for the Portuguese ice creams and sweets it has been making since 1890. Installed in an old hat factory, the confectioners serves *pastéis de nata* (custard pastry), *dom-rodrigos* (almond candy), and other delicacies to its large, faithful clientele. *Rua Sete de Setembro, 137, Centro, tel. (21) 2221-0533. Mon – Fri, 9am – 7pm; Sat, 9am – 1pm.*

More information on restaurants can be found on page 210.

Central do Brasil Metro Station (on the left) and Duque de Caxias Palace

documents are now available online at www.arquivonacional.gov.br. The building, a national heritage site, is open to the public. A reservation is required, however, for access to the collection.
Praça da República, 173, Centro, tel. (21) 3806-6175. Mon - Fri, 8:30am – 5:30pm. Collection consultation closes at 4pm.

❿ ESTAÇÃO CENTRAL DO BRASIL
When the Central do Brasil Railroad system opened in 1858, Estação Central do Brasil Station opened its doors as well. The station has South America's largest four-faced clock tower. The current art deco building dates to 1946. Estação Pedro II – the station's historic name – was called Central do Brasil by locals. The local title became official in 1998 after it served as the setting for Walter Salles's award-winning film *Central Station*. Trains leaving from its thirteen platforms connect the downtown area to Rio's North and West Zones, as well as other cities in the region.
Praça Cristiano Otôni, no #, Centro, tel. (21) 2111-9494. Daily, 5am – 11:40pm.

⓫ PALÁCIO DUQUE DE CAXIAS
The enormous Duque de Caxias Palace (built 1937-1941) was designed by Cristiano Stockler das Neves to replace the Campo de Santana army barracks. The old barracks dated back to 1811; Brazil, in fact, was proclaimed a republic within its walls. The sumptuous palace, all 21 acres of it, was the largest public building of its time. It has a marble façade and beautiful 43-foot stained-glass windows in the foyer. On the tenth floor is the Salão de Honra, a room completely lined with marble *(reservations are required to visit this room)*. It's worth taking a moment to see the bronze statues by Hildegardo Leão Veloso on the tower, as well as the *sucupira*-wood doors. Sitting in front of the palace is the **Panteão de Caxias**, a monument that contains the remains of Duque de Caxias, patriarch of the Brazilian Army and his wife.
Avenida Presidente Vargas, 25, Centro,

PRAÇA TIRADENTES AND ENVIRONS

tel. (21) 2519-5762, 2519-5214. Mon and Wed, 8:30am – 4:30pm; Tue and Thu, 10am – 4:30; Fri, 8am – noon.

⑫ PALÁCIO ITAMARATY

Built by the baron of Itamaraty, the Itamaraty Palace (1851-1854) houses the Museu Histórico e Diplomático (Historical and Diplomatic Museum), the Arquivo Histórico (Historic Archive), the Mapoteca (Map Library), and the Biblioteca do Itamaraty (Itamaraty Library). The museum of history exhibits intaglio prints, china, lamps, and paintings by Debret and Pedro Américo, as well as furniture from Dom Pedro II's office. The archive holds approximately 6 million Brazilian diplomatic documents; the oldest dates back to 1808. The map library contains a vast cartographic collection, with thousands of maps, atlases, nautical charts, and drawings dating back to the 16th century. Finally, the library holds close to 65 thousand volumes relevant to Brazil's history, including the Baron of Rio Branco's personal collection.

The palace has also served as a presidential residence; presidents Deodoro da Fonseca, Floriano Peixoto, and Prudente de Morais all lived here. Reservations are required to visit the palace and must be made in advance by phone.
Avenida Marechal Floriano, 196, Centro, tel. (21) 2223-1284 (reception), 2263-2828 (museum). Mon – Fri, 10am – 5pm.

⑬ CENTRO CULTURAL LIGHT

Built in 1911 to house the Light & Power Electric Company, each piece of the façade arrived in numbered pieces from the United States. Since 1994 the building has housed the Cultural Light Center. Seven exhibition rooms hold the permanent collection. The Espaço Rio Antigo (Old Rio Space) displays photographs of the city by Augusto Malta, who spent three decades (1903-36) recording important moments in Rio's urban history. The Espaço Di Cavalcanti (Di Cavalcanti Space) has four of the painter's canvases on display, produced when he worked for the newspaper *Última hora*, along with some items of furniture from the same newspaper. Planeta Energia (Planet Energy) houses an exhibit of scientific discoveries aimed toward children. The Espaço Bonde (Streetcar Space) has a restored streetcar used for artistic performances, and the Espaço Caminhão Elétrico (Electric Truck Space) explores the company's first means of transporting services. Educational performances and videos can be seen in the Teatro Lamartine (Lamartine Theatre) and Sala de Vídeo (Video Room), respectively, and visitors can read about the company's

19th-century Itamaraty Palace

Samba School parade: an unforgettable experience for both participants and spectators

history in the Espaço Memorial (Memorial Space). Guides are available. *Avenida Marechal Floriano, 168, Centro, tel. (21) 2211-7268. Mon – Fri, 11am – 5pm.*

14 CENTRO CULTURAL CALOUSTE GULBENKIAN
At the Calouste Gulbenkian Cultural Center (built 1971) one can take courses in sculpture, drawing, painting, dance, and decorative arts. The center has two galleries, the Ismael Nery Gallery and Calouste Gulbenkian Gallery, where teachers' and students' artwork is exhibited. Shows, dance performances, and plays are staged in the Teatro Gonzaguinha (Gonzaguinha Theater). Gallery and performance admission is free.
Rua Benedito Hipólito, 125 (Praça Onze), Centro, tel. (21) 2221-6213. Mon – Fri, 9am – 5pm.

15 SAMBÓDROMO
Architect Oscar Niemeyer made the first sketch of Sambódromo Avenue on a paper towel in a bar, the Passarela do Samba, popularly known as the Sambódromo. The avenue was built in just 120 days for the carnival of 1984. Samba schools have been dancing their way down the 710-yard stretch ever since.
A few miles away, the **Centro de Memória do Carnaval**, a kind of carnival museum, has a vast iconographic, phonograph, and bibliographic carnival collection. You must make a reservation in advance in order to tour the museum. *(Avenida Rio Branco, 4, 2nd floor, Centro, tel. (21) 3213-5151; Mon – Fri, 2pm – 6pm).*
Rua Marquês de Sapucaí, no # (Praça Onze), Cidade Nova.

Saúde and Gamboa

No strict boundaries exist between the neighboring ports of Saúde and Gamboa. They are interconnected both geographically and historically. Once a hub for slave trade, the area has become an important center of Afro-Brazilian culture. Historical sites dot the seaside, from the cobbled Morro da Conceição (Conceição Hill) to Pedra do Sal (literally "Salt Rock") to the Cemitério dos Ingleses (British Burial Ground). Recent revitalization projects have attracted several bars and taverns to the area, many featuring the best samba and *choro* music for miles. Rio's first skyscraper stands nearby, in Praça Mauá (Mauá Square), which was originally home to the prestigious Rádio Nacional radio station. To reach Saúde and Gamboa, travel along Avenida Rio Branco, Avenida Rodrigues Alves, or Avenida Presidente Vargas – all major thoroughfares.

Attractions
1. 2. Morro and Fortaleza da Conceição
3. Largo da Prainha
4. Pedra do Sal
5. Igreja de Nossa Senhora da Saúde
6. Centro Cultural José Bonifácio
7. Cidade do Samba
8. Cemitério dos Ingleses
9. Apartamentos operários

Bars
1. Trapiche da Gamboa
2. Cabaret Kalesa

❶ Morro da Conceição and ❷ Fortaleza da Conceição

Built in 1715 to protect Rio from French attack, Fortaleza da Conceição fortress sits atop Morro da Conceição hill, on church land behind the Palácio Episcopal (Episcopal Palace). Its powerful artillery never fired on the French, though, and its only test firing was something of a debacle. The rattle from the explosions damaged some furnishings in the palace, and Bishop Francisco de São Jerônimo, who occupied it, demanded

Detail of Conceição Fortress, built behind the Episcopal Palace in 1715

that the soldiers cease firing. So irked was the bishop that he later successfully sought indemnity from the Portuguese Crown for the damage to the property. Years later, the building, awarded national heritage status in 1938, served as a prison for conspirators in the Inconfidência Mineira independence movement. The fortress is currently headquarters for the Brazilian Army's Geographical Service. Guided tours are available for groups of six or more persons; the tours include a visit to the Museu Cartográfico (Cartography Museum) in the Palácio Episcopal. The 1798 map of the Carta Nova Lusitânia is a tour highlight *(Rua Major Daemon, 81, Centro; tel. (21) 2263-9664; Mon – Thu, 8am – noon and 1pm – 4pm; Fri, 8am – noon)*. Pleasant Morro da Conceição is also worth a stroll, preferably with a stop at the informal **Bar do Odilo**, which is popular among locals despite its irregular hours. Quaint houses along the nearby **Rua do Jogo da Bola** give a glimpse into simpler times of centuries past.

❸ LARGO DA PRAINHA

Samba, carnival-group rehearsals, and *chorinho* music add to the liveliness of Prainha Square. The historic Igreja de São Francisco da

A sentry box at Fortaleza da Conceição

SAÚDE AND GAMBOA

> ### NIGHTLIFE
>
> A mixed crowd sets the relaxed, cheerful vibe at **Trapiche da Gamboa**, a key player in Rio's samba scene since 2004. Women's samba sessions, and samba performances by Eduardo Galotti and Galocantô occur inside the beautiful 1867 mansion *(Rua Sacadura Cabral, 155, Saúde; tel. (21) 2516-0868, 2233-9276; Tue – Thu, 6:30pm – 1am; Fri, 6:30pm – 3am; Sat, 8:30pm – 3am)*. **Cabaret Kalesa**, a popular dancehall in the 80s and 90s, reopened in 2005 with an eclectic, unconventional agenda: an alternative crowd enjoys everything from samba to stripteases. On Fridays, DJ Tom spins MPB (popular Brazilian music) and electronic music. DJs Yuri and Janot spice up Saturdays with MPB and carnival music. Guests can catch fresh air between songs on one of Kalesa's balconies, which overlook Morro da Conceição *(Rua Sacadura Cabral, 61, Saúde; tel. (21) 2516-8332; Fri – Sat, 10pm – 5am)*.

Prainha church, built from 1738 to 1748, sits on the square.
Largo de São Francisco da Prainha, Saúde.

❹ PEDRA DO SAL

A famous meeting place for slaves and migrants, Pedra do Sal ("Salt Rock"), at the foot of Morro da Conceição, also brought together several of Brazil's first carnival groups. Legendary musicians Pixinguinha, Donga, João Baiana and Cartola, have their origins here. By the early 20th century Pedra had become a sacred site; offerings were left to the gods during festivities. Today it's still a popular place for cultural events. The Projeto Sal do Samba hosts a monthly samba session accompanied by *feijoada* (Brazil's traditional black-bean stew). With its roots firmly planted in the history of Morro da Conceição, Pedra do Sal was declared an Afro-Brazilian monument and listed as a state heritage site in 1984.
Rua Argemiro Bulcão, no #, Saúde.

❺ IGREJA DE NOSSA SENHORA DA SAÚDE

Eighteenth-century Portuguese tiles line the interior of Nossa Senhora da Saúde Church, depicting scenes from Joseph's travels in Egypt. Listed on the national heritage registry in 1938, the baroque church was under renovation at press time, but it was due to reopen by May 2007.
Rua Silvino Montenegro, 52, Saúde, Information, tel. (21) 2253-3645.

❻ CENTRO CULTURAL JOSÉ BONIFÁCIO

Inaugurated in 1877 by Dom Pedro I, this building housed the José Bonifácio School until 1966. In 1983, when it became a cultural center, the

Pedra do Sal: an Afro-Brazilian cultural landmark

namesake was retained in homage to Bonifácio, the patriarch of Brazil's independence. Talks, conferences, book fairs, and music and dance performances held here aim to preserve Afro-Brazilian culture. Nicknamed "Zéboni" (a shortening of José Bonifácio), the center features temporary exhibitions by black artists, performances in the 200-seat **Teatro Ruth de Souza** and movies in the tiny **Cine Vídeo Grande Othelo**.
Rua Pedro Ernesto, 80, Gamboa, tel. (21) 2253-6255. Mon – Fri, 9am – 6pm; Sat, 10am – 5pm.

❼ Cidade do Samba

Founded in 2005, Cidade do Samba (literally "Samba City") houses 14 samba schools from veteran carnival group. Visit from November to February to see the workshops in full swing. Catch a glimpse at the early stages of a carnival float or view costumes from the previous year's carnival on display. In the off-season, samba musicians and dancers host smaller shows for tourists. *(2pm, 4pm, and 6pm)*. Members of the samba schools perform in the main square *(Thu, 8pm, no set finishing time).*
Rua Rivadávia Correia, 60, Gamboa, tel. (21) 2213-2503. Wed – Mon, noon and 6pm.

❽ Cemitério dos Ingleses

British ambassador Lord Stranford requested the construction of this British Burial Ground after large numbers of Protestant families began emigrating to the country. Completed in 1809, the grounds were equipped with a quay for offloading those who died at sea. Officials recognized the cemetery as a national heritage site in 1988.
Rua da Gamboa, 181, Gamboa.

❾ Apartamentos Operários

Architects Lúcio Costa and Gregori Warchavchik helped to tackle Rio de Janeiro's already-complex housing problem in 1932 by creating these modernist worker's apartments, the first of their kind aimed at Rio's lower class. Sociologist and anthropologist Gilberto Freyre recognized the designers' efforts in the preface of his 1932 study *Casa-grande & senzala* (published in English as *The Masters and the Slaves*). Although time and weather have run their course, the buildings maintain their original façade – a series of staggered cubes that follow the curve of the street.
Rua Barão da Gamboa, 160, Santo Cristo.

The Port, by Machado de Assis

He walked for a long while, passed Saco do Alferes Beach and Gamboa, stopped in front of the British Burial Ground, with its old graves backing up the hill, and finally reached Saúde. He saw narrow streets, others sloping upwards, houses jammed together in the distance and atop the hills, alleys, lots of old houses, some ancient, decaying, cracked, gutted, the filthy quay, and life inside. And it all gave him a feeling of nostalgia. Much about Rio's port today still resembles the place described in Machado de Assis's 1891 Brazilian classic *Quincas Borba* (published in English as *Philosopher or Dog? Quincas Borba*). But with rapid airport and highway construction, the area no longer holds the title of gateway to the city. It's precisely for this reason that Saúde and Gamboa have managed to retain their traditional aesthetic. These are among the few places left in Rio that can transport visitors back to the 19th century.

São Cristóvão and Environs

Traditional São Cristóvão sits in Rio's Zona Norte (North Zone). The neighborhood took its name from a chapel built by Jesuits in the 16th century. In 1808, a local businessman donated his luxurious country manor to the royal family, who promptly moved into what became known as São Cristóvão Palace. The building now houses the National Museum. By the mid-20th century the neighborhood began to develop an industrial character. To this day a number of small factories, modest shops, low-income residences, bars, and restaurants call São Cristóvão home. If you are traveling by car from the Zona Sul (South Zone), take Túnel Rebouças tunnel; if traveling by metro, take a line 2 train and get off at Estação São Cristóvão or Estação Maracanã.

1. Quinta da Boa Vista
2. Museu Nacional
3. Jardim Zoológico
4. Museu do Primeiro Reinado (Solar da Marquesa de Santos)
5. Feira de São Cristóvão
6. Museu de Astronomia e Ciências Afins
7. Centro de Abastecimento do Estado da Guanabara (Cadeg)
8. Maracanã

1 Quinta da Boa Vista

Boa Vista Estate's lovely garden, landscaped in 1869 by Auguste Glaziou, is dotted with lakes, caves, and marble and bronze statues. A tree-lined avenue leads to the old Palácio São Cristóvão (São Cristóvão Palace), now the Museu Nacional (National Museum), as well as the Jardim Zoológico (Zoo), the Museu da Fauna (Animal Museum), and the alfresco **Quinta da Boa Vista** restaurant, which whips up a selection of tasty dishes for hungry patrons, including their famous *rabada* (oxtail stew) *(tel. (21) 2589-6551, 2589-4279; daily, 11am – 6pm)*.

The National Museum houses extensive collections in natural history, anthropology, and paleontology

The park is quiet and not well-policed, so we recommend you go in a group or with a local guide.
Avenida Pedro II, no #, São Cristóvão. Tue – Sun, 10am – 4pm.

❷ Museu Nacional

The National Museum holdings include a large natural history, paleontology, and anthropology collection that used to belong to the Museu Real (Royal Museum) created in 1818 by Dom João VI. Visitors can see dinosaur fossils, Egyptian mummies and sarcophagi, Greco-Roman pottery, indigenous Brazilian artifacts, and the Bendegó iron meteorite, the largest in the Americas. It also hosts temporary exhibitions. Guided visits are available for groups only and must be booked at least two weeks in advance.
Parque Quinta da Boa Vista, no #, São Cristóvão, tel. (21) 2568-8262. Tue – Sun, 10am – 4pm.

❸ Jardim Zoológico

Located behind the Museu Nacional (National Museum), the Zoological Gardens are home to over 2,100 animals (350 species in all) including reptiles, mammals, and birds. It has several rare species including the king vulture, the ararajuba pygmy owl, and the capuchin monkey, and treats sick and injured animals found on the Rio coast. In the Casa Noturna, a dark, cavern-like space, visitors can watch nocturnal creatures go about their nighttime business. The zoo has a luncheonette and a picnic area. The imposing gate at the entrance was given to Dom João in 1812 by the duke of Northumberland. Guided tours must be booked in advance.
Parque Quinta da Boa Vista, no #, São Cristóvão, tel. (21) 2569-2024. Tours: (21) 2567-9732, 2569-5869. Tue – Sun, 9am – 4:30pm.

❹ Museu do Primeiro Reinado (Solar da Marquesa de Santos)

Dom Pedro I built this spacious two-story home in 1827 for his mistress Domitila de Castro Canto e Melo, Marchioness of Santos. Allegorical paintings by Francisco Pedro do Amaral grace its walls, and the upstairs rooms are still home to some of the marchioness' personal effects, as well as furniture and weapons from Brazil's imperial period. The museum's bas-reliefs are attributed to the brothers Marc and Zépherin Ferrez, members of the French Artistic Mission. Notice the heart-festooned flags on the doors and windows; they were meant to illustrate the Emperor's passion for his mistress.
Avenida Pedro II, 283, São Cristóvão, tel. (21) 2299-2148. Tue – Fri, 11am – 5pm.

❺ Feira de São Cristóvão

The Pavilhão de São Cristóvão (São Cristóvão Pavilion), headquarters of the Centro Luiz Gonzaga de Tradições Nordestinas (Luiz Gonzaga Center for Northeastern Traditions), hosts the São Cristóvão Fair, a street fair of food, arts and crafts, and literature from northeast Brazil. On weekends there is *forró* music and dancing all night long. Long-term patrons complain, however, that the quality of the music has recently dropped off. Parking is available at the pavilion.
Campo de São Cristóvão, no #, São Cristóvão, tel. (21) 2580-0501. Tue – Thu, 10am – 4pm; 10am Friday around the clock until 10pm Sunday.

❻ Museu de Astronomia e Ciências Afins

The Museum of Astronomy and Related Sciences, a research institute created in 1985, is connected to the Ministry of Science and holds a collection of scientific instruments dating back to the 19th century. A variety of lamps, sculptures, crystals, thermometers, and astronomical instruments rotate through its exhibit rooms. Every Saturday the institute hosts activities for children and teenagers, including storytelling, science talks, and planetarium demonstrations. We recommend that you call to ask what's on. Every Wednesday and Saturday the institute opens its doors for star-watching from 6pm to 8pm.
Rua General Bruce, 586, São Cristóvão, tel. (21) 2580-7010. Tue, Thu, and Fri, 10am – 5pm; Wed, 10am – 8pm; Sat, 2pm – 8pm; Sun, 2pm – 6pm.

❼ Centro de Abastecimento do Estado da Guanabara (CADEG)

Located in the neighborhood of Benfica, near São Cristóvão, this enormous municipal market is *the* place to buy all manner of plants and flowers. The Portuguese community throws a lively party here every Saturday. During the rest of the week visitors often choose to unwind with a glass of draft beer and finger food from one of the market stalls.
Rua Capitão Félix, 110, Benfica, tel. (21) 3890-0202. Daily, noon – midnight.

Our Recommendation

🍽 Opposite Centro Luiz Gonzaga de Tradições Nordestinas, the **Adegão Português** restaurant serves a range of cod dishes – all excellent and served in generous portions. For something other than cod, try the highly-praised *leitão assado* (roast suckling pig).
Rua Campo de São Cristóvão, 212, tel. (21) 2580-7288, 2580-8689. Mon – Sat, 11am – 11pm; Sun, 11am – 8pm.

More information on restaurants starts on page 210.

8 Maracanã

A world soccer symbol, Maracanã Stadium (officially called Estádio Jornalista Mário Filho, or Journalist Mário Filho Stadium) was built for the 1950 FIFA World Cup. The stadium seats 80,000, and extensions scheduled to be finished in November 2007 will add another 15,000 to that number. The stadium has hosted shows by a number of famous artists including Frank Sinatra, Paul McCartney, and Madonna. Within the same complex are several other sports venues. Cultural and athletic events are held at the **Maracanãzinho** (Little Maracanã), and three Olympic-size swimming pools are open to the public at the **Parque Aquático** (Aquatic Park). Be sure to visit the hall with photographs of players and the ball with which Pelé kicked his 1,000th goal, and the **Calçada da Fama** (Walk of Fame), where one can see the footprints of Brazil's greatest players. Guided tours cover special seating, the athletes' changing rooms, and the tunnel to the field – with sound effects that simulate a crowded stadium. Tours must be booked in advance. If you have time, try to catch a game at the stadium. *(Tours organized by: Be a Local, tel. (21) 9643-0366, 7816-9581, 7816-9582.)*
Rua Professor Eurico Rabelo, no #, Maracanã, tel. (21) 2566-7800, 2299-2941. Daily, 9am – 5pm.

> ### Modernist Architecture in São Cristóvão
>
> Designed by Affonso Eduardo Reidy in 1947, the **Conjunto Residencial Prefeito Mendes de Morais** complex, better known as "Pedregulho," is a landmark of modernist architecture in Rio de Janeiro. Its first residents were public servants. In addition to residential blocks, the complex also has a nursery, school, grocery store, laundromat, swimming pool, shops, and sports courts. The complex's school has a mosaic by Burle Marx, and the gymnasium has a painted tile panel by Di Cavalcanti.
> *Rua Capitão Félix, 50, São Cristóvão*

Maracanã Stadium: a venue for shows, soccer matches, and guided tours

Lapa

Gangsters, musicians and samba composers. Pimps, prostitutes and poets. Those and assorted other hipsters populate the neighborhood of Lapa and drive Rio de Janeiro's lively bohemian culture. In the 1930s, famous figures such as composer Noel Rosa and former outlaw and drag performer Madame Satã frequented the area, which owes its name to the mid-18th-century church Igreja Nossa Senhora do Carmo da Lapa do Desterro, in Largo da Lapa square. After a period of decline, the area has made a comeback, with music venues, bars, and taverns that cater to varied clienteles with the sounds of samba, *choro*, and MPB (popular Brazilian music). Avenida Mem de Sá has several houses that offer excellent music, *chope* (draft beer), and snacks. Besides nightlife, the neighborhood's main historical attractions are concentrated around Largo da Lapa and on Rua dos Arcos, Rua do Passeio, and Rua do Lavradio. You can get to Lapa by car or bus along Avenida Mem de Sá, Avenida República do Paraguai, and Avenida Augusto Severo.

Attractions
1. Arcos da Lapa
2. Circo Voador
3. Fundição Progresso
4. Teatro Odisséia
5. Feira Rio Antigo
6. Museu da Imagem e do Som (MIS)
7. Escadaria Selarón
8. Sala Cecília Meireles
9. Igreja Nossa Senhora do Carmo da Lapa do Desterro
10. Escola de Música da Universidade Federal do Rio de Janeiro
11. Passeio Público

Bars
1. Comuna do Semente
2. Casa Brasil Mestiço
3. Estrela da Lapa
4. Carioca da Gema
5. Café Cultural Sacrilégio
6. Bar Brasil
7. Nova Capela
8. Clube dos Democráticos
9. Rio Scenarium
10. Mangue Seco

1 Arcos da Lapa

Most of the almost 300-yard-long Aqueduto da Carioca, also known as Arcos da Lapa (Lapa Arches), was built during the first half of the 18th century. To solve the city's chronic water supply problem, the aqueduct connected the Carioca River to the hills of Santa

The Arcos da Lapa Aqueduct, built to improve the city's water supply, features 42 arches

Teresa and Santo Antônio, bringing water from the Carioca River to a large public fountain in the Largo da Carioca (Carioca Square). The Count of Bobadela oversaw its completion in the 1750s, when he was governor of Rio de Janeiro. In 1896 it became a viaduct for Carioca Curvelo streetcars, offering visitors a bird's-eye view of Largo da Lapa (Lapa Square), where many cultural events are held.
Largo da Lapa, no #, Centro.

❷ CIRCO VOADOR
Many seminal events in the recent history of Brazilian pop music have taken place at the Circo Voador. In the 1980s Brazilian rock legends Barão Vermelho, Blitz, Legião Urbana, and Kid Abelha all debuted here and actors like Regina Casé and Luís Fernando Guimarães performed here. In the 1990s it was an obligatory stop for bands and musicians such as Planet Hemp, O Rappa, Cidade Negra, Chico Science and Lenine. Its stage has launched theatre groups such as Intrépida Trupe and Teatro do Anônimo and hosted dance performances by Carlinhos de Jesus, Jayme Arôcha and Déborah Colker. It reopened in 2004 after an eight year hiatus and

---

MALANDROS AND BOHEMIANS

The neighborhood of Lapa has attained an almost mythical status, as a zone in which Rio's shadier elements once rubbed shoulders with bohemians and intellectuals. In the early 20th-century poets, painters, journalists, and musicians walked its streets, along with prostitutes, gamblers, and *malandros*. The latter are still its most memorable symbol: the *malandro* is a romanticized small-time hood, an archetypal figure of the distant past who still inhabits the folklore of Rio de Janeiro. This bohemian Lapa, immortalized in the songs of famous samba composers, went through ups and downs until it went into a steep decline in the 1970s. At the turn of the 21st century, however, it reemerged. Its old mansions are being restored and converted into music venues, bars, and taverns, where typical Brazilian (and local) music can be heard. The neighborhood began to attract a new clientele, especially university students and young people from the middle classes seeking the mixture of tradition and fun that the area has to offer. The newcomers join a rollicking mix of transvestites, beggars, and other characters in the neighborhood's pool parlors, dive bars, strip clubs, and gay nightclubs.

renovation. Some traditional events are still held here, including the dance Domingueira Voadora on Sundays, and the Cine-Circo short film screenings. See www.circovoador.com.br for program details (in Portuguese).
Rua dos Arcos, no #, Lapa, tel. (21) 2533-0354, 2533-6179. Tue – Fri, 7pm until the last person leaves; Sat, Sun, and holidays, 8pm until the last person leaves.

❸ Fundição Progresso
This large cultural center located next to Circo Voador, with seating for 5,000, is pivotal in the Brazilian music world. It features an eclectic program of shows in its enormous arena that includes a stage, dance floor, and stadium seating. During Carnival, thousands of people come to watch the rehearsals of the Monobloco samba group, led by musician Pedro Luís and his band A Parede. The center also offers a range of workshops and serves as the headquarters for companies such as Intrépida Trupe, Teatro do Anônimo, and Vídeo Fundição. Installed in an old oven factory that was once saved from demolition by public protest, it has two floors with spaces of different sizes and styles, and four small theatres. It also hosts parties and fairs, and has served as a film set.
Rua dos Arcos, 24, Lapa, tel. (21) 2220-5070. Daily, 10am – 10pm. Shows: 10pm – 5am.

❹ Teatro Odisséia
Teatro Odisséia inhabits mansion built in 1907 and features one of the most diverse lineup of shows and music in Rio de Janeiro. It hosts both new performers and established groups and singers. Some shows (rock, pop, *baião*, samba, *coco*, and *forró*, etc.) are held on the first floor, where there is a dance floor. There is a mezzanine on the second floor with tables and chairs for less participatory performances. A space for exhibitions and theatrical performances occupies the third floor. There are also parties with Carnival and *maracatu* groups or DJs. The house menu includes bar food with an innovative twist – *rolinhos de moranga e carne seca* (shredded beef and pumpkin rolls), served with curd cheese and mango chutney.

Circo Voador has hosted shows and plays since the 1980s

LAPA

Building façades on Rua do Lavradio, a street lined with antique shops

Avenida Mem de Sá, 66, Lapa, tel. (21) 2224-6367. Tue – Sat, 9pm until the last customer leaves.

❺ FEIRA RIO ANTIGO

Rua do Lavradio, a street with many antique shops, hosts the monthly Rio Antigo Fair, which offers a vast array of furniture, decorative items, paintings, old carpets, and other curios. Music and dance performances, as well as photo exhibits, pepper the event. Visitors can also appreciate the beautiful façades on the street's houses, many of which are now bars and restaurants. The street was once a popular meeting place for politicians and artists.
Rua do Lavradio, Centro, tel. (21) 2224-6693. First Saturday of every month, 10am – 7pm.

❻ MUSEU DA IMAGEM E DO SOM (MIS)

The Lapa branch of the Image and Sound Museum (there is another in Praça Rui Barbosa; *see page 18*) houses the museum's administration section and the sound collections available for research. Highlights include rare recordings collected by MPB (popular Brazilian music) researcher Lúcio Rangel, archives of the Rádio Nacional and the Musician Jacob do Bandolim Collection (the country's most important private collection on the history of *choro*). The Música Popular Brasileira (MPB) Collection includes works by Chiquinha Gonzaga, Noel Rosa, Ari Barroso, Pixinguinha, João Gilberto, Tom Jobim, and Nara Leão.
The pioneering Depoimentos Collection comprises spoken word recordings of the stories of personalities from the arts, science and technology, radio, sports, politics, and Afro-Brazilian religions. The recently renovated museum's material is currently being digitalized, and a new exhibition space has been added for the Rádio Nacional material. Guided tours and research support are available but must be booked in advance.
Rua Visconde de Maranguape, 15, Lapa, tel. (21) 2224-8467. Mon – Fri, 10am – 5pm.

❼ Escadaria Selarón

At the end of Rua Teotônio Regadas (behind Sala Cecília Meireles), a beautiful set of stairs – Selarón Stairs– connects the neighborhoods of Lapa and Santa Teresa. Stunning mosaics of colorful tiles cover the stairs. Brazil-based Chilean artist Jorge Selarón, who brought the tiles from different countries, has been working on the project since 1994.
Rua Teotônio Regadas, no #, Lapa.

❽ Sala Cecília Meireles

Cecília Meireles Music Hall boasts the best acoustics among all of Rio's chamber music halls. The 1896 building was originally intended to be a confectionery, then later housed the famous Grande Hotel da Lapa and, in 1948, the Cine Colonial, a film house. In 1965, when the Brazilian Academy of letters bestowed the Machado de Assis Award upon Cecília Meireles, the venue was inaugurated as a music hall bearing her name. It has been hosting some of Rio's best classical music ever since. It commands a view of Rodolfo Bernardelli's iron and granite **Lampadário Monumental** in Largo da Lapa; the monument is one of the neighborhood's landmarks. A number of renovations have improved the space over the years, adding the **Auditório Guiomar Novaes**, which hosts concerts by young artists, and the **Espaço Ayres de Andrade**, for small receptions.
Largo da Lapa, 47, Centro, tel. (21) 2224-4291. Mon – Fri, 9am – 6pm. Box office: Mon – Fri, 1pm – 6pm; Sat, Sun and holidays, when a show is on, 1pm – 6pm.

❾ Igreja Nossa Senhora do Carmo da Lapa do Desterro

Dom João VI donated an 18th-century chapel and seminar to Carmelite monks, who rebuilt the church in 1827 and renamed it Nossa Senhora do Carmo da Lapa do Desterro Church. Mestre Valentim sculpted the throne of the statue of Our Lady of Carmel inside, along with statues of the apostles. Surrounding these works are other treasures, such as canvases believed to have been painted by João de Souza. Next door is the Capela do Divino Espírito Santo chapel, dating from 1773.
Largo da Lapa, no #, Centro, tel. (21) 3094-8312. Mon – Fri, 6:30am – 1pm and 5pm – 8pm; Sat, 6pm – 8pm; Sun, 7am – 9:30am and 6pm – 8pm.

⓫ Escola de Música da Universidade Federal do Rio de Janeiro (UFRJ)

Brazil's oldest and most traditional music school, University of Rio de Janeiro Music School, occupies a 1922 building with unusual architecture. Framed by the Passeio Público Garden, and within view of the Arcos da Lapa Aqueduct, the building has three halls that host concerts and musical performances from a variety of genres.

Cecília Meireles Music Hall has excellent acoustics

LAPA

Pyramid by Mestre Valentim in the Passeio Público Garden

The Leopoldo Miguez hall, which was inspired by the Salle Gaveau in Paris, is the largest. It holds up to six hundred spectators in addition to a 1950s Italian organ with 5,000 tubes. The other halls – Sala Henrique Oswaldo and Sala da Congregação – each seat a hundred. Phone in advance for information on the program. The building has been undergoing renovations since 2005 and their expected completion date hasn't been announced.
Rua do Passeio, 98, tel. (21) 2240-1391, 2240-1491. Mon – Fri, 8am – 8pm.

⑫ Passeio Público Garden

In 1783, Governor Luís de Vasconcelos e Sousa commissioned this garden near the Largo da Lapa over a landfilled marsh. According to legend, he did it to please a beautiful woman who lived nearby. It was the first leisure area open to the public in Rio and Mestre Valentim designed it, although it was redone in the 1860s by landscaper Auguste Glaziou, who introduced winding paths interspersed with lakes and small bridges. Over time, storms, demolitions, and other construction work have disfigured the garden, leaving only the old gate, the alligator fountain and pyramids by Mestre Valentim, a lead sculpture of child by an unknown artist, and the winding paths. This area is not well policed and should only be visited in groups or with a guide.
Rua do Passeio, no #, Centro.

Lapa's Bars

The bars that occupy Lapa's narrow old houses on Avenida Mem de Sá and Rua do Lavradio, host *choro*, MPB (popular Brazilian music), and samba shows – often several on the same night. The bohemian atmosphere is complemented by the ice-cold *chope* (draft beer) and lively dancing. Saturday nights on Avenida Mem de Sá are very busy, and the queues and ebullient crowds spill out into the streets. Book in advance if you can and arrive early, especially if you want a table.

❶ Comuna do Semente

Located under the Arcos da Lapa, this simple little bar draws top musicians such as Ronaldo do Bandolim, Márcio Bahia, and Yamandu Costa, who play on weeknights after midnight. The menu is modest. Its products are all made at Landless Peasants' Movement (or "MST") settlements. It carries beer produced in the hills behind Rio (Itaipava) and a soft drink made in the interior of the state (Mineirinho), but doesn't serve many of the country's big-brand soft drinks or beers.
Rua Joaquim Silva, 138, Lapa, tel. (21) 2509-3591. Sun – Thu, 8pm – 2am (closed on Fri and Sat).

❷ Casa Brasil Mestiço

Singer and cultural producer Luciane Menezes created this venue to showcase Brazilian popular culture, focusing on *ciranda*, *jongo*, *boi*, *coco*, *maracatu*, *forró*, samba, and *choro*. The second floor is reserved for DJs, who play Brazilian music. The menu includes a selection of snacks and draft beer. Dance workshops are also held here.
Avenida Mem de Sá, 61, Lapa, tel. (21) 2509-7418. Wed, 8pm – 12:30am; Thu, 7:30pm – 1am; Fri, 7pm – 3:30am; Sat, 8pm – 3:30am.

❸ Estrela da Lapa

Housed in a magnificent 1898 mansion, Estrela da Lapa opened in 2005. Architect João Pedro Bailly restored the heritage-listed building, harmoniously combining old and new elements, including old German tiles and art nouveau counters. Its spaces (bar, dance floor, and pavilions) host different kinds of music, such as samba, MPB, jazz, and blues. The menu offers appetizers and innovative new versions of traditional regional dishes.
Avenida Mem de Sá, 69, Lapa, tel. (21) 2507-6686. Tue, 7pm – until the last customer leaves; Wed – Fri, 6pm until the last person leaves; Sat, 7pm until the last person leaves.

❹ Carioca da Gema

After opening in 2000, Carioca da Gema quickly became one of the main venues on Rio's bohemian circuit, thanks to its excellent musical program, which features top samba and *choro* musicians. The menu offers some Brazilian classics, such as the tasty *caldinho de feijão* (bean broth), and *carne-seca* (seasoned, shredded beef). The decor is simple and friendly and there are photographs scattered throughout the premises of favored patrons, including some famous personages.
Avenida Mem de Sá, 79, Lapa, tel. (21) 2221-0043. Mon – Thu, 6pm – 1am; Fri, 6pm – 3am; Sat, 9pm – 3am.

❺ Café Cultural Sacrilégio

Brazilian show-business legends such as Carmen Miranda, Donga, Pixinguinha, and Villa-Lobos performed here in music nights organized by the previous owner, *choro* musician João

History and modernity mix at Estrela da Lapa

LAPA

Pernambuco. Reopened in 2001 after renovations that restored the building's original features, Sacrilégio is still one of the best places in Rio to hear samba and *choro*. Tributes to the greats of Brazilian music comprise the backbone of the extremely danceable program, as well as performances by top samba musicians and groups.
Avenida Mem de Sá, 81, Lapa, tel. (21) 3970-1461, 2222-7345. Mon – Fri, 7pm – 12:30am; Sat, 8:30pm – 3am.

❻ Bar Brasil
This hundred-year-old bar has always sat in an old two-story house on the corner. It serves some of the best *chope* in town and traditional German food. The main room has high ceilings and antique furniture, including a beautiful bronze keg.
Avenida Mem de Sá, Lapa, 90, tel. (21) 2509-5943. Mon – Wed, 11:30am – 11pm; Thu and Fri, 11:30am – midnight; Sat, 11:30am – 6pm.

❼ Nova Capela
This traditional restaurant stays open well into the wee hours, and is a meeting place for musicians, artists, and journalists at the end of the night. Nicknamed Capelinha (Little Chapel), it was inaugurated in 1923, but its original location was later demolished and it reopened at its current address in 1969. The house meets every standard for a great tavern, with good service, tasty snacks, cold *chope* and a relaxed atmosphere. It serves such dishes as *cabrito* (kid goat) with broccoli rice.
Avenida Mem de Sá, 96, Lapa, tel. (21) 2252-6228. Daily, 11am – 4am.

❽ Clube dos Democráticos
This samba club was established in 1867 and is based in a beautiful, if not terribly comfortable, heritage-listed 1930 art deco-style house. Regulars pack in for the excellent samba, *gafieira*, and *forró* nights. The club fills up quickly, spawning a huge queue outside, so arrive early to get a table.
Rua Riachuelo, 91, Lapa, tel. (21) 2252-4611. Wed – Sat, 11pm – 4am; Sun, 8pm – midnight.

❾ Rio Scenarium
Housed in a three-story building, this popular venue receives approximately 2,000 people each weekend. They flock to hear top samba, *choro*, and *gafieira* groups and much on a variety of snacks and Brazilian dishes. The house also functions as an antique shop during the day, with nearly 10,000 pieces for sale or lease. At night, the antiques form part of the ever-changing decor, adding a unique charm to the place. For samba and *choro* lovers, greats such as Walter Alfaiate, Luís Carlos da Vila, and the Henrique Cazes Quartet perform here on a regular basis. Early on Tuesday nights there are *chorinho*, MPB, and samba shows, while Saturdays bring everything from *forró* to *maracatu*.
Rua do Lavradio, 20, Lapa, tel. (21) 3852-5516, 2233-3239. Tue – Sat, 7pm until the last customer leaves.

❿ Mangue Seco
Housed in an early-19th-century mansion, one of Rio's most complete *cachaça* bars offers over 100 labels of Brazil's traditional white rum from all over the country. To accompany the *cachaça*, order *caranguejos* (crabs, which can be chosen from a tank) or some of the house's other famed seafood dishes, such as *bobó de camarão*, *moqueca capixaba* or *moqueca baiana* (Bahian-style stews). Head upstairs to enjoy samba, *choro* and *gafieira* music.
Rua do Lavradio, 23, Centro, tel. (21) 3852-1947. Mon – Sat, 11am – 1am.

Santa Teresa

For decades Santa Teresa has drawn artists, writers, photographers, designers, and tourists with its magnificent views of Rio and quick connections to the downtown area. The bustle of residents and visitors on the hilly neighborhood's slopes doesn't interfere with its small-town atmosphere. Rather, the activity lends it something of a cosmopolitan village feel. Old homes, tidy gardens, guesthouses, bars, artists' studios, and a wide array of cultural attractions line the narrow streets. The streetcar is the most popular way to get to Santa Teresa (this the only place in the country, in fact, where they are still fully operational), but one can also drive there on one of several main thoroughfares: Rua Almirante Alexandrino, Rua Cosme Velho, Rua Alice, Rua Cândido Mendes, Rua Benjamim Constant, Rua Santa Cristina, or Rua Joaquim Murtinho

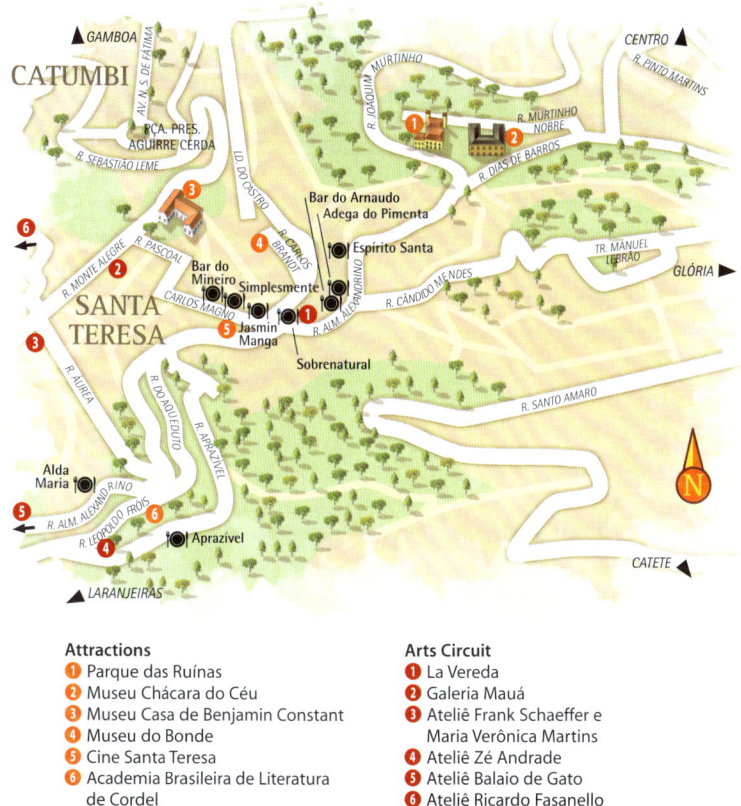

Attractions
1. Parque das Ruínas
2. Museu Chácara do Céu
3. Museu Casa de Benjamin Constant
4. Museu do Bonde
5. Cine Santa Teresa
6. Academia Brasileira de Literatura de Cordel

Arts Circuit
1. La Vereda
2. Galeria Mauá
3. Ateliê Frank Schaeffer e Maria Verônica Martins
4. Ateliê Zé Andrade
5. Ateliê Balaio de Gato
6. Ateliê Ricardo Fasanello

❶ Parque das Ruínas

Next to Chácara do Céu Museum at the top of Santa Teresa's hill, **Ruínas (Ruins) Park** is what remains of the home of arts patroness Laurinda Santos Lobo, nicknamed the "marshal of elegance" by writer João do Rio. From the 1920s to the 1940s the palace was

Santa Teresa

The modernist Chácara do Céu Museum houses a large collection of paintings

the setting for parties and gatherings that brought together the foremost artists and intellectuals of the time. Some of the original walls have been preserved and now stand in contrast with glass and iron structural frames – the result of an award-winning architectural project by Ernâni Freire and Sônia Lopes. The park hosts contemporary art exhibitions, musical performances in a range of genres *(first and last Sunday of each month, 6pm)*, and magic, mime, theater, and music shows for children and teenagers *(first Sunday of each month, 11am)*.
Rua Murtinho Nobre, 169, Santa Teresa, tel. (21) 2252-1039. Tue – Sun, 8am – 8pm.

❷ Museu Chácara do Céu
The Chácara do Céu Museum is located in a beautiful 1957 home. It is one of two Castro Maya art museums *(see Museu do Açude on page 172)*, and houses paintings, drawings, and intaglio prints by Europeans (including Seurat and Miró), Brazilian modernists (Guignard, Di Cavalcanti, Antônio Bandeira, and Portinari), and Braziliana artists (with works by Rugendas, Chamberlain, Taunay, and an important set of intaglio prints by Debret). The gardens, designed by Burle Marx, Brazil's most famous landscape artist, are also worth visiting. The museum's windows offer magnificent views of Rio's main postcard attractions.

Café Filo
Casa da Gente, a grassroots culture center-cum-guesthouse, runs Café Filo, which serves as a venue for evening philosophical debates on a range of pre-defined topics. Music, finger food, and drinks generally accompanies the discussion. The debates take place sometime during the second half of each month, and start at 7:30pm. Call in advance to inquire about the day and topic.
Rua Pinto Martins, 28, Santa Teresa, tel. (21) 2232-2634.

Santa Teresa

Rua Murtinho Nobre, 93, Santa Teresa, tel. (21) 2224-8981, 2224-8524. Wed – Mon, noon – 5pm.

❸ Museu Casa de Benjamin Constant

Benjamin Constant, one of the most important leaders of the campaign to create a Brazilian republic, lived briefly in the mansion-cum-museum that now bears his name. The museum has restored several rooms to look as they did during the illustrious former resident's stay. Original paintings, photographs, furniture, sculptures, clothing, and personal effects help transport visitors back to the 19th century. There is also a library with 26,000 documents, 6,000 books, and 3,000 photographs from Benjamin Constant and his descendents' personal collection *(you must call in advance to see the collection, tel. (21) 2509-1248; Mon – Fri, 10am – 5pm)*. The museum offers half-hour guided tours. Nearby is the **Centro Cultural Laurinda Santos Lobo**, a cultural center with an exhibition space, auditorium, and library that specializes in books about the neighborhood *(Rua Monte Alegre, 306, tel. (21) 2242-9741; Mon – Fri, 9am – 5pm; Sat and Sun, 10am – 4pm)*.

Rua Monte Alegre, 255, Santa Teresa, tel. (21) 2509-1248, 2242-0062. Thu – Sun, 1pm – 5pm.

❹ Museu do Bonde

Streetcars, though now almost completely retired, long served as icons of Rio de Janeiro's modernization. The Streetcar Museum exhibits a wide array of related memorabilia, including a life-size streetcar replica, conductors' uniforms, old tickets, clocks, models, and collections of photos, illustrations, phonograph recordings, and other historical material.

Rua Carlos Brandt, 14, Santa Teresa, tel. (21) 2292-6993. Daily, 9am – 4:30pm.

Benjamim Constant's House Museum

Raymundo Castro Maya

Businessman and industrialist Raymundo Ottoni de Castro Maya was eight years old when, in 1892, he left Paris for Rio de Janeiro, where he lived until his death in 1968. Raymundo was one of the greatest men of culture in his generation: a patron of the arts, a protector of Rio's historical and natural heritage, and an art collector. In 1943 he coordinated the landscape reshaping of Tijuca Forest, and founded the Cem Bibliófilos do Brasil Society, a group dedicated to publishing Brazilian authors. In 1948, he served as the first president of Rio's Museum of Modern Art. That same year, he formed the Os Amigos da Gravura Society, a foundation promoting intaglio printing. In 1963 he created the Castro Maya Foundation. Twenty years later the foundation became the Castro Maya museum system and was incorporated into the Brazilian Institute for National Artistic and Historical Heritage. Visitors can view his magnificent collection of Brazilian, European, and Oriental art at the Museu Chácara do Céu, in Santa Teresa, and at the Museu do Açude, in Alto da Boa Vista.

A streetcar ride is the most charming way to get to know Santa Teresa

❺ Cine Santa Teresa

Santa Teresa Cinema, also known as "Cine Santa," was initially an itinerant theater that screened films in churches, public squares, bars, and schools. In 2005 it was given its own small, permanent theater space in a building that also houses Santa Teresa's regional administration and a police post. Their program is varied and often features Brazilian and foreign art films as well as films for children.

Rua Pascoal Carlos Magno, 136, Santa Teresa, tel. (21) 2507-6841. Daily, 2pm – midnight.

❻ Academia Brasileira de Literatura de Cordel

The pompous-sounding "Brazilian Academy of Cordel Literature" is actually a small shop operating out of *cordelista* Gonçalo Ferreira da Silva's garage. Mr. da Silva sells his own *cordel* literature, as well as works by other *cordelistas*, including reprints of classic and rare titles. Cordel (string) literature is a type of folk literature that encompasses novels, poems, and songs. Street vendors frequently hawk them in northeast Brazil; the booklets are displayed by hanging them from strings, hence the name.

Rua Leopoldo Fróis, 37, Santa Teresa, tel. (21) 2232-4801. Daily, 9am – 7pm.

Streetcar Tour

In addition to the usual streetcar service, there is a special two-hour tour run on Saturdays and Sundays that winds through the streets of Santa Teresa. The tour leaves from Largo da Carioca in downtown Rio, crosses over the Arcos da Lapa Aqueduct, and visits regional attractions.

Rua Professor Lélio Gama, next to the Petrobrás building and Aqueduto da Carioca (Arcos da Lapa Aqueduct), Centro, tel. (21) 2215-8559. Sat and Sun, 10am – 2pm.

Arts Circuit

An artists' haven, Santa Teresa is home to a large number of studios. Many can be visited, but only if arrangements are made in advance. In July, however, the neighborhood hosts **Arte de Portas Abertas** (Art with Open Doors), a festival of local art that includes approximately fifty workshops open to the public, adding an extra dash of spice to the region's colorful cultural life.

La Vereda
La Vereda sells lamps, pottery, tapestries, hammocks, paintings, and furniture made from demolition timber. The nearby depot has pieces from the owners' collection that are worth a quick look.
Rua Almirante Alexandrino, 428, Santa Teresa, tel. (21) 2507-0317. Mon – Sat, 10am – 8pm; Sun, 10:30am – 8pm.

Galeria Mauá
Mauá Gallery, created by the Santa Teresa Visual Artists' Association, operates on the premises of the old Hotel Mauá. It hosts temporary art exhibitions and shows the work of local artists. Call in advance for program details.
Rua Monte Alegre, 277, Santa Teresa, tel. (21) 2507-5352, 2509-5037. Mon – Fri, 9am – 1pm and 2pm – 6pm.

Scrap Sculptures

For years, a wooden shack that looks like a streetcar has served as artist Getúlio Damado's delightful studio. Here he produces enormously popular furniture, dolls, tiny houses, and colorful little streetcars made of wood and scrap materials. Getúlio, who used to make a living fixing pots and pans in the neighborhood, says he would watch the streetcars all day as he worked – and it ultimately inspired him to begin producing his own miniature versions of them. It is best to book your visit in advance.
Rua Leopoldo Fróis, in front of # 15, Santa Teresa, tel. (21) 2531-9066. Daily, 9am – 8pm.

Toys made by Getúlio Damado from scrap materials

Ateliê Frank Schaeffer and Maria Verônica Martins

This artist couple's watercolors, gouaches, and acrylic paintings portray landscapes and architectural details of Rio and other cities. Visits to Frank Schaeffer e Maria Verônica Martins' Studio should be booked in advance.
Rua Monte Alegre, 356 and 303, Santa Teresa, tel. (21) 2252-4576.

Ateliê Zé Andrade

This Bahian artist has made ceramic dolls of more than seventy national personalities, including poet and lyricist Vinicius de Moraes, and musicians Tom Jobim, Cartola, and Pixinguinha. Be sure to call in advance to set up a time to visit Zé Andrade's Studio.
Rua Leopoldo Fróis, 83-A, Santa Teresa, tel. (21) 2242-1415.

Anel ("ring") armchair

Ateliê Balaio de Gato

At Balaio de Gato Studio, designer-artists Luciana Lopes and Márcia Pinto make and display sculptures and jewelry. Jewelry-making courses are sometimes available on weekends. Call before visiting.
Rua Almirante Alexandrino, 2750, apartment 21, Santa Teresa, tel. (21) 9145-5736, (21) 9868-9770.

Ateliê Ricardo Fasanello

Some of celebrated 1960s designer Ricardo Fasanello's most famous creations, including the Arcos table and Anel and Esfera armchairs, are still made in his workshop by professionals trained under Fasanello himself. Now run by the artist's children, Ricardo Fasanello Study is only open for visitors who have called in advance.
Rua do Paraíso, 42, Santa Teresa, tel. (21) 2232-3164.

The studio of Ricardo Fasanello, celebrated furniture designer

Portuguese sweets prepared according to Alda Maria's family recipes

FOOD AND DRINKS IN SANTA TERESA

Near Largo dos Guimarães square in the heart of Santa Teresa are a number of excellent bars, cafés, and restaurants. On Rua Pascoal Carlos Magno, local artists meet at **Bar do Mineiro**, which displays works of folk and contemporary art and offers a great selection of *cachaça* (Brazilian white rum). The menu features traditional dishes from Minas Gerais *(Rua Pascoal Carlos Magno, 99, tel. (21) 2221-9227; Tue – Sun and holidays, 11am – 2am)*. **Simplesmente** is also popular among artists and intellectuals, and hosts samba sessions on Wednesdays *(Rua Pascoal Carlos Magno, 115, tel. (21) 2221-0337; Mon – Thu, 7pm – 3am; Fri and Sat, 7pm – 4:30am)*. At **Jasmim Manga**, a charming cyber-cafe, patrons enjoy delicious sweets, pies, bread, and biscuits *(Rua Pascoal Carlos Magno, 143, tel. (21) 2242-2605; Wed – Mon, 9am – 11pm)*. Not far away, Rua Almirante Alexandrino is home to most of the neighborhood's bars and restaurants. **Espírito Santa** cooks traditional dishes from northern Brazil, including delicious *moqueca* and *bobó* (fish and shrimp stews), as well as excellent *caipirinhas (Rua Almirante Alexandrino, 264, tel. (21) 2508-7095; Mon – Wed, noon – 6pm; Thu – Sat, noon – midnight; Sun, noon – 7pm)*. **Adega do Pimenta** serves traditional German food in a rustic setting *(Rua Almirante Alexandrino, 296, tel. (21) 2224-7554; Mon – Fri, noon – 10pm; Sat, noon – 8pm; Sun, noon – 6pm)*. **Bar do Arnaudo** has been serving food from northeast Brazil for more than thirty years *(Rua Almirante Alexandrino, 316-B, tel. (21) 2252-7246; Mon, noon – 6pm; Tue – Fri, noon – 11pm; Sat and Sun, noon – 9pm)*. Fresh seafood, caught from the owners' own boats, is served at **Sobrenatural** *(Rua Almirante Alexandrino, 432, tel. (21) 2224-1003;*

Pumpkin soup at Espírito Santa

Conveniently located Mama Ruisa Hotel offers delightful views of Rio

daily, noon until the last customer leaves). **Mike's Haus** has a vast selection of Brazilian and imported beers and a very German menu of cold cuts and handmade sausages to match. *(Rua Almirante Alexandrino, 1458, store A, tel. (21) 2509-5248; Tue – Thu and Sun,*

OUR RECOMMENDATION

Relais Solar, also known as "Solar Santa," offers comfort amid lovely décor in a charming colonial mansion. The rooms, which overlook a delightful tropical garden, are decorated with art and furniture by Brazilian designers, and a showroom displays additional arts and crafts. The hotel enjoys wonderful views of Rio. Relais Solar is also home to **Bistrô Solaris**, which serves Brazilian cuisine. *Ladeira do Meireles, 32, Santa Teresa, tel. (21) 2221-2117. Restaurant: Mon – Thu, 3pm – 9pm; Fri – Sun, noon – 9pm.*

At the sophisticated **Mama Ruisa** Hotel, guests are picked up from the airport. Run by Frenchman Jean-Michel, it is a haven of peace and quiet. The rooms are named for famous personalities, including Carmen Miranda and Lévi-Strauss. The hotel offers wonderful views of Rio. *Rua Santa Cristina, 132, Santa Teresa, tel. (21) 2242-1281.*

More hotel information begins on page 205.

noon – midnight; Fri and Sat, noon – 2am). At **Alda Maria's house** patrons enjoy delicious Portuguese sweets. Alda Maria inherited the recipes from her grandmother *(Rua Almirante Alexandrino, 1116, tel. (21) 2232-1320; Tue – Sun, 2pm – 7pm).* Nearby, **Aprazível** offers a beautiful view of the city and Brazilian cuisine with original touches by chef Ana Castilho *(Rua Aprazível, 62, tel. (21) 2508-9174; Thu and Fri, noon – 1pm; Sat, 1pm – 1am; Sun and holidays, 1pm – 7pm).*

ACCOMMODATIONS

Bed and breakfasts are common in Santa Teresa. In addition to the neighborhood's convenient proximity to local attractions, visitors who stay in with locals will also appreciate excellent insider tips on what to see and do in the area. The guesthouses typically offer simple but comfortable rooms, and several also provide sight-seeing opportunities developed in conjunction with the Riotur touring company. *Cama e Café: Rua Pascoal Carlos Magno, 5, Santa Teresa, tel. (21) 2224-5689, 2221-7635. Mon – Fri, 9am – 8pm; Sat, 10am – 5pm.*

Glória and Catete

Sandwiched between the districts of Lapa and Flamengo and close to downtown Rio, Glória and Catete are residential districts dotted with squares and criss-crossed by small streets, some of which can be quite steep. A number of 19th- and early 20th-century buildings are the neighborhoods' main attractions; most line Rua do Catete, Rua da Glória, and Rua do Russel. Eighteenth century Igreja Nossa Senhora da Glória do Outeiro church is the most worthwhile place to visit in Glória, while Catete is home to the Palácio do Catete palace, formerly the seat of the republican government (1897-1960) and now a museum. The nearest metro stations are Glória, Catete, and Largo do Machado. There aren't too many dining options in either neighborhood, but nearby Flamengo has several restaurants *(see page 84)*.

Attractions
1. Chafariz da Glória
2. Igreja Nossa Senhora da Glória do Outeiro
3. Memorial Getúlio Vargas
4. Hotel Glória
5. Parque do Museu da República
6. Museu da República
7. Museu Folclórico Edison Carneiro
8. Largo do Machado

Architecture
1. Praça Paris
2. Templo da Humanidade
3. Beneficência Portuguesa
4. Clube High Life
5. Faculdade de Medicina Souza Marques
6. Delegacia do Catete Police Station
7. Edifício Milton
8. Art nouveau residence by architect Antonio Virzi
9. Edifício Itatiaia
10. Edifício Itacolomy
11. Edifício Ipu
12. Edifício Lage

1 Chafariz da Glória

Glória Fountain was constructed in 1772 at the request of the Marquis of Lavradio. Parts of the fountain were rebuilt in 1905 under Mayor Pereira Passos' administration; it was further restored in the 1960s.
Rua da Glória, 156, Glória.

Nossa Senhora da Glória do Outeiro, an unusually designed church in a beautiful location

❷ Igreja Nossa Senhora da Glória do Outeiro

From its home at the top of a knoll, Nossa Senhora da Glória do Outeiro Church looks out on Guanabara Bay. It was the favorite church of the royal family, whose children were all baptized in its font. Built between 1714 and 1739, the church has an unusual ground plan which shows two elongated octagons fit together. The central portal, made of limestone, displays a medallion of the Virgin Mary. Inside, beautiful Portuguese tile panels show scenes from the bible. Cláudio Gurgel do Amaral who donated the land on which the church was built, is buried under the central mosaic in the sacristy. Behind the church, the church-run **Museu Mauro Ribeiro Viegas** displays beautiful religious objects, including some donated by Dom Pedro II, as well as a canvas by Félix Émile Taunay that depicts Dom Pedro I in a riding accident *(Tue – Fri, 9am – noon and 1pm – 5pm; Sat and Sun, 9am – 1pm)*. To visit the church, take Ladeira da Glória's 100 steps, or hitch a ride on the recently restored inclined elevator, which moves diagonally up the slope *(Rua do Russel, near # 300)*. The elevator is out of service on Mondays. *Praça Nossa Senhora da Glória, 135, Glória, tel. (21) 2557-4600. Mon – Fri, 9am – noon and 1pm – 5pm; Sat and Sun, 9am – noon.*

Panel detail from Gloria Church

❸ Memorial Getúlio Vargas

Architect Henock de Almeida designed this memorial to honor

former Brazilian president (and Rio resident) Getúlio Vargas. The monument consists of two 60-foot-tall marble-covered metal forms in the middle of a reflecting pool. The underground area exhibits photographs, texts, videos, documents, and objects related to Vargas's personal and political life. Memorial Getúlio Vargas also has a café and an auditorium that hosts talks, presentations, and an occasional film screening.
Praça Luís de Camões, no #, Glória, tel. (21) 2557-9444, 2245-7577. Tue – Sun, 10am – 7pm.

❹ Hotel Glória
The eclectic Glória was christened in 1922 by President Epitácio Pessoa during the centennial celebrations of Brazil's independence. Though it is not considered as prestigious as the Copacabana Palace, the Glória has received its share of Presidents – Jânio Quadros lived there for the whole year in 1960, and Getúlio Vargas stayed there for two years (1926 and 1927) when he held the position of secretary of the national treasury – and international celebrities, including Ava Gardner, whose tumultuous stay at the hotel (which involved the starlet throwing a killer tantrum) made headlines. The antique furniture and Persian carpets still bear witness to its glamorous past. In 1970 the **Teatro Glória** (Glória Theatre) was opened in an annex *(tel. (21) 2555-7262).*
Rua do Russel, 632, Glória, tel. (21) 2555-7272. Daily, open 24 hours.

❺ Parque do Museu da República
The extensive garden that surrounds the Museum of the

Glória Hotel, one of the oldest hotels in Rio de Janeiro

The Museum of the Republic preserves the furniture of one of Brazil's most luxurious palaces

Republic was designed by French landscaper Paul Villon in 1897. Many of the park's original features have been preserved: 19th-century French sculptures and an artificial lake, waterfall, and cave. Extending from Rua do Catete to Praia do Flamengo (Flamengo Beach), the 6-acre garden is filled with imperial palms, as well as brazilwood, mango, myrtle, starfruit, tamarind, and avocado trees. The garden hosts a number of cultural events, including theatre, music, and dance performances. A photography fair is held here on the last Sunday of every month from 9am to 5pm and attracts professionals and amateurs alike. Talks, seminars, and contemporary art exhibitions take place at **Galeria do Lago** *(tel. (21) 2558-6350, extension 216; Mon – Fri, 11am – 6pm; Sat, Sun, and holidays, 2pm – 6pm)*. Also in the park, the pleasant **Bistrô Jardins** serves hearty breakfasts, lunches, and afternoon teas *(tel. (21) 2558-2673; daily, 9:30am – 6pm)*.
Rua do Catete, 153, Catete, tel. (21) 2558-6350. Daily, 8am – 9pm.

Museum of the Republic

GLÓRIA AND CATETE

❻ Museu da República

Built between 1862 and 1864 for the baron of Nova Friburgo, Palácio do Catete – now the Museum of the Republic – was the seat of the republican government and served as the official presidential residence from 1897 to 1960. The building became a museum after the nation's capital shifted to Brasília. It was also the setting of one of the most dramatic episodes in Brazil's history: it was here that President Getúlio Vargas committed suicide in 1954 *(see page 109)*. The luxurious palace, with its magnificent paintings, furniture, and sculptures, also has a valuable collection of 20,000 books, 7,000 art objects, and 80,000 historical documents. The room in which Vargas killed himself has been kept just as it was at the time. Visitors can see the revolver he used to shoot himself and his pajamas with a bullet-hole in them. Concerts are held in the museum's auditorium every Wednesday from noon to 1:30pm (tickets must be purchased at least an hour in advance). The museum also has a cinema, Cinema Espaço Museu da República *(tel. (21) 3826-7984)*, and a bookshop, Livraria do Museu da República *(tel. (21) 2556-5828)*.
Rua do Catete, 153, Catete, tel. (21) 2558-6350. Tue, Thu, and Fri, noon – 5pm; Wed, 2pm – 5pm; Sat, Sun, and holidays, 2pm – 6pm.

❼ Museu Folclórico Edison Carneiro

Small and well-organized, the Edison Carneiro Folklore Museum has a collection of over 14,000 pieces of Brazilian folk culture arts and crafts. Approximately 1,400 of these are on permanent display. The museum is housed in two late-19th-century mansions. The complex is also home to the **Galeria Mestre Vitalino** and **Sala do Artista Popular** art galleries, as well as a folk art shop and a folk culture library.
Rua do Catete, 179, Catete, tel. (21) 2285-0441. Tue – Fri, 11am – 6pm; Sat, Sun, and holidays, 3pm – 6pm.

A sculpture of José de Alencar, by Bernadelli

❽ Largo do Machado

Though it officially lies in the neighborhood of Catete, even those familiar with the area often think that Machado Square sits in the district of Flamengo. A haven for Rio's bohemians, the square used to be frequented by intellectuals such as Sérgio Buarque de Holanda, Machado de Assis, and Rui Barbosa. Many of them met at nearby **Café Lamas**. Today there are still several bars in the area *(see information on area bars on page 84)*. As you approach the square, note the sculpture of writer José de Alencar by Rodolfo Bernadelli.

Architectural Circuit

Lovers of architecture and history will enjoy a stroll through Glória and Catete, as the neighborhoods are particularly rich in neoclassical, art deco, and French-style buildings. The French touches arose during the turn-of-the-19th-century administration of Mayor Pereira Passos. **Praça Paris** (Paris Square), in Glória, was built in 1920 and its original fountains and statues remain. Rua Santo Amaro is home to the neoclassical **Beneficência Portuguesa** hospital (built 1840-1858), by architect Luís Hosxe *(Rua Santo Amaro, 80-84, Glória)*. On the same street, the building now occupied by Incra was formerly **Clube High Life**, a club that hosted the most glamorous carnival balls of the early 20th century *(Rua Santo Amaro, 28, Glória)*. Nearby, on Rua Benjamin Constant, is the **Templo da Humanidade** (built 1890-1897), Brazil's first church based on the positivist philosophy *(Rua Benjamin Constant, 74, Glória)*. On Rua do Russel, named after Englishman John Russel, is a 1915 art nouveau residence designed by Antonio Virzi *(Rua do Russel, 784, Glória)*. On the same street one can still see examples of more eclectic architecture in the features of buildings like the 1925 **Edificio Lage** *(Rua do Russel, 300, Glória)*, which was inspired by an Italian style, and the 1929 **Edificio Milton** *(Rua do Russel, 710, Glória)*, which is modeled in a French Renaissance manner. Strong art deco influences can be seen in **Edificio Ipu** (1935) *(Rua do Russel, 496)*, **Edificio Itacolomy** (1937), and **Edificio Itatiaia** (1937) *(Rua do Russel, 680 and 694, respectively)*. Note the unusual baroque architecture of the **Igreja Nossa Senhora da Glória do Outeiro** (1714-1739) *(Rua do Russel, 300)*. This church assumes the form of two prisms with elongated, octagonal bases and a squared-off bell tower. The access ramps are mid-20th-century additions designed by Lúcio Costa. In spite of the architectural abundance on Rua do Russel, the most important construction that's associated with Russel may be the one that was a feat of engineering rather than of architecture: In the 1860s, Russel oversaw the construction of the neighborhood's drainage systems. Several architecturally eclectic residences lie between the Estação Catete metro station and Largo do Machado square along historic Rua do Catete, including the 1908 **Delegacia do Catete** (Catete Police Station) on the corner of Rua Pedro Américo. On the same street stands the imposing, neoclassical **Faculdade de Medicina Souza Marques** (Souza Marques Medical School), built in 1862 *(Rua do Catete, 6, Glória)*.

Beneficência Portuguesa hospital

Laranjeiras and Cosme Velho

Two of the oldest neighborhoods in the city, Laranjeiras and Cosme Velho are joined at the hip. Both of these residential neighborhoods preserve the charm of the 19th century in their old houses and squares and in tree-lined streets that brim with stores, bars and cultural centers. All that remains of their earlier, rural past is the reference to the long-gone orange groves (*laranjeiras* is Portuguese for orange trees). The two neighborhoods developed along the Carioca River as small land holdings there urbanized. Cosme Velho has the honor of being the place where the celebrated writer Machado de Assis lived and wrote some of his best works. The train to the top of Corcovado also leaves from here. The neighborhoods' main streets, Rua das Laranjeiras and Rua Cosme Velho, are continuations of one another. Largo do Machado (Machado Square) is a helpful landmark if you are coming from Flamengo.

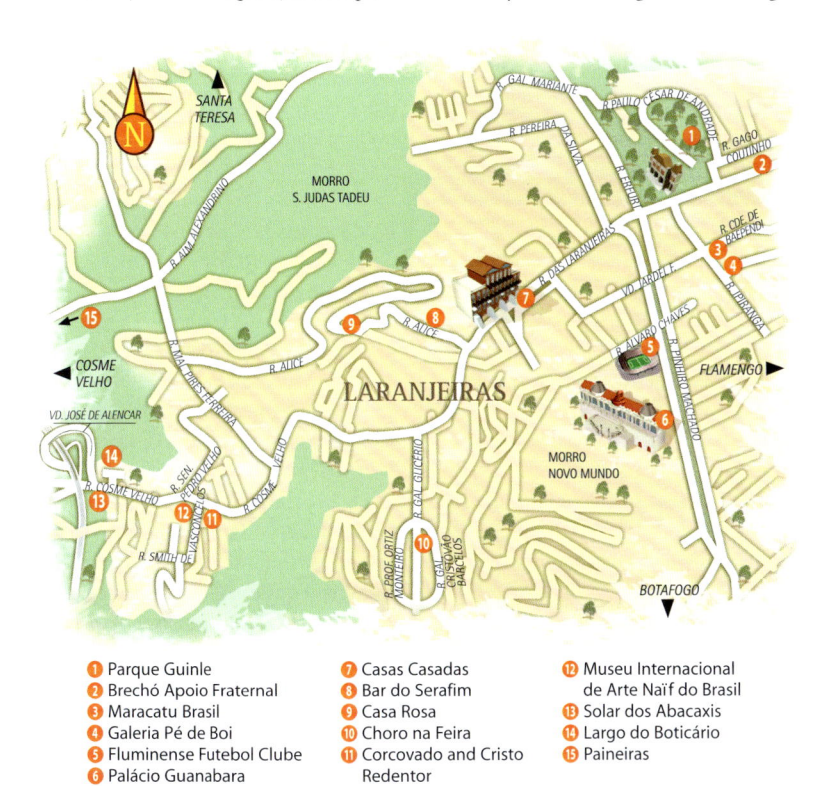

1. Parque Guinle
2. Brechó Apoio Fraternal
3. Maracatu Brasil
4. Galeria Pé de Boi
5. Fluminense Futebol Clube
6. Palácio Guanabara
7. Casas Casadas
8. Bar do Serafim
9. Casa Rosa
10. Choro na Feira
11. Corcovado and Cristo Redentor
12. Museu Internacional de Arte Naïf do Brasil
13. Solar dos Abacaxis
14. Largo do Boticário
15. Paineiras

1 Parque Guinle

Entrepreneur Eduardo Guinle built his house at the beginning of the 20th century on a 6-acre property. Today, **Palácio das Laranjeiras** (Laranjeiras Park), inaugurated in 1914, is the state governor's residence, and its surroundings have been turned into immense French-style gardens, with winding lanes, lawns and a lake at the center. In one part of the park, on the slopes of Morro de Santa Teresa, stand three mid-19th-century residential buildings designed by Lúcio Costa.

Laranjeiras and Cosme Velho

A building designed by Lúcio Costa, in Guinle Park

These are landmarks of modern Brazilian architecture. Another set of buildings, designed by the architectural firm MMM Roberto, went up around the same time. All these buildings contrast with the stylistically eclectic palace, which Armando da Silva Telles designed to rises solemnly from the top of a hill. Visitors can explore the palace's sumptuously decorated rooms, which contain many paintings, sculptures, books, and art objects. Two works by the Dutch painter Frans Post (*Paisagem* and *Índios caçando*) are highlights. The palace is only open for visits on Tuesdays and Thursdays at 2pm and 3pm (*Rua Paulo César de Andrade, 407, Laranjeiras, tel. (21) 2299-5689). Guinle Park: Rua Gago Coutinho, no #, Laranjeiras.*

❷ Brechó Apoio Fraternal
This thrift store is on the second floor of the building that houses the Apoio Fraternal Institution. The institute's primary mission is to help the elderly, and the store sells clothes, shoes, and accessories. Racks of clothes are organized according to type (suits, dresses, shirts, etc.). It's occasionally possible to find brand-new items and prized international labels.
Rua das Laranjeiras, 110, Laranjeiras, tel. (21) 2205-1531. Tue – Fri, 2pm – 5:30pm.

❸ Maracatu Brasil
This combination of a store, music school and studio has new and used drums, and other percussion instruments, available for rental or purchase. It also contains four recording studios. They hold courses in drum, guitar, bass and percussion, as well as in musical theory and appreciation.
Rua Ipiranga, 49, Laranjeiras, tel. (21) 2557-4754. Store: Mon – Fri, noon – 8pm. Lessons: Mon – Fri, noon – 10pm.

❹ Galeria Pé de Boi
This store specializes in Brazilian arts and crafts. Owner Ana Maria Chindler sells pieces mostly from the states of Minas Gerais, Pernambuco and Ceará. The pieces include figures from Vale do Jequitinhonha, Marajoara pottery, wooden sculptures, Indian-made stools, costumes and ornamental accessories used in such folk festivities as *bumba-meu-boi* and *maracatu*, and hand-embroidered Holy Spirit banners from different parts of Brazil. Once a year, usually in August, the gallery holds an exhibition of these items.
Rua Ipiranga, 55, Laranjeiras, tel. (21) 2285-4395. Mon – Fri, 10am – 7pm; Sat, 9am – 1pm.

❺ Fluminense Futebol Clube
Hipólito Pujol designed the Fluminense Soccer Club's majestic building, which was built between

1917 and 1922. Guided visits can be arranged in advance *(Mon – Sat, 11am – noon and 2pm – 3pm)*. These show off such rooms as the Salão Nobre, with its lovely French stained-glass windows, light fittings and frescos, and the Sala dos Troféus, which holds hundreds of items, including an unusual grain of rice that's engraved with the names of the entire 1951 team and the club's shield. The club's restaurant is very popular among local workers *(tel. (21) 2554-4726; daily, 11:30am – 4pm)*. This is also the address of **Estádio das Laranjeiras**, the oldest soccer stadium in the country. The Brazilian national team played its first official game here (and the first game played at the stadium) in 1919. Fans can watch Fluminense's training sessions (phone in advance to check times). The library, which holds around 9,000 books and periodicals, counts some interesting 1950s sports books among its collection.
Rua Álvaro Chaves, 41, Laranjeiras, tel. (21) 2553-7240. Mon – Sat, 10am – noon and 2pm – 3pm.

❻ Palácio Guanabara
Guanabara Palace (1853), the current seat of the state government, is the former residence of Princess Isabel and her husband, the Count of Eu. It was here, in 1888, that the Princess signed the Lei Áurea, which ended slavery in Brazil. After the country became a republic, the palace received many illustrious visitors. Francisco Marcelino Souza Aguiar renovated it in 1908, adding its architecturally eclectic features. French landscaper Paul Villon, a disciple of Auguste Glaziou, designed the palace gardens.
Rua Pinheiro Machado, no #, Laranjeiras, tel. (21) 2554-2000, 2553-6253. Mon – Fri, 9am – 6pm.

❼ Casas Casadas
The family of Count Leite Leal built this set of six neoclassical, two-story terrace houses in 1874. Heritage-listed since 1994, the buildings have been restored and today house the headquarters of the film company Riofilmes. They are not currently open to the public, although there is a project afoot to turn them into a cultural center that would hold cinemas, a media library, and a computerized collection of audio-visual productions.
Rua das Laranjeiras, 307, Laranjeiras, tel. (21) 2225-7082. Mon – Fri, 10am – 6pm.

❽ Bar do Serafim
Open since 1944, this bar serves Portuguese dishes in an informal, welcoming atmosphere. Families and bohemians alike come to savor the celebrated cod dish, *bacalhau à trasmontana*, and the *rabada* (oxtail stew), accompanied by the house's excellent *chope* (draft beer). Friday is the day for a full *feijoada*, Brazil's traditional black-bean dish.
Rua Alice, 24, Laranjeiras, tels. (21) 2225-2843, 2202-5951. Mon – Sat, 11am – midnight; Sun, 11am – 6pm.

❾ Casa Rosa
According to legend, this house was a brothel at the beginning of the 20th century. Nowadays, it's a live-music venue and cultural center that holds percussion, dance, judo, and *capoeira* workshops for children. Friday nights come alive with a variety of musical styles, while Saturday is the day for '80s music, and Sunday is for samba and *feijoada*.
Rua Alice, 550, Laranjeiras, tels. (21) 2557-2562, 9854-1111. Fri and Sat, 11:30 – 5am; Sun, 5pm – midnight.

The Christ the Redeemer statue atop Corcovado looks out on a magnificent view of Guanabara Bay

❿ Choro na Feira

This recurring musical event, known as "*choro* in the market," takes place among street-market stalls on Saturday afternoons. A *cavaquinho* (a kind of ukulele) player named Ignez Perdigão formed the group, bringing together masters such as Bilinho Teixeira, on the guitar, Clarice Magalhães, on the *pandeiro* (a type of tambourine), and Franklin da Flauta and Marcelo Bernardes, on sax and clarinet. The event attracts the city's top names in *choro* and samba music. Perhaps its no coincidence that a stall in the market sells rare Brazilian CDs.
Rua General Glicério, no #, Laranjeiras. Sat, 1pm – 3pm.

Bica da Rainha

Rust-laden water, which was ostensibly medicinal, used to spout from this small stone fountain. Its many users included Dona Maria I, mother of Dom João VI, hence the name (the Queen's Fountain). It is now in disuse and surrounded by iron railings *(Rua Cosme Velho, 109, Cosme Velho).*

⓫ Corcovado and Cristo Redentor

The statue of Christ the Redeemer, which looms over Rio, has become a symbol of the city. The engineer Heitor da Silva Costa designed it and had it built in 1931 on top of Morro do Corcovado. It still stands there, at an altitude of 704 meters (2,310 feet), inside Tijuca National Park. The ascent, is thoroughly enchanting. Despite being touristy, it's an absolute must, for the view from the top is spectacular. The best way to go up is by train, which runs every half hour from Cosme Velho station. Private vehicles have been banned, which has led to a kind of 'mafia' of overpriced taxis and minibuses. While waiting for the train, have a look at the murals and videos in the **Espaço Cultural Trem do Corcovado**, which tell the story of the railway's construction. On the way up, gaze out at the beautiful Parque Nacional da Tijuca national park forest. At the top, an escalator and panoramic lift spare tired visitors from having to climb the 220 steps to the lookout point. Go on a clear day to make the most of the magnificent

view of the city. For more information, log onto www.corcovado.com.br.
Rua Cosme Velho, 513, Cosme Velho, tel. (21) 2558-1329. Daily, 8:30am – 6:30pm.

⑫ Museu Internacional de Arte Naïf do Brasil

Near the road to Corcovado, this International Museum of Brazilian Naïf Art houses more than 6,000 works by Brazilian and international artists. Among these are Lia Mittarakis' richly-detailed 13-foot by 23-foot painting *Rio de Janeiro, gosto de você* (*Rio de Janeiro, I Like You*), and Aparecida Azevedo's almost 80-foot-wide *Brasil, 500 anos* (*Brazil, 500 Years*), which illustrates the history of Brazil in nineteen episodes. A small store sells souvenirs, catalogues, and books on naïf art, which is art by untrained, self-invented artists. Group visits should be arranged in advance. Visitors to the Cristo Redentor statue receive a discount on admission to this

---

MACHADO'S COSME VELHO

It was in the neighborhood where I live. The presence of Corcovado was enough to compare the solidity of the earth with the mobility of man. Thus wrote Machado de Assis in a piece published in *A Semana* newspaper in 1892. The neighborhood in the shadow of Corcovado was Cosme Velho, where the writer lived from 1884 until his death in 1908, and which he described in many articles, stories, and novels. Born in 1839, Joaquim Maria Machado de Assis is one of the greatest Brazilian writers – for many, *the* greatest – and he is so closely associated with the neighborhood that he earned the nickname "Bruxo do Cosme Velho" (Wizard of Cosme Velho). Many of its leafy streets and old houses still evoke that passage from Machado – and others (*The victory of electricity in Cosme Velho and Laranjeiras should be achieved sparing the trees. It can be done.*). The writer's house, however, at 18 Rua Cosme Velho, on the corner of Marechal Pires Ferreira, no longer exists; it has been replaced with an apartment block. A solitary plaque on the wall informs passersby of the illustrious Brazilian who lived and worked there. Some of his furniture and certain other items can be seen in the Espaço Machado de Assis, at the Academia Brasileira de Letras *(see page 21)*; The Fundação Casa Rui Barbosa houses manuscripts and correspondence *(see page 91)*.

museum upon presentation of their ticket to Corcovado.
Rua Cosme Velho, 561, Cosme Velho, tel. (21) 2205-8612. Tue – Fri, 10am – 6pm; Sat, Sun and holidays, noon – 6pm.

⓭ SOLAR DOS ABACAXIS
This mid-19th-century house accommodated the Carneiro de Mendonça family. José Maria Jacinto designed it, incorporating into its lovely façade a motif of iron pineapples (*abacaxis*, hence the name), which were a common decoration at the time and were forged in Minas Gerais.
Rua Cosme Velho, 857, Cosme Velho.

⓮ LARGO DO BOTICÁRIO
Hidden at the end of a small alley off Rua Cosme Velho, this square honors local resident Joaquim Luís da Silva Souto, who served as apothecary to the royal family. Seven restored and well-preserved houses with colonial roofs and façades and centuries-old trees create a nostalgic atmosphere, and the square affords views of a stretch of native Atlantic forest and the Carioca River. Throughout the year, the square serves as a stage for many different artistic and cultural presentations.
In 1920, neo-colonial buildings designed by Lúcio Costa and Gregori Warchavchik and by the diplomat and amateur architect Rodolfo Siqueira replaced a row of early-19th century houses that used to stand here (*Rua Cosme Velho, starting at #822*).

⓯ PAINEIRAS
A trip to Paineiras, near the Christ the Redeemer statue, is a must for nature lovers. Before you get to the statue, the road to Paineiras (via Rua Almirante Alexandrino in Santa Teresa) forks off: it is called Estrada do Corcovado (going to the statue) and Estrada do Redentor (going toward Alto da Boa Vista). On weekends, vehicles are not allowed on the latter, and it becomes a large pedestrian area. Along the road, at various points, you can watch capuchin monkeys, admire the view, walk, run, exercise, skateboard, climb, or bathe in the small waterfalls nearby. On the way to the Christ statue is the old Hotel das Paineiras, where the Brazilian soccer team used to stay.

Largo do Boticário: centuries-old trees and a nostalgic atmosphere await at the end of an alleyway

FLAMENGO

Don't just pass through Flamengo without stopping. The lovely view of Pão de Açúcar (Sugarloaf Mountain) and the neighboring towns of Catete and Glória and Botafogo make Flamengo well worth visiting. The city faces the sea and boasts restaurants, bars, museums, and cultural centers, in addition to Parque do Flamengo, one of the most popular parks in the city. However, with its early 20th-century houses and lovely art deco buildings, Flamengo remains a very residential neighborhood. The main thoroughfare is Avenida Infante Dom Henrique. You could also take the metro to Estação Flamengo, and exit onto Rua Marquês de Abrantes, one of the main streets in the neighborhood. Most of the bars are on this street. (It's less safe to exit the station onto Rua Paulo IV.) Rua Senador Vergueiro, with its old buildings, busy bars and stores, is also worth a visit.

Attractions
1. Oi Futuro
2. Castelinho do Flamengo
3. Casa de Arte e Cultura Julieta de Serpa
4. Centro Cultural Arte Sesc

Art deco buildings
1. Conjunto À Praia do Flamengo
2. Edifício Biarritz
3. Edifício Paissandu
4. Igreja da Santíssima Trindade
5. Edifícios Hicatu and Itaiúba

Nightlife
1. Manoel & Juaquim
2. Bar Devassa
3. Adega do Juca
4. Armazém do Chopp
5. Picote
6. Belmonte

FLAMENGO

Castelinho do Flamengo, an art nouveau building that functions as a cultural center

❶ Oi Futuro

Built in 1918, the old Centro Cultural Telemar stands near Largo do Machado (Machado Square). Renovated and reopened as Oi Futuro in 2005, today it offers a wide range of activities: Its eight high-tech floors host exhibitions, plays, shows, and an internet room. If you want to research the old Companhia Telefônica publications and historical material, make arrangements in advance. On the eighth floor, the bistro **Conexão Sabor** serves lunch, snacks, and desserts.
Rua Dois de Dezembro, 63, Flamengo, tel. (21) 3131-3060. Tue – Sun, 11am – 8pm.

❷ Castelinho do Flamengo

Designed in 1916 by Gino Copede, this is one of the last art nouveau

---

Art Deco Buildings

Countless art deco buildings sprang up in Flamengo in the 1930s and 1940s, when the architectural style was most popular. Today, a stroll around Flamengo reveals architectural treasures like the **Conjunto À Praia do Flamengo**, built in 1940 by Robert R. Prentice. This group of three buildings – Anchieta *(Praia do Flamengo, 186)*, Nobre *(Rua Almirante Tamandaré, 10)*, and Barth *(Rua Machado de Assis, 17)* – stands out with its long, curved balconies. **Edifício Biarritz**, a building designed in 1940 by Henri Paul Pierre Sajous and Auguste Rendu, has curved balconies, railings, and friezes that catch the eye *(Praia do Flamengo, 268)*. **Edifício Paissandu**, designed by Eduardo V. Pederneiras and built in 1929, showcases a relief detail on its façade that produces a surprising juxtaposition of light and shade *(Rua Paissandu, 93)*. You can also see **Igreja da Santíssima Trindade**, a church designed by Sajous and built in 1939. Its ornate tower and interior columns contain beautiful bas-reliefs *(Rua Senador Vergueiro, 141)*. **Hicatu** and **Itaiúba**, twin buildings designed by Rafael Borges Dutra in 1933, have curved balconies and shutters; the area between the buildings holds recreational facilities and parking *(Rua Senador Eusébio, 6 and 10)*.

buildings built in the city. Its official name, Centro Cultural Oduvaldo Vianna Filho, is virtually unused. Everybody calls it "castelinho" (little castle) because its tower resembles a medieval castle. Castelinho offers talks in Portuguese on literature and contemporary art, and shows opera films every two weeks on Fridays at around 3pm. On the first Saturday of every month, the center holds evening concerts, and on the last Saturday, it hosts classical guitar performances at 5pm. To see any of these, simply register on the spot once you arrive. There is also a video library with around 1,000 Brazilian and international films, which includes documentaries, children's films, and musicals. You can view all of these videos in booths equipped with a computer or video player.
Praia do Flamengo, 158, Flamengo, tel. (21) 2205-0276. Tue – Sun, 10am – 8pm.

❸ Casa de Arte e Cultura Julieta de Serpa

Opened in 2003, this sophisticated cultural and gastronomic center is located in the old Seabra Palace (1920), designed by Luiz Morais Júnior. The center includes the **J. Club** piano bar which features live jazz, *choro* music, and bossa nova on Fridays and Saturdays from 9pm; the elegant French restaurant **Blason** *(Mon, noon – 4pm; Tue – Sat, noon – 4pm, and 7pm until the last customer leaves)*; the **Provence** bistro, with its Mediterranean cuisine *(Tue – Sat, noon – 4pm, and 7pm until the last customer leaves; Sun, noon – 5pm)*, and the luxurious **Salon D'Or** tea room *(Tue – Sat, 4pm – 7pm)*. For a lighter meal, snack in the outside area, **Pérgula**. The center also hosts auctions, exhibitions, courses, and talks. Call in advance for information on current events at the center.
Praia do Flamengo, 340, Flamengo, tel. (21) 2551-1278. Daily, 9am – 7pm.

❹ Centro Cultural Arte Sesc

Across from Flamengo station, the Arte Sesc Cultural Center has been operating here since 2003. The building used to belong to the early-20th-century entrepreneur and recording tycoon Frederico Figner. The center's five rooms host art exhibitions, talks, seminars, forums, and fairs on various themes. The ground-floor auditorium holds 250 seats. The center holds feature-length and short film festivals, book launches, dramatic readings, and classical and MPB (popular Brazilian music) musical projects, such as *Sábados Clássicos*, on Saturdays at 5pm.
Rua Marquês de Abrantes, 99, Flamengo, tel. (21) 3138-1343. Tue – Sat, noon – 8pm; Sun, 11am – 5pm.

An old building houses Arte Sesc

Bar Devassa, famous for its traditional draft beer

NIGHTLIFE IN FLAMENGO

Flamengo attracts both Bohemians and food-lovers with its variety of traditional and modern bars. Located near Largo do Machado (Machado Square), **Manoel & Juaquim** serves codfish cakes as well as tasty *chope* (draft beer) *(Rua Almirante Tamandaré, 77, tel. (21) 2556-7488; Tue – Sat, 1pm – 2am; Sun, noon – 2am)*. In 2005, **Bar Devassa** opened a branch in Flamengo. Since its opening, it has attracted customers with its four types of excellent, traditionally brewed *chope* *(Rua Senador Vergueiro, 2, stores. B and C, tel. (21) 2556-0618; daily, 11:30am – 2am)*. Try the skewered sausage to start, and follow it with the famous *picanha* (rump steak) at **Majórica** *(Rua Senador Vergueiro, 11, tel. (21) 2205-6820; Mon – Thu, and Sun, noon – midnight; Fri and Sat, noon – 1am)*. **Lamas** has been in operation for over a century and serves one of the best fillet steaks in the city *(Rua Marquês de Abrantes, 18, tel. (21) 2556-0799; Mon – Fri, 9:30am – 3am; Sat, 9:30am – 4am; Sun, 9:30am – 3am)*. The newest spot in the area, **Adega do Juca,** serves dishes like *bacalhau à transmontano* (codfish with tomatoes, onions and bell peppers), along with a variety of appetizers *(Rua Paissandu, 122, tel. (21) 2245-0858; daily, 8am – 2am)*. Nearby stands **Armazém do Chopp**, opened in 1996, which serves delicious snacks and main dishes *(Rua Marquês de Abrantes, 66, tel. (21) 2557-4052; daily, 11am – 1am)*. For more than forty years, **Picote** has been serving tasty appetizers at its sidewalk tables *(Rua Marquês de Paraná, 128, store C, tel. (21) 2552-1799; daily, 7am – 1am)*. The very popular **Belmonte**, opened in 1952, is always full and serves great *pastéis* (deep-fried pastries), as well as generous dishes such as *risoto de camarão* (shrimp risotto) *(Praia do Flamengo, 300, tel. (21) 2552-3349; daily, 8am – 3am)*.

Parque do Flamengo
(Parque Brigadeiro Eduardo Gomes)

This extensive area on the shoreline of Guanabara Bay between Santos-Dumont Airport and Botafogo Beach began as the Glória landfill project. Material from the bulldozed Santo Antônio Hill ended up in this landfill in the 1950s. Transformed into a park in 1964, and listed as a heritage site the following year, the park is the work of some of Rio's most famous landscapers. These include Lota Macedo Soares, a self-taught architect who conceptualized the park, Affonso Eduardo Reidy, who was responsible for the urban design, and Burle Marx, the landscaper. Known as Aterro do Flamengo, the park links the downtown area and the South Zone with expressways. At the same time, the vast gardens act as a gathering area for residents, with facilities for soccer, volleyball, basketball, tennis, model airplane flying, cycling (bike rentals are available), and skate-boarding.

There is also a children's playground and an artificial beach. Here you will also find the Museu de Arte Moderna, a modern art museum beautifully designed by Reidy. On Sundays and holidays, part of Avenida Infante Dom Henrique is closed to traffic, and the park gets crowded – children, sports enthusiasts, and many others come to walk through the trees and admire Pão de Açúcar (Sugarloaf Mountain). Thirty years after its creation, Aterro do Flamengo is at the center of controversy over the proposed construction of boathouses and buildings at Glória Marina for the 2007 Pan-American Games. The project is meeting with resistance from locals, architects and employees of Iphan (National Institute for Historical and Artistic Heritage). The main attractions at the park have parking facilities. See the following map to pinpoint the park's attractions.

Aterro do Flamengo: one of Brazil's loveliest urban parks

Flamengo

Attractions
1. Aeroporto Santos-Dumont
2. Museu de Arte Moderna
3. Monumento aos Mortos da II Guerra Mundial
4. Marina da Glória
5. Restaurante Porcão
6. Museu Carmen Miranda

1 Aeroporto Santos-Dumont
The Roberto brothers designed the Santos-Dumont Airport (1937). At the front entrance to the airport is the square known as Praça Senador Salgado Filho, which was one of Burle Marx's most important landscaping projects. Later incorporated into Aterro do Flamengo, this square contains Amadeu Zanide's lovely monument for Santos Dumont, Brazil's "father of aviation."
Praça Senador Salgado Filho, no #, Centro, tel. (21) 3814-7070.

2 Museu de Arte Moderna (MAM)
Rio's Museum of Modern Art is Affonso Eduardo Reidy's masterpiece. This horizontal building, suspended on perpendicular V-shaped columns, stands out in the middle of Aterro do Flamengo. The museum opened in 1958, five years after Reidy designed it; Burle Marx landscaped its surroundings. A fire in 1978 destroyed part of the museum's collection, and closed its doors for more than a decade. It now houses approximately 13,000 exhibits, including the paintings *Urutu* by Tarsila do Amaral, *O farol* by Anita Malfatti, and *Number 16*, by Jackson Pollock, as well as Antônio Manuel's installation *O fantasma*, and a sculpture entitled *Mademoiselle Pogany*, by Brancusi. In the garden are two lovely sculptures by Amilcar de Castro and Franz Weissmann. However, there is no permanent exhibition. The temporary exhibitions rotate every two or three months. Guided visits can be arranged by telephone. An annex of MAM houses **Vivo Rio**, a huge national and international musical venue.
Avenida Infante Dom Henrique, 85,

FLAMENGO

Leisure Activities
1. Model airplane flying
2. Dance floor
3. Skateboarding area
4. Full-sized soccer fields
5. Multi-sport courts
6. Tennis courts
7. Puppet theater
8. Outdoor bowls
9. Informal soccer fields

Parque do Flamengo, tel. (21) 2240-4944. Tue – Fri, noon – 6pm; Sat, Sun and holidays, noon – 7pm.

❸ Monumento aos Mortos da Segunda Guerra Mundial

Built in 1960 by architects Marcos Konder Netto and Hélio Ribas Marinho, this is a monument to the Brazilian soldiers killed in World War II. It features a sculpture by Alfredo Ceschiatti honoring the Brazilian armed forces. The monument also contains a museum with a collection of medals, flags, videos on the Brazilian Expeditionary Force, and a mural by Anísio Araújo de Medeiros. The dead soldiers are buried in an underground mausoleum.
Avenida Infante Dom Henrique, 75, Glória, tel. (21) 2240-1333. Tue – Sun, 10am – 4pm.

❹ Marina da Glória

This marina is one of the main centers in the country for water sports and sailing and is the departure point for boat trips. Trips range from quick, two-hour jaunts in vessels that can hold up to 25 people, to all-day private trips in launches for six to twelve people. These trips visit places such as Niterói, located on the other side of the bay. The marina also offers diving trips to Guanabara Bay. Bilingual guides are available.
*(Organizers: **Macuco Rio.** Reservations Mon – Fri, 8am – 5pm, tel. (21) 3286-8130, 7836-5466. Open Mon – Sat, departures at 10am; Sun and holidays, 11am. **Tropical Cruises.** Reservations Mon – Fri, 7am – 8pm, tel. (21) 2487-1687, 9963-6172).* The marina has been chosen to host the 2007 Pan-American Games. Its two large

Flamengo

Boat trips leave from Marina da Glória

pavilions hold business and cultural events, such as **Fashion Rio** and the **Rio Boat Show**, which displays a wide range of nautical equipment. The marina has a lovely view of the mooring area, shops that specialize in boats and boating equipment, restaurants, diving centers, and schools offering sailing and fishing courses. It can house 400 boats and has floating docks. You will also find the Portuguese restaurant **Barracuda**, one of the best restaurants in Rio, which serves fish and seafood in an elegant atmosphere *(tel. (21) 2205-3346; Mon – Sat, noon – midnight; Sun, noon – 6pm).*
Avenida Infante Dom Henrique, no #, Glória, tel. (21) 2205-6716. Daily, 8am – 6pm.

❺ Restaurante Porcão
The best all-you-can-eat restaurant in town serves fantastic meat dishes, as well as an extensive salad buffet. The restaurant's wonderful view of Pão de Açucar (Sugarloaf Mountain) is especially beautiful at night.
Avenida Infante Dom Henrique, no #, Parque do Flamengo, tel. (21) 3461-9020. Sun – Thu, 11:30am – midnight; Fri, 11am – 1am.

❻ Museu Carmen Miranda
Opened in 1976, this museum is housed in a circular building designed by Affonso Eduardo Reidy. Its collection comprises clothes, accessories, and sandals worn by Carmen Miranda, as well as photographs and posters of her films and shows.
Avenida Rui Barbosa, 560, Flamengo, tel. (21) 2299-5586. Wed – Fri, 11am – 5pm; Sat, 1pm – 5pm.

Lota Macedo Soares, a Local Visionary

Maria Carlota Costellat de Macedo Soares (1910 – 1967), known to many as Lota, was one of the most prominent figures in Rio in the 1940s and 1950s. She was a friend to intellectuals and artists and was endowed with a sound knowledge of architecture and city life. Her long-running romance with American poet Elizabeth Bishop ultimately proved her undoing, however. After the affair ended, the crushed Lota died of sleeping pill overdose. With the support of Governor Carlos Lacerda, she coordinated the group responsible for the construction of Aterro do Flamengo. Lota, known for her forceful personality, came into conflict with her team on many occasions, most of all with Burle Marx. Despite the disagreements, she knew how to see her ideas to fruition. It is impossible to think of Rio's landscape today, or of the city's 20th-century history, without invoking her name. She died in 1967, grieving the end of the affair with Bishop.

Botafogo and Humaitá

The calm waters of the bay and the serene poise of Pão de Açúcar (Sugarloaf Mountain) provide a stunning backdrop for the neighborhood of Botafogo, which is the main link between Rio's Centro (downtown area) and Zona Sul (South Zone). The villages of Flamengo and Urca flank one side of Botafogo, and Leme and Copacabana rest on the other. Humaitá, a neighborhood adjoining Lagoa and Jardim Botânico, lies just beyond the border. Since the beginning of the 20th century, Botafogo has grown vertically. Commercial and residential buildings, bars and restaurants, shopping malls, cinemas, theatres and museums have replaced former homes of the Old World aristocracy. The town's main thoroughfares, Rua São Clemente and Rua Voluntários da Pátria, offer access to the Botafogo metro station. Avenida Botafogo leads to the beach of the same name. Despite pollution and advisories against swimming, the 700-meter stretch of beach sees plenty of action among water-sports enthusiasts.

Attractions
1. Fundação Getúlio Vargas
2. Botafogo Praia Shopping
3. Centro de Arquitetura e Urbanismo
4. Fundação Casa de Rui Barbosa
5. Museu do Índio
6. Tempo Glauber
7. Museu Villa-Lobos
8. Pinakotheke Cultural
9. Lurixs Arte Contemporânea
10. Cemitério São João Batista
11. Museu dos Teatros
12. Teatro Poeira
13. Casa da Matriz
14. Espaço Cultural Maurice Valansi
15. Sergio Rodrigues Design e Móveis
16. Cobal do Humaitá
17. Espaço Cultural Sérgio Porto
18. Botafogo de Futebol e Regatas
19. Canecão
20. Rio Sul Shopping Center

Cinemas
1. Unibanco Arteplex
2. Botafogo Praia Shopping
3. Espaço Unibanco de Cinema
4. Estação Botafogo

Botafogo Bay, with Morro da Urca and Sugarloaf Mountain behind it, offers beautiful views

❶ Fundação Getúlio Vargas

The Getúlio Vargas Foundation is one of the most renowned teaching and research institutions in the country. Oscar Niemeyer designed the building, an example of modern Brazilian architecture completed in 1955. Though it's not open to visitors, you can still catch a glimpse of its V-shaped supporting pillars outside. The foundation offers university courses and sponsors important social and economic studies. A resource for important historical research on Brazil, the center also is responsible for calculating the country's main economic indices. The institution's bookstore is on the ground floor. For more information, log onto fgv.br.
Praia de Botafogo, 190, Botafogo, tel. (21) 2559-6000. Mon – Fri, 8am – 10pm.

❷ Botafogo Praia Shopping

This shopping mall opposite Botafogo Bay contains 170 stores spanning eight floors. Don't miss the lovely view of Botafogo Beach and Pão de Açucar (Sugarloaf Mountain) from the eighth-floor food court, a sight even more beautiful at night. Our tip is to grab a table at **Botequim Informal** and enjoy the people-watching with a *chope* (draft beer) and serving of *bolinhos de bacalhau* (savory cod patties) or the manioc patties called *bolinhos de aipim* (*8th floor, tel. (21) 3171-6442; daily, noon – 11:30pm*). The mall also has a multiplex cinema and a temporary art exhibition area.
Praia de Botafogo, 400, Botafogo, tel. (21) 3171-9559. Mon – Sat, 10am – 10pm; Sun, 3pm – 9pm.

❸ Centro de Arquitetura e Urbanismo

Formerly the residence of Portuguese builder Joaquim Fonseca Guimarães, this imposing, gated mansion now serves as the Center of Architecture and Urbanism. Colégio Jacobina, one of Rio's most traditional schools, occupied the site from the mid-1940s until 1980. The house was donated to the city in 1997, and part of the grounds used for the construction of a residential building. The original 1879

façade, featuring intricate stonework with circular motifs in bas-relief, was listed as a national heritage site in 1985. Its eclectic architectural features remain nearly intact.
Rua São Clemente, 117, Botafogo, tel. (21) 2579-2038. Tue – Sun, noon – 8pm.

❹ Fundação Casa de Rui Barbosa

Politician and diplomat Rui Barbosa called this lovely neo-classical building home for 28 years. Today it houses an important library with some 37,000 volumes, in addition to Barbosa's furniture, paintings, decor, and personal effects. Note the library desk, on which the first republican Constitution of Brazil was written. Book-lover Plínio Doyle established the foundation's annex, **Arquivo-Museu de Literatura Brasileira**, a literary treasure trove of objects, documents, and private files belonging to legendary Brazilian writers, including Manuel Bandeira, Clarice Lispector, Vinicius de Moraes, Pedro Nava, Carlos Drummond de Andrade, and Machado de Assis. Items may be perused for research purposes, by prior appointment *(tel. (21) 3289-4655)*. The house–the first to be made a museum in Brazil, and open to the public since 1930–hosts exhibitions of pieces from Barbosa's permanent collection, courses, seminars, and, in the auditorium, literary, theater, cinema and musical performances. Highlights include Série Brasiliana, a series of classical music concerts held the last Tuesday of each month *(6:30pm)*, and Cineclube ABC&D's Saturday screenings of documentaries and short films *(6pm)*. Families should take advantage of the property's large garden and the excellent children's library.
Rua São Clemente, 134, Botafogo, tel. (21) 3289-4600. Tue – Fri, 10am – 5pm; Sat, Sun and holidays, 2pm – 6pm; last Tuesday of the month, 8am – 5pm. Library: Mon – Fri, 9am – 4:30pm. Gardens: Daily, 8am – 5pm.

❺ Museu do Índio

Established in 1953 by world-renowned anthropologist Darcy Ribeiro, the Indian Museum has

occupied this 19th-century mansion since 1978. Part of Funai (The National Indian Foundation), the museum houses more than 14,000 objects, 16,000 national and international publications dedicated to indigenous ethnology, 50,000 pictures, some 200 audio records, and an important exhibit on indigenous groups and their ecological environments. See headdresses made from macaw-tail or toucan feathers, view films documenting life in Indian villages – even come face-to-face with a medicine man (okay, maybe just his picture). In the museum gardens, a reproduction of a traditional Indian dwelling comes alive with sound effects. The adjoining store sells handicrafts such as necklaces and bags.
Rua das Palmeiras, 55, Botafogo, tel. (21) 2286-8899. Mon – Fri, 9am – 5:30pm; Sat, Sun, and holidays, 1pm – 5pm.

❻ Tempo Glauber
Lúcia Rocha, mother of Brazilian filmmaker Glauber Rocha, established this cinematic tribute to her son in 1989. He's perhaps best known as director of *Deus e o diabo na terra do sol* (released in English as *Black God, White Devil*), which was once voted the best Brazilian film of all time. The building sits adjacent to Museu Villa-Lobos, and houses a collection of about 80,000 items, including articles, magazines, manuscripts, and films *(screenings should be arranged in advance). Rua Sorocaba, 190, Botafogo, tel. (21) 2527-5840. Mon – Fri, 10am – 6pm.*

❼ Museu Villa-Lobos
This museum, housed inside a 19th-century building, is dedicated to the memory of local composer Heitor Villa-Lobos (1887-1959). Three rooms of photographs depict different moments in his career. Villa Lobos' widow, Arminda, donated most of the objects on display, among which are medals, hats, musical scores, and a guitar. The exquisite Gaveau piano is a gift from the signature piano makers in recognition of the composer's talent. A library and sound archive are tucked at the back of the house *(Mon, Wed, and Fri, 9am – noon; Tue and Thu, 1pm – 5pm). Rua Sorocaba, 200, Botafogo, tel. (21) 2266-3845. Mon – Fri, 10am – 5:30pm.*

❽ Pinakotheke Cultural
Gallerist Max Perlingeiro moved into his current location on Rua São

---

Cinemas in Botafogo

Botafogo is a great place to catch a film. Rua Voluntários da Pátria is home to **Espaço Unibanco de Cinema** *(#35, tel. (21) 2226-1986; daily, 1pm – 10pm)* and **Estação Botafogo** *(#88, tel. (21) 2226-1988; daily, 1pm – 10pm)*. Fans of independent films will enjoy the former, opened in 1996 and equipped with three screens, a bookstore, and a café. The latter has been in operation since 1980 and also features three screening rooms. International films and film festivals are popular events here. A charming snack bar, **Ateliê Culinário**, serves sweet and savory snacks, such as oven-baked pastries and mini-quiches. Cinephiles can also head to nearby Botafogo Beach, where the new six-screen **Unibanco Arteplex** draws a large weekend crowd *(#316, tel. (21) 2559-8750; daily, 12:30pm – 10pm)*. Commercial and art films share space with a bistro, café, and bookstore. And don't forget **Botafogo Praia Shopping**, which also houses a multiplex cinema *(#400, tel. (21) 3171-9559; Mon – Sat, 10am – 10pm; Sun, 3pm – 9pm)*.

An exhibition of works by José Bechara at Lurixs Arte Contemporânea

Clemente in 1994. The space was designed by Eduardo Pederneiras at the start of the 20th century. Branches of the gallery can be found in São Paulo and Fortaleza. Highlights of the collection include works by renowned modernist Brazilian artists such as Antonio Bandeira, Bruno Giorgi, Di Cavalcanti, Frans Krajcberg, Guignard, Pancetti, and Portinari. Doors are open to the public three months a year, when the gallery puts several of its pieces up for sale. Visits must be arranged in advance otherwise.
Rua São Clemente, 300, Botafogo, tel. (21) 2537-7566.

❾ Lurixs Arte Contemporânea
This is one of Rio de Janeiro's best contemporary art galleries. Renowned artists from the 1960s to the 1980s show alongside lesser-known names. Consider a partial list of contributors: José Bechara, Luciano Figueiredo, Afonso Tostes, Paulo Climachauska, Elizabeth Jobim, Lygia Clark, and Antonio Dias. The gallery, opened in 2003, operates out of a 1938 building.
Rua Paulo Barreto, 77, Botafogo, tel. (21) 2541-4935. Mon – Fri, 2pm – 7pm; Sat, 4:30pm – 8pm.

❿ Cemitério São João Batista
Built in 1851, this cemetery was one of the first in Rio to conduct burials of people from all social classes. The sprawling grounds comprise hundreds of chapels, including one dedicated to Saint John the Baptist. No formal visitor facilities exist, but the curious can stroll past deceased personalities of composer Ari Barroso, singer Carmen Miranda, aviator Santos-Dumont, and musician Tom Jobim, among others.
Rua General Polidoro, no #, Botafogo, tel. (21) 2527-0648. Daily, 7am – 6pm.

⓫ Museu dos Teatros
Museum of Theatres opened its doors in 1950, showcasing a collection of about 36,000 documents and photographs chronicling the history of the Teatro Municipal. Interior sketches by painter Eliseu Visconti hang in the art gallery. Note the original Segundo Reinado (Second Reign) period seating removed from the now-defunct Teatro Lírico, which once stood in the city center. Scores for the opera *Jupira*, by Francisco Braga, are also on display.
Rua São João Batista, 105, Botafogo, tel. (21) 2299-5585. Tue – Fri, 11am – 5pm.

Museu dos Teatros tells the history of a local theater playhouse

⓬ Teatro Poeira

Actresses Andréa Beltrão and Marieta Severo opened this tiny theater in 2005 in an effort to showcase culturally and artistically diverse presentations. The three-tiered arena theater accommodates about 160 spectators, and can be adapted to semi-arena. Grab a quick snack in Poeira's charming café.
Rua São João Batista, 104, Botafogo, tel. (21) 2537-8053. Box Office: Tue – Sat, 3pm – 7:30pm; Sun, 3pm – 7pm.

Our Recommendation

🍴 Local chef Flávia Quaresma serves a rotating menu of seasonal dishes at the acclaimed, sophisticated French eatery **Carême Bistrô**. Call in advance to confirm Quaresma will be on duty when you show up *(Rua Visconde de Caravelas, 113-D, Botafogo; tel. (21) 2537-2274, 2226-0085; Tue – Sat, 8pm – midnight.)*

Additional restaurant information begins on page 210.

⓭ Casa da Matriz

The owners of Lapa hotspot Teatro Odisséia bring the party to Botafogo with Casa da Matriz. Tucked away off a blink-and-you'll-miss-it side street, the nightclub boasts two dance floors and a games room. Expect to hear rock on Monday and Thursday nights, hip-hop and reggae on Wednesdays, MPB (Brazilian popular music) on Fridays, and, on Saturdays, enjoy a mix of rock and electronica.
Rua Henrique de Novais, 107, Botafogo, tel. (21) 2266-1014. Daily, 11pm until the last customer leaves.

⓮ Espaço Cultural Maurice Valansi

Entrepreneur Maurice Valansi founded much of Rio's early cinema scene. The small center that bears his name hosts design courses, classical music recitals, and photography and art exhibitions. We recommend the live jazz and bossa nova sessions held on Wednesdays and Thursdays. If you can nab a seat at the piano bar on

Saturdays beginning at 8pm, you're in for a real treat. Be sure to visit the top floor to browse the chair collection of Maurice's son, architect and center owner Richard Valansi. The 200-plus models from various eras and geographies are awe-inspiring. *Rua Martins Ferreira, 48, Botafogo, tel. (21) 2527-4044. Mon – Sat, 5pm – 1:30am.*

⓯ Sergio Rodrigues Design e Móveis

Sergio Rodrigues, master of design and maker of such award-winning pieces as *Poltrona Mole* (Soft Armchair), has run this shop for two decades. Examples of furniture made in his factory are on display. Tables, chairs, and chests of drawers and sofas, among other items, are made from certified tauari wood (to order only).
Rua Conde de Irajá, 63, Humaitá, tel. (21) 2539-0393, 2286-8792. Mon – Fri, 9am – 6pm.

⓰ Cobal do Humaitá

The Cobal center burst onto the scene in the 1970s as a huge market for fresh produce. Today, in addition to its daytime farmer's market, with countless vendors hawking vegetables, fish, and even wines, the Cobal offers food in its bars, restaurants, pizza parlors, and snack shops. At night, these establishments are a popular meeting place for locals. A video rental library on site features a good selection of classic films and an area for live shows. This spacious spot, complete with plastic chairs, also has an outpost in Leblon.
Rua Voluntários da Pátria, 448, Humaitá, tel. (21) 2537-0186. Fruit and vegetable market: Mon – Sat, 8am – 1pm. Bars and restaurants: Daily, 1pm – 4am.

Our Recommendation

🍽 **Yorubá** operates out of a simple house, where chef Neide Santos prepares typical dishes from Bahia, such as *farofinha de dendê* (manioc flour and *dendê* palm oil). Try the African-inspired *ebubu fulô* – fish cooked in coconut milk, with ginger, fresh and smoked shrimp, plantain purée, and white rice. *(Rua Arnaldo Quintela, 94, Botafogo, tel. (21) 2541-9387; Wed – Fri, 7pm – midnight; Sat, 2pm – 11pm; Sun, noon – 6pm.)*

Additional restaurant information begins on page 210.

⓱ Espaço Cultural Sérgio Porto

This small cultural center favors new and eccentric local artists, and it focuses on music, dance, and the visual and dramatic arts. Opened in 1983, the space was formerly a warehouse used by city government, who still maintain the property. The center also houses an art gallery and theater.
Rua Humaitá, 163, Humaitá, tel. (21) 2266-0896. Tue – Sun, 2pm – 10pm.

Cobal do Humaitá, a popular meeting spot

'Craques do Botafogo' (Botafogo football stars) terracotta figurines by artist Marliete

⑱ Botafogo de Futebol e Regatas
Designed in 1927 by Arquimedes Memória and Francisque Couchet, this soccer club sits a bit beyond its fellow neighborhood attractions. Two arched verandas, terraces, a rooftop pergola, and tiled murals reflect the building's Hispanic-American neo-classical style. Visitors can see the club's prizes on display in the trophy room.
Avenida Venceslau Brás, 72, Botafogo, tel. (21) 2543-7027. Mon – Fri, 10am – 5pm.

⑲ Canecão
Built in 1967 as a large beer hall – hence the name, which means tankard – this performance venue is an old, storied standby. The 3,000-person-capacity space has hosted big-name artists such as Elis Regina, Vinicius de Moraes, and Tom Jobim. Today, many MPB (Brazilian pop) acts can be seen here, and national pop groups and international ballet performances also fill the space from time to time. However, this venue is neither as modern nor as comfortable as some others, which is why some people prefer the likes of Vivo and Claro Hall.
Avenida Venceslau Brás, 215, Botafogo, tel. (21) 2105-2000. Daily, noon – 9:20pm.

⑳ Rio Sul Shopping Center
Opened in 1980, Rio's first shopping mall is a comprehensive 400 stores across six floors. Specializing in women's fashion, the mall also includes a wide range of gift and electronic boutiques, travel agencies, a Federal Police post, and a multi-screen cinema. The following shops are worth a look: **Bumbum**, the world's first exclusive bikini label, has added accessories, bags, sandals and fashion jewelry to its collection *(store D-54, tel. (21) 2543-3392)*; **Salinas**, a beach fashion store *(store D-090/P, tel. (21) 2275-0793)*; **Joana João**, a popular children's clothier *(store B-10, tel. (21) 2541-5941)*; **Osklen**, offering clothes, shoes, and accessories for men and women *(store. C-15, tel. (21) 2542-8410)*; and the **Biscoito Fino** recording studio *(kiosk on the 2nd floor, tel. (21) 2279-3605)*. Extensive renovations on Rio Sul began in 2006, to be completed mid-2007.
Rua Lauro Müller, 116, Botafogo, tel. (21) 3527-7000. Mon – Sat, 10am – 10pm. Sun and holidays, stores open 3pm – 9pm, food court open noon – 9pm.

Urca

This small South Zone neighborhood (next to Botafogo) is home to one of Rio's most important attractions – the cable cars that run to the top of the iconic Pão de Açúcar, which is known to most English speakers as Sugarloaf Mountain. Urca is also the birthplace of the city of Rio de Janeiro: It was at the foot of Urca's Morro Cara de Cão that, in 1565, explorers founded São Sebastião do Rio de Janeiro, the area's first settlement. In the 1930s, Urca rose to prominence as one of Rio's busiest neighborhoods, attracting tourists, artists, and celebrities drawn to the major casino built in the neighborhood. Today, Urca is calm and predominantly residential, with art deco houses and luxury apartment buildings. There are two beaches, Urca and Vermelha. The main thoroughfares are Avenida Pasteur, Avenida Portugal, and Avenida João Luís Alves. No metro lines serve the neighborhood.

❶ Morro da Urca and Pão de Açúcar
❷ Praia Vermelha
❸ Museu de Ciências da Terra
❹ Fórum de Ciência e Cultura da UFRJ
❺ Igreja de Nossa Senhora do Brasil
❻ Fortaleza de São João

❶ Morro da Urca and Pão de Açúcar

Since the route opened in 1912, riding on cable cars to the top of Pão de Açúcar (Sugarloaf Mountain) has been the most popular tourist activity in Rio de Janeiro – as well as one of the most pleasant and most unforgettable ways for anyone to get to know the city. The journey up Pão de Açúcar requires two trips, first to the top of the smaller Morro da Urca, and the second up to the summit of the Sugarloaf itself. Visitors begin at the

The Sugarloaf Mountain cable car: the spectacular view makes this trip a must

cable car station at Praia Vermelha (Vermelha Beach), at the end of Avenida Pasteur. From the station, 75-person cable cars leave every 30 minutes for the 3-minute, 577-yard ascent to the top of Morro da Urca. At 720 feet above sea level, Morro da Urca offers excellent views of Botafogo Beach and Guanabara Bay; the mount also has snack shops, an amphitheater, and a helipad for panoramic helicopter tours *(Organizers: Helisight, tel. (21) 2511-2141, 2542-7895; Cruzeiro Táxi-Aéreo, tel. (21) 3325-6500, 9808-2828).* At Morro da Urca, visitors transfer to another cable car that makes the final 804-yard trip to the top of Pão de Açúcar. Though the summit of the Sugarloaf features several souvenir shops, snack and ice cream shops, an Amsterdam Sauer jewelry store, and the sculpture *Guanabara mitológica* by Remo Bernucci, the view is the undisputed main attraction. At 1300 feet above sea level, the panoramic lookout takes in almost all of Rio de Janeiro, as well as the nearby lakes, the city of Niterói across the bay, and Fiscal Island in the distance. The effect is simply dazzling. Be sure to visit on a sunny day with clear skies, particularly in the afternoon, when you can sit outside and watch the sun set over the city.
Avenida Pasteur, 520, Urca, tel. (21) 2546-8400. Daily, 8am – 9:50pm.

② Praia Vermelha

This tiny beach has been a strategic defensive stronghold for Rio since colonial times. In 1856, officials chose the area for the site of the Batalhão de

---

Shows on Morro da Urca

For four months of the year, from roughly November through February, Morro da Urca plays host to the country's top musical groups (mostly pop and rock bands), in a venue that holds nearly 2,000 people. This annual concert program, now known as **Oi Noites Cariocas**, was started by producer Nelson Motta in 1980. Though the performances stopped for a time in the early 90s, the program was revived in 2004 by the sponsorship of the Oi telephone company. For program details, visit oinoitescariocas.oi.com.br.

Engenheiros (Engineers' Battalion) and Escola Militar (Military School). The beach remained closed to the public until 1938, when Praça General Tibúrcio was inaugurated. The square is now home to the Pão de Açúcar cable car station. When you're in the area, stop in for a *chope* (draft beer) at the restaurant of the **Círculo Militar da Praia Vermelha** club, right in the square. Try for a seat on the terrace, which is shaded by almond trees and has a delightful view of the sea. The restaurant features samba and *choro* performances on Thursdays at 8pm and MPB and *choro* on Saturdays at 6pm (*Praça General Tibúrcio, no #, Urca, tel. (21) 2543-7284; daily, noon – 1am*).

❸ Museu de Ciências da Terra Housed in the eclectic-looking Palácio da História Geológica Brasileira, the Museum of Earth Sciences features several permanent exhibits on minerals, meteorites, and fossils. Two of the exhibits are geared specifically toward children: "Dinossauros do Triângulo" (Dinosaurs of the Triangle), which showcases dinosaur fossils from the Triângulo Mineiro region; and "No Tempo dos Dinossauros" (In the Time of the Dinosaurs), which uses vertebrate fossils found in Brazil to explain the evolution of our planet and its wildlife. The museum library has 90,000 volumes on the geosciences, the largest collection of its kind in South America.
Avenida Pasteur, 404, 2nd floor, Urca, tel. (21) 2295-7596, 2295-4746. Tue – Sun, and holidays, 10am – 4pm.

> ### Musical Gatherings in Urca
>
> Every Saturday at noon, from March to November, the **Escola Portátil de Música do Rio de Janeiro** music school holds gatherings at Urca's UniRio (near the Museu de Ciências da Terra). Though mostly showcasing the school's students, the event also attracts some professional musicians, as well as amateurs and music lovers of all kinds.
> *Avenida Pasteur, 458, Urca, tel. (21) 2242-3597.*

URCA

❹ FÓRUM DE CIÊNCIA E CULTURA DA UFRJ

The university's Science and Culture Forum occupies the grand Palácio da Praia Vermelha. Designed and built in 1852 by Domingos Monteiro, Joaquim Cândido Guillobel, and José Maria Jacinto Rebelo, the building is most impressive for its size and austerity. The interior features a skylight and high ceilings, ornate doors, stairs flanked by statues, and corridors lined with Portuguese tiles. The building was originally constructed to house the Hospício Pedro II hospice, which has cared for such Brazilian luminaries as the writer Lima Barreto and pianist Ernesto Nazaré. When the hospice closed in the 1940s, the Federal University of Rio de Janeiro (UFRJ) bought the building. Decades later, under Brazil's military dictatorship, it was the scene of violent clashes between students and police. Still a part of the university, today the forum hosts debates and musical performances, both classical and choral. The full lineup of events is available at www.forum.ufrj.br.
Avenida Pasteur, 250, 2nd floor, Urca, tel. (21) 2295-1595. Mon – Fri, 8am – 9pm.

❺ IGREJA DE NOSSA SENHORA DO BRASIL

Not the most architecturally unique church in Rio, the Igreja de Nossa Senhora do Brasil was built between 1925 and 1934. Frederico Faro Filho designed it in the Spanish colonial style and placed it here, near Praia da Urca beach.
Avenida Portugal, 772, Urca, tel. (21) 2295-0496. Mon, Tue, and Fri, 8am – noon and 2pm – 6pm; Wed and Sat, 8am – noon; Sunday mass at 9am, 11am, and 6pm.

❻ FORTALEZA DE SÃO JOÃO

In 1565, Estácio de Sá built the São João Fort in the vicinity of Morro Cara de Cão to guard the recently founded village of São Sebastião do Rio de Janeiro. All that remains of the original building are the gate, with its baroque pediment, and the walls, with their rounded guard towers. Within the walls of the fort are a small collection of 16th-century military artifacts. Visits must be booked in advance.
Avenida João Luís Alves, no #, Urca, tel. (21) 2543-3323. Mon – Fri, 9am – noon and 1:30pm – 4pm.

WALKING TRAILS AND CLIMBING ROUTES

With its rugged terrain and high peaks, Urca is a popular adventure sports destination. Walkers can head for the **Pista Cláudio Coutinho** trail, which starts at Praia Vermelha and runs near Morro da Urca and Pão de Açúcar. The 1.5-mile trail is flat and easy, with a beautiful view out to sea. Native forest flanks the path on all sides, offering walkers a complete immersion in nature: Watch for capuchin monkeys and colorful birds along the trail. Forking off from the main path are more difficult trails, such as the **Bem-te-vi** (which leads to Morro da Urca) and the **Costão** (which goes to Pão de Açúcar, with some climbing involved). Professional guides are recommended for both trails. Climbers will find more than forty climbing routes on Pão de Açúcar itself. Most of the climbs are not for beginners, though one big draw of the mountain is that even the most experienced climbers can take the cable car back down. Almost all of the companies that lead guided climbs up the mountain also offer courses.
Organizers: *Trilhas do Rio, tel. (21) 2424-5455, 9207-1360; Cia. da Escalada, tel. (21) 2567-7105, 9393-5060; Rio Hiking, tel. (21) 2552-9204, 9721-0594; Centro de Escalada Limite Vertical, tel. (21) 2527-4938, 9343-8972.*

Leme and Copacabana

Leme and Copacabana together form the graceful curve of coastline that runs from Pedra do Leme (Leme Rock) to the walls of Forte de Copacabana (Copacabana Fort). Avenida Princesa Isabel, the main route into the area from the city center, serves as the divider between the two neighborhoods. Each district has a distinct character: while Leme is calm and quiet, with a tiny beach frequented mostly by families, lively but slightly run-down Copacabana, with its high concentration of hotels, restaurants, and stores, draws travelers from all over the world. The main thoroughfares in the area are Avenida Atlântica, Avenida Nossa Senhora de Copacabana, and Rua Barata Ribeiro. Several bus lines run through the neighborhoods, and there is no shortage of taxis. There are no metro stations serving Leme, but there are two in Copacabana (Cardeal Arcoverde and Siqueira Campos).

Attractions
1. Praia do Leme
2. Pedra do Leme
3. Forte Duque de Caxias
4. Leme Tênis Clube
5. Morro da Babilônia
6. Avenida Princesa Isabel

Leme

❶ Praia do Leme

Leme Beach is a little over half a mile long, running from Avenida Princesa Isabel to Pedra do Leme (Leme Rock). The water at Leme is generally cleaner than at Copacabana, and is usually suitable for bathing. The best waves for surfing are at the end of the beach closest to Pedra do Leme. The volleyball nets dotting the beach are free and open to the public. One of the most popular meeting spots for locals is **Axé**, a kiosk in front of the Iberostar Copacabana hotel that serves appetizers and juices made to order.

LEME AND COPACABANA

❷ Pedra do Leme

This large rock at one end of Leme Beach is an ideal place to enjoy the sunrise or sunset. In addition to its various climbing paths, the rock is ringed by the **Caminho dos Pescadores**, a walkway often occupied by fishing enthusiasts. Kiosks (some open 24 hours) that sell fish and seafood surround the access area leading up to the rock. Sundays feature live samba performances.

❸ Forte Duque de Caxias

This fort was built in 1779, but only later named for the duke and military figure who gained fame in the war against Paraguay. The path to the fort is an attraction in itself: the steep 20-minute climb to the top of Pedra do Leme rewards visitors with a panoramic view of the Copacabana shoreline, Sugarloaf Mountain, Corcovado and the Christ statue, the *favela* of Morro da Babilônia, and even parts of Tijuca Forest. The remaining fortifications include underground passages and cannons. There are walking trails in the immediate area.
Praça Almirante Júlio de Noronha, no #, Leme, tel. (21) 2275-3122. Sat, Sun, and holidays, 9am – 5pm.

❹ Leme Tênis Clube

This tennis club was founded in 1927 by several employees of the electric company Companhia Carris, Luz e Força Rio de Janeiro (now known as Rio Light S.A.). Situated on one of Leme's nicest, quietest streets, Rua Gustavo Sampaio, the club has four clay tennis courts, two squash courts, a multi-sports court, swimming pools, and a games room, plus a bar and restaurant. However, the club's biggest attraction by far is its private stretch of perfectly preserved Atlantic forest. Visitors are admitted for a fee, but only if invited by a member.
Rua Gustavo Sampaio, 74, Leme, tel. (21) 2543-1089. Mon – Fri, 7am – 11:30pm; Sat, Sun, and holidays, 7am – 2am.

❺ Morro da Babilônia

The *favela* of Morro da Babilônia rose to fame in the 1950s, when it served as the setting for Marcel Camus's film *Orfeu Negro* (*Black Orpheus*). Based on the play of the same name by Vinicius de Moraes, the film won the Palme d'Or at the Cannes Film Festival in 1959. Forty years later, filmmaker Eduardo Coutinho also chose Babilônia as the subject of his documentary about *favela* life, *Babilônia 2000*. Ari Barroso, composer of the song *Aquarela do Brasil*, once lived in the

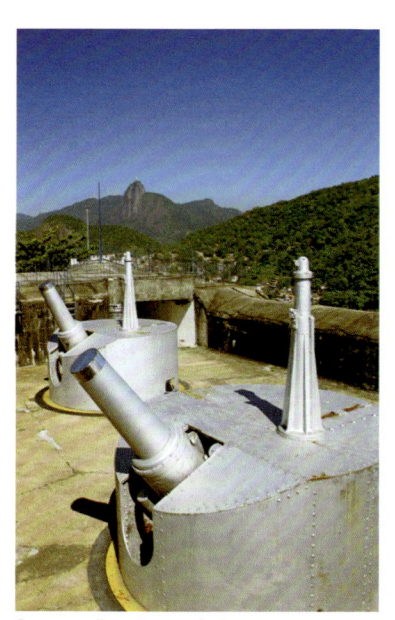

Cannon at Forte Duque de Caxias

Copacabana's neighboring beach, Praia do Leme, is great for bathing

favela. For safety reasons, we do not recommend you visit Morro da Babilônia.

❻ Avenida Princesa Isabel

Princesa Isabel Avenue and **Túnel Novo** (New Tunnel) are the main routes into Copacabana and Leme. The tunnel is one of the first in Rio, opened in 1906 by then-mayor Pereira Passos. Avenida Princesa Isabel, which separates Copacabana from Leme, begins immediately at the tunnel's exit. At the intersection with Rua Barata Ribeiro is a statue of composer João de Barro (better known as Braguinha), one of the biggest names in Brazilian music.

Restaurants in Leme

One of the best places for seafood in Rio is **Marius Crustáceos,** which has a generous tasting menu. You must reserve in advance for the tasting *(Avenida Atlântica, 290; tel. (21) 2104-9002; daily, noon – midnight)*. The traditional **La Fiorentina** prepares pasta, pizza, and meat- and fish-based dishes *(Avenida Atlântica, 458-A; tel. (21) 2543-8395, 2543-8513; Sun – Thu, noon – 2am; Fri and Sat, noon until the last customer leaves)*. Another suggestion is the tiny trattoria **Da Brambini**. The cuisine here is inspired by Crema, a town in the Lombardy region of Italy, where the family has another restaurant *(Avenida Atlântica, 514-B; tel. (21) 2275-4346 and 2542-8357; daily, noon – 1am)*. The tiny, unpretentious **Shirley** serves Spanish food, specializing in generous portions of paella *(Rua Gustavo Sampaio, 610, store A; tel. (21) 2542-1797 and 2275-1398; daily, noon – 1am)*. The Italian restaurant **D'Amici** maintains a stellar reputation thanks to excellent roasts (including duck and lamb shoulder), a highly-praised wine cellar, and impeccable service *(Rua Antônio Vieira, 18-B; tel. (21) 2541-4477 and 2543-1303; Mon – Thu, noon – midnight; Fri – Sun, noon – 1am)*.

Attractions
1. Praia de Copacabana
2. Farmácia do Leme
3. Praça do Lido
4. Parque do Chacrinha
5. Beco das Garrafas
6. Copacabana Palace
7. Charutaria Lollô
8. Modern Sound
9. Túnel Velho
10. Paróquia da Ressureição
11. Clube dos Marimbás
12. Forte de Copacabana

Shopping
1. Shopping Center Cidade de Copacabana
2. Shopping Cassino Atlântico
3. Galeria River
4. Bossa Nova & Cia
5. Baratos da Ribeiro
6. Livraria Argumento

Galleries
1. Novembro Arte Contemporânea
2. Galeria Artur Fidalgo
3. Marcia Barrozo do Amaral Galeria de Arte
4. Athena Galeria de Arte
5. Arte 21

Antique Stores
1. Machado Antigüidades
2. Retrô
3. Ben-Hur Antigüidades
4. Grafos
5. Onze Dinheiros
6. Rue Jadis Antiquário

COPACABANA

Copacabana puts all the contradictions of Rio de Janeiro on vibrant display: sophisticated buildings share space with blocks of cramped studio apartments; well-known celebrities and anonymous locals mingle on sidewalks designed by Burle Marx; high-end hotels stand next to simple corner bars; tiny but charming food stores pop up on every corner, sitting shoulder-to-shoulder with the neighborhood's many fancy boutiques. Despite promising beginnings, however – composers Braguinha and Alberto Ribeiro once christened Copacabana "Princess of the Sea" – the area has lost some of its charm, due largely to the increase in prostitution and sex tourism and a decline in the middle-class population. Nevertheless, the neighborhood is still home to the glamorous Copacabana Palace Hotel, and still takes center stage in Rio's vibrant New Year's Eve celebrations. Copacabana also boasts countless hotels, fine examples of art deco architecture, and numerous art galleries, antique stores, shops, bars, and restaurants.

1 PRAIA DE COPACABANA
The stretch of beach from Posto 2 to Posto 6 (these lifeguard posts are

Architecture
1. Tuyuti
2. Orion
3. América
4. Alagoas
5. Comodoro
6. Solano
7. Ouro Preto
8. Edifício Ophir
9. Guahy
10. Itahy
11. Ceará
12. Almeida Magalhães
13. Edifício Ribeiro Moreira
14. Chopin, Prelúdio, Balada, and Barcarola
15. EdifícioLabourdette
16. Brasil
17. Amazonas
18. Irapuan
19. Edifício Angel Ramirez
20. Edifício Finúsia
21. Edifício Lamberti
22. Jardim Amazonas
23. Edifício Jardim Santa Clara
24. Edifício Embaixador
25. Roxy
26. Edifício Ypiranga

Gay Scene
1. Rainbow
2. Le Boy
3. La Girl

spaced along the beach and serve as localization markers) exemplifies the true *carioca* (meaning "from Rio") spirit. Home to around 20,000 people, Copacabana buzzes day and night – in crowded kiosks, at volleyball games, along the beachfront promenade and cycle paths, and in the crowds that throng to big-name summer shows. Copacabana is the beach favored by older locals, who walk and exercise there. The stretch in front of the **Copacabana Palace**, at Posto 3, attracts many (mostly foreign) tourists, and is considered by many a magnet for petty crime. This part of the beach gets very crowded on weekends, due largely to its proximity to the Cardeal Arcoverde metro station. At Posto 4, children and teenagers can take soccer classes at **Escolinha de Futebol do Júnior**, in front of Rua Figueiredo Magalhães. The best, least crowded stretch of Copacabana is at Posto 5, particularly the area in front of Rua Constante Ramos. The final section of the beach, at Posto 6, is particularly quiet, with fishermen selling what they catch on the spot. At Posto 6 you'll also find a statue of the poet Carlos Drummond de Andrade, sitting on a bench. Though born in Minas Gerais, Andrade lived for some time in Copacabana, and would spend the afternoons looking out to sea in front of Rua Rainha Elisabete.

New kiosks along the beach offer more comfort and amenities for beachgoers

Do not carry valuables or large sums of money while walking along the beach at Copacabana. And be prepared to be mobbed by street vendors, who tend to flock like seagulls around anyone walking along the beach.

Kiosks

Copacabana's new beachfront kiosks, designed by architect Luiz Eduardo Índio da Costa, have become an attraction in and of themselves. More spacious than the traditional kiosks, they have underground restrooms, showers, and lockers, plus security cameras. In the kiosks near the Copacabana Palace (between Posto 2 and Posto 3, in front of Rua República do Peru) you'll find such famous Rio bars as **Bar Luiz,** which serves German food and has been in business for over a hundred years *(kiosk #10, tel. (21) 8702-3078)*, **Caroline Café**, serving sandwiches, aperitifs, and exotic drinks *(kiosk #7, no telephone)*, and **Rainbow**, which caters to gay customers. Near the Othon Palace Hotel, at Posto 5, you will find **Quiosque 35**, which is open 24 hours.

❷ Farmácia do Leme

Originaly opened in Leme, in 1933, this pharmacy moved to Copacabana twenty years later (but never changed its name). Locals have a special place in their hearts for the establishment, which sells all kinds of medication and cosmetic lines. One of the staff members, Zé das Medalhas, has become something of a local celebrity. A resident of Avenida Prado Júnior for forty years, Zé is immediately recognizable by the medals he wears round his neck, and is known for the stories he loves to tell about the neighborhood.
Avenida Prado Júnior, 237-A and B, Copacabana, tel. (21) 3223-9000. Daily, 24 hours.

❸ Praça do Lido

This square was created in 1919 and took its name from one of the city's most elegant restaurants, Lido, which opened on the square in 1922 and was for years a symbol of the neighborhood's glamour. The square was refurbished in the 1960s, when it acquired a bust of the 19th-century painter brothers Rodolfo and Henrique Bernardelli, who lived in the area. Nowadays the square is a meeting place for children and older residents.

❹ Parque Estadual da Chacrinha

This beautiful forest reserve is right in the middle of Copacabana's hustle and bustle; its ecology reflects that of the once-dominant forest that stretched along the Atlantic coast of Brazil. The park is home to several plant species and features sign-posted trails, a children's playground, and recreation areas. Visitors are free to feed fruit to the small monkeys that live in the reserve; fully accustomed to the presence of humans, the monkeys will take pieces of banana from visitors' hands.
Rua Guimarães Natal, no # (Cardeal Arcoverde metro station), Copacabana, tel. (21) 2530-3106. Tue – Sun, 8am – 5pm.

❺ Beco das Garrafas

The closed-off alley between buildings #21 and #37 on Rua Duvivier is known as Beco das Garrafas – literally "Bottle Alley," after the bottles that local residents used to throw at rowdy night-clubbers. As the site of Rio's most popular nightclubs in the 1950s and 60s, this was once one of the most celebrated addresses in the Brazilian music world, playing host to such legendary artists as Dolores Duran, Baden Powell, Elis Regina, Nara Leão, Wilson Simonal, Sérgio Mendes, Luís Eça, Vinicius de Moraes, and Tom Jobim. It was in hotspots such as the Little Club, Baccara, Bottle's, and Ma Griffe that instrumental bossa nova (or samba-jazz as some call it) was born. In addition to its regular evening shows, the Little Club held Sunday jazz and bossa nova sessions where singers, composers, and instrumentalists, both amateur and professional, would come to play and improvise for free. These days, the tiny street has lost most of its charm, though some nightclubs still operate there. The charming bookstore **Bossa Nova & Cia** aims to bring some of that legendary atmosphere back to the once-storied address *(see Bookstores, page 118).*

New Year's Eve in Copacabana

Though there are New Year's Eve festivities held all over Rio – Ipanema, Lagoa Rodrigo de Freitas, Leblon, the Marina da Glória – without a doubt the most exuberant and vibrant celebrations are in Copacabana. Every New Year's Eve, around two million people, most of them dressed in white, crowd onto the two-and-a-half mile beach to watch a fantastic fireworks display that lasts a quarter of an hour. The hotels along Avenida Atlântica host sumptuous parties, followed by elaborate breakfasts. In the days leading up to the end of the year, Copacabana also serves as the site for festivities related to Brazil's various syncretic religions, notably *umbanda* and *candomblé*. On December 31, the main thoroughfares are closed to private cars after 6pm, and bus service is limited. Anyone not staying in Copacabana would do well to take a taxi after 6pm, or park in Ipanema and continue on foot to Copacabana. Despite the huge numbers of people walking about, there are very few disturbances; the beach is heavily policed during the festivities.

❻ Copacabana Palace

The first hotel in Copacabana and a Rio de Janeiro landmark, the heritage site-listed Copacabana Palace Hotel has been the meeting place for the jet set since it opened in 1923. Past guests have included Santos Dumont, Gene Kelly, Orson Welles, Princess Diana, and Arturo Toscanini. The hotel has welcomed presidents, kings, and Hollywood stars, and was the setting for the 1933 film *Flying Down to Rio*, in which Fred Astaire and Ginger Rogers danced together on screen for the first time. Famous for its traditional elegance and sophistication, the Copacabana Palace was built by the entrepreneur Otávio Guinle at the suggestion of the then-president of Brazil, Epitácio Pessoa, who visited France and became enchanted by the fashionable architecture of Paris. The design by French architect Joseph Gire was inspired by the Negresco Hotel in Nice and the Carlton Hotel in Cannes. The hotel's two buildings house two restaurants: the refined **Cipriani**, which serves food from the north of Italy, under the leadership of Francesco Carli *(tel. (21) 2545-8747; Mon – Thu and Sun, 12:30pm – 3pm and 7pm – midnight; Fri and Sat, 12:30am – 3pm and 7pm – 1am)*, and the pool-side **Pérgula**, which serves contemporary cuisine, including tea, breakfast, lunch, and one of the best Sunday brunches in Rio.
Avenida Atlântica, 1702, Copacabana, tel. (21) 2548-7070.

❼ Charutaria Lollô

Opened in 1952, this cigar store stands at one of the busiest spots on Avenida Nossa Senhora de Copacabana, between Rua Santa Clara and Rua Figueiredo Magalhães. It's the perfect place to stop for a quick coffee. Some locals consider the brew served here to be the most traditional and aromatic in the city. Visitors can also buy tobacco, cigars

The sophisticated Copacabana Palace, open since 1923

Modern Sound, one of the city's best music stores

and pipes of different sizes and colors, and souvenirs such as lighters and playing cards.
Avenida Nossa Senhora de Copacabana, 683, Copacabana, tel. (21) 2235-0625. Mon – Sat, 24 hours; Sun, 7am – 11pm.

❽ Modern Sound
This store is among the best of its kind in the city. It stocks a wide variety of DVDs and CDs, including a basement space selling second-hand music books and vinyl records. Featuring musically inspired décor, the shop also sells audio and video equipment, and often marks weekly new music launches on Tuesdays with free shows. **Alegro Bistrô**, inside the store, serves quick meals and sandwiches, and also holds very popular happy hours featuring good live music. Saturday afternoons offer the chance to have lunch in the bistro and listen to veteran instrumentalists performing live.
Rua Barata Ribeiro, 502-D, Copacabana, tel. (21) 2548-5005. Mon – Fri, 9am – 9pm; Sat, 9am – 8pm.

❾ Túnel Velho
Built at the end of the 19th century to connect Botafogo and Copacabana, this so-called Old Tunnel (officially Túnel Alaor Prata) spurred the rapid growth of residential settlements in the latter district. Up to the time of the tunnel's construction, Copacabana and

---

Rua Tonelero, the Road to Change

This road runs from Praça Cardeal Arcoverde to the entrance to the Major Rubens Vaz Tunnel, in the direction of Arpoador. It entered the history books as the scene of the attempt on the life of Carlos Lacerda, editor of the *Tribuna da Imprensa* newspaper at the time and a bitter opponent of then-president Getúlio Vargas. Lacerda was attacked by two gunmen when he arrived home on August 5, 1954. Though he escaped with his life, his bodyguard, Major Rubens Vaz, died. Subsequent investigations revealed that the attackers had been contracted by the chief guard of the presidential palace, Gregório Fortunato. The episode shocked the nation and fairly changed the course of Brazilian political history: an extraordinarily gifted orator, Lacerda intensified his campaign against Vargas after the attempted assassination, leading Vargas to commit suicide soon afterward.

Forte de Copacabana, built in 1914 to defend Guanabara Bay

Leme had been difficult to get to – more of a summer refuge for the elite (including Dom Pedro II) than a place to live. When the Companhia Ferro-Carril do Jardim Botânico decided to run trams out to Copacabana, they opened this tunnel through Morro de Vila Rica – and so the most iconic neighborhood in Rio came into being on July 6, 1892. The tramline was soon extended as far as Forte do Leme (Leme Fort), encouraging the construction of new roads and parceling out of building plots. Avenida Atlântica was inaugurated soon after, in 1906.

🔟 Paróquia da Ressurreição
The tiny church stands between Copacabana and Arpoador. It is home to the statue of Nossa Senhora de Copacabana (Our Lady of Copacabana), removed from the old church that gave the neighborhood of Copacabana its name. The church was designed by Ibsen Vilaça and built in 1956.
Rua Francisco Otaviano, 99, Copacabana, tel. (21) 2522-7698. Tue – Sun, 8am – 11am and 4pm – 7pm.

⓫ Clube dos Marimbás
This leisure club is at Posto 6 on Copacabana Beach, just 22 yards from

Bairro Peixoto, a Calm Area

Bounded by Rua Santa Clara, Rua Figueiredo de Magalhães, and Rua Tonelero, Peixoto is a haven of tranquility within Copacabana, filled with neo-colonial buildings built in the 1940s and 1950s. In addition to its well preserved architecture, the area boasts another major attraction: the *capoeira* classes offered by Mestre Feijão and the Centro Cultural Senzala, offered daily from 7:30pm to 9pm in Praça Edmundo Bittencourt. Visitors interested in participating can talk to the organizers on-site in the *praça*. Perhaps as a result of the area's tradition of martial arts, Peixoto has entered into Rio slang – to say that someone was "born in Peixoto" is to imply that he is tough.

the sea and about 3 miles from Ilhas Cagarras, a great spot for underwater fishing and diving. The club itself features facilities geared primarily toward water sports. Though the club is members-only, it opens to the public during Rio's famous New Year's Eve celebrations. It's worth a visit for the enviable view, which takes in the fireworks over Copacabana on one side and the charming beach at Ipanema on the other. Beach volleyball is the club's hallmark sport: the net is directly in front of the club, and after a hard game, you can choose between a dip in the sea or a shower in the shade of coconut palms. *Praça Colonel Eugênio Franco, 2, Copacabana, tel. (21) 2267-5151, 2267-5152, and 2227-1115. Mon – Fri, 9am – 7pm (office hours).*

⑫ Forte de Copacabana

This fort was built in 1914 to defend Guanabara Bay. It sits on the former site of the Igreja de Nossa Senhora de Copacabana church, which gave the neighborhood its name. The exhibitions at the **Museu Histórico do Exército** (Army History Museum), inside the fort, cover important events in the history of Rio de Janeiro using video presentations and models. A long veranda with a panoramic view of Copacabana Beach stretches the length of the main hall, known as the Salão Nobre. The smaller Salão República has exhibits on the Revolta da Armada (a naval revolt), the Canudos campaign, and the nationalist *tenente* movement. In July 1922, the fort was the site of an uprising known as "*Os 18 do Forte*" ("The Fort 18"), when a group of mutinous officers left the fort to face down troops loyal to the government in the middle of Avenida Atlântico. The on-site **Café do Forte**, with its dazzling view of Copacabana Beach, has the same owners as Confeitaria Colombo, in Centro *(tel. (21) 3201-4049; Tue – Sun, 10am – 8pm)*. The café serves breakfast and afternoon tea at covered outdoor tables. *Praça Colonel Eugênio Franco, 1, Copacabana, tel. (21) 2521-1032, 2521-0443, and 2522-6136.*

Ypiranga's curvy design incorporates aerodynamic elements

ARCHITECTURE IN COPACABANA

ART DECO CIRCUIT

Rio de Janeiro has the most art deco buildings of any city in Brazil, and many of them are in Copacabana. The first art deco edifices were built in the 1930s near Posto 2 (between Avenida Atlântica and Rua Barata Ribeiro), and were symbols of the then elegant, modern Copacabana. Important buildings on Avenida Atlântica include: **Edifício Labourdette**, designed in 1937 by Robert Prentice, with its convex verandas and a central column set back from the façade *(#1880)*; **Edifício Embaixador**, designed in 1935 by architects Freire & Sodré, inspired by the great transatlantic ships of the time *(#3170)*; and **Edifício Ypiranga**, also from 1935, with its eye-catching curves and aerodynamic elements *(#3940)*. Architect Oscar Niemeyer had his office in the Ypiranga building. There are also lovely art deco buildings away from the main avenue, especially near Praça do Lido (Lido Square), around Posto 2. On Avenida Nossa Senhora de Copaca-

Tuyuty, art deco from 1931

bana you'll find **Comodoro** *(#162)*, **Solano** *(#166)*, **Ouro Preto** *(#174)*, **Ceará** *(#209)*, **Itahy** *(#252),* and **Roxy** *(#945)*. The oldest of these, Edifício Solano (built in 1930), has a front entrance finished in granite and a lovely iron gate. Edifício Itahy, from 1932, has a wrought-iron front entrance gate with seaweed designs. The Roxy cinema, opened in 1938, is one of Rio's best examples of art deco, with an eye-catching staircase and a foyer done in an aerodynamic style. The theatre was recently restored and is now divided into three. Rua Ministro Viveiros de Castro is home to **Tuyuti**, from 1931 *(#100)*, **Orion** *(#104)* and **América** *(#110)*, both from 1934, and Alagoas *(#122)*, from 1933. The façades of all of these buildings deserve a close look. Rua Ronald de Carvalho features interesting buildings planned in accordance with the rationalist style that was in vogue at the time. One such example is **Edifício Ribeiro Moreira** *(#21)*, near the intersection with Avenida Atlântica. Designed by Alessandro Baldassini and in its time the tallest skyscraper in Rio, the innovative building (then known as Edifício OK) features split floors, verandas that are incorporated into the body of the building, and a canopied front entrance. The equally imposing **Almeida Magalhães** *(#45)* has generous verandas and a marble-trimmed front entrance. **Edifício Ophir** *(#154)* impresses with the geometric lines of its façade and its lovely entrance gate. A little further on is **Guahy** *(#181)*, with its beveled façade. Further examples of Rio's distinctive art deco style fill the area between Rua República do Peru and Rua Fernando Mendes. On Rua Fernando Mendes, **Brasil** *(#19)*, **Amazonas** *(#25)*, and **Irapuan** *(#31),* all of which were built between 1936 and 1940, feature spacious, sophisticated, eye-catching entrances. **Edifício Lamberti** (1935), in Praça Serzedelo Correia *(#15)* is also worth a look.

Modernist Buildings

Visitors will also find plenty of modernist architecture in Copacabana. Among the cluster of four residential buildings, the **Chopin, Prelúdio, Balada**, and **Barcarola**, all surrounding to the Copacabana Palace, the first stands out the most. Built between 1951 and 1957 from a design by Jacques Pilon, it has enormous windows and spacious apartments. It has hosted ambassadors and ex-presidents, and is most famous today for the lavish parties held by its residents, particularly those held during New Year's Eve *(Avenida Atlântica, #1782)*. **Edifício Angel Ramirez**, designed in 1952 by MMM Roberto Architects and built in 1954, features V-shaped supporting columns and

Edifício Amazonas, on Rua Fernando Mendes

The distinctive, V-shaped columns on Edifício Angel Ramirez

wooden shutters *(Rua República do Peru, 72)*. Though its original marquees and entrance have changed since they were initially designed by the Roberto brothers in 1952, **Edifício Finúsia** is still notable for its geometric façade and its overall opulence *(Rua Barata Ribeiro, 283)*. Nearby is **Edifício Jardim Santa Clara**, a 1966 Álvaro Vital Brasil design that successfully balances the needs of space and functionality *(Rua Santa Clara, 372)*. **Jardim Amazonas**, from 1962, is another example of modern architecture by the same architect *(Rua Anita Garibaldi, 25)*.

Living in Copacabana

With no less than 23 studio apartments per floor (totaling 276 units on 12 floors), the enormous **Edifício Master** houses nearly 500 people. The building's mix of students, retirees, foreigners, actors, transvestites, and prostitutes is emblematic of the cultural diversity that abounds in Copacabana specifically and in Rio de Janeiro as a whole. The building *(Rua Domingos Ferreira, 125)* and its residents were the subject of a documentary by Eduardo Coutinho in 2002. Another famous building of studio apartments is known only by its former street address, **Barata Ribeiro, 200**. It was once the scene of violent fights and police activity. Today, after changes in the administration, the building is much calmer: even the street number has been changed to erase its bad reputation *(Rua Barata Ribeiro, 194)*.

Eating in Copacabana

Bars

The tiny, simple **Bip Bip** is a genuine classic. Customers wanting beer, soda, or water help themselves from the refrigerator. The bar features live samba on Sundays and *choro* on Tuesdays. It is also the site of the traditional carnival group **Rancho Flor do Sereno**, which parades on Carnival Monday *(Rua Almirante Gonçalves, 50-D; tel. (21) 2267-9696; daily, 7pm – 1am)*. **Cervantes** has been one of Rio's most popular traditional spots for decades, thanks to its highly-praised roast pork sandwich with pineapple, its ice-cold *chopes* (draft beers), and opening times that extend into the early hours *(Avenida Prado Júnior, 335, store B; tel. (21) 2275-6147; Tue – Thu and Sun, noon – 4am; Fri and Sat, noon – 5am)*. **Ponto da Bossa Nova** is one of the most popular bars in Copacabana, with a relaxing atmosphere and great savory snacks like French fries with spicy sausage and bacon *(Rua Domingos Ferreira, 215, stores B and C; tel. (21) 2549-7597; Mon, 8am – 1am; Tue – Sat, 8am – 3am)*. Copacabana also has branches of several local bar chains: **Belmonte**, with its *pastel de carne seca* (deep-fried pastry stuffed with shredded beef) and selection of the Brazilian white rum *cachaça* *(Rua Domingos Ferreira, 242; tel. (21) 2255-9696; daily, 8am – 3am)*; and **Manoel & Juaquim**, serving *bolinho de bacalhau* (deep-fried cod patties), and filet mignon with cheese and tomato, served on French bread *(Avenida Atlântica, 3806, Posto 6; tel. (21) 2523-1128; daily, noon – 2am)*.

Coffee and Desserts

Santa Satisfação is a pleasant spot with sidewalk tables, serving sweet and savory snacks and quick meals *(Rua Santa Clara, 36-C; tel. (21) 2255-9349; Mon – Sat, 9am – 11pm)*. **The Bakers** is one of the best bakeries in the city, with an atmosphere similar to that of Santa Satisfação. The bakery serves sandwiches, bread, and a variety of cakes *(Rua Santa Clara, 86-B; tel. (21) 3209-1212; daily, 9am – 8pm)*.

Sunday samba at the unpretentious Bip Bip

LEME AND COPACABANA

JUICE BARS

Juice bars owe their popularity to the need of beachgoers to rehydrate themselves after spending time in the intense Rio sun. Their juices make a refreshing morning treat, as well. All branches of **Kicê Sucos** *(Avenida Nossa Senhora de Copacabana, 1033; tel. (21) 2287-2141; daily, 8am – 2am)* and **Bibi Sucos** *(Rua Miguel Lemos, 31, store A; tel. (21) 2513-6000; Sun – Thu, 8am – 1am; Fri and Sat, 8am – 2am)* serve various juices and *vitaminas* (juice-based drinks, often made with milk or yogurt) made from exotic Brazilian fruits, as well as sandwiches.

RESTAURANTS

Cais da Ribeira, inside the Hotel Pestana, serves smaller portions of contemporary Portuguese dishes. We recommend the *arroz de pato* (rice with duck) and the codfish dish *bacalhau ao Brás (Avenida Atlântica, 2964; tel. (21) 2548-6332; daily, noon – 3pm and 7:30pm – 11:30pm)*. **Le Pré Catelan** is a sophisticated French restaurant inside the Hotel Sofitel, in front of Forte de Copacabana. Chef Roland Villard changes the menu every fortnight *(Avenida Atlântica, 4240; tel. (21) 2525-1160; Mon – Sat, 7:30pm – 11:30pm)*. **A Marisqueira** serves codfish dishes and *caldeirada* (fish and/or seafood stew). On Sundays they feature such dishes as *tripas à moda do Porto*, Porto-style tripe *(Rua Barata Ribeiro, 232; tel. (21) 2547-3920; daily, 11am – midnight)*. The best option at the Portuguese restaurant **Alfaia** is a dinner of the codfish dish *bacalhau à patuscada* followed by *pastel de nata* (custard pastry) for dessert *(Rua Inhangá, 30, store B; tel. (21) 2236-1222; Mon – Sat, noon – midnight; Sun, noon – 11pm)*. **Adega Pérola** focuses on seafood, but also serves a variety of appetizers (including fish, eggplant, and fava beans) at the counter *(Rua Siqueira Campos, 138; tel. (21) 2255-9425; Mon – Sat, 10am – midnight)*. One of the best restaurants for Lebanese food in the city is **Amir,** which serves a varied menu throughout the week and offers several different types of Moroccan couscous on the weekends *(Rua Ronald de Carvalho, 55, store C; tel. (21) 2275-5596; daily, noon – midnight)*. **Siri Mole & Cia** serves first-class food from Bahia, which is far to the north of Rio. Dishes include such specialties as *moqueca de siri mole* (crab stew with coconut milk), *acarajé* (black-eyed pea fritter), *vatapá* (fish and/or shrimp with coconut milk, palm oil, and peanuts), and homemade sweets. A generous Saturday lunch is served buffet style *(Rua Francisco Otaviano, 50, Posto 6; tel. (21) 2267-0894; Mon, 7pm – midnight; Tue – Sun, noon – midnight)*.

THE GAY SCENE

There are gay meeting points all along the beach at Copacabana. **Rainbow** is a 24-hour kiosk that gets very lively in the early hours and features drag shows on weekends *(between Posto 2 and Posto 3, in front of Rua República do Peru)*. The biggest attraction in the neighborhood is the club **Le Boy**, with its outrageous go-go boys and DJs spinning electronica, pop, and 80s (aka "flashback," in local terminology) music *(Rua Raul Pompéia, 102-A, Copacabana; tel. (21) 2513-4993; Tue – Sun, 11pm until the last customer leaves)*. Next door is the female version of this club, **La Girl**, which features great music, go-go girls, and drag shows *(Rua Raul Pompéia, 102-M, Copacabana; tel. (21) 2247-8342; Mon, Wed, and Thu, 9:30pm – 6am; Fri – Sun, 10pm – 6am)*. There are more gay bars and clubs in Ipanema *(see page 126)*.

Carrinho Crítico, by Antonio Dias, on display at Arte 21 Gallery

Shopping

Antique Stores

The **Machado Antigüidades** antique store has two branches in Shopping Center Cidade de Copacabana and another at Rua Francisco Sá, 51. Machado has more than 4,000 antiques, mostly from the 19th and early-20th centuries *(Rua Siqueira Campos, 143, stores 114 and 35; tel. (21) 2235-5788; Mon – Fri, 10am – 7pm; Sat, 10am – 4pm)*. In the Shopping Center Cidade de Copacabana you will also find the following antique stores: **Retrô**, which specializes in art deco pieces and objects from the 1950s and 1970s *(store 159; tel. (21) 2257-1310; Mon – Fri, 11am – 7pm; Sat, 10am – 4pm)*; **Ben-Hur Antigüidades**, which deals in items like Dominici bronze light fittings and L'Atelier furniture *(store 104; tel. (21) 2235-1243; Wed – Sat, 10am – 2pm)*; **Grafos**, which sells originals by Brazilian designers *(stores 1 and 2; tel. (21) 2255-8283; Mon – Fri, 10am – 7pm; Sat, 10am – 2pm)*; and **Onze Dinheiros**, which specializes in pieces from Brazil's imperial period *(stores 144, 145, and 146; tel. (21) 2256-1552; Mon – Fri, 2pm – 7pm; Sat, 10am – 2pm)*. **Rue Jadis Antiquário**, in the Shopping Cassino Atlântico mall, is a great place to find furniture, especially 18th- and 19th-century European pieces *(Avenida Atlântica, 4240, store 334; tel. (21) 2267-4346; Mon – Sat, 11am – 7pm)*.

Art Galleries

The **Novembro Arte Contemporânea** gallery represents young artists such as Matheus Rocha Pitta, Ricardo Becker, and Lais Myrrha *(Shopping Center Cidade de Copacabana, Rua Siqueira Campos, 143, store 118, Copacabana; tel. (21) 2235-8347; Tue – Fri, noon – 7pm; Sat, noon – 5pm)*. **Galeria Artur Fidalgo** is in the same mall and sells works by Artur Barrio, José Damasceno, and Marcos Bonisson, among other contemporary artists *(stores 147, 148, and 149; tel. (21) 2549-6278; Mon – Fri, 2pm – 7pm; Sat, 10am – 2pm)*. There are several galleries in the basement of Shopping Cassino Atlântico *(Avenida Atlântica, 4240)*. The traditional **Marcia Barrozo do Amaral Galeria de Arte** has works by Frans Krajcberg, Anna Letycia, Eduardo Sued, and Franz Weissmann, among others *(store 129; tel.*

(21) 2521-5195; Mon – Fri, 10am – 6pm; Sat, 1pm – 5pm). Next door are **Athena Galeria de Arte**, owned by Liecil Oliveira, which specializes in Brazilian modernists such as Pancetti, Guignard, and Di Cavalcanti *(store 120; tel. (21) 2523-8621 and 3813-2222; Mon – Fri, 3pm – 7pm)*, and **Arte 21**, which deals in contemporary artists such as Emmanuel Nassar and Carlos Vergara *(store 123, tel. (21) 2227-7280 and 2227-7267; Mon – Fri, 10am – 7pm; Sat, noon – 6pm)*.

Bookstores

Bossa Nova & Cia, in Beco das Garrafas, opened in 2006 on the site of the popular 1960s nightclub Ma Griffe. Specializing in bossa nova, MPB (Brazilian pop), samba, and *choro*, it has a vast selection of products, including scores, songbooks, books, magazines, CDs, DVDs, and musical instruments *(Rua Duvivier, 37-A; tel. (21) 2295-8096; Mon – Sat, 9am – 7pm)*. **Baratos da Ribeiro**, one of the friendliest second-hand stores in Rio, buys and sells used books, CDs, vinyl and HQ magazines, children's books, and films on video and DVD. On weekends the store holds free shows by alternative bands *(Rua Barata Ribeiro, 354, store D; tel. (21) 2549-3850; Mon – Fri, 9am – 8pm; Sat, 10am – 2pm)*. A branch of the Leblon bookstore **Livraria Argumento** sells Brazilian and imported books *(Rua Barata Ribeiro, 502-B; tel. 2255-3783; Mon – Sat, 9am – 11pm)*.

Galeria River

Opened in 1967, this shopping arcade features about 60 stores selling gear for sports and leisure, including equipment for surfing, body boarding, roller-skating, adventure sports, and martial arts – plus shops offering tattoos and piercings. The mall is particularly popular with surfers and other water-sports enthusiasts, clubbers, and denizens of Rio's alternative scene. Among the best stores are: **Surf's Co,** which sells surfboards, sportswear, and other accessories for surfing, body boarding, and skateboarding *(store 1; tel. (21) 2522-8727; Mon – Sat, 10am – 8pm; Sun, 10am – 3pm)*; **Ocean Surf Shop**, which rents and sells surfboards made by the store's own team, as well as selling its own clothing label *(store 3; tel. (21) 2522-8794; Mon – Sat, 10am – 1pm and 2pm – 7pm)*; and **Spirit**, which makes surfboards to order, offers surfboard repair services, and sells clothing and accessories *(store 4; tel. (21) 2267-9943; Mon – Sat, 11am – 7pm). Rua Francisco Otaviano, 67, tel. (21) 2267-1709. Mon – Sat, 9am – 7pm.*

Shopping Malls

Some of the best art galleries and antique stores in Rio are housed in two shopping malls in Copacabana. **Shopping Center Cidade de Copacabana,** Rio's first mall, is best known for its antique stores, though it also has stores offering prints, frames, stationery, jewelry, lingerie, decorative items, furniture restoration, and second-hand goods. The mall often holds auctions of antiques, art, and decorative items *(Rua Siqueira Campos, 143, Copacabana; tel. (21) 2549-0650; Mon – Fri, 10am –6pm; Sat, 10am – 2pm)*. As its name implies, **Shopping Cassino Atlântico**, in front of Posto 6, occupies the site of the 1930s Atlântico casino *(Avenida Atlântica, 4240; tel. (21) 2523-8709; Mon – Fri, 9am – 9pm; Sat, 9am – 7pm)*. Connected to **Hotel Sofitel**, this mall holds regular art auctions and, on Saturdays between 11am and 7pm, the Cassino Antique Fair, comprising 90 stalls selling works of art, antique objects, and arts and crafts. Weary shoppers can relax with a beer by the pool in **Atlantis**, the restaurant inside Hotel Sofitel, which offers views of Copacabana.

IPANEMA

Ipanema embodies the image of sunny, cheery Rio de Janeiro, at once laid-back and sophisticated. The neighborhood lies between Arpoador and Leblon, from which the Jardim de Alá canal separates it, providing an outlet to the sea for the Lagoa Rodrigo de Freitas lagoon. One of the most affluent parts of the city, it is mostly residential, with many elegant shops and pleasant bars, hotels, and restaurants. The beachfront offers many leisure options. Four important thoroughfares run the length Ipanema: the glamorous Avenida Vieira Souto (along the beachfront), the commercial street Visconde de Pirajá (in the center of the neighborhood), Avenida Epitácio Pessoa (which borders Rodrigo de Freitas Lagoon), and Rua Prudente de Morais. The best way to get around is on foot or by bike, especially in the late afternoon when bus and taxi traffic grinds to a halt.

Attractions
1. Praia do Arpoador
2. Praia de Ipanema
3. Casa de Cultura Laura Alvim
4. Country Club

Cinemas
1. Estação Laura Alvim
2. Estação Ipanema

IPANEMA BEACHFRONT

① Praia do Arpoador

Located at one end of the Ipanema beachfront, Arpoador Beach stretches from Forte de Copacabana (Copacabana Fort) to where Rua Francisco Otaviano turns into Avenida Vieira Souto. More than a quarter-mile long and with beautiful sand, gym equipment, and volleyball and soccer pitches, it is a critical meeting point for surfers. In the corner, Pedra do Arpoador (Arpoador Rock) offers one of the most beautiful views of Ipanema. In the 1950s and 1960s the beach was a popular among bossa nova musicians, and it maintains a special atmosphere even today. Many like to climb the rock to watch the sunrise or sunset, which always ends with general applause – a true ritual among regulars. Praia do Arpoador disappears during rough weather and at high tide. In the stretch between Forte de Copacabana and the Pedra do Arpoador is Praia do Diabo (Devil's Beach), where there is good surf. Behind Praia do Diabo is **Parque Garota de Ipanema**, a spacious, green park with playground

The Ipanema beachfront, with a view toward Arpoador Rock

equipment. Some pickpocketing does go on in this area, so don't take your valuables to the beach.

② Praia de Ipanema

Democracy rules along Praia de Ipanema, where people of all ages and walks of life frequent the two miles of sand. Over the course of more than half a century, the place has achieved mythical status and acquired an image of hedonism and modernity that fascinates the country and the world. The well-kept bike path along the beachfront is always busy, and joggers and walkers fill the kiosk-lined promenade, which is especially lively on hot days, when the best thing to be had is coconut water, served *estupidamente gelado* ("ridiculously cold," as locals like to say), sucked straight out of the coconut with a straw. Here you will find useful products and services for sale, such as sunscreen *(see box at right)*. Chair- and sun-umbrella rental is also available at various points along the beach.

Families and children hold sway near **Posto 8**, one of many lifeguard posts along the beach. A rainbow flag between Rua Teixeira de Melo and Rua Farme de Amoedo marks the preferred spot of the gay community. A laid-back crowd of university students, actors, and musicians tends to concentrate around **Posto 9**, which sits between Rua Vinicius de Moraes and Rua Joana Angélica. At dusk, bathers in this area applaud the sunset, a tradition

---

Local Characters

In her stall at Posto 9, in addition to selling cookies and drinks and renting out chairs, the friendly and creative **Dona Dilma** sells sunscreen in tiny pots for individual use, and rents out sunglasses at low prices. In 1990, the itinerant vendor **Claudinho** took seventy small plastic bags of frozen fruit juice to the beach. He returned home 20 minutes later with an empty ice chest and a head full of ideas. Today the resourceful Claudinho can be found on the strip of sand in front of the Caesar Park Hotel selling his frozen juice, now a local institution.

Looking toward Leblon from busy Ipanema Beach, the twin rocks Dois Irmãos poke up in the background

that began in the 1960s. The area between Posto 9 and **Posto 10**, near Rua Aníbal de Mendonça, is popular among teenagers and beach-volleyball enthusiasts, who set up their nets here to practice. But beach volleyball is not the only sport played on the sands of Ipanema. Up and down the entire beach, people play soccer, footvolley and even the Samurai martial art *kenjutsu* – a group of devotees meets once a week to practice. The relatively strong waves attract surfers. Only nightfall drives away the crowd. Ipanema after dusk is very quiet.

❸ Casa de Cultura Laura Alvim
Two years after the death of cultural patron Laura Alvim (1900-84), her beachfront house was donated to the state and made into a cultural center. Built between 1906 and 1913, it is one of the few actual houses left in the neighborhood, if not along the entirety of Avenida Vieira Souto. It was and still is frequently visited by artists and intellectuals. When it became a cultural center, Angelo de Aquino, Daniel Senise, Rubens Gerchman, and other artists donated some of their works to the collection. It contains an art gallery, a venue for events and festivals, two theatres, a café, and a cinema *(see page 123)*, and even offers courses.
Avenida Vieira Souto, 176, Ipanema, tel. (21) 2267-1647. Mon – Fri, noon – 10pm; Sat and Sun, 1pm – 9pm.

❹ Country Club
Founded in 1916 in the heart of Ipanema, the Country Club is quite traditional, with tennis courts and tournaments. It also has a swimming pool, a movie projection theatre, a games room, and a playground. In addition to holding courses, it has good services – including a hairdresser – and a beautiful piano bar. Its facilities and organized activities, however, are limited to members and their guests. Nonetheless, or for this very reason, it remains a symbol of Rio's elite.
Rua Prudente de Morais, 1597, Ipanema, tel. (21) 2239-3332.

IPANEMA FOR ALL TASTES

Away from the beach, Ipanema is a pleasant, leafy neighborhood with a mixture of stores, restaurants and residential buildings. The busiest and most sophisticated block is formed by Rua Visconde de Pirajá, Rua Garcia d'Ávila, Rua Barão da Torre, and Rua Aníbal de Mendonça. This area is especially recommended for shoppers and lovers of good food. Other streets also hold pleasant surprises, however: large squares, old churches, cultural centers, and bookstores. Stroll through the neighborhood and you will discover its treasures street by street.

Praça General Osório

The heritage-listed fountain **Chafariz das Saracuras** (1795) stands in the middle of General Osório Square, where Copacabana ends and Ipanema begins, between Rua Visconde de Pirajá, Rua Jangadeiros, Rua Prudente de Morais, and Rua Teixeira de Melo. The work of artist Mestre Valentim, until 1911 it stood in the courtyard of Ajuda Convent in Cinelândia. When the convent was demolished, the fountain was brought to this square. The pyramid shape, typical of Mestre Valentim, is original, but the four *saracura* birds that gave it its name are replicas *(Praça General Osório, no #)*. The square is also venue for the **Feira Hippie** (Hippie Fair), held every Sunday since the 1960s. Wandering among the hundreds of blue-canvas stalls, you'll come across all manner of hand-made objects, many of high quality: decorations, souvenirs, clothes, shoes, handbags, costume jewelry, paintings, intaglio prints, and sculptures. There are also food and drink stalls with everything from hot dogs to Bahian acarajé. The fair gets very busy in the afternoon *(Praça General Osório, no #, Ipanema; Sun, 8am – 6pm)*.

Praça Nossa Senhora da Paz

Right in the heart of Ipanema, this large square is a meeting place for all ages, who come here to take a walk, read, play, and practice sports. Events

The Sunday Feira Hippie in Praça General Osório began in the 1960s

Praça Nossa Senhora da Paz, a meeting place in the heart of the neighborhood

such as theatrical sketches and itinerant exhibitions also take place here. There is a street fair in the area on Fridays, from 6am to 1pm. In the middle of the square is an imposing statue by sculptor Hildegardo Leão Veloso, unveiled in 1931 in homage to Senator Pinheiro Machado, who was murdered in 1915. Facing the square is the church **Igreja Nossa Senhora da Paz** (1918-1920), whose name (Our Lady of Peace) celebrates the end of World War I. It has German stained-glass windows, and the high altar, made of marble, came from Italy. It draws crowds of locals and tourists during the Christmas season, when parishioners set up a large Nativity scene on the sidewalk in front of it. The legendary samba composer Pixinguinha died here, on a carnival Saturday in 1973. To this day, whenever the Banda de Ipanema carnival band passes through the square it plays the song "Carinhoso" in his honor *(tel. (21) 2523-4543. Open: Mon – Sat, 6am – 8pm; Sun, 6:30am – 10pm). Praça Nossa Senhora da Paz, no #, Ipanema. Daily, 7am – 6pm, and 7am – 7pm during daylight savings.*

Cinemas

Ipanema has two movie houses: **Estação Laura Alvim** has three small screening rooms *(Avenida Vieira Souto, 176, tel. (21) 2267-4307)*. **Estação Ipanema**, which belongs to the same chain, has another two *(Rua Visconde de Pirajá, 605, tel. (21) 3221-9221)*. Both have branches of the café **Ateliê Culinário**, which offers excellent savory snacks, oven-baked pastries, and desserts.

Flower stalls paint the streets

IPANEMA

Architecture
1. Horácio Mendes de Oliveira Castro Filho Residence
2. Picasso, Cézanne, and Matisse
3. Bar Lagoa
4. Edifício Alberto de Campos
5. Edifício Santa Cruz
6. Edifício Barão de Gravatá
7. Edifício Jardim Leonor
8. Edifício JK (beachfront)
9. Edifício Vieira Souto
10. Edifício Atlântica Boavista
11. Edifício Estrela de Ipanema

Art Galleries
1. Estúdio Guanabara
2. Silvia Cintra Galeria de Arte and Box 4
3. Laura Marsiaj Arte Contemporânea
4. Bolsa de Arte
5. Galeria Jean Boghici
6. Galeria de Arte Ipanema

Decoration and Design
1. Forma
2. Eleonora Presentes
3. Lillian Rose
4. Florense
5. Empório Beraldin
6. La Lampe
7. Elle et Lui Maison
8. H. Stern Home
9. Scenario Fusion
10. Tissi Valente
11. 021 Móveis Cariocas

Book and Music Stores
1. A Cena Muda
2. Toca do Vinicius
3. Letras & Expressões
4. Livraria da Travessa

THE STREETS OF IPANEMA

RUA VISCONDE DE PIRAJÁ
This long street runs through the entire neighborhood and is the main shopping strip. It starts at Rua Gomes de Carneiro and ends at Avenida Borges de Medeiros, in neighboring Leblon (traffic runs one-way away from Leblon). It has a variety of sophisticated stores and busy galleries (**Ipanema 2000** and **Fórum de Ipanema**) that are worth a longer visit, as well as a branch of the bookshop **Livraria da Travessa** and an interesting second-hand magazine store, **A Cena Muda**. Rio's biggest beach fashion labels – **Blue Man**, **Bumbum Ipanema**, **Lenny**, and **Salinas** – are all here. In addition to **Tissi Valente**, which is one of the best florists in town, delightful flower stalls stand along Visconde de Pirajá.

RUA GARCIA D'ÁVILA
This street begins at Avenida Vieira Souto and runs six blocks back from the beach to Avenida Epitácio Pessoa. It crosses Ipanema's major thoroughfares, such as Rua Visconde de Pirajá and Rua Barão da Torre. It is known to have the most up-market

IPANEMA

Fashion
1. Espaço Lundgren
2. Bia Vasconcellos
3. Vale das Bonecas
4. Mango
5. Tutti Fashion
6. Casa Alberto
7. Natan
8. A Teen
9. Maria Bonita
10. Dama Y Soberana
11. Etra
12. Donna Chita
13. Jujuba Dorme Bem
14. Andrea Saletto
15. Jean-Yves
16. Khós
17. Espaço Fashion
18. Ricardo Filgueiras
19. Galeria Fórum de Ipanema (Blue Man, Bumbum, Lenny)
20. Mara Mac
21. Glorinha Paranaguá
22. Foch
23. Constança Basto
24. Danielle Carvalho
25. Carlos Tufvesson
26. Pselda
27. Richard's
28. Osklen
29. Reserva
30. Bianca Silveira
31. Contemporâneo Brasil
32. Macaca de Ipanema
33. Tear Gas
34. Accessorize
35. Gilson Martins
36. Mixed
37. AmazonLife
38. Louis Vuitton
39. Leeloo
40. Maria Filó
41. Eliza Conde
42. Totem and Totem Kids
43. Galeria Ipanema 2000
44. Cristine Ban
45. Maria Bonita Extra
46. H. Stern
47. Antonio Bernardo
48. Cartier
49. MontBlanc
50. Verve
51. Crystal Care
52. Cristina Cordeiro
53. Casa da Alessa
54. Crystal Hair

Gay Spots
1. Galeria Café
2. Bofetada
3. Dama de Ferro

boutiques in the area, especially international designer labels such as **Louis Vuitton**, and jewelers such as **Antonio Bernardo**, **H. Stern**, **Cartier**, and **MontBlanc**. **Alessandro & Frederico Café** and **Mil Frutas Café** invite a pleasant pause between boutiques.

Rua Barão da Torre
Parallel to Rua Visconde de Pirajá from Rua Jangadeiros to the Jardim de Alá canal, Rua Barão da Torre is a nice place for a stroll, because it is flat, quiet, and leafy. It contains a number of restaurants and bistros, including the famous steak houses **Esplanada Grill** and **Porcão**, and the Mediterranean seafood restaurant **Satyricon**.

Bicycle Rental

Bike Lazer rents out various kinds of bikes by the hour or the day. It also sells sporting equipment, repairs bicycles, and organizes group rides and eco-tourism outings that are accompanied by guides, security personnel, and mechanics *(Rua Visconde de Pirajá, 135-B, tel. (21) 2521-2686; Mon – Fri, 9am – 7pm; Sat, 9am – 2pm)*.

Cheerful colors are a trademark of Totem, the fashion store in Galeria Ipanema 2000

Rua Aníbal de Mendonça

This street perpendicular to Avenida Vieira Souto is one of the busiest in the neighborhood. Find the shopping arcade **Galeria Ipanema 2000**, with the fashion stores **Salinas**, **Elisa Conde**, and **Maria Filó**, on the corner of Rua Visconde de Pirajá. The street is also home to **Maria Bonita Extra**, **Cristine Ban**, and **Cavendish**, as well as top restaurants such as **Gero**, **Forneria** and the extremely popular **Gula Gula**.

Ipanema's Gay Circuit

Posto 8 and Posto 9 on Ipanema Beach mark the main meeting place for Rio's gay scene. After going to the beach, groups get together in bars on Rua Farme de Amoedo, in the block between Rua Visconde de Pirajá and Rua Barão da Torre. One of the most popular is the **Bofetada** *(Rua Farme de Amoedo, 87-A, tel. (21) 2227-1675; daily, 8am until the last customer leaves)*. Nearby, heading toward Lagoa Rodrigo de Freitas, is the bar and nightclub **Dama de Ferro** *(Rua Vinicius de Moraes, 288, tel. (21) 2247-2330; Thu – Sun, 11pm until the last customer leaves)*. Three blocks down, between Rua Prudente de Morais and Rua Visconde de Pirajá, is **Galeria Café**, a café-cum-art gallery *(Rua Teixeira de Melo, 31, stores E and F, tel. (21) 2523-8250; Wed – Sat, 10:30am until the last customer leaves; Sun, noon – 8pm)*. Copacabana *(see page 116)* also has several establishments that are popular on the gay scene.

Other Streets

The heyday of bossa nova focused on Ipanema, where many of the musical genre's creators lived. Many of the busiest streets of the time, which attracted young people and artists with bars that never closed, have since lost their bohemian atmosphere, having been repopulated by commerce and residential buildings. The small **Rua Redentor**, running from Rua Joana Angélica to the Jardim de Alá, is home to establishments such as the fashion store **Khós** and the hairdresser **Jean-Yves**. One block above it, **Rua Nascimento Silva** (where homegrown composer and musical legend Tom Jobim once lived at building #107) has several elegant stores, such as **Andrea Saletto** and **Carlos Tufvesson**. In a bar called Veloso on what was once the Rua Montenegro, inspiration struck poet-lyricist Vinicius de Moraes and Tom Jobim to compose "Garota de Ipanema" ("Girl from Ipanema"). Both street and bar were renamed: the street is now **Rua Vinicius de Moraes**, and the bar could only be called **Garota de Ipanema**. The poet-lyricist's presence can be felt elsewhere in the neighborhood, at **Vinicius Piano Bar** and the bookstore **Toca do Vinicius**.

Art Galleries

Ipanema boasts some of Rio de Janeiro's best art galleries. **Estúdio Guanabara**, specialized in Brazilian art from the 1950s and 60s, gives pride of place to geometric abstraction *(Rua Visconde de Pirajá, 82, underground store 116, Ipanema, tel. (21) 2521-0197; Mon – Fri, 1pm – 7pm)*. Across Praça General Osório, Silvia Cintra runs the **Silvia Cintra Galeria de Arte**, while her daughter Juliana runs **Box 4**. Silvia has been in the contemporary art business for twenty years and has a collection of works by artists such as Amilcar de Castro, Antonio Dias, and Daniel Senise. Juliana holds exhibitions by young, rising talents *(Rua Teixeira de Melo, 53, tel. (21) 2267-9401; Mon – Fri, 10am – 7pm; Sat, noon – 4pm)*. The traditional **Laura Marsiaj Arte Contemporânea** has works by Antonio Dias, Lygia Clark, Ernesto Neto, Mira Schendel, Waltercio Caldas, and Eduardo Sued in its collection *(Rua Teixeira de Melo, 31-C, tel. (21) 2513-2074; Tue – Fri, 10am – 7pm; Sat, noon –6pm)*. Since 1971, **Bolsa de Arte** has been holding auctions at Copacabana Palace Hotel that shape the Brazilian art market. They have auctioned works by artists ranging from Picasso and Torres-García to Ismael Nery, Antônio Parreiras, and contemporary Brazilians. Usually held about four times a year, the auctions follow exhibitions at the Bolsa de Arte headquarters *(Rua Prudente de Morais, 326, tel. (21) 2522-1544; Mon – Fri, 10am – 7pm)*. Near Praça Nossa Senhora da Paz, **Galeria Jean Boghici**, famous for its expensive collection, only opens for clients who make advance arrangements. Art dealer Jean Boghici guarantees the variety and excellence of the works on sale *(Rua Joana Angélica, 180, tel. (21) 2522-4660, 2547-1972)*. The cheery premises that house **Galeria de Arte Ipanema**, display creations by important modernists – Di Cavalcanti, Volpi, and Pancetti – and contemporary artists *(Rua Aníbal de Mendonça, 27, tel. (21) 2512-8832; Mon – Fri, 10am – 7pm; Sat, 10am – 2pm)*.

Galeria Silvia Cintra has been plying contemporary art for twenty years

Shopping and Services

Decorations and Home Furnishings

In the last few years, Ipanema has become a hub of decoration and design in Rio. Many new stores offer a wide range of imported and Brazilian products. **Forma**, a branch of the traditional São Paulo designer furniture store, has many items for the home and office. Its many options include chairs by Philippe Starck and upholstered pieces by Cini Boeri *(Rua Farme de Amoedo, 82-A, tel. (21) 2523-2949; Mon – Fri, 9am – 7pm; Sat, 9:30am – 1pm)*. Offerings at **Eleonora Presentes** range from simple objects for the home to imported vases *(Rua Visconde de Pirajá, 310, store A, tel. (21) 2227-4936, 2287-6021; Mon – Fri, 9am – 7pm; Sat, 9am – 2pm)*. The stationer **Lillian Rose** produces leather office products, and personalized albums and bindings *(Rua Visconde de Pirajá, 365, store 7, tel. (21) 2513-4037; Mon – Fri, 10am – 7pm; Sat, 10am – 2pm)*. **Florense**, the traditional home and office furniture producer from the south of Brazil, has a large store in the neighborhood, with five floors of showrooms *(Rua Joana Angélica, 169, tel. (21) 2247-9488; Mon – Fri, 9am – 8pm; Sat, 9am – 6pm)*. Everything at **Empório Beraldin** is made from organic materials – from silk and linen to coconut fibers and animal horns. In addition to furniture and decorative objects, there are carpets, fabrics and revetting materials *(Rua Nascimento Silva, 330, tel. (21) 3206-7272; Mon – Fri, 9:30am – 7pm; Sat, 10am – 2pm)*. The Rio branch of **La Lampe** designs lighting for interiors and sells its own line of lights and lamps, as well as international brands, including the Italian Artemide and Fontana Arte *(Rua Barão de Jaguaripe, 211, tel. (21) 2523-2484; Mon – Fri, 10am – 8pm; Sat, 10am – 2pm)*. The famous jewelry producer H. Stern has a store with decorations for the home and office, kitchen utensils, and even

Lillian Rose offers stationery and monogrammed items

accessories such as wallets and key rings, **H. Stern Home** *(Rua Garcia d'Ávila, 102-108, tel. (21) 2239-7845; Mon – Fri, 10am – 7pm; Sat, 9am – 3pm).* Nearby, the designer fashion label Elle et Lui also has **Elle et Lui Maison**, with its own line of furniture and exclusive objects imported mostly from Europe *(Rua Garcia d'Ávila, 124, tel. (21) 2239-6749; Mon – Fri, 10am – 7pm; Sat, 10am – 2pm).* **Scenario Fusion** has Brazilian and imported articles for the home *(Rua Aníbal de Mendonça, 55, store G, tel. (21) 2512-4876; Mon – Fri, 10am – 8pm; Sat, 10am – 6pm).* **Tissi Valente** creates elegant floral arrangements, simple or elaborate *(Rua Visconde de Pirajá, 595, upstairs store 308, tel. (21) 2259-1638, 2259-1371; Mon – Fri, 9am – 5pm; Sat, 9am – 1pm).* Young designers Márcio Lewkowicz and Zanini de Zanine created all of the modern furniture and objects at **021 Móveis Cariocas** exclusively for this store *(Rua Paul Redfern, 32, tel. (21) 2249-5506; Mon – Fri, 9am – 7pm; Sat, 10am – 5pm).*

BOOK AND MUSIC STORES
In Ipanema's well-stocked bookstores, in addition to buying books, magazines, CDs and DVDs, you can have a coffee, *chope* (draft beer), or even a meal – in some cases, well after midnight. **Cena Muda** is just a newsstand, but it carries rare publications, such as Brazilian magazines from the 19th century through to the 1970s, in addition to photographs and collectors' card albums *(Rua Visconde de Pirajá, in front of # 54, tel. (21) 2287-8072; Mon – Fri, 10am – 7pm; Sat, 10am – 5pm).* **Toca do Vinicius** specializes in sound. Its sells sheet music, CDs, books, and souvenirs related to Brazilian music, especially bossa nova. The store has a small museum, with manuscripts, personal

Toca do Vinicius specializes in sound

effects, and photographs of musical legends such as Baden Powell, Edu Lobo, Toquinho, Tom Jobim, Miúcha, and, of course, Vinicius de Moraes himself. The Salinha da Bossa (Bossa Room) hosts talks, debates, and DVD exhibitions. On Sundays, even the sidewalk in front of the bookstore gets hopping, with performances of Brazilian music *(Rua Vinicius de Moraes, 129, tel. (21) 2247-5227; daily, 9am – 8pm).* The Ipanema branch of **Letras & Expressões** carries an excellent range of books and magazines. On the third floor, Bar do Zira – named after the famous Brazilian cartoonist Ziraldo, who is a patron – holds literary readings and music nights. While you watch, order a "*sanduíche literário*" ("literary sandwich") and a *chope* (draft beer). Inside the bookstore is Café Ubaldo, well-known for its cappuccinos *(Rua Visconde de Pirajá, 276, tel. (21) 2521-6110; Sun – Thu, 8am – midnight; Fri and Sat, 8am – 2am).* **Livraria da Travessa**, with three branches in the city, has an excellent range of books about Rio. On the mezzanine there are CDs and DVDs, as well as the restaurant

Livraria da Travessa offers a good range of titles

B!, which serves meals and snacks *(Rua Visconde de Pirajá, 572, Ipanema, tel. (21) 3205-9002; Mon – Sat, 9am – midnight; Sun, 11am – midnight)*.

Fashion Accessories

In business for more than 60 years, **Casa Alberto** specializes in fabrics, but it also sells accessories from international designer labels *(Rua Visconde de Pirajá, 302, tel. (21) 2522-1552; Mon – Fri, 10am – 7pm; Sat, 10am – 3pm)*. **Macaca de Ipanema** sells colorful and humorous accessories, as well as items of hand-embroidered women's clothes *(Rua Visconde de Pirajá, 444, store 113, tel. (21) 2247-8348; Mon – Fri, 10am – 7pm; Sat, 10am – 3pm)*. The Ipanema branch of the British chain **Accessorize** sells a stylish range of handbags, flip-flops, handkerchiefs, costume jewelery, and purses *(Rua Visconde de Pirajá, 462, store A, tel. (21) 2247-6588; Mon – Fri, 10am – 8pm; Sat, 10am – 6pm)*. At **Etra** you can find hand-made accessories produced by exclusive artisans *(Rua Joana Angélica, 192, store 201, tel. (21) 3813-3124; Mon – Fri, 11am – 7pm; Sat, 10am – 2pm)*.

Handbags and Shoes

Glorinha Paranaguá makes handbags and accessories in cloth, crochet, leather, wood, and bamboo. Some items are intended for everyday use, and others for special occasions *(Rua Visconde de Pirajá, 365, store 2, tel. (21) 2522-8203, 2267-4295; Mon – Fri, 9am – 7pm; Sat, 9am – 2pm)*. Designer **Constança Basto** has four stores in Brazil and one in Manhattan, and she sells her exclusive line of shoes at each. She invariably uses special or unusual materials. She also runs the brand **Peach**, whose more casual trends appeal to young people *(Rua Visconde de Pirajá, 371, upstairs store 206, tel. (21) 2247-9932; Mon – Fri, 10am – 7pm; Sat, 10am – 2pm)*. **Danielle Carvalho** creates handbags in a range of styles *(Rua Visconde de Pirajá, 371, store 202, tel. (21) 2287-7607; Mon – Fri, 10am – 7pm; Sat, 10am – 2pm)*. The handbags, purses, and shoes at **Bianca Silveira** are made from fine fabrics (*Rua Visconde de Pirajá, 414, store 109, tel. (21) 2227-2496; Mon – Fri, 9am – 7pm; Sat, 10am – 3pm)*, while the leather, plastic, and vinyl handbags at **Gilson Martins** are fun and exotic, with shapes like a soccer ball, or Sugarloaf Mountain *(Rua Visconde de Pirajá, 462-B, tel. (21) 2227-6178; Mon – Sat, 10am – 8pm)*. **AmazonLife** sells a wide range of handbags, backpacks, and travel bags, all made from plant materials *(Rua Visconde de Pirajá, 499, upstairs, tel. (21) 2511-7686; Mon – Fri, 10am – 8pm; Sat, 10am – 4pm)*. There is also a **Louis Vuitton** store in the neighborhood *(Rua Garcia d'Ávila, 114, tel. (21) 2511-5839; Mon – Fri, 10am – 8pm; Sat, 10am – 4pm)*.

Stylists

Some Ipanema stores carry exclusive creations by celebrated fashion designers. **Eliza Conde**, who has another two addresses in the city, uses only fine fabrics such as silk, satin, and crepe *(Rua Visconde de Pirajá, 547, store 226, tel. (21) 2239-6765; Mon – Fri, 9:30am – 7:30pm; Sat, 9:30am – 3:30pm)*. The very feminine clothes designed by **Andrea Saletto** are made from imported fabrics. She also offers a secondary brand, **Permanente**, with simpler designs and more accessible prices *(Rua Nascimento Silva, 244, tel. (21) 2267-9361; Mon – Fri, 10am – 8pm; Sat, 10am – 2pm)*. **Carlos Tufvesson** makes party dresses, often tailoring them while they hang on the client's own body *(Rua Nascimento Silva, 304, tel. (21) 2523-9200; Mon – Fri, 10am – 7pm; Sat, 10am – 2pm)*. **Cristine Ban** is especially known for her knitwear *(Rua Aníbal de Mendonça, 123, store A, tel. (21) 2259-2676; Mon – Fri, 9:30am – 7:30pm; Sat, 9:30am – 2:30pm)*. In her studio **Cristina Cordeiro** creates exclusive clothes using hand-painted fabrics *(Rua Garcia d'Ávila, 194, tel. (21) 2267-7195; Mon – Fri, 10am – 8pm; Sat, 10am – 6pm)*.

WOMEN'S AND MEN'S CLOTHES

The Spanish brand **Mango** has a wide variety of items at good prices *(Rua Visconde de Pirajá, 250-A, tel. (21) 2521-4793; Mon – Fri, 9am – 8pm; Sat, 9am – 5pm; Sun, noon – 5pm)*. The romantic, delicate clothes at **Espaço Fashion** are designed with young people in mind *(Rua Visconde de Pirajá, 351, store 201, tel. (21) 2247-7633, 2521-3237; Mon – Fri, 10am – 8pm; Sat, 10am – 3pm)*. **Mara Mac** has modern, provocative items made from top-quality fabrics with impeccable cuts *(Rua Visconde de Pirajá, 365, store A, tel. (21) 2523-2340; Mon – Fri, 9am – 7pm; Sat, 9am – 3pm)*. **Tear Gas** focuses on in street wear. The house is famous for extremely colorful jeans and t-shirts *(Rua Visconde de Pirajá, 444, upstairs store 20, tel. (21) 2267-6598; Mon – Sat, 10am – 8pm)*. **Mixed** has jeans, basic wardrobe items, party clothes, shoes, and accessories *(Rua Visconde de Pirajá, 476, store upstairs, tel. (21) 2259-9544; Mon – Fri, 10am – 8pm; Sat, 10am – 4pm)*. With extremely

Fashion designer Andrea Salleto's store proffers elegant women's wear

IPANEMA

Leeloo sells both party threads and casual clothes

feminine designs, **Leeloo** is a big hit in Rio. It carries casual and party clothes, accessories, and even home decorations *(Rua Visconde de Pirajá, 547, tel. (21) 2540-6389; Mon – Fri, 10am – 8pm; Sat, 10am – 7pm; holidays, 11am – 5pm).* **Maria Filó** entered the market in 1997 and has made a name for itself as a brand for young people who are romantically inclined, as is so typical of native *cariocas (Rua Visconde de Pirajá, 547, store K, tel. (21) 2259-9230; Mon – Fri, 9:30am – 7:30pm).* At **Totem,** you'll find comfortable clothes for a laid-back lifestyle, including trousers, shirts, skirts, blouses, and beachwear for men and women, as well as an entire floor just for kids *(Rua Visconde de Pirajá, 547, store F, tel. (21) 2540-0661; Mon – Fri, 10am – 8pm; Sat, 10am – 6pm).* Designer Alessa Migani, of **Casa da Alessa**, produces colorful, daring women's clothes, lingerie, and accessories *(Rua Nascimento Silva, 399, tel. (21) 2287-9939; Mon – Fri, 10am – 7pm; Sat, 10am – 3pm).* **Dama Y Soberana** makes elegant, modern clothes, and often treats customers to tea and prosecco wine in the afternoons *(Rua Barão de Jaguaripe, 94 D, tel. (21) 3813-0082; Mon – Fri, 10am – 8pm; Sat, 10am – 2pm).* The fun pieces for sale at **Vale das Bonecas** – from skirts and dresses to bikinis – have an artsy touch *(Rua Farme de Amoedo, 75, store C, tel. (21) 2523-1794; Mon – Fri, 10am – 8pm; Sat, 10am – 2pm).* The traditional **Maria Bonita** has elegant, feminine pieces, and a collection of evening gowns *(Rua Vinicius de Moraes, 149, tel. (21) 2523-4093; Mon – Fri, 9am – 8pm and Sat, 9am – 4pm);* **Maria Bonita Extra** is a younger, sportier version of the same brand *(Rua Aníbal de Mendonça, 135, C and D, tel. (21) 2540-5354; Mon – Fri, 9am – 8pm; Sat, 9am – 4pm).* The local label **A Teen** carries clothes for young women, ranging from everyday items to formal evening gowns *(Rua Joana Angélica, 108, stores C and D, tel. (21) 2522-1878; Mon – Fri, 10am – 8pm; Sat, 10am – 3pm).* For men, **Reserva** carries basic attire and also athletic items; it's especially great for finding classy jeans *(Rua Maria Quitéria, 77, store F, tel. (21) 2255-3279; Mon – Fri, 9am – 6pm; Sat, 10am – 6pm; Sun, 11am – 5pm).* **Osklen** also produces men's and women's fashion, with casual clothes and dress wear *(Rua Maria Quitéria, 85, tel. (21) 2227-2911, 2227-2930; Mon – Fri, 9am – 8pm; Sat; 9am – 6pm; Sun, 11am – 5pm).* While impeccably cut shirts are **Richard's** signature specialty, the famous men's fashion brand also has an interesting women's collection *(Rua Maria Quitéria, 95, tel. (21) 2522-1245; Mon – Fri, 9am – 8pm).*

CHILDREN'S WEAR

Beachwear for kids can be found at **Totem Kids**, on the mezzanine at Galeria Ipanema 2000 *(Rua Visconde de Pirajá, 547, store 212, tel. (21)*

2540-0661; Mon – Fri, 10am – 8pm; Sat, 10am – 6pm). **Donna Chita** has various brands of clothing for children up to age eight *(Rua Joana Angélica, 192, upstairs store 103, tel. (21) 2267-5127; Mon – Fri, 9am – 7pm; Sat, 9am – 2pm).* The elegant **Jujuba Dorme Bem** has everything for babies, from diaper-bags to blankets and sheets *(Rua Joana Angélica, 192-203, tel. (21) 2247-8799; Mon – Fri, 10am – 7pm).*

Underwear and Lingerie
Foch is a men's brand for all kinds of clothes, but it specializes in men's underwear and modern-looking swimsuits *(Rua Visconde de Pirajá, 365 B, ground floor, store 10, tel. (21) 2521-1172; Mon – Fri, 10am – 8pm; Sat, 10am – 4pm).* **Verve** sells romantic, delicate women's underwear with unique patterns *(Rua Garcia d'Ávila, 149, tel. (21) 3202-2680; Mon – Sat, 10am – 7pm).* **Pselda** carries sexy lingerie and erotic accessories *(Rua Maria Quitéria, 121, upstairs store 21, tel. (21) 2247-2047, 2521-7901; Mon – Fri, 10am – 7pm; Sat, 10am – 2pm).*

Jewelery
Ricardo Filgueiras designs modern jewelery that's then produced by artisans and sold here *(Rua Visconde de Pirajá, 351, store 203, tel. (21) 2287-1090; Mon – Fri, 10am – 7pm; Sat 10am – 2pm).* In her studio, where she receives visitors only by appointment, **Bia Vasconcellos** produces exclusive pieces, including jewelery, paintings, painted ceramics and glass, and even eyewear *(Rua Barão da Torre, 107-A, house 4, apartment 201, tel. (21) 2287-4870).* The celebrated **Antonio Bernardo** has two stores in Ipanema, where he showcases his beautiful creations of gold, silver, and precious metals *(Rua Garcia d'Ávila, 121, tel. (21) 2512-7204; Mon – Fri, 10am – 8pm; Sat, 10am – 4pm; also Rua Visconde de Pirajá, 351, store 104, tel. (21) 2523-3192; same hours).* The neighborhood also has branches of famous international and Brazilian brands, including **Natan** *(Rua Visconde de Pirajá, 309, store A, tel. (21) 2525-5555; Mon – Fri, 10am – 7pm; Sat, 10am – 2pm);* **H. Stern** offers guided tours through the gem-cutting area and has a collection of gemstones and jewels on display *(Rua Visconde de Pirajá, 490, tel. (21) 2274-3447; Mon – Fri, 10am – 7pm; Sat, 10am – 3pm);* **Cartier** *(Rua Garcia d'Ávila, 129, tel. (21) 2274-0104. Mon – Fri, 10am – 7pm; Sat, 11am – 3pm);* **MontBlanc** *(Rua Garcia d'Ávila, 145, store A, tel. (21) 3813-6464; Mon – Fri, 10am – 7pm; Sat, 10am – 2pm).*

Reserva carries classic styles and sportswear lines

Balanço, Puzzle and Fold rings, by Antonio Bernardo

Bumbum and Blue Man, famous beachwear brands

Multibrand Stores

On the Ipanema beachfront, the enormous **Espaço Lundgren** sells famous Brazilian and international clothing brands *(Avenida Vieira Souto, 234, tel. (21) 2523-2522; Mon – Fri, 10am – 8pm; Sat, 10am – 6pm)*. **Tutti Fashion** sells elegant and classical women's clothes, such as suits and coats *(Rua Visconde de Pirajá, 282, store A, tel. (21) 2247-1756; Mon – Fri, 9am – 8pm; Sat, 9am – 3pm)*. At **Contemporâneo Brasil**, one can find clothes for men, women, and children, as well as accessories, shoes, and costume jewelry from brands such as Alexandre Herchcovitch and Glória Coelho *(Rua Visconde de Pirajá, 437, upstairs, tel. (21) 2287-6204; Mon – Sat, 10am – 8pm)*. **Khós** has clothes and accessories for all ages and styles, from party dresses to jeans *(Rua Redentor, 23, 2nd floor, tel. (21) 3813-2879; Mon – Fri, 10am – 7pm; Sat, 10am – 2pm)*.

Beachwear

Ipanema's top beachwear stores are concentrated in the block formed by Ruas Barão da Torre, Garcia d'Ávila, Visconde de Pirajá, and Aníbal de Mendonça, not far from the beach. The shopping arcade **Galeria Fórum de Ipanema** has **Blue Man**, famous for its bikinis *(Rua Visconde de Pirajá, 351, stores C and D, tel. (21) 2247-4905; Mon – Fri, 9am – 8pm; Sat, 9am – 6pm)*; **Bumbum**, which, in addition to beachwear, sells sandals, beach bags, and accessories *(Rua Visconde de Pirajá, 351, tel. (21) 2521-3859; Mon – Fri, 9am – 8pm; Sat, 9am – 4pm)*; and **Lenny**, which carries swimwear that range from discreet to daring, in addition to accessories and clothes *(Rua Visconde de Pirajá, 351, stores 114 and 115, tel. (21) 2523-3796; Mon – Fri, 10am – 8pm; Sat, 10am – 3pm)*. The arcade **Galeria Ipanema 2000** has **Salinas**, with beachwear for adults and children *(Rua Visconde de Pirajá, 547, stores 204 and 205, tel. (21) 2274-0644; Mon – Fri, 9am – 7pm; Sat, 10am – 5pm)*; and **Totem**, whose beachwear is full of color and cheer *(Rua Visconde de Pirajá, 547, store F, tel. (21) 2540-0661; Mon – Fri, 10am – 8pm; Sat, 10am – 6pm)*.

Beauty Salons

Ipanema has some of the best hairdressers and beauty salons in Rio. **Jean-Yves**, run by Frenchman Jean-Yves Satre, offers exclusive hair treatments, such as *fotohair* – a laser-straightening technique – and shiatsu for the scalp. Book in advance to have your hair cut by the master himself *(Rua Redentor, 4, tel. (21) 2522-8650; Tue – Fri, 10am – 7:30pm; Sat, 10am – 6pm).*

At **Crystal Hair**, one Rio's top salons, clients receive relaxing massages while they get their hair done *(Rua Barão de Jaguaribe, 243, tel. (21) 2523-1542; Tue - Sat, 9am – 9pm).* **Crystal Care**, on the same street, also offers excellent services and has a pleasant, leafy veranda with deck chairs, where you can enjoy a sandwich or glass of prosecco while waiting *(Rua Barão de Jaguaribe, 289, tel. (21) 3813-0560; Mon – Sat, 9am – 9pm).*

Food

Cheap, Tasty Snacks

Ipanema contains a plethora of bars, taverns, and simple restaurants that offer no-fuss, tasty food in hearty portions. The traditional Brazilian finger foods on offer send shivers up the spines of the diet-conscious, but are irresistible to mere mortals – especially if accompanied by a cold glass of *chope* (draft beer). **Barril 1800** serves finger food, pizzas, and a variety of dishes that are ideal for satisfying one's hunger after an active day at the beach *(Avenida Vieira Souto, 110, tel. (21) 2523-0085; daily, 11am – 1am).* There is also the traditional **Belmonte**, with delicious pastries and Brazilian white rum, aka *cachaça (Rua Teixeira de Melo, 53-B, tel. (21) 2267-9909; daily, 10am until the last customer leaves)*, **Bar Devassa**, with its handmade *chope (Rua Prudente de Morais, 416, tel. (21) 2522-0627; Mon – Thu, 5pm – 2am; Fri, Sat, and Sun, noon – 3am)*, **Manoel & Juaquim**, which serves meat dishes and *bolinho de bacalhau* (cod deep-fried in batter) *(Rua Barão da Torre, 162, tel. (21) 2522-1863; Mon – Fri, 5pm – 1am; Sat, Sun, and holidays, noon until the last customer leaves)*, **Botequim Informal**, with a variety of cheeses and antipasti *(Rua Barão da Torre, 348, tel. (21) 2247-6711; Sun – Wed, noon – 2am; Thu, Fri, and Sat, noon – 3am)*, and **Conversa Fiada**, with sandwiches, finger foods, and snacks *(Rua Maria Quitéria, 46, tel. (21) 2247-8609; daily, noon – 4am).*

Cafés and Sweets

There are several places to recharge your energies as you wander through Ipanema. **The Bakers** serves pies, brownies, and a chocolate cake called *teia de aranha*, which means "the spider's web" *(Rua Visconde de Pirajá, 330, tel. (21) 3201-5050; Mon – Fri, 9am – 7pm, Sat; 9am – 2pm).* The **Armazém do**

Conversa Fiada conveys a relaxed atmosphere

The Casa da Feijoada serves traditional Brazilian feijoada at lunch and dinner

Café has a vast selection of top-quality coffees, as well as waffles and brownies *(Rua Maria Quitéria, 77-G, tel. (21) 2522-5039; Mon – Fri, 8:30am – 8pm; Sat, 9am – 6pm)*. **Alessandro & Frederico Café** serves a hearty breakfast and sandwiches on homemade bread *(Rua Garcia d'Ávila, 134, store D, tel. (21) 2521-0828; daily, 9am – 2pm)*.

RESTAURANTS

In Ipanema, there is a restaurant for every palate. Open for lunch and dinner, the **Casa da Feijoada** serves a traditional *feijoada*, with bowls of black beans and meat, duly accompanied by sliced orange, grated collard greens, and manioc flour *(Rua Prudente de Morais, 10-B, tel. (21) 2247-2776; daily, noon – midnight)*. The **Satyricon** is considered a temple of seafood in Rio *(Rua Barão da Torre, 192, tel. (21) 2521-0627; daily, noon until the last customer leaves)*. The steakhouse **Porcão** has a wide range of top-quality meats, brought to you endlessly, until you're sated, on spits right from the fire, in a *prix fixe* dining system that Brazilians call *rodízio* *(Rua Barão da Torre, 218, tel. (21) 3202-9155; Mon – Thu, 11:30am – 12:30am; Fri and Sat, 11:30am – 1am; Sun, 11:30am – midnight)*. On the same street, **Expand Wine Bar** – an importer of some 2,000 labels – has a restaurant at the back of the premises that serves meat dishes and seafood *(Rua Barão da Torre, 358, tel. (21) 2123-7900; Mon – Sat, noon – midnight)*. Those seeking pizza should try the suggestions at the always-lively **Capricciosa**, which has a menu of thirty-some different pizzas *(Rua Vinicius de Moraes, 134, tel. (21) 2523-3394; Sun – Thu, 6pm – 1am; Fri and Sat, 6pm – 2am)*. **Forneria** offers sandwiches and top-quality pastas with a menu designed by chef Salvatore Loi *(Rua Aníbal de Mendonça, 112, tel. (21) 2540-8045; Mon – Sat, noon – 3am; Sun, noon – 2am)*. Salads, grilled meats and fish, and light dishes can be found at the delightful **Gula Gula** *(Rua Aníbal de Mendonça, 132, tel. (21) 2259-3084; Sun – Thu, noon – midnight; Fri and Sat, noon – 1am)*. The Ipanema branch of the São Paulo restaurant **Gero** is a big hit among locals seeking quality Italian food *(Rua Aníbal de Mendonça, 157, tel. (21) 2239-8158; Mon – Fri, noon – 4pm and 7pm – 1am; Sat, noon – 2am; Sun, noon – midnight)*. The **Margutta** is a favorite among lovers of seafood and

Italian cooking. Regulars lavish praise upon the menu of starters *(Avenida Henrique Dumont, 62, tel. (21) 2259-3718; Mon – Fri, 6pm – 1am; Sat and holidays, noon – 1am; Sun, noon – midnight)*.

JUICE AND ICE CREAM PARLORS

Juice parlors lie scattered throughout Rio de Janeiro. One of the best-known is in Ipanema: **Polis Sucos** has been creating innumerable fruit combinations for over thirty years *(Rua Maria Quitéria, 70-A, tel. (21) 2247-2518; daily, 7am – 12:30am)*. The Ipanema branch of **Mil Frutas**, famous for its juices and homemade ice creams, also serves coffee, soups, and salads *(Rua Garcia d'Ávila, 134, store A, tel. (21) 2521-1384; Mon – Thu, 10:30am – midnight; Fri and Sat, 9:30am – 1:30am; Sun, 9:30am – 12:30am)*. Other good ice cream parlors are **Sorvetes Chaika** *(Rua Visconde de Pirajá, 321-A, tel. (21) 2267-3838; daily, 9am – 1am)* and **Sorvete Itália** *(Avenida Henrique Dumont, 71, store C, tel. (21) 2239-1396; Mon – Thu, 9am – 9pm; Fri – Sun and holidays, 9am – 10pm)*.

CARNIVAL GROUPS

The traditional street carnival groups, **Simpatia é Quase Amor**, **Banda de Ipanema**, and **Monobloco** draw crowds of samba dancers and curious onlookers. At night the sessions take place parallel to the official samba-school parade. **Simpatia é Quase Amor** *(photo)* meets on Rua Teixeira de Melo, in front of Praça General Osório, on carnival Saturday evening and Sunday during the day. The famous **Banda de Ipanema**, founded by journalist Albino Pinheiro in the 1960s, starts partying a little earlier than the rest: Its parades, to the sound of traditional *marchinhas* and sambas, take place on the two Saturdays prior to carnival and the Saturday and Tuesday after carnival. It leaves Ipanema and parades into the neighborhood of Leblon, drawing a lively gay crowd along the way. **Monobloco**, born out of a percussion workshop with the band Pedro Luís e a Parede, plays samba, *coco*, funk, and *charm*, as well as classics by composers Tim Maia and Luiz Gonzaga. Thousands flock to see the parade, which departs from Posto 12, in neighboring Leblon, on the Sunday after carnival.

Architectural Itinerary

One of Rio's most charming neighborhoods, Ipanema and its long, flat, leafy streets and avenues have always been home to elegant, avant-garde architecture. In addition to providing *cariocas* with meeting places in the form of its many bars, restaurants, and stores, the district and its neighbors have luxurious and functional buildings in a variety of styles, although modernist and art deco architecture predominate.

Modern Architecture Circuit

Edifício Picasso, **Edifício Cézanne**, and **Edifício Matisse** are among the modernist buildings scattered throughout Ipanema. Designed by Waldemar Ferreira and Luiz Mário de Sá Freire in 1949, the triumvirate provides good examples of middle class buildings that reproduce, on a small scale, the characteristics of luxury buildings of that era *(Avenida Epitácio Pessoa, 2214)*. **Edifício Alberto de Campos** (1978), has wooden sun baffles on the balconies, which control the light and create intriguing visual effects on the façade *(Rua Alberto de Campos, 250)*. Not far from there, **Edifício Barão de Gravatá**, designed by Sérgio Bernardes in 1952, is noteworthy for the contrast between the daring glass façade and its traditional sides and rear *(Rua Barão da Torre, 42)*. **Edifício Jardim Leonor**, designed by Álvaro Vital Brazil in 1954, presents a fascinating contrast between the imposing volume of the building and the single, almost-delicate-looking central pillar on which it rests *(Rua Prudente de Morais, 65)*. On Avenida Vieira Souto you can see **Edifício JK**, designed by **Oscar Niemeyer** in 1960. With only four floors (three of which hold just one occupant), the building owes its elegance to the frugal use of different architectural elements *(#206)*. Nearby, the 1958 **Edifício Vieira Souto** *(#350)*, another of Álvaro Vital Brazil's projects, shows off aluminum window frames. Facing onto Rua Prudente de Morais, **Edifício Atlântica Boavista** (1978), by Luiz Paulo Conde and Mauro Neves, has a modernist façade and brick sun baffles *(#630)*. Designed by Paulo Casé in 1967, **Edifício Estrela de Ipanema** is an example of brutalist architecture, with exposed lighting structures *(#765)*.

Art Deco Circuit

Avenida Epitácio Pessoa has three examples of art deco style. A small house that Freire & Sodré built in 1937 for **Horácio Mendes de Oliveira Castro Filho** is still enchanting for its circular terrace and the playful interaction of straight and curved lines *(#2500)*. Near Lagoa Rodrigo de Freitas is **Bar Lagoa** (1934), noteworthy for its round chandeliers made of inlaid-wood and glass, and the marble walls and floors *(#1674)*; **Edifício Santa Cruz**, built in the same year, has preserved its pure lines, horizontal furrows above the windows, and a large central section that's reminiscent of a ship's bridge – such elements were common in coastal buildings of the time *(#186)*. In Ipanema, on Rua Rainha Elizabete, the U-shape of **Edifício Itayá** (1937) ensures ample light and ventilation *(#729)*. On Praça Nossa Senhora da Paz, the **Monumento a Pinheiro Machado** (1931), also manifests art deco with its friezes in bas-relief.

LEBLON

An affluent residential neighborhood with sophisticated shops, good food, and a busy cultural scene and nightlife, charming Leblon owes its name to the Frenchman Charles Le Blond, the owner of a fishery with a property here in 1836. Leblon rubs shoulders with Ipanema on one side, Gávea, on the other, and backs onto the Lagoa and Jardim Botânico. Baixo Leblon (Lower Leblon) is a kind of sub-neighborhood, revolving around the busy Rua Dias Ferreira. Alto Leblon (Upper Leblon) has classy residences on streets often closed off with barriers. Quartered by Avenida Ataúlfo de Paiva (running towards Ipanema) and Avenida Bartolomeu Mitre (running from the beach towards Jardim Botânico), Leblon's other main thoroughfares are Avenida Delfim Moreira (along the beachfront) and Avenida Visconde de Albuquerque.

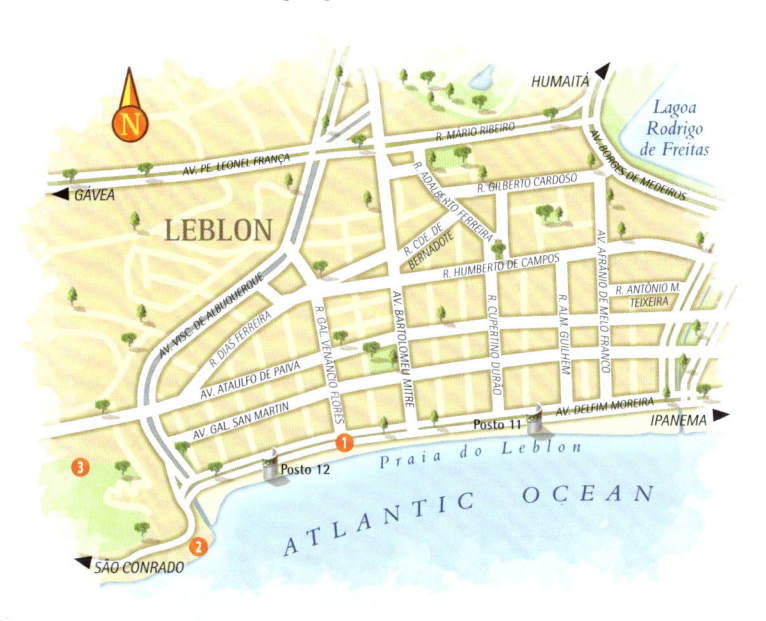

1. Baixo Bebê
2. Mirante do Leblon
3. Parque do Penhasco Dois Irmãos

Praia

Mile-long Leblon Beach starts at the stretch of sand where the Jardim de Alá Canal flows into the sea, between Posto 10 and Posto 11, and ends after Posto 12, the last life-guard post in Rio's South Zone. The vitality of Leblon's beachfront is reflected in the promenade, cycle path, volleyball school, and children's play area, called Baixo Bebê *(see page 140)*, which is in front of Rua General Venâncio Flores. A bike ride – there are several bike rental outfits at the end of the beach – through the area is especially pleasant. The cycle path is well signposted, although do watch out for pedestrians wandering across it (choose a bike with a bell or horn). Drink ice-cold coconut water at one of the kiosks

View of the sea and the shore from Mirante do Leblon

scattered along the promenade and if you want to swim head for the Ipanema end of the beach, as far as possible from Rua Visconde de Albuquerque, where the water quality is worse. You can always rent chairs and sun-umbrellas for a few *reais*. Posto 10, between Ipanema and Leblon beaches, is one of the best. It attracts a crowd that used to hang around Posto 9, who migrated down the beach for a bit more peace and quiet.

❶ Baixo Bebê
What used to be an ordinary kiosk has become one of the most fun places in the region for little ones. Standing between Posto 11 and Posto 12 (closer to 12), Baixo Bebê ("bebê" means baby in Portuguese) has a padded diaper-changing area, and the owners, Nilza and Wanilma, supply diapers and baby wipes for free. There are walkers and strollers on the sidewalk, and cubby houses, castles, and slides in the sand. The kiosk employees daily sift, wash, sweep, and level the strip of sand by the kiosk. They also clean and reassemble the equipment every day.
Praia do Leblon, in front of Rua General Venâncio Flores.

❷ Mirante do Leblon
At the end of Praia do Leblon, right in front of Morro Dois Irmãos, the Leblon Lookout offers a breathtaking view of the sea and rocky shore, especially when the waves are rough. To get there from Leblon, ascend Avenida Niemeyer toward Vidigal and São Conrado. It is an ideal stop for those who want to take a rest during an early-morning walk or watch the sunset as they drink coconut water at one of the charming kiosks. At night it is popular among couples, who come here for romantic encounters by moonlight. A reassuring police presence is relatively constant, but be alert as you approach on Avenida Niemeyer, which has some poorly lit stretches.

❸ Parque do Penhasco Dois Irmãos
This municipal park, still relatively unexplored by locals and tourists, is an

alternative place to watch the sunset or enjoy the cityscape. Its nearly 100 acres have dirt walking trails, soccer fields, a playground, a small arena theatre, and four lookouts: **Mirante do Sétimo Céu** affords visitors a view of the beaches, from Leblon to Arpoador. If you follow a narrow cobbled path, you will come across, in order: **Mirante do Anfiteatro**, from which you can see Vidigal Hill and the Cagarras Islands; **Mirante da Sede**, with a view of Leblon and Ipanema beaches, and the city of Niterói in the background (on clear days); and finally, **Mirante da Lagoa**, which looks out over Rodrigo de Freitas Lagoon, Gávea Horseracing Track, the Jockey Club, Botafogo Bay, and the neighborhoods of Jardim Botânico, Leblon, Ipanema, and Arpoador. On weekdays the park is visited by hippies, who meditate to the sound of the waves. On Saturdays and Sundays it tends to attract couples and families with children.
Rua Aperana, Leblon, tel. (21) 2503-2779. Daily, 8am – 6pm.

Leblon for All Tastes

Leblon has all manner of nooks and crannies that can be explored at leisure. Strolling through its delightful streets makes a pleasant outing at any time of day, whether to enjoy the local cultural attractions (including cinemas, theaters, and bookstores), or to the various shops and excellent eateries (some of Rio's most famous are located in this neighborhood). The main attractions are on Avenida Ataúlfo de Paiva and Rua Dias Ferreira. The former, which runs through the center of the neighborhood, is quite busy and offers bars, juice parlors, confectioners, restaurants, luncheonettes, bookstores, cinemas, shopping centers, fashion boutiques, decoration stores, and hairdressing salons. On the latter, restaurants, shops, bookstores, taverns, and coffee shops stand shoulder to shoulder.

Shopping and Services

Shopping Centers

Rio Design Leblon, originally specialized in furniture and design, but has recently invested in the triad of fashion, beauty, and food, and has become one of the most popular places in the area. It has seventy stores and six restaurants, including **Gula Gula**, **Joe & Leo's**, and **Cafeína**, which serves a tasty breakfast, as well as a cinema that seats 95 and **Armazém Digital Leblon**, a combination bookstore, bistro, cinema, and music venue *(see page 146)*. Among the fashion and accessory outlets are **Cris Menezes**, **Mara Mac**, **Verve**, **Osklen**, and **Rupee Rupee** *(Avenida Ataúlfo de Paiva, 270, tel. (21) 2430-3024; daily, 10am – 10pm)*.

Shopping Leblon, which opened at the end of 2006, contains 190 stores selling both Brazilian and foreign labels. Highlights are the large branch of **Livraria Travessa** bookstore and the fashion labels **Fórum Tufi Duek**, **Armani Exchange**, **Miele by Carlos Miele**, **Ferragamo**, and **Calvin Klein**. The food court has a lovely view of Rodrigo de Freitas Lagoon. Construction on a cultural center including a theater, cinema, library, art workshops, and auditoriums should be finished by mid 2007. The shopping center offers a shuttle service to and from the major hotels in Copacabana, Ipanema, and Leblon.
Avenida Afrânio de Melo Franco, 290, Leblon, tel. (21) 2131-3100. Mon – Sat, 10am – 10pm; Sun and holidays, 3pm – 7pm.

Home Goods and Decoration

The irreverent **Design Caffè** sells picture frames, cushions, lamps, handbags, accessories, and even customized t-shirts *(Avenida Ataúlfo de Paiva, 270, store 303, tel. (21) 2512-8480; Mon – Sat, 10am – 10pm; Sun, 3pm – 9pm)*. **Daqui** brings together fine art, folk art, and design concepts in personal accessories and items by various designers *(Avenida Ataúlfo de Paiva, 1174-F, tel. (21) 2529-8576; Mon – Fri, 10am – 8pm; Sat, 10am – 4pm)*. **Melon** provides personalized items for the bedroom, bathroom and dining table – napkins, linens, bathrobes, toiletry bags, pajamas, and pillows *(Rua Rainha Guilhermina, 249, mezzanine store 202, tel. (21) 2294-0222; Mon – Fri, 10am – 6pm)*. A traditional manufacturer of replicas of old European furniture, **Oficina Inglesa** produces items in rustic, aged, and unfinished wood, among other

Shopping Centers and Bookstores
1. Shopping Leblon
2. Rio Design Leblon
3. Livraria do Conde
4. Livraria Argumento
5. Beco das Virtudes
6. Banca Piauí
7. Letras & Expressões

Leisure
1. Teatro Café Pequeno
2. Cine Leblon
3. Galeria Espaço Cultural Leblon
4. Teatro Leblon
5. Arte em Dobro

LEBLON

Nightlife
1. Armazém Digital Leblon
2. Bar do Tom
3. Bardot
4. Guapo Louco
5. Melt

Fashion and Decoration
1. Oficina Inglesa
2. Doce Beauté
3. Cavendish
4. Cris Menezes
5. Design Caffé
6. Cantão
7. Ophicina do Cabelo
8. Carla Bokel
9. Maria com Graça
10. Daqui
11. Clutch
12. Roberta Wright
13. Ateliê Ibô
14. Melon
15. Lucci
16. Eliane Carvalho

materials *(Avenida Ataúlfo de Paiva, 80-B, tel. (21) 2512-9911; Mon – Fri, 10am – 7pm; Sat, 10am – 2pm)*.

BOOKSTORES

One of Leblon's main attractions is its bookstores, which offer far more than just books and magazines. In these relaxing spots, you can have a coffee, eat a meal, and have a good chat with friends. Open 24 hours a day, **Letras & Expressões** sells books, magazines, international newspapers, and CDs, and also boasts a tobacconist shop, a cyber café, and Café Antônio Torres, a excellent place for a maté tea, coffee, or late-night snack. It also hosts literary events and gatherings *(Avenida Ataúlfo de Paiva, 1292, store C, tel. (21) 2511-5085)*. Inside Galeria Espaço Cultural Leblon *(see page 145)*, **Livraria da Conde** sells books, CDs and DVDs, and has a lounge, where events are held, as well as a pleasant coffee shop *(Rua Conde de Bernadote, 26, store 125, tel. (21) 2274-0359)*. One of the best known bookstores, **Livraria Argumento** stands at the confluence of the neighborhood's most popular streets. With an avant-garde tradition, during the last military regime it numbered among the few places that sold titles by prohibited authors Brazilian and imported books on a range of subjects, as well as rare titles, sit well-organized on the shelves. It also sells CDs and has two coffee shops. **Severino** serves sandwiches and light meals, while Café Argumento offers cappuccinos and *beirute* sandwiches in Lebanese bread *(Rua Dias Ferreira, 417, tel. (21) 2239-*

Open 24/7, Livraria Letras & Expressões holds literary gatherings and events

5294; Mon – Fri, 9am – 12:30am; Sat and Sun, 10am – 12:30am). For those who love trawling for great works, a visit to the tiny **Beco das Virtudes** is indispensable: there you will find art books, intaglio prints, and limited-edition catalogues. There are also titles on Brazilian and contemporary art. Find it in an old arcade, at the end of a corridor that houses tattoo shops and even a bicycle workshop *(Avenida Ataúlfo de Paiva, 1174, store 3, tel. (21) 2249-9525; Mon – Fri, 10am – 1pm and 3pm –7pm; Sat, 10am – 3pm)*. The newsstand **Banca Piauí**, a fixture for more than forty years in Leblon, specializes in foreign magazines and always has the latest releases *(Avenida Ataúlfo de Paiva, in front of #1273, tel. (21) 2511-5822; daily, 5am – 1am)*.

Fashion
Handbags and Footwear
Plastic, resin, and cloth are just a few of the materials designer **Cris Menezes** uses to make handbags, cushions, and hats *(Avenida Ataúlfo de Paiva, 270, kiosk 4, tel. (21) 2259-6595; Mon – Sat 10am – 10pm; Sun, 3pm – 9pm)*. Specializing in handbags, with an exclusive range in leather, mois, and Italian silk, **Clutch** mostly deals with retailers, but also sells to individual buyers *(Rua Aristides Espínola, 121, apartment 202, tel. (21) 2274-4288; Mon – Fri, 10am – 6pm; Sat, 10am – 2pm)*. **Roberta Wright** produces sling-backs, pumps, and sandals on a small scale *(Rua Aristides Espínola, 121-202, tel. (21) 2512-3343; Mon – Fri, 10am – 7pm; Sat, 10am – 3pm)*.

Women's and Men's Fashions
Clothing stores abound. Aimed at the younger generation, **Cantão**, a Rio brand born in 1969, sells brightly colored and patterned t-shirts, Bermuda shorts, and sandals *(Avenida Ataúlfo de Paiva, 566, stores A and B, tel. (21) 2294-7211; Mon – Sat, 9am – 8pm)*. At **Maria com Graça** you will find clothes and accessories with embroidery, crochet, and *fuxico* patchwork, as well as retro styles *(Avenida Ataúlfo de Paiva, 1079, store 117, Vitrine do Leblon*

Galeria, tel. (21) 2540-5111; Mon – Fri 10am – 7pm; Sat, 10am – 1pm). The charming **Lucci** carries basic but high-quality items for women, as well as articles that use pure silk and muslin, embroidery and French lace *(Rua Dias Ferreira, 247, tel. (21) 2540-6970, 9976-2483; Mon – Fri, 10am – 8pm; Sat, 10am – 3pm).* The sisters Paula and Carla make light, comfortable items at **Cavendish**, all produced with creativity and good taste, rich in interesting cuts and details *(Avenida Ataúlfo de Paiva, 270, store 214, tel. (21) 2512-2137; Mon – Sat, 10am – 10pm; Sun, 3pm – 9pm).* A cross between tea house and boutique, **Eliane Carvalho** sells fashion accessories and costume jewelry *(Rua Dias Ferreira, 242, tel. (21) 2540-5438. Boutique: Tue – Fri, 10am – 8pm; Sat, 10am – 7pm; Sun, 11am – 5pm. Cafe: Tue – Fri, 1pm – 7:30pm; Sat, 10am – 7pm; Sun, 11am – 5pm).* **Ateliê Ibô** purveys the creations of Isabela Capeto, who is famous for her embroidery and patterns. Along with skirts and trousers, the store carries menswear, accessories, costume jewelry, shoes, and beachwear *(Rua Dias Ferreira, 45, store B, tel. (21) 2540-5232; Mon – Fri, 10am – 8pm; Sat, 10am – 6pm).* The creations of stylist **Carla Bokel** – skirts, blouses, and dresses in silk, organza, muslin, and chiffon – reflect both sophistication and simplicity, mostly in neutral colors *(Rua General Urquisa, 25, apartment 101, tel. (21) 2294-6392. Appointment required).*

Beauty Salons
Run for 25 years by beautician Docelina Gomes, aka Doce ("Sweet"), **Doce Beauté** is one of the most traditional and sophisticated beauty salons in Rio de Janeiro. In addition to cutting, dying, and styling hair, the professionals also offer a range of treatments for the face and body *(Avenida Ataúlfo de Paiva, 135, 3rd floor, stores 314 and 321, Galeria Cidade do Leblon, tel. (21) 2239-9799; Mon, 2pm – 8pm; Tue – Sat, 9am – 8pm).* **Ophicina do Cabelo** has a great team of professionals, including some of Rio's best hairdressers, such as Gilberto Moraes *(Avenida Delfim Moreira, 630, 4th floor, Hotel Marina Palace, tel. (21) 2274-7798; Tue – Sat, 9am – 8:30pm).*

Leisure

Art Gallery
Arte em Dobro holds temporary exhibitions of paintings, photographs, and sculptures. Young artists, such as Felipe Barbosa, share space with the gallery's collection of contemporary art by the likes of José Bento, Luiz Hermano, and Walton Hoffmann.
Rua Dias Ferreira, 417 and 205, Leblon, tel. (21) 2294-8284. Mon – Fri, 10am – 6pm.

Galeria Espaço Cultural Leblon
Inaugurated in 1977, Galeria Espaço Cultural Leblon houses high points of the neighborhood such as **Teatro Leblon** (Leblon Theatre) and **Livraria da Conde** bookshop. In addition to cultural attractions, typically Rio-style bars and restaurants inhabit the space, including **Botequim Informal** and **Academia da Cachaça**, both popular among local residents.
Rua Conde de Bernadote, 26, Leblon, tel. (21) 2259-5346. Daily, 7am – 3am.

Theater and Cinema
Two theatres play a role in Leblon's cultural life. The **Teatro Leblon** complex in the lively Galeria Espaço Cultural Leblon, whose two halls seat 414 and 472, respectively, hosts a

Mexican food and dance music at the cheery Guapo Loco

range of performances in different genres, above all light comedies *(Rua Conde de Bernadote, 26, tel. (21) 2274-3536; Tue – Sun, 3pm – 8pm)*. **Teatro Café Pequeno**'s single stage seats 120 with chairs, tables and a bar all in the same physical space. In addition to theatrical performances, shows and musical comedies are staged here *(Avenida Ataúlfo de Paiva, 269, tel. (21) 2294-4480; Tue – Sat, 3pm – 9pm; Sun, 3pm – 8pm)*. The traditional **Cine Leblon**, with two large movie halls and wide seats, is a draw for cinephiles. Unlike other multiplex cinemas around the city, its old architecture and decoration have been preserved, and it draws audiences interested both in the arts and culture and in Hollywood blockbusters *(Avenida Ataúlfo de Paiva, 391, tel. (21) 3221-9292)*.

Nightlife

Leblon provides options for all tastes at night. At **Bar do Tom**, the main musical genres are bossa nova, MPB (Brazilian popular music), and samba, with some jazz presentations *(Rua Adalberto Ferreira, 32, tel. (21) 2274-4022; no fixed hours)*. **Armazém Digital Leblon** has become a meeting place for the new bossa nova generation with a bookstore, bistro, cinema, and space for live jazz and MPB, among other musical genres *(Avenida Ataúlfo de Paiva, 270, store SS 104, Rio Design Leblon, tel. (21) 2274-5999; Mon – Sat, 10am – 10pm; Sun, 3pm – 9pm)*. To dance, flirt, or chat over a light snack, the place to go is **Bardot** *(Rua Dias Ferreira, 247-A, tel. (21) 2274-5590, 2274-5587; Wed and Thu, 8:30pm – 1am; Fri and Sat, 9pm – 4am)*. **Guapo Loco** can guarantee a night of Mexican color and fun with music and dancing *(Rua Rainha Guilhermina, 48, tel. (21) 2294-8148; Mon – Fri, 6pm – midnight; Sat, noon – midnight; Sun, noon – 7pm)*. If you are looking for a variety of rhythms, from hip hop to salsa to samba-rock, head for **Melt** *(Rua Rita Ludolf, 47, tel. (21) 2512-1662, 2249-9309; daily, 10pm until the last customer leaves; happy hour, 6pm – 9pm)*.

Food

Cobal

More than a market, Cobal is a meeting place for local residents with *al fresco* bars and restaurants, such as **Pizza Parque**, which serves *chope* (draft beer), pizza, and finger food. While this laid-back locale lacks infrastructure, it contains many interesting food stalls. At **Deli Gil**, there are delights such as Parma ham, pecans, and pickled artichoke hearts entice, while **Cantinela** sells an excellent range of pastas, as well as pies and quiches. *Rua Gilberto Cardoso, no #, Leblon, tel. (21) 2540-0604 (administration). Fruit and vegetable area: 8am – 6pm. Bars and restaurants: 9am – 4pm.*

Tasty Snacks

Leblon has many good bars for any time of the day or night. Those who appreciate a nice cold *chope* will love **Botequim Informal**, where the draft beer is poured from two taps, one just for foam, because Brazilians typically love a layer of froth on top *(Rua Humberto de Campos, 646, tel. (21) 2259-6967, 2274-8980; Mon – Thu, noon – 1:30am; Fri – Sun, noon – 2am).* The traditional **Belmonte**, offering finger foods and *cachaça*, has branches in the neighborhoods of Copacabana, Flamengo, Ipanema, and Lapa *(Rua Dias Ferreira, 521, tel. (21) 2294-2849; daily, 8am until the last customer leaves).* With a range of delicious snacks, **Jobi** is an excellent place for a late-night drink *(Avenida Ataúlfo de Paiva, 1166, tel. (21) 2274-0547, 2274-5055; daily, 9am – 5am).* **Conversa Fiada** has a pool table and hors d'oeuvre counter, and sells quick meals to accompany your *chope (Avenida Ataúlfo de Paiva, 900, tel. (21) 2512-9767; Mon – Fri, 5:30pm until the last customer leaves; Sat and Sun, noon until the last customer leaves).* **Bar Bracarense** is famous for its finger foods, such as the *bolinhos de camarão com catupiry* (deep-fried prawn and *catupiry* cheese balls) *(Rua José Linhares, 85-B, tel. (21) 2294-3549; Mon – Sat, 9am – midnight; Sun, 9:30am – 10pm).* The micro-brewed *chope* at **Bar Devassa**, which has a couple of branches around town, is

Jobi, a great place for a late night meal, offers an extensive and tasty menu

popular among locals *(Avenida General San Martin, 1241, tel. (21) 2540-6087; Mon – Fri, 5pm until the last customer leaves; Sat and Sun, 2pm until late).*

COFFEE AND SWEETS

Late afternoons in Leblon practically beg you to stop for a coffee and something sweet. **Ateliê Culinário** offers light meals, mouthwatering sweets, and savory snacks, as well as breakfast *(Rua Dias Ferreira, 45, store A, tel. (21) 2239-2825, 2529-6856; Mon – Thu, noon – 11pm; Fri, noon – 1am; Sat, 10am – 1am; Sun, 10am – 11pm).* A less sugary option is a Sachertorte (chocolate gateau with apricot jam filling) at the German **Kurt** *(Rua Geberal Urquisa, 117, store B, tel. (21) 2294-0599, 2512-4943; Mon – Fri, 8am – 7pm; Sat, 8am – 5pm).* **Esch Café**, a combination restaurant and tobacconist, serves finger foods, sandwiches, and hot meals. In addition to the nearly twenty types of special cigars, its cellar stocks some 200 wines *(Rua Dias Ferreira, 78-A, Leblon, tel. (21) 2512-5651; daily, noon – 2am).* **Armazém do Café** has a vast selection of high quality coffees *(Rua Rita Ludolf, 87-B, tel. (21) 2259-0170; Sun – Thu, 8am – midnight; Sat, 8am – 1am).* Try the truffles and chocolate bars with different flavors and fillings from **Cacau Noir** *(Rua Ataúlfo de Paiva, 270, 2nd floor, Rio Design Leblon, tel. (21) 2529-6977; Mon – Sat, 10am – 10pm; Sun, 3pm – 9pm).* **Envídia** offers forty different types of chocolate, hand-made with Belgian ingredients – one of the best is the bonbon with orange and pink peppercorns. The menu also has hot chocolate and different types of tea *(Rua Dias Ferreira, 106, store A, tel. (21) 2512-1313; Mon – Sun, 11:40am – 8pm; holidays, 11:40am – 8pm).* **Aquim** has delicious bonbons made with Belgian chocolate *(Avenida Ataúlfo de Paiva, 1321, store C, tel. (21) 2274-1001; Mon – Fri, 11am – 8pm; Sat, 10am – 7pm).* Hand-made sweets, such as the classic *brigadeiro* (a soft Brazilian sweet made of melted chocolate and condensed milk) and the *rocambole de chocolate* (chocolate-filled roly-poly) are some of the highlights at the charming **Colher de Pau** *(Rua Rita Ludolf, 90-A, tel. (21) 2274-8295; daily, 10am – 7pm).* Ice cream lovers can choose between branches of the famous American chain **Häagen-Dazs** *(Rua Rainha Guilhermina, 95, tel. (21) 2279-6082; Mon – Fri, noon – 11pm; Sat and Sun, noon – midnight),* the Brazilian **La Basque** *(Rua Rainha Guilhermina, 90, store B, tel. (21) 2294-4194; Mon – Thu and Sun, 9am – midnight; Fri and Sat, 9am – 1am),* and the Italian **Sorvete Itália**, which has unusual flavors like mango and ginger *(Rua Almirante Guilherme, 317, store 320, tel. (21) 2540-9954; Mon – Thu, 10am – 9pm; Fri, Sat, and Sun, 11am – 10pm).*

Cake at Colher de Pau

RESTAURANTS

One of the foremost culinary centers in Rio, Leblon has something for everyone, from fast-food lovers to those with more refined palates. Good options include **Joe & Leo's**, which is decorated like an American burger joint and offers fifteen creative variations on the hamburger, including a vegetarian version *(Avenida Ataúlfo de Paiva, 270, tel. (21) 3204-9347).* The popular **Küpper** specializes in hand-made hotdogs *(Rua Cupertino Durão, 79, store B, tel. (21) 2512-6640; Mon, 6pm – midnight; Tue – Fri, 10:30am – midnight; Sat and Sun, noon – 2pm).* At **Álvaro's**, the

A traditional pit stop for Rio's night owls, Álvaro's serves hearty portions of finger food

big hit is the crunchy mini *pastéis* (deep-fried pastries with a variety of fillings), which comes in a hearty serving *(Avenida Ataúlfo de Paiva, 500, tel. (21) 2294-2148; daily, 11am – 2am)*. The informal **Degrau** is the place to go after the beach if you are hungry *(Avenida Ataúlfo de Paiva, 517-B, tel. (21) 2259-3648, 2259-2842; daily, 11am – 2am)*. The specialties at **Pavelka**, originally from the city of Petrópolis, are its sandwiches and the famous meat or chicken croquettes served with cold beer *(Rua João Lira, 97, store B, tel. (21) 2294-1745; Sun – Thu, 9am – 10pm; Fri and Sat, 9am – 11pm)*. **Plataforma** offers tender barbequed meats *(Rua Adalberto Ferreira, 32, tel. (21) 2274-4022; Mon – Thu, noon – midnight; Fri and Sat, noon – 1am; Sun, noon – 1am)*. If you crave regional food, **Academia da Cachaça** has the best Brazilian recipes and a bar stocked with seventy liquors *(Rua Conde Bernadote, 26, store G, tel. (21) 2239-1542; Sun – Thu, noon – 1am; Fri and Sat, noon – 3am)*. **Adega do Pimenta**, headquartered in Santa Teresa, has top quality German cuisine, with delicacies such as pork knuckle (eisbein) with sauerkraut *(Rua Conde Bernadote, 26, store D, tel. (21) 2229-9673; Mon – Fri, 5pm – 10pm; Sat, noon – 8pm; Sun and holidays, noon – 6pm)*. The bakery and delicatessen **Talho Capixaba** serves a popular breakfast, with more than thirty kinds of bread, twenty pastas, and a variety of cheeses, cold cuts, and antipasti *(Avenida Ataúlfo de Paiva, 1022, stores A and B, tel. (21) 2512-8760; Mon – Sat, 7am – 9pm; Sun, 8am – 9pm)*. **Sushi Leblon** is one of the oldest Japanese restaurants in town and also one of the busiest *(Rua Dias Ferreira, 256, tel. (21) 2512-7830; Mon – Fri, noon – 4pm and 7pm – 1:30am; Sat, noon – 1:30am; Sun, 1pm – midnight)*. **Zuka**, under the same ownership as Sushi Leblon, serves creative, contemporary dishes *(Rua Dias Ferreira, 233, tel. (21) 3205-7154; Mon, 7pm – 1am; Tue – Fri, noon – 4pm and 7pm – 1am; Sat, 1pm – 1am; Sun, 1pm – midnight)*. The calorie-conscious can choose from the colorful salads at the popular **Celeiro** *(Rua Dias Ferreira, 199, stores A, B and C, tel. (21) 2274-7843; Mon – Sat, 11:30am – 5pm)*. The Rio branch of **Carlota** serves the creations of São Paulo chef Carla Pernambuco *(Rua*

LEBLON

The sophisticated Garcia & Rodrigues

Dias Ferreira, 64, tel. (21) 2540-6821; Tue – Thu, 7pm – midnight; Fri – Sat, 1pm – 5pm and 7:30pm – 12:30am; Sun, 1:30pm – 10:30pm). A Rio landmark is the traditional **Pizzaria Guanabara**, which serves pizzas in four different sizes, baked in an electric oven *(Avenida Ataúlfo de Paiva, 1228, tel. (21) 2294-0797; daily, 24/7).* At the sophisticated **Garcia & Rodrigues**, a gourmet complex with a confectioner's, delicatessen, wine cellar, bakery, and restaurant, chef Christophe Lidy adapts his French cooking to the Brazilian palate *(Avenida Ataúlfo de Paiva, 1251, stores A and B, tel. (21) 3206-4120; daily, 8am – 12:30am).* Lidy's **La Cigale** serves a variety of dishes at lunch, and takes on French airs at night with à la carte creations by the chef-owner himself *(Rua Aristides Espínola, 88, stores A and C, tel. (21) 2279-4473; Mon – Sat, noon – 4pm and 8pm until the last customer leaves).* **Gula Gula** offers salads and grilled meats, prepared in accordance with a light, health-oriented philosophy *(Rua Rita Ludolf, 87, store A tel., (21) 2294-0650; Sun – Thu, noon – midnight; Fri and Sat, noon – 1am).* The impeccable **Antiquarius** prepares Portuguese delicacies, including sublime cod dishes *(Rua Aristides Espínola, 19, tel. (21) 2294-1049, 2294-1496; daily, noon – 2am).*

JUICES

Juice parlors form a peculiar but popular Leblon institution. One of the most famous, the **Balada Sumos**, furnishes dozens of flavors and unusual mixtures, as well as tasty sandwiches *(Avenida Ataúlfo de Paiva, 620, store A, tel. (21) 2239-2699; Sun – Thu, 7am – 2am; Fri and Sat, 7am – 3am).* The Leblon branch of **Bibi Sucos** has a varied menu *(Rua Ataúlfo de Paiva, 591-A, tel. (21) 2259-4298; Sun – Thu, 8am – 2am; Fri and Sat, 8am – 3am).* At **Juice Co.**, the drinks have no added sugar or water and are made only with fresh fruits and vegetables *(Avenida General San Martin, 889, tel. (21) 2294-0048; Mon – Wed, 6pm – midnight; Thu – Sat, noon – 1am; Sun, noon – midnight).* The busy **BB Lanches** offers fifty kinds of fruits in juices and shakes *(Rua Aristides Espínola, 64-A, tel. (21) 2294-1397; Mon – Thu, and Sun, 8:30am – 3am; Fri and Sat, 8:30am – 5am).*

Lagoa Rodrigo de Freitas

The neighborhood that sprang up around Rodrigo de Freitas Lake, in Rio's South Zone, features residential patches and a laid-back atmosphere. The area is popular with joggers and cyclists, as well as those attracted by the area's lively bars and restaurants. To get there from the North Zone, take Túnel Rebouças. From the West Zone, take Avenida das Américas, followed by Avenida Armando Lombardi, Elevado das Bandeiras, Avenida Professor Mendes de Morais, and Túnel Zuzu Angel which opens onto Avenida Borges de Medeiros, one of the neighborhood's main thoroughfares.

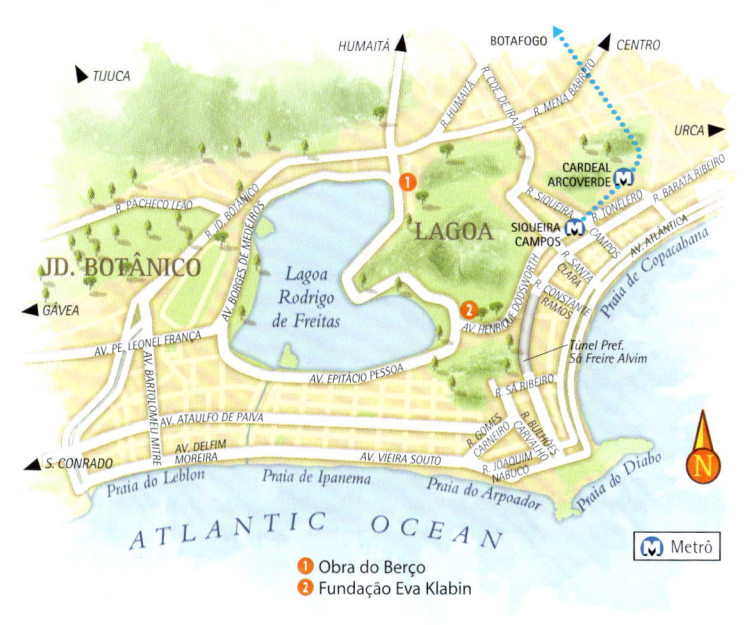

❶ Obra do Berço
❷ Fundação Eva Klabin

Outings and Sports in Lagoa

Lagoa is a salt-water lake, surrounded by mountains and green areas and ringed by the neighborhoods of Humaitá, Copacabana, Ipanema, Leblon, Gávea, and Jardim Botânico. A man-made canal, the Canal do Jardim de Alá, connects the lake to the sea. In addition to the 4.5 miles of biking, walking, and jogging paths that ring the lake, the banks feature countless options for sports and outdoor enthusiasts, including parks, paddleboats, kiosks, tennis courts, a roller-skating rink, a skateboarding half pipe, a heliport, and sports clubs. Visitors can rent bicycles and quadricycles between the parks Corte do Cantagalo and Curva do Calombo, near the paddleboats, and in Parque dos Patins (Skate Park) *(see page 152)*. The area at the edge of the lake hosts shows and children's activities. The kiosks offer Japanese, Italian, and German cuisine, and keep the area busy at night with live music performances. The best kiosks are in Parque dos Patins and Corte do Cantagalo. Some kiosks are also popular breakfast spots on weekends. Other stalls sell coconut water, sodas, and beer. Avoid poorly-lit areas at night; there is not a

LAGOA RODRIGO DE FREITAS

large police presence around the lake. In December, people come from all over the city to see the traditional Christmas tree, glittering with lights. Many find this a less crowded alternative to the New Year's Eve fireworks show held on Copacabana Beach.
Avenida Epitácio Pessoa (called Avenida Borges de Medeiros in Leblon and Jardim Botânico).

Parks
Nicknamed **Parque da Catacumba** (Catacomb Park), Parque Carlos Lacerda is near Corte do Cantagalo. Scattered among the park's beautiful fruit trees are some thirty sculptures by artists such as Roberto Moriconi, Bruno Giorgi, and Caribé. A short (but tiring) climbing trail winds up Morro dos Cabritos to Mirante do Sacopã (Sacopã Lookout), some 140 yards up *(Avenida Epitácio Pessoa, 3000).* The area surrounding the lake is made up of a number of smaller parks within the larger **Parque Tom Jobim**. **Parque dos Patins** (formerly known as Espaço Vítor Assis Brasil) features a roller-skating rink, an amphitheater, a soccer field, multiuse sports facilities, a playground, a busy cultural program, and activities for children *(Avenida Borges de Medeiros, no #).* **Parque das Taboas**, between the Clube de Regatas Flamengo and Clube Caiçaras, has soccer fields, tennis courts, and a mini-ramp for skateboards *(Avenida Borges de Medeiros, no #).* **Parque do Cantagalo**, in front of Corte do Cantagalo, has baseball, soccer, hockey facilities, as well as paddle boats *(Avenida Epitácio Pessoa, no #).*

Kiosks
Nighttime revelers are drawn primarily to the kiosks around the lake. Getting a table in the summer takes patience, but it's worth the wait. The pleasant **Palaphita Kitch** has an extensive menu of northeastern Brazilian dishes. The great drinks, pleasant background music, and al fresco tables make it an ideal place to chat with friends *(Parque das Taboas, kiosk 20, Avenida Borges de Medeiros, no #; tel. (21) 2227-0837; daily, 6pm until the last customer leaves).* **Café Del Lago** features Italian cuisine (mostly meat and pasta dishes, plus pizzas) and live Brazilian music *(Parque dos Patins, Avenida Borges de Medeiros, no #, kiosk 8; tel. (21) 2239-9005; Mon – Fri, noon until the last customer leaves; Sat, Sun, and holidays, 10am until the last customer leaves).* One of the busiest kiosks is **Arab**, which specializes in Syrian and Lebanese food. Arab is also a great spot for live music, with a range of different Brazilian musical traditions featured regularly *(Parque dos Patins, kiosks 7 and 9, Avenida Borges de Medeiros, no #; tel. (21) 2540-0747; daily, 9am – 2pm).* Popular with

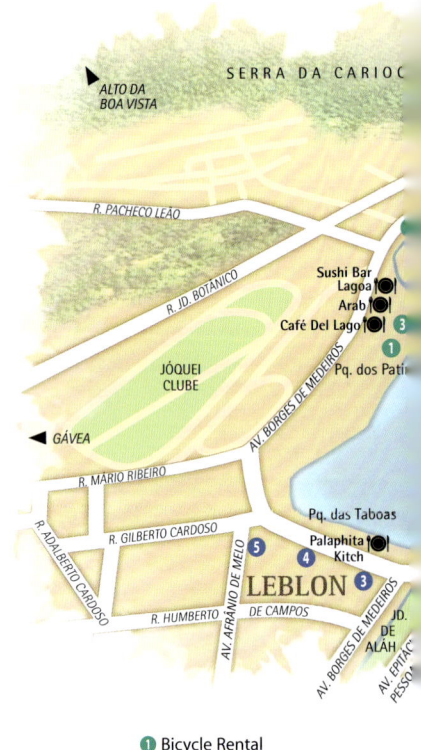

Sports Clubs
① Club de Regatas Vasco da Gama
② Clube dos Caiçaras
③ Clube Monte Líbano
④ Associação Atlética do Banco do Brasil (AABB)
⑤ Paissandu Atlético Clube

locals and visitors alike, **Sushi Bar Lagoa** complements its menu of drinks, Japanese food, and traditional appetizers such as *bolinho de bacalhau* (cod fritters) with a nightly lineup of live music *(Parque dos Patins, kiosk 6, Avenida Borges de Medeiros, no #; tel. (21) 3205-8836; Mon – Fri, 5pm until the last customer leaves; Sat, Sun, and holidays, 11am until the last customer leaves)*.

Sports Clubs

There are several athletic clubs in the area around Lagoa Rodrigo de Freitas, many of them excellent examples of Modernist architecture. Designed by Américo Rodrigues Campelo in 1948, **Clube de Regatas Vasco da Gama** stands on cylindrical piles. The building that houses the club's rowboats features a tiled panel designed by Roberto Burle Marx *(Rua General Tasso Fragoso, 65)*.

The **Clube dos Caiçaras** boathouse, designed by Ivan Oest de Carvalho in 1961, has a simple design, with exposed concrete, brick walls, and ceramic *brise soleils (Avenida Epitácio Pessoa, no #, near Praça Jardim de Alá)*. In **Clube Monte Líbano** (1946), architect João Khair made ample use of domes and slanting planes *(Avenida Borges de Medeiros, 701)*. Carlos Frederico Ferreira and Raif César Habib built **Associação Atlética do Banco do Brasil** (1955), an athletic facility with two buildings connected by sports fields *(Avenida Borges de Medeiros, 829)*.

Obra do Berço

Its name literally translating to "Cradle Work," this was noted Brazilian architect Oscar Niemeyer's first project. Built in 1937 to house a crèche and maternity ward, the design

Lagoa Rodrigo de Freitas

One of the display rooms at the Fundação Eva Klabin

showcases the play of volumes and light forms that is a hallmark of all Niemeyer's work.
Rua Cícero Góis Monteiro, 19, Lagoa.

Fundação Eva Klabin

The former personal residence of art collector Eva Klabin, this gallery opened to the public in 1995 to exhibit her personal collection. The house was one of the first in the area around Lagoa Rodrigo de Freitas, built in 1931. When Klabin bought the building in 1952, she immediately began renovations, most notably adding classical lines and details to the structure. The collection itself is displayed in ten different rooms. There are over 2600 catalogued pieces, including works by 18th-century English artists like Joshua Reynolds, Thomas Lawrence, and Thomas Gainsborough, as well as Italian renaissance masters such as Tintoretto, Botticelli, Donatello, and Della Robbia. Other highlights of the collection are the ancient Egyptian and Roman pieces (such as sculptures, bottles, and even a cat sarcophagus), 17th-century Dutch and Flemish works by Gerard ter Borch and Rembrandt, Tang dynasty terra cottas, bronzes from the first Chinese dynasties, and an important collection of decorative arts. The foundation also hosts excellent contemporary art exhibitions.
Avenida Epitácio Pessoa, 2480, Lagoa, tel. (21) 2523-3471. Wed – Sun, 2pm – 6pm. Guided visits: 2:30pm – 4pm.

Our Recommendation

Sushi Bar Lagoa would be worth a visit just for its art deco architectural flourishes and the view of Lagoa Rodrigo de Freitas from its veranda. But there is more: diners will find a bar serving excellent *chopes* (draft beer) and a wide selection of German and Brazilian dishes *(Avenida Epitácio Pessoa, 1674, Lagoa; tel. (21) 2523-1135; Mon, 6pm – 2am; Tue – Sun, noon – 2am).*

More information on restaurants starts on page 210.

Jardim Botânico

The middle-to upper-class neighborhood of Jardim Botânico surrounds its namesake park (literally meaning 'botanical garden'), created in 1808 and open to the public since 1819. Located in Rio's Zona Sul (South Zone), its neighbors include Lagoa Rodrigo de Freitas *(see page 151)* and Gávea *(see page 163)*. Flanked by mountains, these lush, green environs are pleasant to walk around. Most sites of interest are on Rua Jardim Botânico and Rua Pacheco Leão, including shops, artist studios, galleries, and restaurants. There are plenty of taxis and buses in the area, especially on Rua Jardim Botânico.

Attractions
1. Jardim Botânico
2. Horto Florestal
3. Parque Lage

Art Studios and Galleries
1. Ateliê Alice Felzenszwalb
2. O Sol
3. Marido e Mulher
4. FMourão
5. Daniella Martins
6. Nina Becker
7. H.A.P. Galeria

Architecture
1. Hospital da Lagoa
2. Igreja de São José
3. Edifício Antônio Ceppas
4. The buildings along Rua Joaquim Campos Porto

Books and Music
1. Livraria Ponte de Tábuas
2. Bis Espaço Musical

Clothes and Accessories
1. Dona Coisa
2. Parceria Carioca
3. Betty Borges

① Jardim Botânico

More than 8,000 species of plants make this park one of the ten most important botanical gardens in the world. Created by Dom João shortly after the Portuguese royal family moved to Brazil in 1808, Jardim Botânico was named a biosphere

Jardim Botânico

reserve by Unesco in 1992. It is almost impossible to remain unmoved by the imperial palms and enormous *pau-mulato* trees covering these lovely 338-acres. Don't miss the **orquidário** (orchid garden), with approximately 1,000 different species of orchids, many of them rare. The giant Amazon water lilies in **Lago Frei Leandro** (Frei Leandro Lake) lend it the nickname Lago da Vitória Régia. And just beyond Café Botânico lies the **cactário** (cactus garden), reopened to the public after ten years.

Other garden highlights include the old gunpowder factory **Museu Casa dos Pilões** and the pediment of the former **Escola de Belas-Artes** (School of Fine Arts), designed by Grandjean de Montigny and brought here after the school was demolished in the city center in 1938. *Eco* and *Narciso,* the two sculptures by master sculptor Mestre Valentim, are some of the artist's first to be cast in Brazil. The central fountain, designed by Herbert W. Hogg in cast iron, was brought to Brazil in 1895 and transferred from Lapa Square to Jardim Botânico in 1905. Recent additions to the park include the **Caminho da Mata Atlântica** (Atlantic Forest Trail) and the **Jardim dos Beija-Flores** (Hummingbird Garden) with more than fifty species of plants to attract the fluttering flock. A walk along the "trilha da floração" ("flowering trail"), offers a look at several flowering species. Be sure to book this and other guided visits in advance. The **Associação de Amigos** (Friends' Association) organizes a monthly bird-watching excursion during the weekend. If you're a fan, Jardim Botânico is one of your best bets for sightings. Call in advance to find out the group's meeting date *(tel. (21) 2239-9742).* A cultural center dedicated to Tom Jobim, a great admirer of the Jardim Botânico, houses the artist's digital and audiovisual collection. **Espaço Cultural Tom Jobim** comprises 10,000 items, from texts to photos,

The stunning botanical gardens

JARDIM BOTÂNICO

musical scores to films. A permanent exhibition displays photos, essay excerpts, biographies, statements, and CD covers. Every two weeks, the garden's Sábados Musicais (Musical Saturdays) attract visitors to an on-site theatre with a variety of jazz, traditional samba, and MPB (popular Brazilian music). While you're down this way, head toward the Tijuca Forest. You'll stumble upon a rustic, heritage-listed workers' villa, where contemporary artists such as Gabriela Machado, Adriana Varejão, and Beatriz Milhazes have their studios. (Unfortunately the artists' spaces are not open to the public.) Take the Estrada Dona Castorina, the road to Tijuca National Park *(see page 169)*, to visit **Impa (National Institute of Pure and Applied Mathematics)**, an important scientific research institution.
Rua Jardim Botânico, 1008, Jardim Botânico, tel. (21) 3874-1808. Daily, 8am – 5pm.

❷ HORTO FLORESTAL
Next door to the Jardim Botânico, this plant nursery sells more than 400 types of seedlings, including fruit trees, exotic species, and trees typical of the Atlantic forest and the Amazon. Inside Horto Florestal is **Solar da Imperatriz** (The Empress' Mansion), built in 1750. The current name came about when Dom Pedro I gave the mansion to his wife as a present in 1829. Its current occupant, the **Escola Nacional de Botânica Tropical** (National School of Tropical Botany), is one of the largest botanical institutions in the country, with an even more impressive roster of researcher graduates. The school boasts a computerized herbarium, with more than 300,000 records of Brazilian and world species of flora, with an emphasis on the Atlantic forest and the Amazon.
Rua Pacheco Leão, 2040, Jardim Botânico, tel. (21) 3875-6211. Mon – Fri, 9am – 11am and 2pm – 4pm.

❸ PARQUE LAGE
Amidst Lage Park's lush greenery sits a large 20th-century mansion built by Italian architect Mario Vrodet for ship chandler Henrique Lage, husband of lyrical singer Gabriela Bezanzoni Lage. Surrounded by 43 acres of gardens, the mansion's interior features beautiful marble-faced walls, floors, and bathrooms. Look for the rare art deco bathtub in one of the women's bathrooms. It was used on the set of the 1969 film *Macunaíma*. When you arrive at the inner courtyard, cast your eyes toward the sky for a glimpse of the unforgettable Christ statue. The mansion also houses the **Escola de Artes Visuais** (Visual Arts School), now three decades old. After your tour, grab a snack after **Café du Lage**, which serves a popular breakfast on weekends with live instrumental music. In 2000, the **Cavalariças** exhibition space was opened in the

OUR RECOMMENDATION

🍴 Minutes from Lagoa Rodrigo de Freitas, the highly praised **Escola do Pão** serves one of Rio's best breakfasts. Juice, tea, and hot chocolate complement a comforting array of breads and cakes. By night, the restaurant morphs into a cheerful bistro. Impeccable service contributes to its excellent reputation. *(Rua General Garzon, 10, Jardim Botânico; tel. (21) 2294-0027, 3205-7275; Breakfast: Sat, Sun, and holidays, 9am – 1pm; bistro: Tue – Sat, 4pm – midnight.)*

For more information on restaurants, see page 210.

Parque Lage attracts visitors with its gardens, a beautiful mansion, and a space for art exhibitions

old stable. The gallery hosts several contemporary artists throughout the year. Make sure you go for a stroll through the exuberant gardens while you're there.
Rua Jardim Botânico, 414, Jardim Botânico, tel. (21) 2538-1879, 2538-1091, 2226-8125. Escola de Artes Visuais: daily, 8am – 5pm; Café du Lage: Mon – Thu, 9am – 10:30pm; Fri – Sun, 9am – 5pm; Cavalariças: Tue – Thu, 10am – 9pm; Fri – Sun, 10am – 5pm.

Jardim Botânico for All Tastes

Jardim Botânico has a wealth of interesting shops, including bookstores, fashion boutiques, arts-and-crafts stores, charming art studios – even a place to listen to good MPB (Brazilian pop). Once you've worked up an appetite, head for one of the area's many distinct eateries. Dining options abound at small bistros, taverns, cafes, sophisticated and casual hotspots, and ice cream parlors. The following is a small taste of what you'll find.

Artists' Studios
Tucked away among resident homes, the studios of Jardim Botânico's artists produce and sell exclusive pieces and original jewelry. Some only receive visitors by appointment. With a bit of patience, you're sure to find some great bargains. Ceramic accessories and home décor crowd **Ateliê Alice Felzenszwalb**, including vases, lamps, plates, and mugs produced by Alice Felzenszwalb herself. The artist also teaches courses in her craft *(Rua Lopes Quintas, 732, Jardim Botânico; tel. (21) 2512-5034; Mon and Tue, 9am – 10pm; Wed – Fri, 9am – 6pm; Sat, 9am – noon)*. For more than 40 years, the **O Sol (Obra Social Leste)** organization has compiled a nationwide portfolio of work by folk native artists and artisans and displayed the results in an

ongoing, permanent fair. The exhibit distinguishes peculiarities of each region of Brazil: Vale do Jequitinhonha, Resende Costa, São João del-Rei, Ouro Preto, and Tracunhaém, among others. You can also purchase embroidery, costume jewelry, baskets, paintings, pottery, and other items are organized by state of origin *(Rua Corcovado, 213, Jardim Botânico; tel. (21) 2294-5099, 2294-6198; Mon – Fri, 9am – 6pm; Sat, 9am – 1pm)*. Husband and wife Jany Mosso and Carlos César Pinto design clothes for their respective genders at **Marido e Mulher**, Jany creates women's wear (some items offered in plus sizes), while Carlos produces modern menswear *(Rua Lopes Quintas, 201, Jardim Botânico; tel. (21) 2511-2929, 9899-3177; Mon – Fri, 1pm – 7pm; Sat, 10am – 2pm)*. **FMourão** stocks a great selection of women's clothing and accessories. Browsing the racks, you'll find embroidered pieces by designer Joana Coutinho, sold under the label Filhas da Mãe. Ana Borschiver accessories come in glass, resin, coconut, and bamboo. Mosaics by Fátima Mourão, intaglio prints by Claudio Roberto Castilho, objects and sculptures by Verônica Rizzo, and paintings by Lúcia Pinto complete the shop's eccentric inventory *(Rua Saturnino de Brito, 67, Jardim Botânico; tel. (21) 3206-0437; Mon – Fri, 10 am – 5pm)*. At **Daniella Martins**, the exclusivity of the pieces justifies the prices of these handmade women's clothes by the namesake designer, who uses knits, velvet, satin, and silk to create skirts, blouses, dresses, handbags, and costume jewelry *(Rua Jardim Botânico, 656, Jardim Botânico, mezzanine store 602; tel. (21) 2294-8804; Mon – Fri, 9am – 5:30pm)*.

Artists' Villa and Arts Circuit

At the end of Rua Engenheiro Pena Chaves (near Rua Lopes Quintas) sits a quaint villa of colorful dwellings, home to about 10 artist studios. Once the site of a major industrial textile factory, the area now supports lush greenery and the bargain-hunting curiosity of tourist and local alike. Each artist hawks his or her specialty: **Claudia Melli**, paintings and drawings; **Lincoln José**, small artisan crafts and trinkets; **Bia Amaral**, paintings and intaglio prints; **Sueli Fefer,** paintings and antiques; **Thereza and Paula Lino**, costume jewelry; and **Renata and Lúcio Tapajós**, mosaic, marquetry, and silver jewelry. Come on a Thursday, between 2pm and 6pm, because studios keep irregular hours during the rest of the week *(Rua Engenheiro Pena Chaves, 6, Jardim Botânico)*. Sometime between June and August, more than 50 village artists open their studios to passersby for the annual three-day **Circuito das Artes do Jardim Botânico** (Jardim Botânico Arts Circuit). Begun in 1997, the event also features lessons in pottery, painting, photography – even cooking and music. Visitors can catch kombi shuttles departing from Parque dos Patins. For information on the circuit contact Cattia Capistrano *(tel. (21) 3874-5889)* or Gabriella Civitate *(tel. (21) 2511-1191)*.

JARDIM BOTÂNICO

A Tour of Modern Architecture

The modernists left an impressive mark on Jardim Botânico. Resting between Lagoa Rodrigo de Freitas and Rua Jardim Botânico, **Hospital da Lagoa** boasts Rio de Janeiro's first V-shaped columns, a structural technique allowing for better space management. Designed by Oscar Niemeyer and Hélio Uchoa and completed in 1952, the site's lower block, facing the lake, has a curved facade and glass walls *(Rua Jardim Botânico, 501)*. Near the hospital is **Igreja de São José** *(right photo)*, a montage of glass mosaic tiles, aluminum, and dark windows built between 1961 and 1964 with design by Edgard Fonceca *(Avenida Borges de Medeiros, 2735)*. The ramp to **Edificio Antônio Ceppas** goes to the ground floor, replete with curves in the gardens and wall facings. Designed by Jorge Machado Moreira in 1946, the complex displays apartments of all shapes and sizes like works of art, accented with tiles by Burle Marx *(Rua Benjamin Batista, 180)*. Two addresses on **Rua Joaquim Campos Porto** also exhibit dazzling modernist lines. Numbers 441 and 457, built in 1966, were designed by the Pontual Arquitetos Associados to mimic the slope of the land. The barrel-vaulted roofs and exposed bricks you'll see were typical of residential architecture at the time.

Singer **Nina Becker**, a vocalist with the Orquestra Imperial, began her fashion career making costumes for shows. She now produces tailor-made pieces in tulle, taffeta, and other fabrics *(Rua Engenheiro Pena Chaves, 27, Jardim Botânico; tel. (21) 2249-1200; daily, prior bookings required)*.
Ana Petrik crafts her beautiful earrings, necklaces, and key rings from beads made of resin, wood, crystal, and other raw materials *(tel. (21) 8836-4050; daily, prior bookings required)*. Pen lids and hairclips are transformed into quirky but beautiful accessories, mobiles, decorations, and gifts in the hands of **Mana Bernardes**. Though the artist does not receive visitors in her studio, she will cordially make house calls upon request. Her necklaces have garnered international acclaim, and can be found in Paris and New York *(tel. (21) 2511-5289; daily, prior bookings required)*. **Dirceu Krepel** makes beautiful custom jewelry, table mobiles, and paintings on paper using a mixture of techniques. To reach Krepel at his studio in Jardim Botânico, visit www.dirceukrepel.com.

H.A.P. Galeria

Not far from the Jardim Botânico, Heloísa Amaral Peixoto's pleasant and charming H.A.P. Galeria rotates exhibits from the permanent house collection and solo installations by different contemporary Brazilian artists. The gallery is housed in a restored 20th-century, heritage-listed house. Cildo Meireles, Gabriela Machado, Lygia Pape, Antonio Manuel, Nelson Felix, and Carlos Zílio are among the artists whose work is on display. *Rua Abreu Fialho, 11, Jardim Botânico, tel. (21) 3874-2830, 3874-2726. Mon – Fri, 10am – 7pm; Sat, 2pm – 7pm.*

FOOD

BISTROS

The sidewalk tables at **Caroline Café** invite you to stop for a quick *chope* (draft beer), but we couldn't resist staying for a full meal. A restaurant, bistro, and coffeehouse all rolled into one, Caroline even operates a sushi bar after sunset *(Rua J. J. Seabra, 10, Jardim Botânico; tel. (21) 2540-0705; Mon – Wed, noon – 1am; Thu – Sat, noon – 4am; Sun, noon – 2am)*. Formerly Boteco 66, the **66 Bistrô** still houses the talents of chef Claude Troisgros. Offerings include a buffet lunch of salads, grilled meats, and desserts, and an à la carte menu at dinner. We suggest the *carré de cordeiro* (rack of lamb) *(Avenida Alexandre Ferreira, 66, Jardim Botânico; tel. (21) 2266-0838; Tue – Fri, noon – 4pm and 7:30pm until the last customer leaves; Sat, noon – 6pm and 7:30pm until the last customer leaves; Sun, noon – 6pm)*. **Bistrô Itália** features Italian and French dishes by chef Antônio Costa *(Rua Frei Leandro, 20, Jardim Botânico; tel. (21) 2226-1038; Mon – Sat, 7:30pm – midnight; Sun, noon – 6pm)*. For a delicious *caipirinha* in a pleasant scenery, spend an evening at **Bar da Graça** *(Rua Pacheco Leão, 780, Jardim Botânico; tel. (21) 2249-5484; Tue – Sun, noon – 2am)*.

TAVERNS AND BARS

The handmade *chope* (draft beer) at **Bar Devassa** is an acclaimed favorite *(Avenida Lineu de Paula Machado, 696, Jardim Botânico; tel. (21) 2274-1513; Mon – Thu, 5pm – 2am; Fri, 5pm – 3am; Sat, 2pm – 3am; Sun, 2pm – 1am)*, while the more traditional **Belmonte** appeases its customers with savory snacks and *cachaça* *(Rua Jardim Botânico, 117, Jardim Botânico; tel. (21) 2239-1649; daily, 8am – 3am)*. A few doors down, **Conversa Fiada** serves up tasty sandwiches and finger foods *(Rua Jardim Botânico, 129, Jardim Botânico; tel. (21) 2286-2111; Mon – Fri, 5pm until the last customer leaves; Sat and Sun, noon until the last customer leaves)*.

RESTAURANTS

Chef Silvana Bianchi lends her special touch to the **Quadrifoglio**, one of the best Italian restaurants in town *(Rua J. J. Seabra, 19, Jardim Botânico; tel. (21) 2294-1433; Mon – Fri, noon – 3:30pm and 7:30pm – midnight; Sat, 7:30pm – 1am; Sun, 12:30pm – 5pm)*. At **Roberta Sudbrack**, the signature chef serves her Brazilian dishes on two floors: lunch on the first, and, on Friday and Saturday, a tasting menu of up to 14 dishes on the second *(Rua Lineu de Paula Machado, 916, Jardim Botânico, tel. (21) 3874-0139. Tue – Thu, noon – 3pm and 8:30pm – 10:30pm; Fri, noon – 3pm and 9pm – midnight; Sat, 9pm – midnight)*. Brazilian ingredients get the French treatment at **Olympe**, under French chef Claude Troisgros *(Rua Custódio Serrão, 62, Jardim Botânico; tel. (21) 2539-4542; Mon – Thu,*

Caroline Café serves up contemporary cuisine

Jardim Botânico

7:30pm – 12:30am; Fri, 12:30pm – 4pm and 7:30pm – 12:30am; Sat, 7:30pm – 12:30am). **Capricciosa**, Ipanema's famous pizzeria, also has an outpost in Jardim Botânico *(Rua Maria Angélica, 37, Jardim Botânico; tel. (21) 2527-2656; Sun – Thu, 6pm – 1am; Fri and Sat, 6pm – 2am)*. For generous servings of traditional cuisine, such as the *filé à Oswaldo Aranha*, **Filé de Ouro** is a must *(Rua Jardim Botânico, 731, Jardim Botânico; tel. (21) 2259-2396; Tue – Sat, noon – 11pm; Sun, noon – 7pm)*.

Juices and Ice Creams

Looking for an afternoon pick-me-up? Try **Bibi Sucos** *(Rua Jardim Botânico, 632-A, Jardim Botânico; tel. (21) 3874-0051; Sun – Thu, 8am – 2am; Fri and Sat, 8am – 3am)* or **Mil Frutas**, one of Rio's best ice cream parlors. Guava and cheese is a popular flavor *(Rua J. J. Seabra, no #, Jardim Botânico; tel. (21) 2511-2550; Mon – Thu, 10:30am – 12:30am; Sat, 9:30am – 1am; Sun, 9:30am – 12:30pm)*.

Shopping and Leisure

Books

A local favorite, **Livraria Ponte de Tábuas** bookstore attracts visitors with its variety of books and the pleasant **Maçã Café**, serving up oven-baked pastries, salads, quiches, cheese cake, and different kinds of coffee *(Rua Jardim Botânico, 585, Jardim Botânico; tel. (21) 2259-8686; daily, 11am – 11pm)*.

Clothes and Accessories

Dona Coisa has a little of everything: designer fashions, stationary, accessories, shoes, and perfumes *(Rua Lopes Quintas, 153, Jardim Botânico; tel. (21) 2249-2336; Mon – Fri, 11am – 8pm; Sat, 11am – 3pm)*. **Café Sudbrack**, on the store's mezzanine, features a menu that includes sweets, good salads, and sandwiches *(tel. (21) 2249-2336; daily, except holidays, 11am – 8pm)*. Since 1998, **Parceria Carioca** has been selling small treasures by artisans from various cooperatives and organizations. Bracelets, necklaces, costume jewelry, handbags, and shoes are among the chic temptations *(Rua Jardim Botânico, 728, store 108, Jardim Botânico; tel. (21) 2259-1437; Mon – Fri, 10 am – 7pm; Sat, 10am – 2pm)*. Vintage clothing and bargain hunters will want to check out **Betty Borges**, a second-hand boutique specializing in clothes and costume jewelry *(Rua J. J. Seabra, 6, Jardim Botânico; tel. (21) 2512-2697, 2294-7578; daily, 10am – 10pm)*.

Music

Bis Espaço Musical is one of the newest show venues in town. Bossa nova, MPB, choro, jazz, and classical musicians have called this small, intricate space home *(Rua Frei Leandro, 20, 2nd floor, Jardim Botânico; tel. (21) 2226-1038; daily, 7pm until the last customer leaves)*.

Artisans display their work at Parceria Carioca

GÁVEA

Surrounded by Jardim Botânico, Leblon, Rocinha and São Conrado, Gávea is predominantly residential, but there are good outdoor activities and nightlife options every day of the week. The neighborhood owes its name to a rock, standing some 2625 feet tall, that resembles a topsail (*gávea*) on an old sailing boat. The area's busiest street, home to most attractions, is Rua Marquês de São Vicente. The main routes into Gávea from the Zona Sul run along Rua Jardim Botânico and Avenida Bartolomeu Mitre. From Barra da Tijuca and São Conrado, take Auto-Estrada Lagoa–Barra, through the Túnel Zuzu Angel, which goes under the Conjunto Residencial Marquês de São Vicente apartment complex.

Attractions
1. Jockey Club Brasileiro
2. Praça Santos Dumont
3. Shopping da Gávea
4. Planetário
5. PUC-Rio
6. Instituto Moreira Salles (IMS)
7. Museu Histórico da Cidade do Rio de Janeiro

Modern Architecture
1. Conjunto Residencial Marquês de São Vicente
2. Hélio Fraga's Residence
3. Helena Costa's Residence
4. Martin Holzmeister's Residence

Galleries
1. Galeria Anna Maria Niemeyer
2. Galeria 90 Arte Contemporânea
3. Mercedes Viegas Arte Contemporânea

1 JOCKEY CLUB BRASILEIRO

The imposing Jockey Club, designed in an offbeat style by Francisco Cuchet and Arquimedes Memória, opened in 1926, with the name Hipódromo da Gávea. Part of the club is reserved for members and their guests, but entry to the public area is free, and there are betting booths. This is where you will find **Turff Bet & Sports Bar**, which has a good selection of drinks *(tel. (21) 2259-5077; daily, 1pm –4am)*. You'll also find **Complexo Victoria**, a collection of several restaurants serving nouveau cuisine food, Japanese, and pizza *(tel. (21) 2512-7115; daily, 8pm until the last customer leaves)*, **Photochart**, with its varied and sophisticated menu *(tel. (21)*

Anyone can watching – and bet on – the races at the Jockey Club

2515-2247; *daily, noon – 2am)*, and **Restaurante Placé**, which serves a generous and varied buffet *(tel. (21) 2274-1867; Fri – Sun, noon – 9:30pm; Mon, 4pm – midnight)*. TVs in the public area broadcast the races from Jockey de São Paulo (you can bet on these races at the Jockey Club). Visitors can visit the stables if they make advance arrangements *(tel. (21) 2512-9988, ext. 294)*. The club also hosts the Grande Prêmio Brasil de Turfe, an annual race held on the first Sunday in August. **Espaço Nirvana**, also within the club, offers fitness activities, including yoga and pilates, therapeutic massage and a health food restaurant *(tel. (21) 2187-0100; Mon – Fri, 7am – 10pm; Sat, 9am – 8pm; Sun, 10am – 4pm)*. **Babilônia Feira Hype**, a weekend fair with shows, courses, modern clothing, objets d'art and decorative items, showcases at the club every two weeks *(more information at: babiloniahype.com.br)*.
Rua Jardim Botânico, 1003, Gávea, tel. (21) 2512-9988. Races: Mon, from 6pm; Fri, from 4pm; Sat and Sun, from 2pm.

❷ Praça Santos Dumont
A Gávea landmark, the so-called Praça do Jockey (Jockey Square) has gardens, a fountain and a children's playground. The square is surrounded by bars, pubs and restaurants – a dense district called **Baixo Gávea** – that stay open till the early hours to serve the youthful clientele. The best include **Braseiro da Gávea** *(#116, tel. (21) 2239-7494; Mon – Thu and Sun, 11am – 1am; Fri and Sat, 11am – 3am)*, which serves great *picanha* (rump steak), **Hipódromo** bar and restaurant *(#108, tel. (21) 2274-9720; Sun – Thu, 10am – 1am; Fri and Sat, 10am – 3am)*, **Garota da Gávea** *(#148, tel. (21) 2274-2347; Sun – Fri, 11:30am – 1am; Sat, noon – 2am)*, **Bacalhau do Rei** *(Rua Marquês de São Vicente, 11-A, tel. (21) 2239-8945; Mon – Thu, 8:30am – 1am; Fri and Sat, 8:30 – 2am; Sun, 8:30am – 10pm)* and **Guimas**, with its French and Brazilian dishes *(Rua José Roberto Macedo Soares, 5, tel. (21) 2259-7996; daily, noon – 1am)*. Throngs of young people fill the surrounding streets from early evening until well after midnight. Sundays,

Mondays and Thursdays are the busiest nights. On Sunday mornings, the *feirinha de artes e antiguidades*, an **art and antiques fair** organized by the local antiques association, takes over the square. This fair, held near Rua Marquês de São Vicente, recreates the atmosphere of the traditional fair at Praça Quinze. You can bargain with stallholders for crockery, jewelry, costume jewelry, clothes, silverware, rugs, cameras, radios, telephones, and books *(9am – 5pm)*. There are no food stalls, so it's best to have a look round the fair and then catch lunch in one of the nearby family-oriented restaurants.

❸ Shopping da Gávea

This shopping mall mainly caters to families with children interested in amusements and electronic games. Its main attractions are the theaters: **Teatro dos Quatro**, **Teatro das Artes**, **Teatro Clara Nunes** and **Teatro Vanucci**, which put on plays and live music shows for all ages. These tend to sell out days before an event, so it's essential to buy tickets in advance. The mall's stores feature famous labels, especially in women's fashion. **Tangerina** sells dolls, arts and crafts, decorations and chocolate. **Area Objetos** imports furniture, light fixtures, cushions, baskets, and rugs from Asia. **Livraria New Books** sells a wide variety of books, CDs and DVDs, in addition to offering Internet access within its friendly café. **Casa do Porto** offers wine tasting. Try the crispy, creamy millefeuille at **Cézanne**. **Parceria Carioca** sells jewelry, bags, and other decorations made by artisans from several co-ops. Many interesting artworks, mostly modern pieces, are for sale at **Contorno**. **Acrilo** makes and sells acrylic furniture, **Secrets de Famille** specializes in French country style furniture, **Lalla Bortolini** sells antique European chandeliers and furniture, and **Rupee Rupee** has Asian furniture, among other items. Near Shopping da Gávea you will find **Gávea Trade Center,** a slightly smaller mall. But it has good shops like **Tea**

Teatro das Artes is one of several excellent theaters at Shopping da Gávea

Gávea's planetarium is modern and well equipped

Pot, which sells high-quality sheets, towels, and tablecloths *(Rua Marquês de São Vicente, 124).*
Rua Marquês de São Vicente, 52, Gávea, tel. (21) 2294-1096. Mon – Sat, 10am – 10pm; Sun, noon – 9pm.

❹ Planetário

The Planetarium, which is considered to be one of the most modern in Latin America, has two domes. One, the **Universarium VIII** planetarium, measures 75 feet in diameter and can display up to 9,000 projected stars. The other dome, with a 41-foot diameter, houses **Spacemaster**. The equipment in that planetarium can simulate the movements of stars and can recreate a sky with 6,500 stars. There is also the Museu do Universo, with dozens of interactive experiments, including a kinetic sculpture of the solar system. After a night session, extend your visit to include a stop at 00 **(Zero Zero)**. This open-air bar-restaurant serves Mediterranean food with Asian accents, and DJs liven up the dance floor with electronica and rock music *(take the entrance at Avenida Padre Leonel Franca, 240, Gávea, tel. (21) 2540-8041; dinner: Tue – Sun, from 8pm; music: Tue – Sat, from 10pm; Sun, from 9pm).*
Rua Vice-Governador Rubens Bernardo, 100, Gávea, tel. (21) 2274-0046. Star observation: Tue – Thu, 6:30pm – 8:30pm; dome sessions: Sat, Sun and holidays, 4pm – 5:30pm (children) and 7pm (adults).

❺ Pontifícia Universidade Católica (puc-Rio)

This is the site of the first Catholic university in Brazil. Founded in 1941, and officially accredited in 1946, Rio's Pontifícia Universidade Católica (puc-Rio) opened its Gávea campus in 1955.

Art Galleries

Galeria Anna Maria Niemeyer, inside Shopping da Gávea, has been exhibiting artists such as Franz Weissmann, Iole de Freitas, Nelson Leirner, and Oscar Niemeyer since 1977 *(Shopping da Gávea, store 205, Rua Marquês de São Vicente, 52, tel. (21) 2239-9144; Mon – Sat, 10am – 10pm)*. Anna Maria opened another branch featuring contemporary pieces amid the hustle and bustle of Baixo Gávea *(Praça Santos Dumont, 140; Mon – Fri, 2pm – 8pm)*. **Galeria 90 Arte Contemporânea** is a good choice for anyone wanting to see new talent. The gallery is inside a charming house and is a popular spot with locals. It has a significant collection *(Vila 90, Rua Marquês de São Vicente, 90, tel. (21) 2529-6588, 2513-7144; Mon – Fri, 2pm – 7pm; Sat, noon – 5pm)*. The highly respected **Mercedes Viegas Arte Contemporânea** has been showing works by Beatriz Milhazes, Daniel Feingold, Daniel Senise, José Bechara, Luiz Zerbini, and Dudi Maia Rosa since 1983. Its exhibitions are quite innovative *(Rua João Borges, 86, tel. (21) 2294-4305; Mon – Fri, 2pm – 7pm; Sat, 4pm – 8pm)*.

Its 23 departments have educated such individuals as composer Edu Lobo, filmmakers Cacá Diegues and Walter Salles, journalist Arnaldo Jabor, and actor José Wilker. The economic team that developed the Plano Real, a 1990s economic plan to stabilize Brazil's currency, also graduated from PUC. Throughout the year, the university opens its doors to the public for cultural events, talks, exhibitions and book fairs. The campus houses **Solar Grandjean de Montigny**, the residence of French architect Grandjean de Montigny This is one of the few places in the city that preserves his work. This grand neo-classical house has become a cultural center, with exhibition rooms and a library specializing in art, architecture and design *(tel. (21) 3527-1435; Mon – Fri, 9am – 6pm).*
Rua Marquês de São Vicente, 225, Gávea, tel. (21) 3527-1001.

6 Instituto Moreira Salles (IMS)
Formerly the residence of the Moreira Salles family, this lovely modernist building now houses a renowned arts institute. Architect Olavo Redig de Campos designed the building, and Burle Marx completed the landscaping and the mosaic behind the outside fountain. The architecture, with extensive gardens cut through by a stream, is a sight in itself. The building houses an important cultural center, with a cinema, exhibition rooms, café, art shop and studio, in addition to a large music and photography collection. The **Reserva Técnica Musical** includes at least 100,000 recordings dating back as far as 1922, including songs by Noel Rosa, Orlando Silva, Pixinguinha, Ernesto Nazaré, and Chiquinha Gonzaga. The **Reserva Técnica Fotográfica** has more than 450,000 photographs by artists such as Marc Ferrez, Georges Leuzinger, Marcel Gautherot, and José Medeiros. Visits to the photo collection should be arranged in advance. IMS also has a literature and visual arts collection, with 600 modern and contemporary paintings. Its collection includes the *Highcliffe album*, one of the most valuable collections from 19th-

The modernist Instituto Moreira Salles contains important music and photography collections

century Brazil, *Ukiyo-e*, a collection of 18th and 19th-century Japanese engravings, watercolors by the Danish artist Paul Harro-Harring, and a Pernambuco landscape that Frans Post painted in 1667. The program of events is available on the institute website, www.ims.com.br.
Rua Marquês de São Vicente, 476, Gávea, tel. (21) 3284-7400. Tue – Sun, 1pm – 8pm.

❼ Museu Histórico da Cidade do Rio de Janeiro

This museum stands in the Parque da Cidade and tells the history of Rio de Janeiro from the very beginning. Marquês de São Vicente was the original owner of the building that houses the museum. Built in 1809 with just one story, its second floor was added at the end of the 19th century, and 1995 renovation improved the roof, verandas, and floor. The original decorative painting was rediscovered during this renovation. The permanent exhibition includes a model of Rio around the time it was founded, as well as photographs of the old museum buildings, statues, and sculptures from the 18th-century onwards, armor from 15th and 16th centuries, paintings, porcelain tableware and furniture from the Imperial Palace, as well as a cattle-branding iron, a whipping cane, shackles, and other items from the slavery era. Temporary exhibitions also rotate through the museum, which has had 24-hour guards since a high-profile robbery occurred during the 2006 carnival. The Capela de São João Batista, a chapel built in 1920, stands on the same grounds. Inside, painter Carlos Bastos incorporated figures of people from his daily life into a painting of the life of Saint John the Baptist. The work caused great controversy and remains unfinished.
Estrada de Santa Marinha, no #, Gávea, tel. (21) 2512-2353. Tue – Fri, 10am – 4pm; Sat, Sun and holidays, 10am – 3pm. Chapel: Wed, Sat, Sun, and holidays, subject to prior arrangements.

Modern Art Circuit

Gávea was one of the first neighborhoods in Rio to acquire modern architecture, although much of it has since been demolished. The residences known as **Conjunto Residencial Marquês de São Vicente**, for example, were designed by Affonso Eduardo Reidy in 1952 to be much more substantial than they are. Only one portion of his plan was built, and it was then radically modified a few years later. Funding constraints caused him to dispense with elevators, so residents had to reach the duplex apartments on the upper floors via an esplanade. The most unusual aspect of the building is its tunnel. Cars go under the building through the Zuzu Angel Tunnel, which was built some years later along Avenida Padre Leonel Franca. Despite its modern design, Hélio Fraga's residence at Rua Cedro, 34, which Carlos Leão designed in 1951, uses elements from earlier architectural periods. The courtyard that unites the entire space is a good example of this. Lúcio Costa designed Helena Costa's residence, at Rua Caio Mário, 200, as a gift for his daughter. This house also harmoniously combines modern and traditional elements, including Arab-style latticed windows, porches, balconies, skylights, and concrete verandas. The highlight of Martin Holmeister's residence at Avenida Jaime Silvado, 20, is the garden designed by Burle Marx. In 1955, Paulo Everard Nunes Pires, Paulo F. dos Santos, and Paulo de Tarso F. dos Santos designed the house, as well as a carefully constructed façade that shields it from the afternoon sun.

Parque Nacional da Tijuca

Tijuca National Park officially opened in 1961 and occupies approximately 80,000 acres in the heart of the city. Depending on personal interests, one can explore the park in a few hours or in a few days. Options exist for experienced sports enthusiasts as well as for people who just want to go for a walk. Within the forest there are historical buildings, trails, waterfalls, climbing and picnic areas, and lovely lookout points. The park also has two very pleasant restaurants.

The park's forest, Floresta da Tijuca, spreads out along the slopes of the Tijuca massif, a huge stone mass composed of gneiss rock. It is one of the oldest rock formations in the world, with mountain peaks emerging from the treetops. The forest also contains many underground caves. During Brazil's colonial and imperial periods, this area attracted explorers and naturalists. The Brazilian Royal Family often came here to enjoy the wood's mild temperatures. But this patch of paradise almost became a victim of expanding coffee plantations in the 19th century. This threatened the source of many of the region's rivers. However, in 1861, Dom Pedro II ordered the re-forestation of the woods with native trees and a few exotic species, thus preventing the total collapse of Rio's water supply system and guaranteeing the survival of local fauna and flora. To this day, about 10% of water supplied to Rio de Janeiro comes from the park. The reforestation project was one of the first of its kind in the world. The Baron of Bom Retiro spearheaded the project, assisted by Major Manoel Gomes Archer and six of his slaves. They planted around 100,000 seedlings in just over a decade.

Parque Nacional da Tijuca

Map legend:
1. Pico da Tijuca
2. Trilha da Cova da Onça
3. Cascatinha do Taunay
4. Bico do Papagaio
5. Museu do Açude
6. Caminho das Grutas
7. Corcovado
8. Pedra da Gávea
9. Pedra Bonita

The Barão D'Escragnolle continued on with the Major's work, and, in time, nature reclaimed her place on the mountain slopes. Tijuca, today one of the biggest urban forests in the world, boasts trees such as *ipês-amarelos*, *angicos*, *jequitibás*, and *embaúbas*. These species provide a habitat for coatis, capuchin monkeys, crab-eating foxes, sloths, and several species of birds and butterflies. The park, just thirty minutes from the city center by car, has four sectors: Floresta da Tijuca (Sector A); Serra da Carioca (Sector B); Pedra Bonita and Pedra da Gávea (Sector C); and Serra dos Pretos Forros and Covanca (Sector D). The last sector, being the newest, lacks a full complement of tourist facilities. The **Centro de Visitantes** (Visitors' Center) provides detailed information and maps. The well-marked trails make independent access easy. Nevertheless, we recommend that you hire a guide, as it is common for visitors to get lost in the park. It is very important to bring insect repellent, sunscreen, water, and snacks, as well as some warm clothing – temperatures in the park are lower than in the city. Anyone who doesn't want to hike can take a motor tour on the park's 25 miles of surfaced roads.

Contact: Companhia da Escalada, tel. (21) 2567-7105, 9393-5060; Rio Hiking, tel. (21) 2552-9204, 9721-0594; Trilharte, tel. (21) 2556-3848, 2245-5584; Trilhas

São Conrado

The view from the Zona Sul (South Zone) neighborhood of São Conrado is stunning: The rocks of Pedra da Gávea and Pedra Bonita, the hill Morro Dois Irmãos, and Praia de São Conrado (São Conrado Beach) lie just ahead on the horizon. São Conrado's signature upper-class condiminums border the neighborhoods of Leblon, Gávea, Barra da Tijuca, and the *favela da* Rocinha. Beyond its prime residential space, São Conrado offers some irresistible tourist attractions, from surfing to hang- and paragliding (touch down on beautiful Praia do Pepino beach!) to upscale shopping. Here you'll find one of the city's most vibrant and important retail centers. To reach São Conrado from the Zona Sul (South Zone), take Avenida Niemeyer or Auto-Estrada Lagoa–Barra. Alternatively, the scenic Estrada do Joá boasts a spectacular view of Morro da Joatinga hill. From here, you're a short distance from the neighborhood of Joatinga and Clube Costa Brava, a club perched spectacularly atop a small, rocky peninsula. Túnel São Conrado tunnel connects São Conrado with Joá, in the Zona Oeste (West Zone). Túnel Zuzu Angel (formerly Túnel Dois Irmãos) links to Gávea.

Attractions
1. Praia de São Conrado
2. Hang-gliding and Paragliding
3. São Conrado Fashion Mall
4. Casa das Canoas

Studios
1. Mucki
2. Inês

1 Praia de São Conrado
Officially named Praia da Gávea, São Conrado Beach is nearly two miles long, stretching from the end of Avenida Niemeyer to Túnel São Conrado.

Hang-gliders and paragliders who lift off from Pedra Bonita land at the beach's far south end, known as Praia do Pepino. Nearby residents and surfers frequent the beach for its good waves.

SÃO CONRADO

❷ HANG-GLIDING AND PARAGLIDING

Hang-gliding and paragliding lessons are popular activities in São Conrado. A long take-off ramp at Pedra Bonita lends hang-gliders what some may call safer conditions. We strongly recommend you hire instructors accredited by the Associação de Vôo Livre do Rio de Janeiro (AVLRJ), whose headquarters on Praia do Pepino are located on Estrada das Canoas, a narrow road leading to the take-off ramp. Flights are offered for individuals or tandem (with a professional), and last approximately 15 minutes. Following a short training session and instructions from the pilot, you'll rise to almost 1720 feet above sea level. From here the scenery is breathtaking: Take in aerial views of Gávea Golf Club, Gávea Rock, and a panorama of the ocean and the South Zone beaches surrounded by the Tijuca Forest. You'll touch ground at Praia do Pepino. Paragliding flights also last an average of 15 minutes, departing from Pedra Bonita. Two-time Brazilian paragliding champion Ruy Marra is one of the best pilots available. When poor weather conditions prohibit hang- or paragliding in São Conrado, an alternative ramp – though somewhat less exciting – can be found at Parque da Cidade, in Niterói.
Contact: AVLRJ, tel. (21) 3322-4176.

❸ SÃO CONRADO FASHION MALL

One of the oldest and most upscale shopping centers in Rio, the São Conrado Fashion Mall is home to several international designer boutiques, restaurants, four movie theatres, and a central open-air area ideal for people-watching. Label-friendly shoppers will delight in the **Diesel**, **Emporio Armani**, and **Ermenegildo Zegna**. Danish electronics store **Bang & Olufsen** and the Brazilian **Clube Chocolate** add to the high-end mix. (The latter sells fashion goods by Prada Sport, Miu Miu, and Helmut Lang.) **Par.is** stocks locally-produced and imported items, such as jeans by French label April 77. Find all your sleepwear needs at **Nuit Nuit**, which specializes indelicate and romantic robes, nightgowns, and pajamas. **Illiá** imports a range of items, including furniture and handbags from Asia, Africa, and India. For great gift ideas, swing by any of the following: **Bhara** features an eclectic mix of costume jewelry, clothes, and accessories alongside incense, oil burners, home decorations, and books; kitchen goods of all prices and styles can be found at **Image**, including classic cookware by Le Creuset and Christofle; **Oliviers & Co** stocks olive oils from around the world. *Estrada da Gávea, 899, São Conrado, tel. (21) 2111-4444. Mon – Sat, 10am – 10pm; Sun, 3pm – 9pm.*

ARTISTS' STUDIOS IN SÃO CONRADO

Unbeknownst to many visitors, São Conrado is home to several artist and stylist studios, many of them open to the public. At **Mucki**, visitors can watch the always-enchanting Mucki Skowronski fashion the pieces sold in her stores at São Conrado Fashion Mall and Galeria Ipanema 2000 *(Rua Jornalista Costa Rego, 99, tel. (21) 3322-1672; Mon – Fri, 10am – 6pm)*. Artist **Inês Rache** creates textiles of paint and pure silk for her signature boutique, as well as decorations such as acrylic light-switch plates and cloth lampshades *(Estrada das Canoas, 290, tel. (21) 3322-3918; no set hours; call in advance)*.

Casa das Canoas, a shining example of Oscar Niemeyer's modernist architecture

❹ Casa das Canoas

Oscar Niemeyer designed Casa das Canoas as his own residence in 1951. Its curvy shape mimics the uneven terrain beneath, reflecting the architect's organic tendency to integrate nature with design. Today this landmark in Brazilian modernist architecture houses a permanent exhibition of Niemeyer's furniture, drawings, and models.
Estrada das Canoas, 2310, São Conrado, tel. (21) 3322-3581. Tue – Fri, 1pm – 5pm. Groups visits should be booked in advance.

Oscar Niemeyer

Born in Rio de Janeiro in 1907, Oscar Niemeyer graduated from the Escola de Belas Artes in the 1930s, when modern architecture was just garnering attention in Brazil. In 1936, Niemeyer was part of the team – led by Lúcio Costa – that designed the Ministry of Education and Health building, now Palácio Gustavo Capanema. Built with the guidance of Le Corbusier, the Ministry complex is today an international modernist landmark. In the 1940s, at the request of Juscelino Kubitschek, then mayor of Belo Horizonte, Niemeyer designed the Pampulha complex. It is here you can spot the curved shapes and large reinforced-concrete structures that were to characterize much of his work. Costa and Niemeyer teamed up again in 1958 to design the new capital building in Brasília. His most significant works include Obra do Berço and Casa das Canoas, in Rio, the Museum of Contemporary Art, in Niterói, Ibirapuera Park and the Copan building, in São Paulo, the headquarters of the French Communist Party, the head office of the Mondadori publishing house, in Milan, and the University of Constantine, in Algeria.

SÃO CONRADO

ROCINHA

At the top of Morro Dois Irmãos, between Gávea and São Conrado, lies Latin America's biggest *favela*, Rocinha. Founded in the 1920s and elevated to the status of "neighborhood" in 1993, Rocinha now houses more than 250,000 residents across more than 173 acres. At night, lights from these thousands of huts create an image as typical of Rio as its golden beaches and forest-clad mountains. The hilltop *favela* has one of the most spectacular views of Rio de Janeiro. A short distance from Tijuca Forest, in a privileged part of the city, Rocinha enjoys an infrastructure uncommon in other *favelas*: successful bars, restaurants, bakeries, pharmacies, shops, crèches, and samba schools operate with the town limits. Cultural and social projects abound: a community TV station, TV **Roc**; the **Casa de Cultura da Rocinha** cultural center; respected clothes factory **Copa Roca** (which sells designer labels); and **Escola de Música**, a music school offering choir and popular music lessons. In the last few years, Rocinha has become a tourist attraction. Air-conditioned vans carry visitors up the hill to catch a glimpse of local life. After outlining basic safety tips and explaining the area's organized crime and notorious relationship between drug lords and the community, the guides – who speak English, French, Spanish, Italian, and German – show visitors how the *favela* is organized, from its energy supply systems to the layout of huts. Locals hawk handicrafts and other goods on the street. You'll find products from the north and northeast at **Largo dos Boiadeiros**, a traditional street fair. A tour of Rocinha lasts approximately three hours and ends in **Favela Vila Canoas**, near the more affluent part of São Conrado *(Contact: Favela Tour, tel. (21) 3322-2727, 9989-0074, 9772-1133)*. Rocinha is also home to the samba school **Acadêmicos da Rocinha**. Founded in 1988 following the merge of three community street-carnival blocks, in 2006 the samba school paraded in Rio's special carnival group, a privilege reserved for only the best schools. Every Saturday, starting at 10pm, the percussion section delights visitors who come to watch the public rehearsals. Even popular samba artists perform at the academy from time to time. The renovated facilities now feature – in addition to new locker rooms – a covered area for spectators *(Rua Berta Lutz, 80, Rocinha; tel. (21) 3205-3303; Sat, 10pm)*.

Favela da Rocinha, atop Morro Dois Irmãos

Barra da Tijuca

Until the end of the 1960s, the stretch of coast between Morro do Joá and Pontal de Sernambetiba remained almost unaltered from its natural state, in which it was a vast stretch of sand dunes. When Viaduto do Joá bridge was built in the 1970s, and city planner Lúcio Costa was developing an urban plan for the area, Barra da Tijuca became a magnet for new growth. Costa's objective was to lay out streets in a way that integrated natural beauty with the new buildings. But after the first buildings were built, the plan changed and Costa's vision never materialized. Barra da Tijuca, which is in the Zona Oeste (West Zone) but very close to the Zona Sul, is unlike other parts of Rio. It doesn't have the bakeries, juice parlors, and corner bars typical of other neighborhoods. In fact, there aren't many corners at all: The neighborhood has a few wide avenues, lots of condominiums, and dozens of shopping centers and supermarkets. Everything is set in beautiful natural surroundings, including beaches caressed by powerful waves and dunes sprinkled with vegetation. It also has plenty of movie theatres, and a few playhouses and cultural centers. However, Barra da Tijuca's modern urban design has introduced its share of problems. The neighborhood is essentially one large avenue, Avenida das Américas, with a secondary thoroughfare, Avenida Sernambetiba, running along the beachfront. Consequently, when the traffic gets heavy, the lack of alternative routes causes serious bottlenecks. Also, there are few places to backtrack on the main thoroughfares, so drivers must pay attention to signs so as to avoiding missing their turnoff. The most beautiful way into the area is along Avenida Niemeyer, passing through São Conrado and following the coast. Another option is Estrada das Furnas, which cuts through Tijuca Forest, then Estrada da Barra da Tijuca as far as Avenida Armando Lombardi. For those coming from the Zona Norte, the yellow line is the quickest route, although it requires paying a toll.

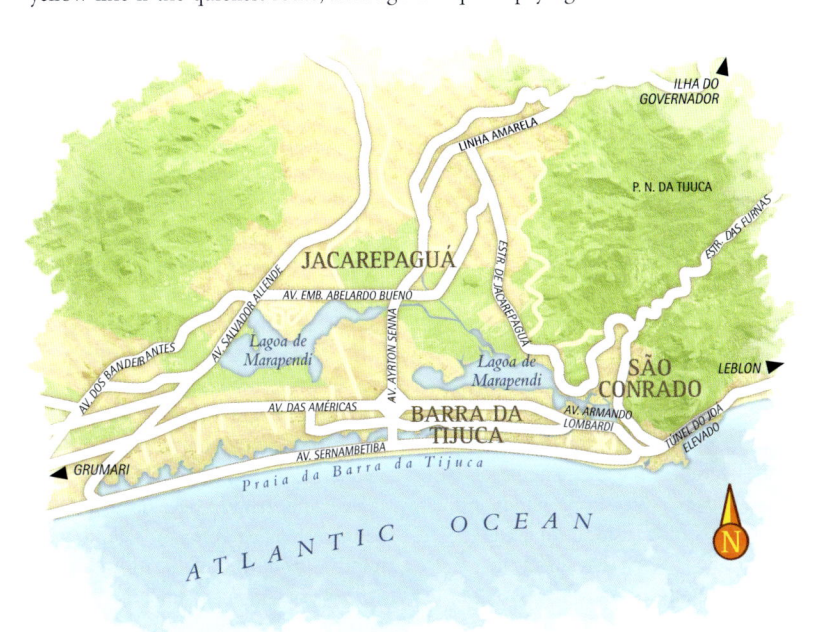

Barra da Tijuca's long beach and bike path are ideal for a variety of sports

Beaches

Praia do Pepê

This 300-yard stretch of beach gets fairly busy in summer. Artists, athletes, and bathers converge here. People play foot-volley, surf, kite surf, and windsurf. The beach stretches from Posto 1 to Posto 2, which is right at the edge of Barra da Tijuca and is on the far left if you are facing the sea. To get there take Avenida Sernambetiba, this strip of which is informally known as Avenida do Pepê. In their names, both the beach and the avenue pay homage to Pedro Paulo Lopes, an adventure sportsman and one of the first people to set up a sandwich stand in the area. Pepê died in 1991 in a hang-gliding accident, but his stand, which is still operating, remains the most famous in the area. The beach has course sand, and its strong winds and high waves make it ideal for water sports. The foot-volley nets in the sand are highly coveted.

Praia da Barra da Tijuca

Stretching for eleven miles, Rio's longest beach has clean – but rough – green waters that draw fishermen and strong winds that attract surfers, windsurfers, and body boarders. It doesn't get as busy as Ipanema and Copacabana beaches, but it's similarly well equipped, with kiosks, showers, bathrooms, and a cycle path. The more-urbanized end of the beach is the half that is closer to Praia do Pepê. People flock to the neighborhood's shopping centers, bars, and restaurants. So, for beachgoers coming from the Zona Sul, heavy traffic can complicate arrival. You're best off going before 10am or after 4pm, when the traffic lets up. Beach-volleyball nets are scattered along the beach, while foot-volley games tend to develop around the marker called Posto 3. At Posto 4, almost in front of the Sheraton Hotel, is Brazil's oldest surf school; there are now many such schools along the entire beach. Although the water is suitable for swimming, the underwater portion of the beach is very steep on the end near Recreio, which sometimes causes powerful waves to surge up unexpectedly. We recommend avoiding the area near Avenida Ayrton Senna, which gets clogged with bus passengers emerging from the nearby terminus of several lines. The deserted area known as Reserva, between Posto 9 and 10, is off limits. The whole beach is poorly lit at night.

Sports

The beaches of Rio's Zona Oeste (West Zone) are suitable for a range of outdoor sports, including surfing, kite surfing, windsurfing, foot-volley, volleyball, soccer, and *frescobol* (beach paddleball). Some have well defined areas set aside for specific sports, and players are careful not to invade each other's spaces. Praia do Pepê hosts perhaps the widest athletic diversity of any local beach.

❶ Surfing

The entire beach from Praia do Pepê to Praia da Macumba (in Recreio) has powerful waves, and surfers tend to populate the whole stretch. There are some particularly popular spots, however. Surf championships are held in the middle of Praia da Barra, in a mile-long stretch around building number 3100, Avenida Sernambetiba, where the waves can get up to six feet high. The waves can vary from three to seven feet at Praia da Macumba, on Estrada do Pontal, at Prainha, and in Grumari. The sport has become so popular that there is even a special bus service for transporting surfers and their boards *(Surf Bus: tel. (21) 2539-7555, 8702-2837)*.
Schools: Bagé Surf Style, tel. (21) 9637-0818; Frajola Kitesurf School (K-08), tel. (21) 2494-4869, 8747-1648; Pedro Müller, tel. (21) 2428-2271, 8121-8641; Recreio Open Sport's, tel. (21) 9922-9584; Rico de Souza, tel. (21) 2438-1692.

❷ Windsurfing

The place to windsurf is at Farol da Barra, on Praia do Pepê, Posto 2.
Schools: Frajola Kitesurf School (K-08), tel. (21) 2494-4869, 7895-1233; KS Naish – Kitecenter, tel. (21) 2495-7815, 8111-5600, 9935-6247; Rio de Janeiro Windsurf Club, tel. (21) 2494-3662, 9872-5700; Rio Wind, tel. (21) 2438-2273, 9106-1045.

❸ Kite Surfing

Praia do Pepê is also the place to kite surf. Seek out the surf post in front of the stall Barraca do Pepê.
Schools: Frajola Kitesurf School (K-08), tel. (21) 2494-4869, 8747-1548.

Strong breezes make for good windsurfing

BARRA DA TIJUCA

RECREIO DOS BANDEIRANTES

BARRA DA TIJUCA

ESTR. BEMVINDO DE NOVAIS
AV. SALVADOR ALLENDE
AV. DAS AMÉRICAS
AV. SERNAMBETIBA

Praia do Abricó
Prainha
Praia da Macumba
Praia do Pontal
Praia dos Bandeirantes

Sports
1. Surfing
2. Windsurfing
3. Kite Surfing
4. Diving
5. Fishing
6. Foot-Volley
7. Volleyball and Soccer
8. Skateboarding
9. Parachuting

4 Diving

Laje do Recreio dos Bandeirantes is the place for diving. From the beach, in front of the stand of pine trees near the beach, you have to swim nearly a mile or walk approximately 546 yards through the rocks, to get to the diving spot. This is a spot for experienced divers, not newbies. Water depth ranges from 6 to 30 feet and visibility from 10 to 30 feet.

5 Flyfishing

All of Praia da Barra is good for fishing, especially from late afternoon until early morning. But fishermen tend to gather around the left end of Praia da Barra, at Praia do Pepê, on the pier, and at the entrance of Lagoa de Marapendi. One can catch a variety of species here. The concentration of bathers and surfers, however, makes it impossible to fish on summer weekends.

6 Foot-Volley

Foot-volley (which is a beach volleyball played without the use of hands; only your head, feet, and chest are allowed), is very popular among soccer players in front of Condomínio Barramares and Posto 3. There are also nets on Praia do Pepê.

7 Volleyball and Soccer

Along every beach, there are volleyball nets and soccer goal posts set up every 100 yards or so. Locals join pickup games that last all day.

8 Skateboarding

The main skateboarding spots in Barra da Tijuca are Cebolão, as the 10-foot by 26-foot Trevo das Palmeiras half pipe is known, and Condomínio Riviera Dei Fiori, which is a small hollow with rounded edges.

BARRA DA TIJUCA

Gyms
1. Academia da Praia
2. KS Academia
3. Downtown Fitness
4. A! Body Tech
5. Cia. Athlética
6. Rio Sport Center

9. **PARACHUTING**

Planes take parachuters on panoramic flights over Barra da Tijuca. After about 25 minutes, it's time to jump – from an altitude of 10,000 feet. The freefall lasts about 35 seconds before

Foot-volley on Praia do Pepê

the parachute opens. Jumpers then float down for another five minutes and return to earth next to the Jacarepaguá airport. Instructors accompany jumpers, and beginners are allowed to participate.
Contact: Skydive Rio, tel. (21) 3410-4599, 7845-7119.

Gyms

For those who are averse to outdoor sports, the Barra da Tijuca district has numerous gyms. Most offer daily and weekly memberships, as well as longer plans. **A! Body Tech**, in Shopping Cittá América, has excellent facilities that fill a space of almost 130,000 square feet. A gymnastics space for children sets it apart from the competition. The gym has a well-respected and highly professional staff that includes award-winning ballerina Ana Botafogo, volleyball coach Bernardinho, and beach-volleyball coach Tande. At night, DJ sets the atmosphere. *(Avenida das Américas, 700, 1ª floor, tel. (21) 2132-7222; Mon – Fri, 6am – 11:30pm; Sat, 9am – 7:30pm; Sun, 10am – 3pm.)* **Cia. Athlética**, in Shopping New York City Center, has special programs for every age group, starting at the tender age of six months. There are classes for hydro-bike, flex-circuit, and street-dance, among other unusual forms of fitness. Scheduling panels throughout the complex show class times and other events, such as public tournaments and beach-running groups. *(Avenida das Américas, 5000, stores 112-113, tel. (21) 3431-5000; Mon – Fri, 5:30am – midnight; Sat, 9am – 8pm; Sun, 9am – 5pm; holidays, 9am – 5pm.)* **Academia da Praia** also offers unusual classes, including Aero Mix (aerobics that involves boxing movements) and Strip Dance (a kind of dance that adds movements from strip-tease). Staff organize activities such as beach volleyball and group walks through Tijuca Forest or around Angra dos Reis, a coastal town south of Rio. *(Avenida Érico Veríssimo, 390, tel. (21) 2494-4028, 2493-8454; Mon – Fri, 5:30am – 11pm; Sat, 8am – 8pm; Sun, 9am – 4pm; holidays, 9am – 4pm.)* Older and in slightly lesser repair than other local gyms, **KS Academia** offers acrobatics classes and a squash court that can be rented by the hour. *(Avenida Armando Lombardi, 663, tel. (21) 2494-2540; Mon – Fri, 6am – 11pm; Sat, 8am – 2pm and 5pm – 8pm; Sun, 9am – 2pm; holidays, 8am – 2pm and 5pm – 8pm.)* **Rio Sport Center** prides itself on having an instructor for every four members and over one hundred pieces of exercise equipment. However, its loud music might be a turnoff for some. It also has a branch in Recreio. *(Avenida Ayrton Senna, 2541, tel. (21) 3325-6644; Mon – Thu, 6am – 10:30pm; Fri, 6am – 10pm; Sat, 8am – 8pm; Sun, 9am – 1pm.)* A much more modest gym than the rest, **Downtown Fitness** is located in the Downtown shopping center. Its most recommendable feature is its sundeck, which has a sauna that's very popular on summer weekends. *(Avenida das Américas, 500, block 18, top floor, tel. (21) 2494-7802; Mon – Fri, 6am – 10pm; Sat, 9am – 2pm and 5pm – 8pm; Sun, 9am – 2pm; holidays, 8am – 2pm and 5pm – 8pm.)*

Other Attractions

❶ Casa de Cultura da Estácio de Sá

This delightful cultural space belongs to Estácio de Sá University and contains an auditorium, art gallery, bookshop, café, and restaurant. The colorful façade makes the entrance welcoming. The 180-seat auditorium hosts plays, shows, and lectures. The café next to the bookshop occasionally holds literary events. Galeria Tarsila do Amaral holds rotating photography and art exhibitions. **Estácio Gourmet Sabores do Mundo** offers a full buffet, and diners pay for food by the kilo. For program details visit: casadecultura.estacio.br.

The cafe at Casa de Cultura da Estácio de Sá holds literary events

Avenida Érico Veríssimo, 359, Barra da Tijuca, tel. (21) 2494-1023. Daily, including holidays, 9am – 11pm or the end of the event.

❷ Centro Cultural Suassuna

Easily missed by people hurrying down Avenida das Américas, the versatile Suassuna Cultural Center, which opened in 2002, has a varied cultural program for all ages. There are theatrical performances, ballets, exhibitions, shows, and other events. The 300-seat theatre hosts inexpensive plays for adults and children. There is also an exhibition room, cafeteria, bookshop, and comic shop. For program details visit www.centroculturalsuassuna.com.br.
Avenida das Américas, 2603, Barra da Tijuca, tel. (21) 2439-8002. Mon and Thu, noon – 7pm; Tue, noon – 8pm; Wed, noon – 6pm; Fri, noon – 11pm; Sat, 2pm – 11pm; Sun, 2pm – 10pm.

❸ Bosque da Barra

Parque Municipal Arruda Câmara (Arruda Câmara Municipal Park), known as Bosque da Barra (the Barra Woods), is a conservation area that preserves a bit of the original ecosystem of Baixada de Jacarepaguá. Joggers and cyclists frequent its its 131 lush acres of peace and quiet on weekdays, and families flock here on weekends. The park has a 1.2-mile jogging track, children's climbing equipment made out of tree trunks and rope, barbecue pits, an artificial lake, parking, a seed laboratory, nursery, and a wide range of plants and animals. Many of the park's plant species are endangered, such as the glorybushes, the *murtilo*, and the strawberry guava. Native animals include crab-eating raccoons, which approach visitors, as well as ferrets, skunks, capybaras, and sloths. Birdlife includes egrets, cormorants, teals, hawks, wood rails, and jacanas. An "ecotheater" group performs on weekends under the shade of the jambolan trees.
Avenida das Américas, km 6, Barra da Tijuca, tel. (21) 2509-5099, 9322-8685. Tue – Sun, 8am – 5pm.

BARRA DA TIJUCA

Attractions
1. Casa de Cultura da Estácio de Sá
2. Centro Cultural Suassuna
3. Bosque da Barra
4. Autódromo Nelson Piquet

Theaters
1. Garden Hall
2. Teatro dos Grandes Atores
3. Teatro Antônio Fagundes

Cinemas
1. Estação Barra Point
2. Cinemark
3. UCI
4. Severiano Ribeiro
5. Espaço Rio Design

4 AUTÓDROMO NELSON PIQUET

Since 1977, the Jacarepaguá racetrack, now called Autódromo Nelson Piquet in homage to the three-time world Formula 1- racing champion, hosts many Brazilian and international sporting events. It has a temporary, 2-mile-long track that's to be replaced by the end of 2008. Surrounded by greenery and mountains, it is one of Brazil's most modern speedways and has been selected as a venue for events in the 2007 Pan American Games. The stadium seating can hold up to 41,000. The public is only allowed in on race days, as there are no guided visits. *Rua Embaixador Abelardo Bueno, no #, Barra da Tijuca, tel. (21) 2220-1546, 2220-1547.*

THEATERS

Barra da Tijuca's theaters stage excellent shows for all ages. In the small Shopping Barra Square, **Teatro dos Grandes Atores** has two somewhat-rundown stages, each with seating for 400 *(Avenida das Américas, 3555, tel. (21) 2430-7000; Mon – Fri, 10am – 10pm; Sun, 3pm – 9pm).* **Teatro Antônio Fagundes**, situated in the Centro de Educação e Cultura, has seating for more than 400 and modern audio and lighting infrastructure *(Avenida Ayrton Senna, 2541-A, tel. (21) 2432-4000).* **Garden Hall**, inside Barra Garden, has seating for 900. Although it is used

---

OUR RECOMMENDATION

The wine importer **Expand** has a cozy restaurant at the back of the shop, with a maître d' and sommelier. The menu has meat dishes, including wild pig and other game, as well as lamb and fish *(Avenida Érico Veríssimo, 901, store A, tel. (21) 2493-6161. Mon – Sat, 5pm – midnight).*

More information on restaurants starts on page 210.

BARRA DA TIJUCA

Bars and Nightclubs
1. Shenanigan's
2. Bar Devassa
3. Guapo Loco
4. Borsalino
5. Academia da Cachaça
6. Nuth Lounge
7. Botequim Informal
8. Na Pressão
9. Surf Adventures
10. Manoel & Juaquim
11. Condado dos Cascais
12. Loft
13. Hard Rock Café
14. Cervantes
15. Barril 8000

Shopping
1. Downtown
2. Citta América
3. Barra Garden
4. Barra Square
5. Barra Shopping
6. New York City Center
7. Casa Shopping
8. Via Parque
9. Rio Design Barra

mostly for business events, there are occasionally plays *(Avenida das Américas, 3255, tel. (21) 3151-3302; Mon – Sat, 2pm – 10pm; Sun, 3pm – 9pm).*

Cinemas

The neighborhood has a variety of cinemas that screen films for all tastes. They're all in shopping centers. If you are looking for something other than Hollywood movies, there is **Espaço Rio Design**, in the shopping center of the same name *(Avenida das Américas, 7777, tel. (21) 2430-3024; Mon – Sat, 10am – 10pm; Sun, 3pm – 9pm)* and **Estação Barra Point**, in Barra Point *(Avenida Armando Lombardi, 350, tel. (21) 2491-3306; Mon – Fri, 10am – 10pm; Sun and holidays, 3pm – 9pm).* At Shopping Downtown, **Cinemark** has fifteen theaters *(Avenida das Américas, 500, tel. (21) 2494-7072; Mon – Fri, 10am – 10pm; Sun, 3pm – 9pm; holidays, 3pm – 9pm).* The eighteen UCI theaters are the big attraction at the New York City Center *(Avenida das Américas, 5000, tel. (21) 2461-1818; Mon – Thu, 1pm – 10:30pm; Fri, 1pm – 12:30am; Sat, 11am – 12:30am; Sun, 11am – 10:30pm).* One of the best in the region is the **Severiano Ribeiro**, at Via Parque *(Avenida Ayrton Senna, 3000, tel. (21) 2421-9222; Mon – Sat, 10am – 10pm; Sun, 3pm – 9pm; holidays, 3pm – 9pm).*

Bars and Nightclubs

The neighborhood's nightclubs, bars and restaurants fill up at night. The best options for dancing are the nightclub **Nuth Lounge**, which has two connected spaces and a variety of musical styles *(Avenida Armando Lombardi, 999, tel. (21) 3153-8595; Mon – Sat, 9pm – 4am; Sun, 7pm – 1am),* and the Rio branch of the **Hard Rock Café** *(Avenida das Américas, 700, 3rd floor, Shopping Cittá América, tel. (21) 2132-*

Manoel & Juaquim, at Shopping Downtown, offers Portuguese finger foods

8000; restaurant open daily from noon; nightclub open Fri and Sat, 10pm until the last customer leaves, and Sun, 7pm until the last customer leaves). **Rua Olegário Maciel** has bars, luncheonettes, restaurants, pizzerias, and juice and fondue parlors. **Shopping Downtown** has several bars with live music and others that are ideal for a happy hour *(Avenida das Américas, 500)*. **Botequim Informal** *(store 107, tel. (21) 2492-2995; daily, noon – 2am)* serves good *chope* (draft beer) and finger food, as does **Na Pressão** *(tel. (21) 2493-2060, 2493-2062. Mon – Fri, 5pm until the last customer leaves; Sat, sun and holidays, noon until the last customer leaves)*. **Surf Adventures** has hamburgers and vegetarian sandwiches *(stores 126 and 127, tel. (21) 3982-2153; Mon – Thu, noon – midnight; Fri, noon – 2am; Sat and Sun, 6pm – midnight)*. Highlights at **Manoel & Juaquim** are the yummy Portuguese finger-foods *(store 143, tel. (21) 2492-1045; Mon – Thu, 4pm – 1am; Fri and Sat, 4pm until the last customer leaves)*. Other hotspots are the **Condado do Cascais**, with several bars and restaurants, and the culinary center **Loft**, whose excellent delicatessen deserves a visit. The local branch of the **Cervantes**, a traditional bar in Copacabana, is famous for its *abacaxi com filé ou lingüiça*, which is pineapple served with steak or sausage *(Avenida Ayrton Senna, 3000, store 2068, Via Parque Shopping, tel. (21) 2421-1068; Avenida das Américas, 5777, store 112, tel. (21) 2438-1458)*. On the beachfront, **Barril 8000** has live music from Monday to Thursday *(Avenida Sernambetiba, 8000, tel. (21) 2433-1730; Mon, 11am – 2am; Tue and Wed, 11am – midnight; Thu – Sat, and holidays, 11am – 4am; Sun, 11am – midnight)*. Popular spots on **Avenida Armando Lombardi** are **Academia da Cachaça**, with over 60 labels of *cachaça* (Brazilian white rum) *(#800, store L, tel. (21) 2492-1159; Sun – Thu, noon – 1am; Fri and Sat, noon –*

3am); the Mexican restaurant **Guapo Loco**, whose success is largely due to its spicy menu and DJ music *(#493, tel. (21) 2491-5427, 2495-2995; Tue – Sat, 7pm – midnight; Sun, noon – midnight)*; the Irish bar **Shenanigan's**, which serves imported beer to the sound of popular rock *(#333, tel. (21) 2492-2798; Sun – Thu, 6pm – 2am; Fri and Sat, 6pm – 4am)*; and **Bar Devassa**, which serves its own house *chope,* or draft beer *(#483, stores A and B, tel. (21) 2494-7626; Mon – Sat, 6pm until the last customer leaves; Sun, 3pm until the last customer leaves).* Also on the avenue is the restaurant **Borsalino**, which serves Mediterranean cuisine in four delightful areas, including a highly sought-after terrace *(#633, tel. (21) 2491-4288. Mon, 6pm – 1am; Tue – Thu and Sun, noon – 1am; Fri and Sat, noon – 2am).*

Shopping Centers

Barra da Tijuca's famous shopping centers are mostly concentrated on Avenida das Américas. **BarraShopping** is considered the largest in Latin America. Women's and men's clothes and accessories are mainly found along Barra Fashion, a corridor of top labels. In Mercado Praça XV you can buy fruits, vegetables, legumes, and dairy products, or have a prepared meal in cozy surroundings. The complex was nearly finished with renovations in early 2007. *(Avenida das Américas, 4666, tel. (21) 3089-1100. Stores: Mon – Sat, 10am – 10pm; Sun, 3pm – 9pm; holidays, 3pm – 9pm. Food and leisure: daily, 10am – 11pm. Mercado Praça XV: Mon – Sat, 10am – 10pm; Sun and holidays, 3pm – 9pm.)* Next door to BarraShopping, is the **New York City Center**. Dining options include Outback, Friday's, and the tavern Na Pressão *(Avenida das Américas, 5000, tel. (21) 3089-1100, 2432-4980; Mon – Sat, 10am – 10pm; Sun and holidays, 3pm – 9pm)*. Originally a home decoration center, **Rio Design Barra** now also contains several acclaimed fashion outlets. It offers a diverse food

Charming Borsalino specializes in Mediterranean food

court with Italian, Arab, and Japanese eateries, and one of the best pizzerias in Rio, the Fiammetta. *(Avenida das Américas, 7777, tel. (21) 2430-3024. Stores: Mon – Sat, 10am – 10pm; Sun and holidays, 3pm – 9pm. Restaurants: noon until the last customer leaves.)* With Rio Design's change of focus, **Casa Shopping** has become the neighborhood's mainstay for home decoration, with more than 140 stores. Casa Bazar sells products from all of the shops at a discount *(Avenida Ayrton Senna, 2150, tel. (21) 2429-8000, 2108-8000; Mon, noon – 10pm; Tue – Sat, 10am – 10pm; Sun, 3pm – 9pm).* **Downtown**, a tree-filled open-air shopping center, brought offices from downtown Rio to Barra da Tijuca. Its enormous area has places to grab a bite, a cinema, bars and women's fashion stores, as well as gymnasiums *(Avenida das Américas, 500, tel. (21) 2494-7072; Mon – Fri, 10am – 10pm; Sun and holidays, 3pm – 9pm).* Outdone by the neighboring Downtown, **Città América**'s only real draws are the Hard Rock Café and the A! Body Tech Academia, since it doesn't have many stores. Twice a year it holds the Top Fashion Bazar, with discounts as high as 70% *(Avenida das Américas, 700, tel. (21) 2132-7777; different stores' hours vary).* **Via Parque** is the best place to buy things for children. Some 40 stores carry furniture, home decorations, clothes, toys, and shoes, and there's a recreation area for kids, too. The show venue Claro Hall is also located here *(Avenida Ayrton Senna, 3000, tel. (21) 2421-9222; Mon – Sat, 10am – 10pm; Sun and holidays, 3pm – 9pm).* At **Barra Garden** the attraction is Barra On Ice, an ice-skating rink loved by kids *(Avenida das Américas, 3255, tel. (21) 2136-9191; Mon – Sat, 10am – 10pm; Sun, 3pm – 9pm).* In addition to the Teatro dos Grandes Atores *(see page 186)*, **Barra Square** has a bowling alley Boliche In Club and a food court *(Avenida das Américas, 3555, tel. (21) 2430-7000; Mon – Sat, 10am – 10pm; Sun, noon – 9pm).*

Artefacto, one of the 140 stores at Casa Shopping, specializes in interior decoration

RECREIO AND ENVIRONS

Although almost an extension of Barra da Tijuca, Recreio dos Bandeirantes has historically been far less urbanized. That has made it a prime target for the current wave of urban development. All along Avenida das Américas – the main thoroughfare – countless condominium complexes are under construction. But large areas are, as yet, unoccupied. The beaches here are relatively quiet, too. At the far end of the district, natural beauties lie hidden. These include: Praia de Grumari, a nice beach with clear waters; tiny, charming Prainha beach; the unspoiled coastal strip called Restinga de Marambaia; and other half-deserted beaches that are only accessible by walking trails. Sítio Roberto Burle Marx, the former home of the remarkable landscaper, deserves a lengthy visit. And the tranquil, charming neighborhood of Vargem Grande offers a variety of culinary experiences. You can reach Recreio by the same roads that lead to Barra da Tijuca.

1. Praia do Recreio
2. Praia da Macumba
3. Prainha
4. Praia de Grumari
5. Casa do Pontal
6. Barra de Guaratiba
7. Restinga de Marambaia
8. Beaches reached by trails
9. Sítio Roberto Burle Marx
10. Vargem Grande

1 PRAIA DO RECREIO

This beach, just over a mile long, lies at the end of Avenida Sernambetiba. It is much quieter than its neighbor, Praia da Barra, and is frequented mostly by locals. However, it has been discovered by a crowd of late-night partiers, who have made it a little noisier than it once was. An ideal spot for surfing, cycling or walking, it has green waters, strong waves and a narrow expanse of coarse, dark sand, where you can play beach-volleyball. An area of dense shrubbery demarks the promenade, which boasts several kiosks, some of which offering amusements for children. The end of the beach, near Praia da Macumba, was recently refurbished and now has its own promenade and kiosks. Several bus lines serve the area, and cars can drive to the beach either along the coast or on Avenida das Américas.

❷ Praia da Macumba

The greenery-surrounded curve at the far end of Praia do Recreio is known as Praia da Macumba, or "Black Magic Beach." Crowded on weekends, this windy beach is a meeting point for surfers and surf-school students, despite the lack of waves at certain times of year. The sea is rough here, which makes swimming inadvisable and dangerous. The beach itself is a short strip of powdery sand. Kiosks and beach sellers provide simple food options. A huge rock unofficially divides the swimming and surfing areas. The sea is calmest near the rock.

❸ Prainha

Tiny, charming Prainha (Little Beach) gets busy on weekends. Reachable by a small road, it stands in a nature reserve just past Praia da Macumba. The beach is a bit less than half a mile long and is surrounded by hills and vegetation-covered dunes. The sea, strong winds, and tall, rolling waves that break close to the beach make this spot a favorite among surfers. Three kiosks sell snacks and items such as surf-board wax and sunscreen. You can also buy water and soft drinks right on the beach. The sand is a little coarser here than it is on neighboring beaches. Prainha stands next to a nature park that has toilet facilities. To get there, take Avenida das Américas.

❹ Praia de Grumari

This long beach stands in a preserved area and has waves that break near the shore. The cleanest beach on the whole coast, it has powdery, coarse, reddish sand and green waters. Vegetation-covered dunes surround the narrow strip of beach. There are calm and rough stretches of sea, but waves form all along the beach. Surfers gather in the area of the beach that is closest to

Praia da Macumba, surrounded by greenery, has powerful winds and powdery sand

Strong, long-lasting waves make Prainha a favorite surfing spot

Prainha. The opposite end is where tourists buses park. The beach draws a variety of visitors, including families, locals, and people from Rio's South Zone. There are only two food kiosks, but there are restaurants nearby. It is best to arrive at the beach before 11am. Paid parking is available in front of the beach, where there is also a nature reserve and some trails. One way to get to Praia de Grumari is by driving through the dazzling landscape of the Serra do Grumari mountains. In summer the road is almost impassable due to traffic and at times authorities limit the number of cars on that route. A continuation of Praia de Grumari called **Abricó** is nothing more than a tiny strip of sand, but it is an official nude beach.

A clay figurine of an outlaw

⑤ Casa do Pontal

The museum Casa do Pontal has the largest collection of folk art in Rio. Its pieces portray daily life in Brazil as represented by some 200 artisans from all over the country. Since 1950, they have contributed sculptures, figures, carvings, clay sculptures, and miniatures with moving parts to this wide-ranging collection. Materials used include clay, wood, fabric, sand, iron, aluminum, bread, straw and wire. The permanent exhibition has explanatory texts in English and more than 5,000 works organized by theme: festive, everyday, imaginary and religious activities. French designer and collector Jacques van de Beuque, who died in 2000, amassed the collection. The museum is currently run by his widow and son. Don't miss the surrounding two acres of gardens, which are part of an ecological reserve.

Estrada do Pontal, 3295, Recreio dos Bandeirantes, tel. (21) 2490-3278, 2490-4013. Tue – Sun, 9:30am – 5pm.

Sítio Burle Marx, a pleasant place to appreciate a diversity of flora

❻ Barra de Guaratiba

This small beach has calm, green waters. Its firm sands gets crowded in summer. Several bus lines serve the beach, which draws all tiers of Brazilian society. Trees surround the beach, and houses cover the adjacent hills. On one side stands the Restinga de Marambaia, a restricted military area. Among the beachside restaurants specializing in seafood, **Tia Palmira** is the best. Take Estrada de Guaratiba to get to restaurant. It's worth waiting for the splendid sunset.

❼ Restinga de Marambaia

A beach of calm waters and muddy sand, Restinga de Marambaia stands on Navy property and is off limits to the public. A strip of native Atlantic forest runs along 26 miles of untouched beaches. **Point do Grumari**, a restaurant at the top of the mountain range, offers an unforgettable view of the region, which looks particularly spectacular at sunset: in the foreground, an immense expanse of greenery; in the background, the deserted beach. The restaurant lies on the road to Grumari.

❽ Beaches Reached by Trails

Even farther from Recreio, there are numerous wild, half-deserted beaches that are accessible only by trails to the west of the Pedra Branca Mountains, or by boat. Its isolation can make the trip there dangerous, so visiting with a

---

Our Recommendation

🍽 **Tia Palmira** is a simple restaurant with tasty food. For a prix-fixe, it offers generous portions of a variety of delightful starters and mains, as well as dessert. Seafood and dishes from Bahia are the house specialties. It's a little more expensive than other restaurants in the area, but it's worth it *(Rua Caminho do Sousa, 18, Barra de Guaratiba, tel. (21) 2410-8169; Tue – Fri, 11:30am – 5pm; Sat, Sun, and holidays, 11:30 – 6pm).*

Additional information on restaurants starts on page 210.

group is a good idea. Parking is available on residential streets near the trailheads. Some beaches have campsites, but there are no food kiosks, so you need to take provisions and supplies with you. **Perigosinho**, **Praia do Meio**, **Funda**, and **Praia do Inferno** are the beaches most popular among surfers. They all have white sand and strong waves. Tiny **Pedra de Guaratiba**, a simple beach used by fishermen, has calm waters, but it is not suitable for bathing; the main attractions here are the restaurants.

9 Sítio Roberto Burle Marx

Renowned landscape artist Roberto Burle Marx lived in this home from 1949 to 1994, the year he died. The grounds have been donated to Iphan, which is the National Institute for Historical and Artistic Heritage. A visit here takes in the immense garden, with innumerable examples of Brazilian and international flora; a 17th-century chapel that still hosts masses and weddings; the artist's studio; and the farmhouse, built in colonial style, where the **Museu-Casa de Roberto Burle Marx** has operated since 1999. Burle Marx obtained the stones for his studio's façade from a demolished building in the city center. Exhibits include 17th- and 18th-century paintings, murals, and furniture, such as the bed where Burle Marx slept, sculptures, and folk art and crystal that he bought on his many travels. The heavy front door came from a church in Pernambuco, the piano from Germany, and the collection of Baroque saints from the Brazilian state of Minas Gerais. The printing studio displays a unique chandelier, which Burle Marx made from plants and dried fruits. The Cozinha de Pedra pavilion, built in the 1960s, has a Burle Marx mosaic, a wood-fired oven, and a waterfall formed by the property's own spring. The studio-house roof was sculpted in Styrofoam, and then modeled in fresh cement. Among thousands of plant species on the

Parque Estadual da Pedra Branca is one of the world's largest urban parks

property are palm, fig, and mango trees that are more than eighty years old, Brazilian ironwoods, more than a dozen types of bromeliad that Burle Marx himself introduced, African tulip trees, aloe vera, pencil trees, floss silk trees, staghorn ferns, calabash trees (used to make musical instruments and handcrafted items), torch ginger, assai palms, cacao trees, velvet bean trees, flamingo lilies, and giant ferns. Spring is the best time to visit, because the property is at its most colorful then; the jade vine is particularly beautiful in spring. Insect repellent is essential. An interesting point: More than two dozen species of plants carry Burle Marx's name, since he discovered them in the course of his travels. Visits must be arranged in advance.
Estrada Roberto Burle Marx (former Estrada da Barra de Guaratiba), 2019, Barra de Guaratiba, tel. (21) 2410-1412. Tue – Sat, 9:30am and 1:30pm; Sun, 9:30am.

10 VARGEM GRANDE

Sitting inside Parque Estadual da Pedra Branca (Pedra Branca State Park), this picturesque neighborhood is far from the hustle and bustle of Rio de Janeiro. Its earthen roads convey the simple air of a country town, and friendly locals go about on foot or bicycles. Within a patch of Atlantic forest, it has trails and small waterfalls, as well as several breeding studs and houses belonging to famous artists, which stand in stark contrast to the nearby *favela*, or shantytown. It offers a wide variety of restaurants that serving mainly Brazilian or varied cuisine. Among the best options for lunch is **Quinta**, which serves a popular roast duck dish that comes with seasonal fruit jelly. Customers sitting on the veranda have semi-domesticated marmosets for company *(Rua Luciano Gallet, 150, Vargem Grande, tel. (21) 2428-1396, 2428-2568; Fri, Sat, Sun and holidays, 1pm – 7pm).*

Niterói

Niterói faces Rio de Janeiro from across Guanabara Bay. The city has tiny hilltop churches, historical forts, beautiful old buildings, museums, white-sand beaches, bars, and restaurants. Many places in the city offer stunning panoramic views of the Rio's beachfront, across the bay. To get to Niterói from Rio, take a boat (a 20-minute ride) or catamaran (8 minutes) from Praça Quinze de Novembro, or cross the Rio–Niterói Bridge by car. Opened in 1973, the impressive bridge is about 8 miles long and has a central span that stands almost 230 feet high.

1. Museu de Arte Contemporânea de Niterói
2. Caminho Niemeyer
3. Fortaleza da Santa Cruz
4. Teatro Municipal João Caetano
5. Solar do Jambeiro
6. Museu Antônio Parreiras
7. Museu de História e Artes do Rio de Janeiro
8. Igreja São Lourenço dos Índios
9. Parque da Cidade

1 Museu de Arte Contemporânea (MAC) de Niterói

Designed by Oscar Niemeyer, and surrounded by an enormous reflecting pool, the Niterói Museum of Contemporary Art opened in 1996. It is a circular building, with a 164-foot-diameter dome resting on a 30-foot base atop the Mirante da Boa Viagem lookout. A large continuous wall of glass forms a ring around the middle of the building, and affords a breathtaking view of the city of Rio de Janeiro. The museum houses the collection of art collector and dealer João Sattamini. It has about 1200 pieces of contemporary Brazilian art, featuring works by artists including Hélio Oiticica, Tomie Ohtake, and José Rezende. The museum is the first building along the Caminho Niemeyer (Niemeyer Path). *Mirante da Boa Viagem, no #, Boa Viagem, tel. (21) 2620-2400. Tue – Sun, 10am – 6pm (7pm during daylight savings).*

Fortaleza de Santa Cruz (right) has views of Sugarloaf Mountain and much of Rio's beachfront

❷ Caminho Niemeyer

This path is a work in progress. According to the plan, this path will have nine buildings and a plaza. Its inception will make Niterói the city with the highest number of works by Niemeyer after Brasília. The buildings – many of which are in different phases of planning and construction – will occupy a stretch of beach between Centro and Praia da Boa Viagem. Those that have already been built include the contemporary art museum (mentioned above) and **Praça Juscelino Kubitschek**, in front of Plaza Shopping. Two sculptures in the Praça Juscelino Kubitschek pay homage to former Brazilian president Juscelino Kubitschek and to Niemeyer himself. **Memorial Roberto Silveira**, named in honor of the former governor of Rio de Janeiro, resembles an Indian dwelling. It will house the city's historical and iconographic archives. As of late 2006, visitors could only enter the building itself, not yet the archives *(Avenida Visconde do Rio Branco, no #, former Vila Olímpica, Centro, tel. (21) 2613-2251; Mon – Fri, 9am – 1pm)*. The **Teatro Popular**, whose silhouette is reminiscent of Sugarloaf Mountain, has been recently completed, but it is not yet open to the public. There are still no set opening dates for the other projects.

❸ Fortaleza de Santa Cruz

Niterói has at least six historical forts. Fortaleza de Santa Cruz is the most noteworthy of these. Its builders constructed it out of Portuguese stones in the place where, in 1555, two cannons protected the entrance to the bay. Over time, it underwent modifications and even briefly operated as a prison. One can still see the prisoners' cells and the bullet marks in the firing-squad wall. **Capela de Santa Bárbara** (Santa Bárbara Chapel), was built in the 17th century and rebuilt in the early 20th century. The outdoor area, next to the old cannons, provides inviting views of the sea and of Sugarloaf Mountain on the other side of the bay.
Estrada General Eurico Gaspar Dutra, no #, Jurujuba, tel. (21) 2710-7840. Tue – Fri, noon – 5pm; Sat, Sun, and holidays, 9am – 5pm.

④ TEATRO MUNICIPAL JOÃO CAETANO
One of the oldest theaters in the country, João Caetano Municipal Theater opened in 1827. Most now consider its architecture to be eclectic in style, especially after several renovations. Details such as the elaborate paintings in the Salão Nobre (auditorium) were restored in 1995. The theater features paintings by German Thomas Driendl, who was initially hired in 1888 to work on set design and decoration. There is also a room for talks and workshops. Show details are available at www.tmnit.com.br.
Rua Quinze de Novembro, 35, Centro, tel. (21) 2620-1624. Box Office: Tue – Fri, 10am – 1pm and 1:30pm – 6pm; Sat and Sun, 3pm – 6pm; on show days, until the show starts.

⑤ SOLAR DO JAMBEIRO
Built in 1872 by a Portuguese businessman, Solar do Jambeiro is an example of 19th-century urban residential architecture. Its façade has Portuguese tiles, while large, hand-painted roof tiles from the Portuguese city of Porto cover the eves. The manor house, which is home to a collection of intaglio prints and paintings by the artists Hilda and Quirino Campofiorito, also holds temporary exhibitions.
Rua Presidente Domiciano, 195, São Domingos, tel. (21) 2109-2222. Tue – Sun, 1pm – 6pm.

⑥ MUSEU ANTÔNIO PARREIRAS
This museum occupies a late 19th-century house designed by Ramos de Azevedo. The painter Antônio Parreiras (1860-1937) lived here, and it now holds about fifty of his works.
Rua Tiradentes, 47, Ingá, tel. (21) 2299-9578. Tue – Fri, 11am – 5pm; Sat, 2pm – 5pm.)

⑦ MUSEU DE HISTÓRIA E ARTES DO RIO DE JANEIRO
Also known as Museu do Ingá, this museum holds a collection of folk art and modern Brazilian art. Workshops taught by Anna Letycia in this museum produced some important intaglio printers in the 1970s and 1980s.
Rua Presidente Pedreira, 78, Ingá, tel. (21) 2299-9577. Tue – Sun, 1pm – 5pm.

8 Igreja São Lourenço dos Índios

With its Jesuit architecture and heritage-site status, the Igreja São Lourenço dos Índios Church is the oldest church in the city. It has a statue of St. Lawrence, a 17th-century retable, and a beautiful baptismal basin. It occupies the spot where a wattle-and-daub chapel used to stand, replaced in the 18th century by this stone and lime construction. The church was restored in 2000 and 2001.
Praça General Rondon, no #, Morro de São Lourenço, tel. (21) 2613-6527. Mass: Sun, 9am. On other days visits must be booked in advance.

9 Parque da Cidade

Situated in an environmental refuge almost 886 feet above sea level, Parque da Cidade (City Park) offers a panoramic view of Piratininga and Itaipu lakes, Guanabara Bay, and the beaches and skyline of Rio de Janeiro. It has a tourist center, a cafeteria, and hang-gliding and paragliding ramps. Hang-gliding and paragliding flights from here are shorter than those from Pedra Bonita, in São Conrado, Rio *(see page 174)*, because they start from a lower altitude. To find instructors, contact the Associação de Vôo Livre do Rio de Janeiro, on Praia do Pepino beach in São Conrado *(tel. (21) 3322-4176).*
Estrada da Viração, São Francisco, tel. (21) 2722-9094 (a public phone booth). Daily, 8am – 5pm.

Beaches

The beaches near the entrance to the bay are the most popular. **Piratininga**, **Camboinhas**, and **Itaipu** beaches all have stretches of calm waters and white sand, and simple restaurants and bars serve fresh seafood. Camboinhas is popular among sailors and windsurfers. Itaipu, where is home to a fishing village, has a beautiful view of Rio de Janeiro and has the **Museu de Arqueologia** (Archeology Museum). This museum displays objects from archeological sites *(Praça de Itaipu, no #, Itaipu, tel. (21) 2709-4079; Wed – Sun, 1pm – 5pm).*
Further away, the beach of **Itacoatiara** has rougher waters, which attract surfers and young people. The bars and restaurants, which line the promenades of beaches such as **São Francisco** and **Charitas**, can get quite lively at night.

Niterói Museum of Contemporary Art: Niemeyer's design makes the most of the superb view

Major Thoroughfares in and around Rio de Janeiro

Highways

Several major federal highways pass through the city of Rio de Janeiro. Each is run by a concessionaire, which is a company that charge tolls and oversees maintenance of certain highways. Concessionaire-run highways are generally in better condition than other roads. The BR-116, also known as Rodovia Presidente Dutra, is run by concessionaire Nova Dutra, and connects Rio to the city of São Paulo, passing along the way through Belford Roxo, Resende, and Barra Mansa. The BR-116, aka Rodovia Rio-Bahia, connects Além Paraíba, in Minas Gerais, to Barra Mansa. The BR-040, aka Rodovia Washington Luís (run by the concessionaire Concer), leaves Rio and passes through Petrópolis and Três Rios, heading toward Belo Horizonte, which is the capital of Minas Gerais state. The BR-101, aka Rodovia Mário Covas, crosses the state of Rio de Janeiro from north to south, passing through Campos dos Goitacases, Niterói, Rio (the city), and Paraty. The BR-101 becomes known as Rodovia Rio-Santos in the stretch from the city of Rio to the port city of Santos.

Toll roads tend to have rest areas and offer emergency medical, towing, and rescue services. Before setting out on a journey, check with the state and federal highway patrols about road conditions on the highways you are planning to take.

Information about the state of the highways can be obtained at: www.dnit.gov.br
Polícia Rodoviária Estadual (State Highway Patrol) – Tel. (21) 3399-4857
Polícia Rodoviária Federal (Federal Highway Patrol) – Tel. (21) 2489-0582

Concessionaires

Concer (runs the BR-040) – Tel 0800-2820040; www.concer.com.br
Nova Dutra (runs the BR-116) – Tel 0800-0173536; www.novadutra.com.br

Major Thoroughfares

The BR-116 (Dutra) and BR-101 highways are the most important routes into Rio. Those coming from the south, via BR-116, will converge on to the long Avenida Brasil, while those coming from the north (along the continuation of BR-101) will inevitably end up on the Rio–Niterói Bridge (Presidente Costa e Silva). There is also the BR-040, which connects Rio to the cities of Brasília, Belo Horizonte, and Petrópolis – and flows into BR-101. In all of these situations, the expressway known as the **Linha Vermelha** (Red Line) is the most useful geographical point of reference. The expressway has exits to the neighborhoods in the Centro (Downtown Rio) and Zona Sul (South Zone). A warning: the neighborhood exit signs on the Linha Vermelha are very close to the exits themselves, so stay on the lookout.

The **Linha Amarela** (Yellow Line), which starts in the middle of the Linha Vermelha, is far from the beachfront but is the quickest route to Barra da Tijuca and environs. Both the Linha Vermelha and the Linha Amarela pass through outlying areas of the city, which are not terribly safe. It is easier to keep your bearings along the coastal avenues, since you have the ocean as a reference. Plus, hugging the coastline is more enjoyable because you can appreciate the beauty of the beaches.

The most important thoroughfares along Rio's beachfront, starting from the north and working south, are: Avenida Rodrigues Alves and Avenida Perimetral (in the port area); Avenida Infante Dom Henrique (also known as Aterro do Flamengo, and which passes through the neighborhoods of Glória and Flamengo); Avenida das Nações Unidas (which passes through Botafogo); Avenida Atlântica (through Leme and Copacabana); Avenida Vieira Souto (through Ipanema); Avenida Delfim Moreira (through Leblon); Avenida Niemeyer (through Vidigal); Auto-Estrada Lagoa–Barra (through São Conrado); Elevado das Bandeiras (through São Conrado/Barra da Tijuca); and, in Barra da Tijuca, Avenida Lúcio Costa – also called Sernambetiba. The most important routes through Centro are Avenida Rio Branco, which connects the downtown area with the port area (Avenida Rodrigues Alves), Enseada da Glória (near Avenida Infante Dom Henrique), and Avenida Presidente Vargas, which goes from Candelária to the beginning of Elevado Engenheiro Freyssinet. In Jardim Botânico and Gávea, major thoroughfares are Rua Jardim Botânico (continuation of Humaitá), Rua Marquês de São Vicente, and Estrada da Gávea. If you are in Centro (downtown Rio) or Zona Sul (the South Zone) and want to go to Floresta da Tijuca (Tijuca Forest), take Rua Pacheco Leão and continue on Estrada Dona Castorina. To go to Corcovado from Botafogo, take Rua das Laranjeiras and Rua Cosme Velho, and then Estrada das Paineiras and Estrada do Corcovado. To get to Corcovado from the Lagoa Rodrigo de Freitas region, take Túnel Rebouças. In Barra da Tijuca, the main thoroughfare crossing the neighborhood is the long Avenida das Américas.

Taxis

Most taxis are painted yellow with a blue stripe; taxis companies number the body of their vehicles. For safety reasons, we recommend you go to a proper stand to get a taxi or call for one. You're better off ignoring hotel porters' recommendations, since they often have agreements with taxi drivers who do not have proper credentials. Taxi rates are fixed by the city council and calculated according to the number of kilometers traveled, plus the call-out fee, plus fractions of time in which the car is at a halt. From Monday to Friday, from 9pm to 6am, and on Sundays and public holidays, the call-out fee is 20% more expensive. There are companies who offer a fixed price per ride, others who have a fixed price according to neighborhoods, and yet others who charge by the hour.

Teleblon – Tel (21) 2512-5547
JB Táxi – Tel (21) 2178-4000, 2501-3026
Transcootour – Tel (21) 2590-2220, 2590-2300
Transcoopass – Tel (21) 2560-4888

Metro

Two lines operate in the city: 1 and 2. Line 1 goes from Estação Siqueira Campos, in Copacabana (South), to Praça Saens Peña, in Tijuca (North). Line 2 connects two points in the north region and goes from Estação Estácio to the outer suburb of Pavuna. The metro system integrates with a range of bus lines. Ticket prices vary according to your destination. The stations that integrate with the bus lines are Siqueira Campos, Cardeal Arcoverde, Botafogo, Largo do Machado, Carioca, Estácio, São Francisco Xavier, and Saens Peña (all on line 1) and Estácio e Del Castilho (on line 2). From Estação Siqueira Campos (line 1) buses leave for Copacabana/end stretch, Ipanema, and Gávea.

The buses that leave Estação Largo do Machado (line 1) go to Corcovado, Palácio da Guanabara, and Teatro Cacilda Becker. Buses headed for the neighborhood of Urca leave from Estação Botafogo. With the **Rio Card** system, metro passengers can also take one bus in a period of up to two hours, at a lower rate than the usual. There are various types of RioCard, but the best one for tourists is called the "vale-transporte rápido," and can be bought at branches of Unibanco.
Tel. 0800-5951111. Mon – Sat, 5am – midnight; Sun and holidays, 7am – 11pm.
www.metrorio.com.br

Buses and Vans

Rio's buses, interconnected with the metro and train lines, go to a range of points in the city. There are also passenger vans that take the bus routes. Be wary, however, of illegal bus operations, without city council identification. Some shopping centers have private lines that take tourists to other places in the neighborhood for free. There are also air-conditioned buses known as "frescão," which go along the beachfront every 30 minutes. The fare is higher than on the normal buses, but worth it.
Tel. 0800-2828664. Daily, 4am – 10pm. Some lines run late into the night, but more sporadically.
www.rio.rj.gov.br/smtr

See useful information on page 242.

Major Thoroughfares in and around Rio de Janeiro

Services

Hotels, Restaurants, Show Venues, Nightclubs, and Shopping

The following pages list Rio's top business establishments in alphabetical order and describe the services and amenities that each offers. Quoted hotel prices are the daily rates for a couple. Restaurant prices were calculated based on the price of the most popular dish, plus a 10% service charge, which is considered appropriate in Brazil. (See the bottom of each page for a key to price ranges.) Many hotels operate a day-use system, in which guests who don't need overnight accommodations can pay a reduced fee for daytime use of the facilities. Also, many beachfront hotels offer what they call a "beach service" (*serviço de praia*), which usually consists of staff providing a complimentary towel to each beachgoer and maintaining beachside restrooms, cold showers, and a small snack bar or kiosk with umbrella-shaded tables. Addresses, telephone numbers, hours, and prices were supplied by the establishments in question and verified by our team of field researchers. Nevertheless, there may have been subsequent changes; we recommend that, whenever possible, readers double-check information before visiting an establishment.

From the top and clockwise: snacks at Tia Palmira's; samba at Comuna do Semente; veranda at Mama Ruisa's hotel; and Beco das Virtudes bookstore

RIO DE JANEIRO

HOTELS BY NEIGHBORHOOD

Arpoador
Mercure Apt Arpoador

Barra da Tijuca
Sheraton Barra Hotel & Suites

Copacabana
Best Western Rio Copa
Copacabana Palace
JW Marriott
Lancaster Othon Travel
Ouro Verde Hotel
Portinari Design Hotel
Royal Rio Palace Hotel

Sofitel Rio de Janeiro

Flamengo
Hotel Novo Mundo

Gávea
La Maison

Glória
Hotel Glória

Ipanema
Adventure Hostel
Caesar Park Ipanema Hotel

Everest Rio Hotel
Fasano Hotel e Restaurante
Ipanema Plaza Hotel

Leblon
Marina All Suites
Sheraton Rio Hotel & Towers

Leme
Iberostar Copacabana

Santa Teresa
Mama Ruisa
Relais Solar (Solar Santa)

WHERE TO STAY

Adventure Hostel $$
Rua Vinicius de Moraes, 174, Ipanema
(Between Rua Barão da Torre and Rua Nascimento Silva)
TEL (21) 3813-2726 FAX (21) 3813-2726
This small youth hostel is simple, but comfortable. It has four communal bathrooms. Staff can provide tips on tour and adventure sport operators, and they offer classes in Portuguese for foreigners. The room rate includes breakfast. ACCOMMODATIONS 8 suites that sleep four people each and 2 two-room suites, each with air-conditioning and a safe. FACILITIES AND SERVICES Internet access (broadband); bar; cyber cafe; shops; video room, garden, bike rental, surfboards and towels; bilingual staff; kitchen open until 10:30pm; shuttles to airport and attractions.
www.adventurehostel.com.br
CREDIT CARDS Not accepted

Best Western Rio Copa Hotel $$
Avenida Princesa Isabel, 370, Copacabana
(Between Rua Ministro Viveiros de Castro and Rua Barata Ribeiro)
TEL (21) 2546-9500, 3875-9191, 0800-7615001
FAX (21) 2275-5545, 3875-9192
Some 200 meters from the beach, this establishment caters mainly to business travelers. The décor is classic and the rooms simple. The room rate includes breakfast. ACCOMMODATIONS 109 rooms, of which 30 are non-smoking and 2 have facilities for the disabled. Rooms have Internet access (broadband); air-conditioning; bathroom; safe; mini bar; hairdryer; telephone; pay TV. FACILITIES AND SERVICES Internet access (broadband wi-fi); public computers available); bar; parking; swimming pool; restaurant; convention room; sauna; bicycles; gym;

cell phone rental; bilingual staff; business center; currency exchange; valet parking; pool, beach, and room service from 6am to 11:40pm.
www.riocopa.com
CREDIT CARDS AmEx; Diners; MasterCard; Visa

Caesar Park Ipanema Hotel $$$$
Avenida Vieira Souto, 460, Ipanema
(Between Rua Joana Angélica and Rua Maria Quitéria)
TEL (21) 2525-2525 FAX (21) 2521-6000
This elegant hotel has excellent service and spacious, well-decorated rooms, most of which afford a wonderful view of the beach. The chill-in area and Italian restaurant Galani are on the top floor. There is live music in the foyer at night. Basic room rates do not include breakfast, but it can be added for a fee. Rooms can also be booked for day-use (6-hour period). ACCOMMODATIONS 222 rooms, of which 2 are handicapped accessible. Rooms have Internet access (broadband wi-fi); air-conditioning; bathroom; safe; DVD player (in one suite); mini bar; hairdryer; telephone; pay TV. FACILITIES AND SERVICES Internet access (broadband; wi-fi); bar; parking; swimming pool; restaurant; masseuse; sauna; bicycles; horse riding, launch, diving, and abseiling (booked through the concierge); gym; travel agency; laptop rental; bilingual staff; business center; currency exchange; 24-hour kitchen; guides for walks; valet parking; first aid service; lifesaver; pool and beach service; shuttles to airport and attractions.
www.caesarpark-rio.com
CREDIT CARDS AmEx; Diners; MasterCard; Visa

Copacabana Palace $$$$
Avenida Atlântica, 1702, Copacabana
(Between Rua Fernando Mendes and Rua Rodolfo Dantas)
TEL (21) 2548-7070 FAX 2235-7330. Reservations required

PRICES	HOTELS (couple)	$ up to R$150	$$ from R$151 up to R$300	$$$ from R$301 up to R$500	$$$$ above R$500

Open since 1923, the Copacabana Palace is recognized as a cultural heritage site and is an enduring Rio landmark. It has received famous artists and authorities from all over the world. The hotel contains two restaurants, the sophisticated Cipriani (serving Italian) and the Pérgula (contemporary cuisine); the latter overlooking the swimming pool. Some packages include breakfast. **ACCOMMODATIONS** 225 rooms, with Internet access (broadband); air-conditioning; bathroom; safe; DVD player; mini bar; hairdryer; telephone; pay TV. **FACILITIES AND SERVICES** Internet access (broadband wi-fi; public computer available); bar; parking; shops; swimming pool; heated pool; restaurant; convention room; beauty salon; bicycles; tennis court; gym; bilingual staff; business center; currency exchange; 24-hour kitchen; masseuse; first aid service; lifesaver; pool and beach service; airport shuttle; shuttles to attractions and nearby cities.
www.copacabanapalace.com.br
CREDIT CARDS AmEx; Diners; MasterCard; Visa

Everest Rio Hotel $$$$
Rua Prudente de Morais, 1117, Ipanema
(Between Rua Maria Quitéria and Rua Garcia D'Ávila)
TEL (21) 2525-2200, 0800-7092220 **FAX** (21) 2521-3198
The comfortable executive suites here have views of the beach or of the lake, Lagoa Rodrigo de Freitas. The restaurant, Grill 360º, has live bossa nova on Wednesdays. There is also a Japanese restaurant called Domburi Edo. Room rates include breakfast. The hotel also rents rooms for daytime-only use, by 12-hour periods. **ACCOMMODATIONS** 156 rooms, of which 109 are non-smoking. Rooms have Internet access (broadband wi-fi); air-conditioning; bathroom; safe; mini bar; hairdryer; telephone; pay TV. **FACILITIES AND SERVICES** Internet access (broadband wi-fi; public computers available); bar; cyber cafe; parking; swimming pool; restaurant; convention room; bilingual staff; business center; currency exchange; 24-hour kitchen; valet parking; lifesaver; 24-hour room service; pool and beach service; airport shuttle; shuttles to attractions and nearby cities.
www.everest.com.br
CREDIT CARDS AmEx; Diners; MasterCard; Visa

Fasano Hotel and Restaurant
Avenida Vieira Souto, 80, Ipanema
TEL (11) 3896-4000, 3896-4155
The Fasano Group, a brand of quality and sophistication in hospitality, was due to open a hotel in Ipanema in June 2007.

Hotel Glória $$$
Rua do Russel, 632, Glória
(Between Rua Silveira Martins and Praça Luís de Camões)
TEL (21) 2555-7272, 2555-7283 **FAX** (21) 2555-7283
A symbol of sophistication, Hotel Glória has beautifully decorated rooms, some with a view of Guanabara Bay. It has four restaurants, and overnight guests get free breakfast. The hotel also operates on a day-use system (6-hour period). **ACCOMMODATIONS** 610 rooms, of which 31 have facilities for the disabled and 284 are specially outfitted to be hypoallergenic, for guests with allergies. Rooms have Internet access (broadband); air-conditioning; bathroom; safe; mini bar; telephone; pay TV. **FACILITIES AND SERVICES** Internet access (broadband); bar; parking; shops; swimming pool; heated pool; restaurant; magazine stand; convention and sports facilities; masseuse; beauty salon; sauna; gardens; playground; gym; bilingual staff; business center; currency exchange; 24-hour kitchen; helipad; first aid service; lifesaver; 24-hour room service; shuttles to airport and attractions.
www.hotelgloriario.com.br
CREDIT CARDS AmEx; Diners; MasterCard; Visa

Hotel Novo Mundo $$
Praia do Flamengo, 20, Flamengo
(Corner of Rua Silveira Martins)
TEL (21) 2105-7000 **FAX** (21) 2265-2369. Reservations required
This hotel is close to Centro (Downtown Rio) and the Zona Sul (South Zone). The junior, executive, and presidential suites have views of Guanabara Bay, the Catete Palace gardens, and Sugarloaf Mountain. Room rates include breakfast. The hotel also operates on a day-use system (6-hour period). **ACCOMMODATIONS** 231 rooms, of which 3 have facilities for the disabled and 86 are hypoallergenic, for guests with allergies. Rooms have Internet access (broadband); air-conditioning; bathroom; safe; mini bar; telephone; pay TV. **FACILITIES AND SERVICES** Internet access (broadband; public computers available); bar; coffee shop; parking; TV room; beauty salon; gym; business center; currency exchange; 24-hour kitchen; valet parking.
www.hotelnovomundo-rio.com.br
CREDIT CARDS AmEx; Diners; MasterCard; Visa

Iberostar Copacabana $$$
Avenida Atlântica, 1020, Leme
(Corner of Avenida Princesa Isabel)
TEL (21) 3873-8888, 3873-8788 **RESERVATIONS** 0800-257171, 3873-8850 **FAX** (21) 3873-8777. Reservations required
The former Le Meridién is well-equipped for conventions, business visitors, and tourists. It had been closed for renovations but is due to reopen in December 2007. Rates do not include breakfast. The hotel also operates on a day-use system (up to 6 hours), for which advance reservations are recommended. **ACCOMMODATIONS** 496 rooms, of which 2 have facilities for the disabled. Rooms have Internet access (broadband wi-fi); air-conditioning; bathroom; safe; DVD player (in some); mini bar; hairdryer; telephone. **FACILITIES AND SERVICES** Internet access (broadband wi-fi; public computers available); wine cellar; bar; parking; convenience store; shops; heated pool; restaurant; magazine stand; convention rooms; masseuse; beauty salon; sauna; golf course (make reservations with the concierge); gym;

bilingual staff; business center; currency exchange; 24-hour kitchen; guides for walks; valet parking; first aid service; lifesaver; pool and beach service; airport shuttle; shuttles to attractions and nearby cities.
www.iberostar.com.br
CREDIT CARDS AmEx; Diners; MasterCard; Visa

Ipanema Plaza Hotel $$$
Rua Farme de Amoedo, 34, Ipanema
(Corner of Rua Prudente de Morais)
TEL (21) 3687-2000 FAX (21) 3687-2001
Just 165 feet from the beach, this exquisitely decorated boutique hotel offers highly personalized service. On the top floor is the Chez Pierre Bar e Bistrô, which specializes in contemporary cuisine. Rates include breakfast. The hotel also operates on a day-use system (12-hour period). ACCOMMODATIONS 140 rooms with Internet access (broadband, in some); air-conditioning; safe; DVD player (in the rooms on the Ipanema Floor); mini bar; Jacuzzi tub (in 3 suites); telephone; pay TV. FACILITIES AND SERVICES Internet access (broadband wi-fi; public computers available); bar; parking; swimming pool; restaurant; convention room; sauna; bicycles; gym; bilingual staff; business center; 24-hour kitchen; valet parking; lifesaver; 24-hour room service; pool and beach service; shuttles to airport and attractions.
www.ipanemaplazahotel.com
CREDIT CARDS AmEx; Diners; MasterCard; Visa

JW Marriott Hotel Rio de Janeiro $$$$
Avenida Atlântica, 2600, Copacabana
(Between Rua Santa Clara and Rua Figueiredo de Magalhães)
TEL (21) 2545-6500 FAX (21) 2545-6555. Reservations required
This hotel offers comfortable facilities and good service. The rooms have a view of either the beach or a sophisticated atrium. The hotel's Terraneo restaurant serves Mediterranean food, and the Taiyou Sushi & Sake Bar specializes in Japanese cuisine. ACCOMMODATIONS 245 rooms, of which 175 are non-smoking, and 2 have facilities for the disabled. Rooms have Internet access (broadband); air-conditioning; bathroom; safe; DVD player (in the executive rooms and suites); mini bar; hairdryer; telephone; pay TV. FACILITIES AND SERVICES Internet access (broadband); bar; parking; convenience store; shops; swimming pool; restaurant; magazine stand; convention facilities; masseuse; sauna; spa; gym; bilingual staff; business center; currency exchange; 24-hour kitchen; valet parking; pool and beach service; shuttles to airport and attractions.
www.marriottbrasil.com
CREDIT CARDS AmEx; Diners; MasterCard; Visa

La Maison $$$$
Rua Sérgio Porto, 58, Gávea
(Between Estrada da Gávea and Auto-Estrada Lagoa–Barra)
TEL (21) 3205-3585 FAX (21) 2540-0554. Reservations required
This tiny hotel operates out of a charming house with thematic decorations in the rooms. The communal areas have books on design, architecture and decoration for visitors to peruse. The dining room serves dishes that combine traditional French cooking with the flavors of Brazil. Rates include breakfast. ACCOMMODATIONS 5 rooms, with air-conditioning (in 2 suites); bathroom; pay TV. FACILITIES AND SERVICES Internet access (broadband; public computers available); bar; parking; swimming pool; masseuse; shuttles to airport and attractions.
CREDIT CARDS Not accepted

Lancaster Othon Travel $$
Avenida Atlântica, 1470, Copacabana
(Between Rua Duvivier and Rua Ronald de Carvalho)
TEL (21) 2169-8300 FAX (21) 2169-8300
This older hotel doesn't have many leisure facilities. The rooms are comfortable but no-frills. The service in the bar and restaurant is good and proper. The room rate includes breakfast. The hotel also operates on a day-use system (12-hour period). ACCOMMODATIONS 69 rooms, of which 6 are non-smoking and 2 have facilities for the disabled. Rooms have Internet access (broadband); air-conditioning; bathroom; safe; mini bar; telephone; pay TV. FACILITIES AND SERVICES Internet access (broadband wi-fi; public computers available); bar; restaurant; bilingual staff; business center; beach service; airport shuttle.
www.hoteis-othon.com.br
CREDIT CARDS AmEx; Diners; MasterCard; Visa

Mama Ruisa $$$
Rua Santa Cristina, 132, Santa Teresa
(Between Rua Cândido Mendes and Rua Almirante Alexandrino)
TEL (21) 2242-1281 FAX (21) 2210-0361. Reservations required
This mansion dates back to 1871 and is surrounded by greenery. Its balconies afford views of Sugarloaf Mountain. The large rooms are decorated with antiques found in Lapa. The room rate includes breakfast. ACCOMMODATIONS 7 rooms, with air-conditioning; bathroom; mini bar; telephone; pay TV. FACILITIES AND SERVICES Internet access (wi-fi; public computers available); bar; parking; swimming pool; masseuse; garden; bilingual staff; currency exchange; 24-hour kitchen; guides for walks; valet parking; airport shuttle.
www.mamaruisa.com
CREDIT CARDS AmEx; Visa

Marina All Suites $$$$
Avenida Delfim Moreira, 696, Leblon
(Between Rua General Urquisa and Rua Bartolomeu Mitri)
TEL (21) 2172-1100 RESERVATIONS (21) 2172-1001 FAX (21) 2172-1110. Reservations required
This is considered one of Rio's best hotels. Although it has few rooms, all of them have ocean views. The Bar

| HOTELS (couple) | $ up to R$150 | $$ from R$151 up to R$300 | $$$ from R$301 up to R$500 | $$$$ above R$500 |

D'Hotel restaurant serves French cuisine, while the Café D'Hotel serves quick meals. Rates do not include breakfast. ACCOMMODATIONS 38 rooms with Internet access (broadband wi-fi); air-conditioning; bathroom; safe; DVD player (in 1 suite); mini bar; Jacuzzi tub (in 4 suites); hairdryer; telephone; pay TV (1 suite has 2). FACILITIES AND SERVICES Internet access (broadband wi-fi; public computers available); bar; parking; swimming pool; restaurant; masseuse; meeting room; video room; sauna; gym; cell phone rental; bilingual staff; babysitter; business center; currency exchange; valet parking; first aid service; lifesaver; 24-hour room service; pool and beach service.
www.hoteismarina.com.br
CREDIT CARDS AmEx; Diners; MasterCard; Visa

Mercure Apt Arpoador $$
Rua Francisco Otaviano, 61, Arpoador
(Between Rua Raul Pompéia and Avenida Nossa Senhora de Copacabana)
TEL (21) 3222-9600 FAX (21) 3222-9605 OTHER LOCATIONS (1) Rua João Lira, 95, Leblon TEL (21) 2511-2442; (2) Rua Rainha Elizabeth, 440, Ipanema TEL (21) 3222-9100; (3) Rua Sorocaba, 305, Botafogo TEL (21) 2266-9200
There is no lack of bars, restaurants, and shopping centers near this hotel. Guests tend to be business travelers who want comfort at a reasonable price. Rates do not include breakfast. The hotel also operates on a day-use system (6-hour period). ACCOMMODATIONS 40 rooms, of which 35 are non-smoking. Rooms have Internet access (broadband); air-conditioning; bathroom; safe; DVD player; cooker; mini bar; microwave oven; hairdryer; telephone; pay TV. FACILITIES AND SERVICES Internet access (broadband wi-fi; public computers available); parking; swimming pool; sauna; gym; bilingual staff; business center; valet parking; beach service; shuttles to airport and attractions.
www.accorhotels.com.br
CREDIT CARDS AmEx; Diners; MasterCard; Visa

Ouro Verde Hotel $$$
Avenida Atlântica, 1456, Copacabana
(Between Rua Duvivier and Praça do Lido)
TEL (21) 2543-4123 FAX (21) 2543-4776
Operating out of a 1950s art deco building, this boutique hotel has 31 rooms with ocean views and other rooms with views of the Christ Statue that overlooks Rio and of the city's iconic Sugarloaf Mountain. There is an in-house restaurant, and breakfast is included in the room rate. The hotel also operates on a day-use system (6-hour period). ACCOMMODATIONS 64 rooms, of which 12 are non-smoking. Rooms have Internet access (dial-up); air-conditioning; bathroom; safe; mini bar; telephone; pay TV. FACILITIES AND SERVICES Internet access (broadband in the business center); bar; parking (nearby); restaurant; bilingual staff; business center; currency exchange; valet parking; beach service.
www.grandarrell.com.br/ouroverde/gouro.htm
CREDIT CARDS AmEx; Diners; MasterCard; Visa

Portinari Design Hotel $$$
Rua Francisco Sá, 17, Copacabana
(Between Rua Júlio de Caxias and Rua Souza Lima)
TEL (21) 3222 8800 FAX (21) 3222 8803
Each of the 11 floors has been decorated by a renowned Brazilian architect. The restaurant Brodowski offers a light, refined menu. Rates include breakfast. ACCOMMODATIONS 66 rooms, of which 12 are non-smoking, including 22 suites. Rooms have Internet access (broadband; suites contain computers for guests' use); air-conditioning; bathroom; safe; DVD player (in the suites); mini bar; hairdryer (in the suites); telephone; pay TV. FACILITIES AND SERVICES Internet access (broadband wi-fi); bar; parking; restaurant; convention room; sauna; spa with Jacuzzi, hydromassage tub, and waterfall; gym; bilingual staff; business center; currency exchange; 24-hour kitchen; valet parking; beach service; airport shuttle; shuttles to attractions and nearby cities.
www.hotelportinari.com.br
CREDIT CARDS AmEx; Diners; MasterCard; Visa

Relais Solar $$$
Ladeira do Meirelles, 32, Santa Teresa
(In front of Largo dos Guimarães, at the intersection with Rua Almirante Alexandrino)
TEL (21) 2221-2117 FAX (21) 2221-6679. Reservations required
This place is for those who want some peace and quiet. Operating out of a colonial building, its rooms are large and look onto a tropical garden. A showroom displays and sells arts and crafts and fashionable design objects. The restaurant Bistrô Solaris serves Brazilian dishes. Room rates include breakfast. ACCOMMODATIONS 5 rooms, all with Internet access (wi-fi, in the suites); air-conditioning; bathroom; safe; hairdryer; telephone; ceiling fan. FACILITIES AND SERVICES Internet access (broadband wi-fi; public computers available); video room; masseuse; garden; bilingual staff; business center; currency exchange; guides for walks; shuttles to airport and attractions.
www.solardesanta.com
CREDIT CARDS AmEx; Visa

Royal Rio Palace Hotel $$
Rua Duvivier, 82, Copacabana
(Between Rua Barata Ribeiro and Rua Ministro Viveiros de Castro)
TEL (21) 2122-9292 FAX (21) 2122-9293
Comfortable room contains modern décor. The top floor has views of the beach. The poolside bar serves good drinks and quick meals, while the restaurant serves Brazilian and international cuisine. The room rate includes breakfast. ACCOMMODATIONS 236 rooms, of which 30 are non-smoking and 2 can be adapted for disabled guests. Rooms have Internet access (broadband); air-conditioning; bathroom; safe; mini bar; Jacuzzi tub (in the 4 suites); hairdryer; telephone; pay TV. FACILITIES AND SERVICES Internet access (broadband); bar; parking; swimming pools; heated pool; sauna;

| PRICES | HOTELS (couple) | $ up to R$150 | $$ from R$151 up to R$300 | $$$ from R$301 up to R$500 | $$$$ above R$500 |

gym; travel agency; bilingual staff; currency exchange; 24-hour kitchen; valet parking; pool service; shuttles to airport and attractions.
www.royalrio.com
CREDIT CARDS AmEx; Diners; MasterCard; Visa

Sheraton Barra Hotel & Suites $$$$
Avenida Lúcio Costa, 3150, Barra da Tijuca
(Between Avenida Peregrino Junior and Rua Gastão Formenti)
TEL (21) 3139-8000 **FAX** (21) 3139-8085
All of the rooms have beach views. The restaurant Terral serves contemporary cuisine, with Mediterranean and Thai touches. Light meals are available in the Bar das Palmeiras. On Saturdays, there's live music or DJs in the lounge. On weekends, breakfast is included for all guests. **ACCOMMODATIONS** 292 rooms, of which 108 are non-smoking. Rooms have Internet access (broadband); DVD player (in the luxury suites); Jacuzzi tub (in the 96 suites); telephone; pay TV. **FACILITIES AND SERVICES** Internet access (wi-fi; public computers available); wine cellar; bar; parking; convenience store; shops; ofuro tub; heated pool; restaurant; magazine stand; convention facilities; masseuse; beauty salon; sauna; spa; garden; playground; squash court; gym; bilingual staff; babysitter; business center; currency exchange; 24-hour kitchen and room service; guides for walks; valet parking; first aid service; lifesaver; pool and beach service; shuttles to airport and attractions, including Barra Shopping.
www.sheraton-barra.com.br
CREDIT CARDS AmEx; Diners; MasterCard; Visa

Sheraton Rio Hotel & Towers $$$$
Avenida Niemeyer, 121, Leblon
(Near Avenida Visconde de Albuquerque and Praça Rubem Dário)
TEL (21) 2274-1122 **FAX** (21) 2239-5643
This enormous sea-front hotel has a large leisure area, and rooms have balconies with panoramic views. The three restaurants serve contemporary and Latin American cuisine. Free transport is provided to Leblon, Ipanema, and Copacabana beaches, as well as Shopping Rio Sul. The hotel also operates on a day-use system (8am – 6pm). **ACCOMMODATIONS** 559 rooms, of which 240 are non-smoking and 2 have facilities for the handicapped. Rooms have Internet access (dial-up and broadband); air-conditioning; bathroom; safe; mini bar; hairdryer; telephone; pay TV. **FACILITIES AND SERVICES** Internet access (broadband wi-fi; public computers available); bar; children's nursery; parking; convenience store; shops; restaurant; magazine stand; convention room; games room; masseuse; spa; tennis court; gym; cell phone rental; bilingual staff; business center; currency exchange; 24-hour kitchen and room service; babysitters; recreational activities for children; valet parking; first aid service; lifesaver; pool and beach service; shuttles to airport and attractions.
www.sheraton.com/rio
CREDIT CARDS AmEx; Diners; MasterCard; Visa

Sofitel Rio de Janeiro $$$$
Avenida Atlântica, 4240, Copacabana
(Between Rua Joaquim Nabuco and Rua Francisco Otaviano)
TEL (21) 2525-1232 **FAX** (21) 2525-1200
The rooms have balconies and beach views. Next to the hotel, the Shopping Cassino Atlântico has antiques shops and art galleries, and even holds art auctions. The restaurant Le Pré Catelan serves a French menu, while the Atlantis has a range of buffets and also serves traditional Brazilian *feijoada* (a pork-and-bean stew) on Saturdays. The hotel also operates on a day-use system. **ACCOMMODATIONS** 388 rooms, of which 112 are non-smoking and 5 have facilities for the disabled. Rooms have Internet access (broadband); air-conditioning; bathroom; safe; mini bar; telephone; pay TV. **FACILITIES AND SERVICES** Internet access (broadband); bar; library; coffeeshop; convenience store; magazine stand; parking; Jacuzzi tub; swimming pool; restaurant; convention facilities; masseuse; sauna; boat; bicycles; golf course; jet-skis; motorboat; scuba diving (make reservations with the concierge); gym; travel agency; bilingual staff; babysitter; business center; currency exchange; laundry; car rental; valet parking; first aid service; lifesaver; pool and beach service; airport shuttle.
www.accorhotels.com.br
CREDIT CARDS AmEx; Diners; MasterCard; Visa

| HOTELS (couple) | $ up to R$150 | $$ from R$151 up to R$300 | $$$ from R$301 up to R$500 | $$$$ above R$500 |

RESTAURANTS BY NEIGHBORHOOD

Arpoador
Azul Marinho

Barra da Tijuca
Barril 8000
Borsalino
Candy Delicatessen
Enotria
La Botticella
Na Pressão
Rosita Café
Shenanigan's
Surf Adventures

Barra de Guaratiba
Bira
Tia Palmira

Botafogo
Adega do Valentim
Carême Bistrô
Champanheria Ovelha Negra
Mentha
Miam Miam
Museu da Cadeira
Yorubá

Centro
Albamar
Atrium
Bar do Zé
Bar Luiz
Beco do Carmo
Cais do Oriente
Casa Cavé
Casa Paladino
Confeitaria Colombo
Eça
Escondidinho
Oásis
Penafiel
Rio Minho

Cinelândia
Amarelinho

Copacabana
Adega Pérola
Alfaia
Amir
Azumi

Bip Bip
Cais da Ribeira
Caranguejo
Cervantes
Cipriani
Copa Café
Kicê Sucos
Le Pré Catelan
A Marisqueira
Pérgula
Siri Mole & Cia
The Bakers
Traiteurs de France

Engenho de Dentro
Manoel & Juaquim

Flamengo
Alcaparra
Barracuda
Belmonte
Laguiole
Lamas
Majórica

Gávea
00
Bacalhau do Rei
Braseiro da Gávea
Chez Anne
Guimas
Hipódromo

Ipanema
Alessandro & Frederico Café
Armazém do Café
B!
Bofetada
Capricciosa
Casa da Feijoada
Delírio Tropical
Esplanada Grill
Expand Wine Bar
Forneria
Gero
Gula Gula
Margutta
Mil Frutas Café
Milano DOC
Olivier Cozan

Osteria Dell'Angolo
Polis Sucos
Porcão
Satyricon
Sorvete Itália
Sorvetes Chaika
Ten Kai
Terzetto
Zazá Bistrô Tropical

Jardim Botânico
66 Bistrô
Bistrô Itália
Café du Lage
Café Sudbrack
Caroline Café
Da Graça
Filé de Ouro
Maçã Café
Mil Frutas
Olympe
Quadrifoglio
Roberta Sudbrack
Yumê

Lagoa
Bar Lagoa
Escola do Pão
Mr. Lam

Lapa
Bar Brasil
Carioca da Gema
Comuna do Semente
Mangue Seco
Rio Scenarium

Laranjeiras
Bar do Serafim

Leblon
Academia da Cachaça
Álvaro's
Antiquarius
Ateliê Culinário
Balada Sumos
Bar Devassa
Bibi Sucos
Botequim Informal
Bracarense
Café Severino
Carlota

Celeiro
Colher de Pau
Conversa Fiada
Degrau
Garcia & Rodrigues
Jobi
Juice & Co.
Küpper
Kurt
La Cigale
Nam Thai
Pizzaria Guanabara
Plataforma
Sushi Leblon
Talho Capixaba
Zuka

Leme
D'Amici
Da Brambini
La Fiorentina
Marius Crustáceos
Shirley

Pedra de Guaratiba
476

Santa Teresa
Adega do Pimenta
Alda Maria Doces Portugueses
Aprazível
Bar do Arnaudo
Espírito Santa
Simplesmente
Sobrenatural

São Conrado
Alfredo di Roma
Joe & Leo's
Torta & Cia.

São Cristóvão
Adegão Português
Quinta da Boa Vista

Urca
Bar e Restaurante Urca

Vargem Grande
Quinta

RESTAURANTS BY CUISINE TYPE

Appetizers
Academia da Cachaça
Amarelinho
Bar Brasil
Bar Devassa
Bar do Serafim
Bar do Zé
Bar Lagoa
Bar Luiz
Barril 8000
Belmonte
Bip Bip
Bira
Bofetada
Botequim Informal
Bracarense
Carioca da Gema
Cervantes
Comuna do Semente
Conversa Fiada
Jobi
Na Pressão
Rio Scenarium
Simplesmente

Arabic
Amir

Brazilian
Academia da Cachaça
Amarelinho
Bar do Arnaudo
Bar do Serafim
Bar do Zé
Bip Bip
Bofetada
Carioca da Gema
Casa da Feijoada
Espírito Santa
Guimas
Jobi
Filé de Ouro
Lamas
Pérgula
Quinta
Siri Mole & Cia.
Sobrenatural
Yorubá

Breads
Escola do Pão
Talho Capixaba

Chinese
Mr. Lam

Contemporary
Aprazível
Atrium
B!
Café Sudbrack
Carême Bistrô
Carlota
Caroline Café
Copa Café
Da Graça
Eça
Laguiole
Mentha
Na Pressão
Pérgula
Quinta

Roberta Sudbrack
Terzetto
Zazá Bistrô Tropical
00
Zuka

French
Bistrô Itália
Café du Lage
Carême Bistrô
Escola do Pão
Guimas
La Cigale
Laguiole
Le Pré Catelan
Museu da Cadeira
Olivier Cozan
Olympe
66 Bistrô
Traiteurs de France

German
Adega do Pimenta
Bar Brasil
Bar Lagoa
Bar Luiz

Ice Cream
Mil Frutas
Mil Frutas Café
Sorvete Itália
Sorvetes Chaika

Italian
Alfredo di Roma
Beco do Carmo
Bistrô Itália
Borsalino
Cipriani
D'Amici
Da Brambini
Enotria
Forneria
Gero
La Botticella
La Fiorentina
Margutta
Milano DOC
Osteria Dell'Angolo
Quadrifoglio
Satyricon
Terzetto

Japanese
Azumi
Sushi Leblon
Ten Kai
Yumê
00

Juices
Balada Sumos
Bibi Sucos
Juice Co.
Kicê Sucos
Polis Sucos

Meats and Barbecue
Braseiro da Gávea
Esplanada Grill
Filé de Ouro

Hipódromo
La Cigale
Majórica
Manoel & Juaquim
Oásis
Plataforma
Porcão

Pizza
Capricciosa
Hipódromo
Manoel & Juaquim
Milano DOC
Pizzaria Guanabara
Surf Adventures

Portuguese
Adega do Valentim
Adega Pérola
Adegão Português
Alfaia
Antiquarius
Bacalhau do Rei
Barracuda
Cais da Ribeira
Candy Delicatessen
Jobi
A Marisqueira
Penafiel

Salads
Celeiro
Delírio Tropical
Maçã Café
Mil Frutas Café

Sandwiches
Alessandro & Frederico Café
Balada Sumos
Café du Lage
Café Sudbrack
Casa Paladino
Cervantes
Champanheria Ovelha Negra
Comuna do Semente
Confeitaria Colombo
Conversa Fiada
Copa Café
Delírio Tropical
Joe & Leo's
Juice Co.
Kicê Sucos
Küpper
Maçã Café
Mil Frutas Café
Polis Sucos
Rosita Café
Surf Adventures
Talho Capixaba
The Bakers

Sea Food
Adega Pérola
Albamar
Alcaparra
Azul Marinho
Bar e Restaurante Urca
Barracuda
Beco do Carmo
Bira
Caranguejo

Majórica
Mangue Seco
Manoel & Juaquim
Marius Crustáceos
Milano DOC
476
Rio Minho
Satyricon
Sobrenatural
Tia Palmira

Spanish
Shirley

Sweet and Savory Snacks
Alessandro & Frederico Café
Armazém do Café
Ateliê Culinário
B!
Café Severino
Chez Anne
Colher de Pau
Maçã Café
Museu da Cadeira

Sweets and Cakes
Alda Maria Doces Portugueses
Armazém do Café
Ateliê Culinário
Casa Cavé
Chez Anne
Colher de Pau
Kurt
The Bakers
Torta & Cia.

Thai
Nam Thai

Varied
Álvaro's
Atrium
Bar Devassa
Barril 8000
Belmonte
Botequim Informal
Cais do Oriente
Cervantes
Confeitaria Colombo
D'Amici
Da Graça
Degrau
Escondidinho
Expand Wine Bar
Garcia & Rodrigues
Gula Gula
La Cigale
La Fiorentina
Maçã Café
Manoel & Juaquim
Mentha
Miam Miam
Plataforma
Quinta da Boa Vista
Rio Scenarium
Rosita Café
Shenanigan's
Surf Adventures
Traiteurs de France

Hotels, Restaurants, and Services

WHERE TO EAT

00 $$
Avenida Padre Leonel Franca, 240, Gávea
(Between Rua General Álcio Souto and Rua Doutor Alberto Gonçalves)
TEL (21) 2540-8041. Thu – Sun, 8:30pm – 3am
CUISINE Contemporary; Japanese. Inside the Planetário da Gávea, this bar and restaurant serves such dishes as grilled filet steak with *mandioquinha* (a type of parsnip) purée, plantain tempura and wasabi. Theater and short film screenings are held here on weekends. DJs and bands liven up the atmosphere after 10pm on the weekend *(see Nightclubs, page 229)*
CREDIT CARDS AmEx; Diners; MasterCard; Visa

66 Bistrô $$
Avenida Alexandre Ferreira, 66, Jardim Botânico
(Between Rua Jardim Botânico and Rua Borges Medeiros)
TEL (21) 2266-0838. Tue – Fri, noon – 4pm and 7:30 until the last customer leaves; Sat, noon – 6pm and 7:30pm until the last customer leaves; Sun, noon – 6pm. Reservations recommended
CUISINE French chef Claude Troisgros changes his recipes every three months. Lunch is buffet-style (salads, grills, and dessert). At night, service is à la carte. Rack of lamb is a popular choice.
CREDIT CARDS MasterCard; Visa

476 $$$
Rua Barros Alarcão, 476, Pedra de Guaratiba
(Almost on the corner of Rua Saião Lobato)
TEL (21) 2417-1716. Wed – Fri, 11:30am – 6pm; Sat and Sun, 11:30am – 7pm **ALSO AT** Ilha da Coroa, 20, Barra da Tijuca **TEL** (21) 2493-4444
CUISINE Seafood; fish. Overlooking the lovely coastal strip known as Restinga de Marambaia, this is an excellent spot to relax far from the city center. Try a fruit cocktail and a shrimp *pastel* (deep-fried pastry). For a main course, choose shrimp curry with mango chutney, sweet-sour pickles, peanuts, banana, and egg salad.
CREDIT CARDS AmEx; Diners; MasterCard; Visa

Academia da Cachaça $$
Rua Conde Bernadote, 26, store G, Leblon
(Between Rua Bartolomeu Mitre and Rua José Linhares)
TEL (21) 2239-1542. Sun – Thu, noon – 1am; Fri and Sat, noon – 3am **ALSO AT** Shopping Condado de Cascais: Rua Armando Lombardi, 800, store L, Barra da Tijuca **TEL** (21) 2492-1159
CUISINE Brazilian; northeastern regional. As the name suggests, this "academy" specializes in the white rum known as *cachaça* – it offers about seventy kinds in all – as well as *caipirinhas*, which are made with *cachaça*, and fruit cocktails. To accompany your drinks, try the *escondidinho* (shredded beef jerky topped with manioc purée) and the traditional *feijoada* (pork-and-bean stew).
CREDIT CARDS Diners; MasterCard; Visa

Adega do Pimenta $$
Rua Almirante Alexandrino, 296, Santa Teresa
(Between Rua Bernardino dos Santos and Rua André Cavalcanti)
TEL (21) 2224-7554. Mon – Fri, 11:30am – 10pm; Sat, 11:30am – 8pm; Sun and holidays, 11:30am – 6pm. Reservations recommended. **ALSO AT** Espaço Cultural Leblon: Rua Conde Bernadote, 26, store D, Leblon **TEL** (21) 2229-9673; Estrada União e Indústria, 11811, Itaipava (Petrópolis) **TEL** (24) 2222-3252
CUISINE German. This restaurant is in the artsy Santa Teresa neighborhood. House specialties are German delicacies such as *eisbein* (pork knuckle), with sauerkraut and several kinds of sausage. The waiters' rudeness is legendary, but it doesn't deter regulars.
CREDIT CARDS Visa

Adega do Valentim $$$
Rua da Passagem, 176-8, Botafogo
(Between Rua Arnaldo Quintela and Rua Álvaro Ramos. The beginning of Rua General Góis Monteiro)
TEL (21) 2295-2748. Mon – Sat, noon – 1am; Sun, noon – midnight
CUISINE Portuguese. Specializing in cod, this restaurant offers eighteen variations on that fish, all served in generous portions. The menu also includes such options as kid, suckling pig, rump of lamb, squid, octopus and sardines. Portuguese desserts round off the meal.
CREDIT CARDS AmEx; Diners; MasterCard; Visa

Adega Pérola $$
Rua Siqueira Campos, 138, Copacabana
(Between Rua Figueiredo Magalhães and Ladeira dos Tabajaras)
TEL (21) 2255-9425. Mon – Sat, 10am – midnight
CUISINE Seafood; Portuguese. Opened in 1958, this restaurant used to be the haunt of artists and audiences from the Tereza Raquel and Opinião theaters. The communal tables give it a relaxed air. The appetizer counter offers fish, eggplant and fava beans.
CREDIT CARDS AmEx; Diners; MasterCard; Visa

Adegão Português $$$
Rua Campo de São Cristóvão, 212, São Cristóvão
(On the corner of Rua Senador Alencar)
TEL (21) 2580-7288, 2580-8689. Mon – Sat, 11am – 11pm; Sun, 11am – 8pm **ALSO AT** Shopping Rio Design: Avenida das Américas, 7777, stores 337-343, Barra da Tijuca **TEL** (21) 2431-2958
CUISINE Portuguese; fish. A classic in the North Zone, this restaurant takes cod seriously. The list of cod dishes, which are more than generously served, is almost endless.
CREDIT CARDS AmEx; Diners; MasterCard; Visa

Albamar $$
Praça Marechal Âncora, 184, Centro
(Between Rua Cais Pharoux and Avenida Alfred Agache, near Praça Quinze)
TEL (21) 2240-8428. Daily, 11:30am – 6pm
CUISINE Seafood; fish. Operating in the surviving tower of

| PRICES | RESTAURANTS | $ up to R$25 | $$ from R$26 up to R$50 | $$$ from R$51 up to R$100 | $$$$ above R$100 |

the old municipal market in Praça Quinze, this is one of the most storied fish restaurants in Rio. Portions are very generous. Try the caviar, a rarity in other local restaurants.
CREDIT CARDS AmEx; Diners; MasterCard; Visa

Alcaparra $$$
Praia do Flamengo, 150, Flamengo
(On the corner of Rua Buarque de Macedo)
TEL (21) 2557-7236, 2557-6271. Daily, noon – 1am
CUISINE Seafood; fish. The menu favors shellfish and fish, for example, grilled codfish with onions, boiled potatoes and broccoli, or grilled trout in almond sauce with boiled potatoes. There are more than twenty dessert options.
CREDIT CARDS AmEx; Diners; MasterCard; Visa

Alda Maria Doces Portugueses $
Rua Almirante Alexandrino, 1116, Santa Teresa
(On the corner of Rua Áurea)
TEL (21) 2232-1320, 2242-3110. Tue – Sun, 2pm – 8pm
CUISINE Portuguese sweets. Friendly Alda Maria sells delicious homemade delights from her own home, using the recipes her Portuguese grandmother taught her. *Dom-Rodrigo* (a sweet treat made with almonds and egg custard) and tamarind-and-almond sweets are the most popular.
CREDIT CARDS Not accepted

Alessandro & Frederico Café $
Rua Garcia d'Ávila, 134, Ipanema
(Between Rua Redentor and Rua Visconde de Pirajá)
TEL (21) 2521-0828. Daily, 9am – 2am
CUISINE Coffee; fast food; sandwiches. More than twenty kinds of sandwiches are prepared using homemade bread, including the tasty "Ana Paula" (apricot and brie with Parma ham). They also serve quiches, pasta and salads, as well as breakfast at any time, from 9am – 2am.
CREDIT CARDS AmEx; Diners; MasterCard; Visa

Alfaia $$$
Rua Inhangá, 30, store B, Copacabana
(Between Rua Barata Ribeiro and Rua Nossa Senhora de Copacabana)
TEL (21) 2236-1222. Mon – Fri, noon – midnight; Sun, noon – 11pm
CUISINE Portuguese. The most famous dish is *bacalhau à patuscada* (codfish cutlet, quartered and browned in olive oil, served with broccoli, potatoes and boiled eggs). Round off your meal with a delicious *pastel de nata* (custard tart).
CREDIT CARDS AmEx; Diners; MasterCard; Visa

Alfredo di Roma $$
Avenida Prefeito Mendes de Morais, 222 (Hotel Intercontinental), São Conrado
(Between Avenida Aquarela do Brasil and the access road to Avenida Niemeyer)
TEL (21) 3323-2200. Daily, 7pm – 11:30pm
CUISINE Italian. This elegant restaurant serves delicious recipes, such as fettuccine Alfredo, using hand-made pasta, with butter and Grana Padano cheese sauce. The meat and seafood dishes are also good.
CREDIT CARDS AmEx; Diners; MasterCard; Visa

Álvaro's $
Avenida Ataulfo de Paiva, 500, Leblon
(On the corner of Rua Cupertino Durão)
TEL (21) 2294-2148. Daily, noon – 2am
CUISINE Varied. This traditional restaurant serves highly praised *pastéis* (deep-fried pastries). Choose from shrimp, cheese, beef, cheese and onion, heart of palm, and *catupiry* cream cheese. The grilled octopus is a highlights, as are the codfish and the daily specials. Portions are all generous. A good choice for happy hour.
CREDIT CARDS AmEx; Diners; MasterCard; Visa

Amarelinho $
Praça Floriano, 55-B, Centro
(On the corner of Avenida Rio Branco)
TEL (21) 2240-8434. Daily, 10am – 2am ALSO AT Ladeira da Glória, 8, Glória TEL (21) 2558-3502
CUISINE Brazilian. This unpretentious bar has been a local institution since 1920. It serves full *feijoada* and many other dishes, but the biggest appeal by far is its long history.
CREDIT CARDS AmEx; Diners; MasterCard; Visa

Amir $$
Rua Ronald de Carvalho, 55, store C, Copacabana
(Opposite Praça do Lido)
TEL (21) 2275-5596. Mon – Sun, noon – midnight
CUISINE Arabic. One of the best Lebanese restaurants and it has a varied and reasonably priced menu. The long list of typical dishes includes hummus, falafel, *mishwe* (grilled meats), *esfiha* (savory pastries), *kofta*, *kibbeh*. They serve Moroccan couscous on weekends.
CREDIT CARDS AmEx; Diners; MasterCard; Visa

Antiquarius $$$
Rua Aristides Espínola, 19, Leblon
(Between Avenida General San Martin and Avenida Delfim Moreira)
TEL (21) 2294-1049, 2294-1496. Daily, noon – 2am
CUISINE Portuguese. The mezzanine is a waiting room-cum-antique store. This restaurant serves delicious Portuguese food, including its own versions of the revered codfish and its highly praised *arroz de pato* (duck with rice).
CREDIT CARDS Diners; MasterCard

Aprazível $$$
Rua Aprazível, 62, Santa Teresa
(Parallel to Rua Almirante Alexandrino)
TEL (21) 2508-9174, 3852-4935. Thu – Sat, noon – 1am; Sun and holidays, 1pm – 7:30pm
CUISINE Contemporary. With a magnificent view of the city, this restaurant serves modern dishes with traditional Brazilian ingredients, such as tropical fish, grilled and served in orange sauce, with coconut rice and roasted plantain.
CREDIT CARDS AmEx; Diners; MasterCard; Visa

RESTAURANTS $ up to R$25 $$ from R$26 up to R$50 $$$ from R$51 up to R$100 $$$$ above R$100

HOTELS, RESTAURANTS, AND SERVICES

Armazém do Café $
Rua Maria Quitéria, 77-G, Ipanema
(Opposite Praça Nossa Senhora da Paz)
TEL (21) 2522-5039. Mon – Fri, 8:30am – 8pm; Sat, 9am – 6pm ALSO AT Rua Visconde de Pirajá, 261, Ipanema TEL (21) 2287-5742; Rua Rita Ludolf, 87-B, Leblon TEL (21) 2259-0170; Rua do Ouvidor, 77, Centro TEL (21) 2242-5173.
CUISINE Coffee; sweets and cakes. This café takes coffee seriously, offering an extensive selection of fine beans. It also serves waffles, croissants, toast, *pastéis* (deep-fried pastries), brownies, and ice cream. Accessories such as coffeepots, kettles, cups, and even cigars and books are also for sale.
CREDIT CARDS AmEx; Diners; MasterCard; Visa

Ateliê Culinário $
Rua Dias Ferreira, 45, store A, Leblon
(Between Rua Aristides Espínola and Avenida Ataulfo de Paiva)
TEL (21) 2239-2825, 2529-6856. Mon – Thu, noon – 11pm; Fri, noon – 1am; Sat, 10am – 1am; Sun, 10am – 11pm ALSO AT Cine Estação Ipanema: Rua Visconde de Pirajá, 605, store 0, Ipanema TEL (21) 2279-4709; Cine Estação Botafogo: Rua Voluntários da Pátria, 88, Botafogo TEL (21) 2226-1989; Cine Odeon: Praça Floriano, 7, Cinelândia TEL (21) 2240-2573. Two further branches
CUISINE Fast food; sweet and savory snacks. They serve excellent savories, including oven-baked pastries, mini-quiches, sandwiches, and hot dishes. The most popular desserts are cheesecake, pecan pie, and tiramisu.
CREDIT CARDS Visa

Atrium $$$
Praça Quinze, 48, Centro
(Between Rua Primeiro de Março and Rua da Assembléia)
TEL (21) 2220-0193/3282. Mon – Fri, 11:30am – 3:30pm
CUISINE Contemporary; varied. We suggest the mushroom risotto with fillet steak strips or beef medallion in Madeira sauce with asparagus risotto. Or the pear au gratin. You can't go wrong with either.
CREDIT CARDS AmEx; Diners; MasterCard; Visa

Azul Marinho $$$
Avenida Francisco Otaviano, 177
(Hotel Arpoador Inn), Arpoador
(Between Rua Francisco Bhering and Rua Joaquim Nabuco)
TEL 2513-5014. Daily, 7am – 10:30am and noon until the last customer leaves.
CUISINE Seafood; fish. Choose from *moqueca azul-marinho*, a seafood stew with squid, shrimp, fish and octopus, or *camarão na moranga* (shrimp served in a pumpkin shell). The sidewalk tables overlook Arpoador Beach. Breakfast is also served.
CREDIT CARDS AmEx; Diners; MasterCard; Visa

Azumi $$
Rua Ministro Viveiros de Castro, 127, Copacabana
(Between Rua Rodolfo Dantas and Rua Ronald de Carvalho)
TEL (21) 2541-4294, 2295-1098. Tue – Thu and Sun, 7pm – midnight; Fri and Sat, 7pm – 1am
CUISINE Japanese. They serve excellent sushi and unusual hot dishes. Highlights are the breaded oysters and shrimp gyoza. Ask about the daily special, which usually isn't mentioned in the menu.
CREDIT CARDS AmEx; Visa

B! $$
Rua Visconde de Pirajá, 572, Ipanema
(Between Avenida Henrique Dumont and Rua Aníbal de Mendonça)
TEL 2249-4977. Tue – Sat, 10am – midnight; Sun and Mon, noon – midnight
CUISINE Contemporary; sweet and savory snacks. On the mezzanine floor of the bookstore Livraria da Travessa, they serve breakfast, grills, quick meals, as well as sandwiches and sweet snacks.
CREDIT CARDS AmEx; Diners; MasterCard; Visa

Bacalhau do Rei $
Rua Marquês de São Vicente, 11-A, Gávea
(Between Praça Santos Dumont and Rua Artur Araripe)
TEL (21) 2239-8945. Mon – Thu, 8:30am – 1am; Fri and Sat, 8:30am – 2am; Sun, 8:30am – 10pm
CUISINE Portuguese. This bar serves fantastic shrimp pastries and codfish cakes. Try a well-pulled draft beer to go with them.
CREDIT CARDS AmEx; Visa

Balada Sumos $
Avenida Ataulfo de Paiva, 620, store A, Leblon
(Between Rua João Lira and Rua José Linhares)
TEL (21) 2239-2699. Sun – Thu, 7am – 2am; Fri and Sat, 7am – 3am
CUISINE Sandwiches; juices. The most popular juices are orange with eggplant, *fruta-do-conde* (sugar-apple), tangerine, and strawberry with vanilla ice cream. Try their fillet steak and cheese sandwich.
CREDIT CARDS MasterCard

Bar Brasil $$
Avenida Mem de Sá, 90, Lapa
(On the corner of Rua do Lavradio)
TEL (21) 2509-5943. Mon – Wed, 11:30am – 11pm; Thu and Fri, 11:30am – midnight; Sat, 11:30am – 6pm
CUISINE German. This place is known for its *chope* (draft beer), which can be accompanied by such German dishes as *kassler à mineira* (smoked pork loin served with bean purée, rice and collard greens).
CREDIT CARDS Diners; MasterCard; Visa

Bar Devassa $
Avenida General San Martin, 1241, Leblon
(Between Rua Rita Ludolf and Praça Atahualpa)
TEL (21) 2540-6087. Mon – Thu, 5pm – 2am; Fri, 5pm – 3am; Sat, 2pm – 3am; Sun, 2pm – 1am. ALSO AT Rua Senador Vergueiro, 2, stores B and C, Flamengo TEL (21) 2556-0618; Avenida Lineu de Paula Machado, 696, Jardim Botânico TEL (21) 2274-1513.

| PRICES | RESTAURANTS | $ up to R$25 | $$ from R$26 up to R$50 | $$$ from R$51 up to R$100 | $$$$ above R$100 |

CUISINE Varied. The main attraction here is the traditionally brewed *chope* (draft beer), which comes in four styles: loura (blonde), ruiva (red), negra (black), and mulata (brunette). The menu offers meat dishes, seafood, fish, and appetizers. The dining room gets very crowded.
CREDIT CARDS AmEx; Diners; MasterCard

Bar do Arnaudo $$
Rua Almirante Alexandrino, 316-B, Santa Teresa
(Between Rua André Cavalcanti and Rua Bernardino dos Santos)
TEL (21) 2252-7246. Mon, noon – 6pm; Tue – Fri, noon – 11pm; Sat and Sun, noon – 9pm
CUISINE Northeastern Brazilian. The standard for northeastern cooking in Rio, this restaurant serves that region's classic sun-dried beef with manioc, black-eyed peas, curd cheese and pumpkin.
CREDIT CARDS Diners; MasterCard; Visa

Bar do Serafim $$
Rua Alice, 24, Laranjeiras
(On the corner of Rua das Laranjeiras)
TEL (21) 2225-2843, 2205-5951. Daily, 11am – midnight
CUISINE Brazilian; Portuguese. This bar has an informal, welcoming atmosphere. The house specialty is codfish *à trasmontana*, but they also serve a delicious *rabada* (oxtail).
CREDIT CARDS AmEx; Diners; MasterCard; Visa

Bar do Zé $
Rua do Carmo, 38, Centro
(On the corner of Rua Sete de Setembro)
TEL (21) 2517-3587. Mon – Fri, noon until the last customer leaves
CUISINE Brazilian. One of the owners, José Antônio Esteves (nicknamed Zé), honors his namesakes with photos and illustrations of anonymous and famous Josés who went by "Zé." They serve their popular *feijoada* on Fridays.
CREDIT CARDS AmEx; Visa

Bar e Restaurante Urca $$$
Rua Cândido Gaffrée, 205, Urca
(Between Rua Otávio Correia and Avenida São Sebastião)
TEL (21) 2295-8744. Tue – Sat, 11am – 11pm; Sun, 11am – 7pm
CUISINE Seafood; fish. The most traditional bar in Urca has informal, sea-themed décor and serves fresh fish, for example, *moqueca baiana* and *lula espanhola* (Spanish-style squid).
CREDIT CARDS Diners; MasterCard; Visa

Bar Lagoa $$
Avenida Epitácio Pessoa, 1674, Lagoa
(Between Rua Joana Angélica and Rua Vinicius de Moraes)
TEL (21) 2523-1135. Mon, 6pm – 2am; Tue – Sun, noon – 2am
CUISINE German. Inside a lovely art deco building with high ceilings, this bar is known for its draft beer. It serves German dishes, as well as other options like grilled *badejo* (grouper) with vegetables and breaded fillet steak.
CREDIT CARDS AmEx; Diners; MasterCard; Visa

Bar Luiz $
Rua da Carioca, 39, Centro
(Between Rua Ramalho Ortigão and Avenida República do Paraguai)
TEL (21) 2262-6900. Mon – Sat, 11am – 11:30pm; Sun, 11am – 5pm ALSO AT the kiosk in front of the Copacabana Palace Hotel: Avenida Atlântica, deck 10 TEL (21) 8702-3078
CUISINE German. Among the city's most famous drafthouses, Bar Luiz serves special *chope* (draft beer) and German food. Try breaded beef, frankfurter with salad or potatoes and *eisbein* (pork knuckle).
CREDIT CARDS AmEx; Diners; MasterCard; Visa

Barracuda $$$$
Avenida Infante Dom Henrique, no #,
Aterro do Flamengo
(Inside Glória Marina)
TEL (21) 2205-3346, 2265-4641. Mon – Sat, noon – midnight; Sun, noon – 6pm
CUISINE Seafood; Portuguese. In front of Hotel Glória, with a lovely view of the excursion boats. House specialties are fish and seafood, especially baked codfish. Try the Portuguese desserts.
CREDIT CARDS AmEx; Diners; MasterCard; Visa

Barril 8000 $$
Avenida Sernambetiba (Lúcio Costa), 8000,
Barra da Tijuca
(On Barra da Tijuca beach, after Posto 8)
TEL (21) 2433-1730. Mon – Wed, 11am – 2am; Thu – Sun, 11am – 4am ALSO AT Shopping Downtown: Avenida das Américas, 500, block 6, stores 105-107, Barra da Tijuca TEL (21) 3153-7740; Shopping Condado de Cascais: Avenida Armando Lombardi, 800, stores A/B, Barra da Tijuca TEL (21) 2494-8214
CUISINE Varied. At night the young customers enjoy the samba shows. To accompany the Brahma draft beer, order rosti potatoes with either bacon and onion or the four-cheese topping.
CREDIT CARDS AmEx; Diners; MasterCard; Visa

Beco do Carmo $$$
Rua do Carmo, 55, Centro
(Between Rua do Ouvidor and Rua Sete de Setembro)
TEL (21) 2508-9400. Mon – Fri, noon – 5pm
CUISINE Seafood, Mediterranean, fish. Nicely positioned tables and Mediterranean-inspired dishes. Special mention for the *cavaquinha magistrale*, which is a type of lobster in pineapple and leek sauce, served with Grana Padano cheese risotto.
CREDIT CARDS AmEx; Diners; MasterCard; Visa

Belmonte $
Praia do Flamengo, 300, Flamengo
(Between Rua Tucumã and Rua Cruz Lima)

RESTAURANTS $ up to R$25 $$ from R$26 up to R$50 $$$ from R$51 up to R$100 $$$$ above R$100

TEL (21) 2552-3349. Daily, 8am – 3am **ALSO AT** Rua Jardim Botânico, 117, Jardim Botânico TEL (21) 2239-1649; Rua Dias Ferreira, 521, Leblon TEL (21) 2294-2849; Rua Teixeira de Melo, 53-B, Ipanema TEL (21) 2267-9909; Rua Domingos Ferreira, 242, Copacabana TEL (21) 2555-9696; Rua do Lavradio, 116, Lapa TEL (21) 2507-2807
CUISINE Varied. The main branch of this chain of bars has a faithful clientele. Among the appetizers they serve, the specialty is the *pastel de carne seca* (deep-fried pastry filled with shredded beef), ideally accompanied by a Brahma *chope* (draft beer). They also have about 30 *cachaças* from the state of Minas Gerais.
CREDIT CARDS Not accepted

Bibi Sucos $
Avenida Ataulfo de Paiva, 591-A, Leblon
(On the corner of Rua José Linhares)
TEL (21) 2259-4298. Sun – Thu, 8am – 2am; Fri and Sat, 8am – 3am **ALSO AT** Rua Jardim Botânico, 632-A, Jardim Botânico TEL (21) 3874-0051; Rua Miguel Lemos, 31, store A, Copacabana TEL (21) 2513-6000
CUISINE Juices. A good spot for a refreshing drink after the beach or on a hot night out. More than thirty varieties include strawberry with yogurt, *cajá* fruit, orange with cacao, and red fruits. They also have sandwiches.
CREDIT CARDS AmEx; Diners; MasterCard; Visa

Bip Bip $
Rua Almirante Gonçalves, 50, store D, Copacabana
(Between Rua Djalma Ulrich and Rua Sá Ferreira)
TEL (21) 2267-9696. Daily, 7pm – 1pm
CUISINE Brazilian, appetizers. This tiny spot attracts a lot of customers thanks to its live music, samba on Sundays, *chorinho* on Tuesdays, and bossa nova or samba on Wednesdays. They serve traditional appetizers such as codfish cakes, salami and kibbeh (see Nightclubs, page 229).
CREDIT CARDS Not accepted

Bira $$$$
Estrada da Vendinha, 68-A, Barra de Guaratiba
(This road is after the entrance to Restinga da Marambaia)
TEL (21) 2410-8304. Thu and Fri, noon – 6pm; Sat and Sun, noon – 8pm
CUISINE Seafood, fish. This simple restaurant has a lovely view of the coastal shrubbery strip known as Restinga da Marambaia. They serve many types of *moqueca* (fish or seafood stew), fresh fish, and shellfish.
CREDIT CARDS Not accepted

Bistrô Itália $$$
Rua Frei Leandro, 20, Jardim Botânico
(Between Rua Jardim Botânico and Rua Alexandre Ferreira)
TEL (21) 2226-1038. Mon – Sat, 7:30pm – midnight; Sun noon – 6pm,
CUISINE French, Italian. Chef Antônio Costa offers such dishes as foie gras escalope with cashew fruit confit, and *cherne* (grouper) with a mixture of mushrooms in olive oil, served with yam purée. The wine list has around 170 vintages.
CREDIT CARDS AmEx; Diners; MasterCard; Visa

Bofetada $
Rua Farme de Amoedo, 87, store A, Ipanema
(Between Rua Visconde de Pirajá and Rua Barão da Torre)
TEL (21) 2227-1675. Daily, 8am – 3am
CUISINE Brazilian. This unpretentious, traditional bar attracts a gay and lesbian crowd. The huge variety of *caipirinha* cocktails deserves a special mention. If hungry, order the raginly popular *carne seca desfiada* (shredded beef jerky).
CREDIT CARDS AmEx

Borsalino $$
**Avenida Amando Lombardi, 633
(Shopping Market Street), Barra da Tijuca**
(Between Rua Georgina de Albuquerque and Avenida Fernando Matos)
TEL (21) 2491-4288. Mon, 6pm – 1am; Tue – Thu and Sun, noon – 1am; Fri and Sat, noon – 2am. Reservations required
CUISINE Italian, Mediterranean. The Mediterranean-inspired Italian dishes are developed by Italian chefs Paolo and Pietro Neroni. The specialty is farfalle pasta with shrimp and saffron. The terrace is the most popular of four dining areas.
CREDIT CARDS AmEx; Diners; MasterCard; Visa

Botequim Informal $$
Rua Humberto de Campos, 646, Leblon
(Between Rua Cupertino Durão and Rua José Linhares)
TEL (21) 2259-6967, 2274-8980. Daily, noon – 2am **ALSO AT** Rua Conde Bernadote, 36, Leblon TEL (21) 2540-5504; Shopping Downtown: Avenida das Américas, 500, block. 22, store 107, Barra da Tijuca TEL (21) 2492-2995; Rua Barão da Torre, 348, Ipanema TEL (21) 2247-6711.
CUISINE Varied. They serve excellent draft beer. The appetizers counter includes a variety of cheeses and antipasti. Among those on offer are cubes of fillet steak with onions, melted cheese and fried manioc, or manioc cakes with shrimp and *catupiry* cream cheese.
CREDIT CARDS AmEx; Visa

Bracarense $
Rua José Linhares, 85-B, Leblon
(Between Avenida Ataulfo de Paiva and Rua Humberto de Campos)
TEL (21) 2294-3549. Mon – Fri, 7am – midnight; Sat, 9am – midnight; Sun, 9am – 10pm
CUISINE Appetizers. One of the most popular bars in Rio. The attraction here is the well-pulled, ice-cold *chope* (draft beer). Appetizers include codfish cakes, manioc cakes stuffed with shrimp, and *catupiry* cream cheese. Try the chicken with okra or shrimp risotto.
CREDIT CARDS MasterCard

| PRICES | RESTAURANTS | $ up to R$25 | $$ from R$26 up to R$50 | $$$ from R$51 up to R$100 | $$$$ above R$100 |

HOTELS, RESTAURANTS, AND SERVICES

Braseiro da Gávea $$
Praça Santos Dumont, 116, Gávea
(Between Rua José Roberto Macedo Soares and Rua Orsina da Fonseca)
TEL (21) 2239-7494. Mon – Thu and Sun, 11am – 1am; Fri and Sat, 11am – 3am
CUISINE Meat dishes. Huge portions of tasty rump steak get served up with broccoli rice, egg and banana farofa (seasoned manioc flour), french fries and pickled salad. Spring chicken in oil and garlic is another good choice.
CREDIT CARDS AmEx; Diners; MasterCard; Visa

Café Severino $
Rua Dias Ferreira, 417
(Livraria Argumento bookstore), Leblon
(On the corner of Rua General Artigas)
TEL (21) 2239-5294. Mon – Fri, 9am – 12:30am; Sat and Sun, 10am – 12:30am
CUISINE Savory and sweet snacks, varied. Inside Livraria Argumento, this café-restaurant serves pasta, salads, sandwiches and soups, as well as crepes, cakes and tarts. They also serve coffee, wine, beer and juices.
CREDIT CARDS AmEx; Diners; MasterCard; Visa

Café du Lage $
Rua Jardim Botânico, 414, Jardim Botânico
(Between Rua Maria Angélica and Rua Benjamim Batista)
TEL (21) 2226-8125. Mon – Thu, 9am – 10:30pm; Fri – Sun, 9am – 5pm
CUISINE French, Italian. Inside Parque Lage, Café du Lage serves tasty dishes and a breakfast buffet, with live instrumental music on weekends. Savories, sweets such as brownies and cookies, and hot drinks are served.
CREDIT CADRS Not accepted

Café Sudbrack $
Rua Lopes Quintas, 153, Jardim Botânico
(Between Rua Jardim Botânico and Rua Corcovado)
TEL (21) 2249-2336. Mon – Fri, noon – 10pm; Sat, 11am – 3pm
CUISINE Contemporary, sandwiches. Inside Dona Coisa store, this modern café's menu is created by chef Roberta Sudbrack. Try asparagus, quinoa and shrimp ceviche or panini grego: pitta bread with tomato, cucumber, spices, roast beef and curd cheese.
CREDIT CARDS AmEx; Diners; MasterCard; Visa

Cais da Ribeira $$$
Avenida Atlântica, 2964 (Hotel Pestana Rio), Copacabana
(Between Rua Constante Ramos and Rua Barão de Ipanema)
TEL (21) 2548-6332. Daily, 6am – 10:30am, noon – 3pm and 7:30pm – 11:30pm
CUISINE Portuguese. Chef Leonel Pereira has created a contemporary menu with smaller portions than in other, similar restaurants. Try the duck and codfish rice or codfish à lagareira.
CREDIT CARDS AmEx; Diners; MasterCard; Visa

Cais do Oriente $$
Rua Visconde de Itaboraí, 8, Centro
(Between Rua do Mercado and Rua Primeiro de Março)
TEL (21) 2233-2531, 2203-0178. Tue – Sat, noon – midnight; Sun and Mon, noon – 4pm
CUISINE Mediterranean, Asian. Try the mariscada, which includes steamed octopus, shrimp, cavaquinha (a type of lobster) and potatoes. They also serve poultry and meat dishes, for example partridge risotto with mushrooms, and Mediterranean-style veal. They have a piano bar with live jazz, blues and Brazilian pop on Friday and Saturday nights (see Nightclubs, page 229).
CREDIT CARDS AmEx; Visa

Candy Delicatessen $$$
Avenida Ayrton Senna, 1791, boxes 1 – 5, Barra da Tijuca
(Between Avenida Luís Carlos Prestes and Avenida das Américas)
TEL (21) 3325-1446, 2431-7664. Advance reservations only
CUISINE Portuguese. This tiny restaurant serves such dishes as duck with rice, and char-grilled codfish with potatoes and eggplant. Owner-chef David Leitão makes an excellent roast suckling pig, but it must be ordered two days in advance.
CREDIT CARDS AmEx; Diners; MasterCard; Visa

Capricciosa $$
Rua Vinicius de Moraes, 134, Ipanema
(On the corner of Rua Barão da Torre)
TEL (21) 2523-3394. Mon – Sat, 6pm – 2am; Sun, 5pm – 2am ALSO AT Rua Maria Angélica, 37, Jardim Botânico TEL (21) 2527-2656; Rua Domingos Ferreira, 187, Copacabana TEL (21) 2255-2598; Avenida Olegário Maciel, 108, Barra da Tijuca TEL (21) 2454-2212
CUISINE Pizza. Locals say Capricciosa serves the best pizza in Brazil. Choose from more than thirty options, like pizza marguerita gourmet (traditional buffalo mozzarella, pachino tomatoes, parmesan flakes and basil).
CREDIT CARDS AmEx; Diners; MasterCard

Caranguejo $$
Rua Barata Ribeiro, 771, Copacabana
(Between Rua Xavier da Silveira and Rua Bolívar)
TEL (21) 2235-1249. Tue – Sun, 9am – 2am
CUISINE Seafood, fish. This restaurant serves fish fresh from the São José market in Niterói. The house specialty is the sinfonia do mar (shrimp, lobster, octopus, squid, cherne (a type of grouper) fish eggs, thickened sauce and broccoli rice). The badejo (grouper) fillet in shrimp sauce with mashed potatoes is also a good choice.
CREDIT CARDS Not accepted

Carême Bistrô $$$
Rua Visconde de Caravelas, 113-D, Botafogo
(Between Rua Conde de Irajá and Rua Capitão Salomão, parallel to Avenida Voluntários da Pátria)
TEL (21) 2537-2274, 2226-0085. Tue – Sat, 8pm – midnight
CUISINE French. A classic dish here is lamb cutlet served with polenta, mushroom ragout, crispy Parma ham and

RESTAURANTS $ up to R$25 $$ from R$26 up to R$50 $$$ from R$51 up to R$100 $$$$ above R$100

cacao sauce. For dessert, try the *tartaran* (an upside-down apple tart topped with crème brûlée) or *cupuaçu* fruit mousse with brazilnut ice cream. The restaurant was slated to move to Leblon in late 2007.
CREDIT CARDS AmEx; Diners; MasterCard; Visa

Carioca da Gema $
Avenida Mem de Sá, 79, Lapa
(Between Rua Gomes Freire and Rua do Lavradio)
TEL (21) 2221-0043. Mon – Thu, 6pm – 1am; Fri, 6pm – 3am; Sat, 9pm – 3am
CUISINE Brazilian. Live samba and *chorinho* play here daily, starting at 9pm. The quick meals and appetizers on the menu have names that honor samba classics: the *caldinho de feijão* (bean broth) with bacon and parsley has been christened Feijoada Completa; the beef jerky with onion and *farofa* (seasoned manioc flour) is called Amor de Malandro. To accompany the food, have a *caipirinha* or bottled beer *(see Nightclubs, page 229)*.
CREDIT CARDS Not accepted

Carlota $$$
Rua Dias Ferreira, 64, Leblon
(Between Rua Rainha Guilhermina and Avenida Ataulfo de Paiva)
TEL (21) 2540-6821. Tue – Thu, 7:30pm – midnight; Fri, 7:30pm – 12:30am; Sat, 1pm – 5pm and 7:30pm – 12:30am; Sun, 1:30pm – 10:30pm. Reservations recommended
CUISINE Contemporary. In this branch of Carlota in São Paulo, mandarin duck with tangerine and baked potatoes tossed in olive oil has proved a great success. Try guava soufflé topped with *catupiry* cream cheese syrup.
CREDIT CARDS AmEx; Diners; MasterCard; Visa

Caroline Café $
Rua J. J. Seabra, 10, Jardim Botânico
(Between Rua Jardim Botânico and Avenida Borges de Medeiros)
TEL (21) 2540-0705. Mon – Wed, noon – 1am; Thu – Sat, noon – 4am; Sun, noon – 2am ALSO AT Avenida Atlântica, no #, kiosk 7, Copacabana
CUISINE Contemporary. They serve a variety of dishes, such as pork ribs with barbecue sauce, as well as salads, for example *primavera* (curly and iceberg lettuce, arugula, fruits in season and house dressing). They also serve sushi nightly starting at 6pm, but many patrons come just for the *chope* (draft beer).
CREDIT CARDS AmEx; Diners MasterCard; Visa

Casa Cavé $
Rua Sete de Setembro, 137, Centro
(Between Rua Gonçalves Dias. And Rua do Ouvidor)
TEL (21) 2221-0533, 2222-2358. Mon – Fri, 9am – 7pm; Sat, 9am – 1pm
CUISINE Sweets and cakes. Famous for their *pastel de nata* (custard tart) – according to some, the best in Brazil – they also serve *toucinhos do céu* (sweet cakes made with egg yolks sugar and almonds), *Dom Rodrigo* (a sweet tart made with almonds and egg paste 'threads'), mille-feuilles and other sweet Portuguese creations.
CREDIT CARDS MasterCard; Visa

Casa da Feijoada $$
Rua Prudente de Morais, 10-B, Ipanema
(Opposite Praça General Osório)
TEL (21) 2247-2776, 2523-4994 (delivery). Daily, noon – midnight
CUISINE Brazilian. They serve one of the most popular *feijoadas* in the city. Bowls of beans and meat are laid out on the tables, with orange slices, collard greens and *farofa* (seasoned manioc flour). They also have a good range of old-fashioned distilled *cachaças*.
CREDIT CARDS AmEx; Diners; MasterCard; Visa

Casa Paladino $
Rua Uruguaiana, 224, Centro
(On the corner of Avenida Marechal Floriano)
TEL (21) 2263-2094. Mon – Fri, 7am – 8:30pm; Sat, 8am – noon
CUISINE Sandwiches. A blend of a bar and a delicatessen, this local fixture has a simple menu. Omelets are the specialty (choose from cod, shrimp or mixed, among others). Cold-cut sandwiches are made with French bread.
CREDIT CARDS Not accepted

Celeiro $$
Rua Dias Ferreira, 199, stores A, B, C, Leblon
(Between Rua Aristides Espínola and Rua Rainha Guilhermina)
TEL (21) 2274-7843. Mon – Sat, 11am – 5pm
CUISINE Salads. They serve 30 different salads at a self-service buffet, as well as soups, bread, meat dishes, pasta and quiches. There is usually a long line of people waiting to eat.
CREDIT CARDS Diners; MasterCard; Visa

Cervantes $
Avenida Prado Junior, 335, store B, Copacabana
(Between Rua Barata Ribeiro and Praça Demétrio Ribeiro)
TEL (21) 2275-6147. Tue – Thu and Sun, noon – 4am; Fri and Sat, noon – 6am ALSO AT Via Parque Shopping: Avenida Ayrton Senna, 3000, store 2068, Barra da Tijuca TEL (21) 2421-1068; Comercial Park Palace: Avenida das Américas, 5777, store 112, Barra da Tijuca TEL (21) 2438-1458
CUISINE Sandwiches; varied. Delicious sandwiches; the highly praised roast pork with pineapple can be readied in a jiffy.
CREDIT CARDS Visa

Champanheria Ovelha Negra $$
Rua Bambina, 120, Botafogo
(Between Rua São Clemente and Rua Muniz de Barreto)
TEL (21) 2226-1064. Mon – Fri, 5pm – 11pm
CUISINE Sandwiches. They serve sparkling wines and non-alcoholic drinks and open only during the week. Three types of sandwiches, bruschettas and cold cuts are also on offer.
CREDIT CARDS AmEx; Diners; MasterCard; Visa

PRICES	RESTAURANTS	$ up to R$25	$$ from R$26 up to R$50	$$$ from R$51 up to R$100	$$$$ above R$100

HOTELS, RESTAURANTS, AND SERVICES

Chez Anne $$
Rua Marquês de São Vicente, 52, store 171 (Shopping da Gávea), Gávea
(Between Rua General Rabelo and Praça Santos-Dumont)
TEL (21) 2294-0298. Mon – Sat, 10am – 10pm; Sun, noon – 9pm
CUISINE Sweet and savory snacks. They serve éclairs, mille-feuilles, *pastéis de Belem* (custard tarts) and more than 30 tarts and cakes, including a swiss roll with strawberries, cream and chocolate mousse. They also serve quick meat and pasta dishes.
CREDIT CARDS Not accepted

Cipriani $$$
Avenida Atlântica, 1702 (Copacabana Palace), Copacabana
(Between Rua Fernando Mendes and Rua Rodolfo Dantas)
TEL (21) 2545-8747. Sun – Thu, 12:30pm – 3pm and 7pm – midnight; Fri and Sat, 12:30pm – 3pm and 7pm – 1am
CUISINE Italian. This restaurant serves such dishes as oven-roasted suckling pig with collard greens, spicy potatoes, and fruit mustard, or grilled veal fillet with *pupunha* palm fruit and shiitake mushrooms. For dessert, try the tiramisu *veneziano* or dark chocolate soufflé with crème brulée. They offer a good wine list.
CREDIT CARDS AmEx; Diners; MasterCard; Visa

Colher de Pau $
Rua Rita Ludolf, 90-A, Leblon
(On the corner of Avenida General San Martin)
TEL (21) 2274-8295. Mon – Sun, 10am – 7pm ALSO AT Rua Farme de Amoedo, 39, Ipanema TEL (21) 2523-3018
CUISINE Sweet and savory snacks. Try the hand-made sweet delights such as *brigadeiro* (chocolate balls made with condensed milk), bolo negro, the most popular cake, chocolate roll filled with *baba-de-moça* (coconut cream), and *toalha felpuda*, a creamy coconut pie. For a savory option, try battered shrimp with *catupiry* cream cheese filling.
CREDIT CARDS Diners; MasterCard; Visa

Comuna do Semente $
Rua Joaquim Silva, 138, Lapa
(Under the Lapa Arches, near Rua Riachuelo)
TEL (21) 9781-2451. Sun – Thu, 8pm – 2am (closed Fri and Sat)
CUISINE Cold cuts; sandwiches. Instrumental music on Mondays, samba and *choro* on Tuesdays, Wednesdays and Sundays, and Latin American on Thursdays. Try the *napolitano* sandwich (provolone cheese, tomato and arugula with olive oil. Itapaiva is the only beer sold here (see Nightclubs, page 229).
CREDIT CARDS Not accepted

Confeitaria Colombo $$
Rua Gonçalves Dias, 32, Centro
(Between Rua do Ouvidor and Rua Sete de Setembro)
TEL (21) 2232-2300. Mon – Fri, 8am – 8pm; Sat and holidays, 9am – 5pm
CUISINE Sandwiches; varied. This great spot harkens back to Rio's *belle époque* and serves dishes that were ordered by such celebrities as Santos Dumont and Leila Diniz. The traditional afternoon tea is served à la carte and includes tea, honey, jelly, butter, a variety of bread, cold cuts, toast, cake, orange juice, fruit, mini sandwiches, and sweet and savory morsels. Try *pastel de nata* (custard tart), *trouxinha de ovos* (puff pastries with egg custard) and *ovos moles* (egg custards). The waffles are wonderful with ice cream.
CREDIT CARDS AmEx; Diners; MasterCard; Visa

Conversa Fiada $$
Avenida Ataulfo de Paiva, 900, Leblon
(Between Rua General Urquiza and Rua Conde Bernadote)
TEL (21) 2512-9767. Mon – Fri, 5pm until the last customer leaves; Sat and Sun, noon until the last customer leaves ALSO AT Shopping Condado de Cascais: Avenida Armando Lombardi, 800, stores J and K, Barra da Tijuca TEL (21) 2496-3222; Rua Jardim Botânico, 129, Jardim Botânico TEL (21) 2286-2111.
CUISINE Appetizers; sandwiches. They offer a counter of small *tapas* and a menu that has everything from sausage sandwiches, deep-fried pastries and rice with seafood or Argentinian rump steak. Waitresses circulate with skewers, savory snacks, and appetizers. They serve several types of *caipirinha*.
CREDIT CARDS Diners; MasterCard; Visa

Copa Café $$
Avenida Atlântica, 3056, store B, Copacabana
(Between Rua Barão de Ipanema and Rua Bolívar)
TEL (21) 2235-2947. Mon – Thu, 7pm – 1am; Fri and Sat, 7pm – 2am
CUISINE Contemporary; hamburgers. There are eight types of homemade burgers, including such variety as lamb with red wine, herbs and mint sauce served on potato *galette*.
CREDIT CARDS AmEx; Diners; MasterCard; Visa

D'Amici $$$
Rua Antônio Vieira, 18-B, Leme
(On the corner of Rua Gustavo Sampaio)
TEL (21) 2541-4477, 2543-1303. Daily, noon – 1am
CUISINE Italian; varied. The roast dishes are the highlight here, for example shoulder of lamb with arugula risotto, but the semolina-flour pasta dishes are also worth trying.
CREDIT CARDS AmEx; Diners; MasterCard; Visa

Da Brambini $$
Avenida Atlântica, 514-B, Leme
(Between Rua Anchieta and Rua Martim Afonso)
TEL (21) 2275-4346, 2542-8357. Daily, noon – 1am
CUISINE Italian. The food here is inspired by the cuisine of Italy's Lombardy region. In addition to the veal, pasta, and fish dishes, a good suggestion is the risotto brambini, with shrimp flambéed in brandy, served with pineapple.
CREDIT CARDS AmEx; Diners; MasterCard; Visa

RESTAURANTS $ up to R$25 $$ from R$26 up to R$50 $$$ from R$51 up to R$100 $$$$ above R$100

HOTELS, RESTAURANTS, AND SERVICES

Da Graça $$
Rua Pacheco Leão, 780, Jardim Botânico
(On the corner of Rua Abreu Fialho)
TEL (21) 2249-5484. Mon, 5pm until the last customer leaves; Tue – Sun, 11:30am until the last customer leaves
CUISINE Contemporary; varied. They serve dishes like *namorado* (sand perch) in butter and walnut sauce, accompanied by jasmine rice or Moroccan couscous. Candlelight guarantees a romantic atmosphere at night.
CREDIT CARDS AmEx; Visa

Degrau $$
Avenida Ataulfo de Paiva, 517-B, Leblon
(Between Rua José Linhares and Rua Cupertino Durão)
TEL (21) 2259-3648, 2259-2842. Daily, 11am – 1am
CUISINE Varied. Their *pastéis* (deep-fried pastries) with beef, cheese or shrimp filling are among the best in the city. They serve *feijoada* on Saturdays; on Sunday it's *cozido* (beef ribs or vegetables stew).
CREDIT CARDS AmEx; Diners; MasterCard; Visa

Delírio Tropical $
Rua Garcia D'Ávila, 48, Ipanema
(Between Rua Visconde de Pirajá and
Avenida Vieira Souto)
TEL (21) 3201-2977. Mon – Sat, 8am –10pm; Sun, 8am – 9pm ALSO AT Rua da Assembléia, 36-A to 38-A, Centro TEL (21) 2242-6369; Rua do Rosário, 135 – 137, Centro TEL (21) 2509-4944; Shopping Cittá América: Avenida das Américas, 700, block 8, stores 114 B, C and D.
CUISINE Salads; sandwiches. Highlights include the 16 types of salads, and they also serve grilled meats, sandwiches, pies, crêpes and soups.
CREDIT CARDS AmEx; Diners; MasterCard; Visa

Eça $$$
Avenida Rio Branco, 128, Centro
(On the corner of Rua Sete de Setembro)
TEL (21) 2524-2300. Mon – Fri, noon – 4pm
CUISINE Contemporary. Various poultry and fish dishes. Suggestions for starter, main course and dessert change daily. Choose from chocolate *fondant* and Belgian chocolates for dessert.
CREDIT CARDS AmEx; Diners; MasterCard; Visa

Enotria $$$
Avenida das Américas, 4666, store 129-B
(Barra Shopping Expansão), Barra da Tijuca
(Gate 1 entrance)
TEL (21) 2431-9119. Daily, noon – 4pm and 7pm – midnight
CUISINE Italian. We recommend grilled duck breast in honey and mango sauce, or grilled lamb cutlets with rosemary sauce and mushroom risotto.
CREDIT CARDS AmEx; Diners; MasterCard; Visa

Escola do Pão $$
Rua General Garzon, 10, Lagoa
(Between Avenida Lineu de Paula Machado
and Rua Jardim Botânico)
TEL (21) 2294-0027, 3205-7275. Tue – Fri, 5pm – midnight; Sat, Sun and holidays, 9am – 1pm
CUISINE French, Italian, bread and cakes. On Saturdays and Sundays they offer one of the most highly praised breakfasts in the city; furthermore, it's all-you-can-eat! The place also functions as a charming bistro.
CREDIT CARDS AmEx; Diners; MasterCard; Visa

Escondidinho $$
Beco dos Barbeiros, 12 A and B, Centro
(Between Rua Sete de Setembro and Rua do Ouvidor)
TEL (21) 2242-2234. Mon – Fri, 11am – 4pm
CUISINE Varied. This restaurant opens for lunch only, and just during the week. They serve generous portions, and the beef ribs deserve a special mention. For dessert try fruit compôte.
CREDIT CARDS AmEx; Diners; MasterCard; Visa

Espírito Santa $$
Rua Almirante Alexandrino, 264, Santa Teresa
(Largo dos Guimarães)
TEL (21) 2508-7095. Mon – Wed, noon – 6pm; Thu, Fri, and Sat, noon – midnight; Sun noon – 7pm
CUISINE Brazilian; Pará. This restaurant serves dishes typical of the city of Pará. Freshwater fish, such as *tambaqui* and *pirarucu*, and regional fruits like *cupuaçu*, are the menu's highlights.
CREDIT CARDS AmEx; Diners; MasterCard; Visa

Esplanada Grill $$$
Rua Barão da Torre, 600, Ipanema
(On the corner of Rua Aníbal Mendonça)
TEL (21) 2512-2970. Mon – Thu, noon – 4pm and 7pm until the last customer leaves; Fri – Sun, noon until the last customer leaves
CUISINE Meats; barbecue. They serve a wide variety of meats, including ostrich and veal. We recommend the *chorizo* steak or traditional *picanha* (rump). Customers choose the side dishes.
CREDIT CARDS AmEx; Diners; MasterCard; Visa

Expand Wine Bar $$
Rua Barão da Torre, 358, Ipanema
(Between Rua Joana Angélica and Rua Maria Quitéria)
TEL (21) 2123-7900. Mon – Sat, noon – midnight ALSO AT Avenida Érico Veríssimo, 901, store A, Barra da Tijuca (main branch) TEL (21) 2493-6161; Avenida Erasmo Braga, 299, Centro TEL (21) 2220-1887; Rua Senador Dantas, 100, store A, Centro TEL (21) 2532-7332
CUISINE Varied. This wine importer sells more than 2,000 types of wine and has a charming restaurant at the back of the wine store in Ipanema. Meats such as *javali* (wild boar) and lamb, in addition to fish, are on the menu.
CREDIT CARDS AmEx; Diners; MasterCard; Visa

Filé de Ouro $$
Rua Jardim Botânico, 731, Jardim Botânico
(Between Rua Pacheco Leão and Rua Lopes Quintas)
TEL (21) 2259-2396. Tue – Sat, noon – 11pm; Sun, noon – 7pm
CUISINE Brazilian; meats. Simple surroundings but excel-

| PRICES | RESTAURANTS | $ up to R$25 | $$ from R$26 up to R$50 | $$$ from R$51 up to R$100 | $$$$ above R$100 |

lent food (and, unfortunately, queues worthy of more famous restaurants. Try the classic beef dish *filé à Oswaldo Aranha*, with garlic, rice, beans, *farofa de ovo* (seasoned manioc flour with egg), and potatoes.
CREDIT CARDS Not accepted

Forneria $$
Rua Aníbal de Mendonça, 112, Ipanema
(Between Avenida Visconde de Pirajá and Rua Barão da Torre)
TEL (21) 2540-8045. Mon – Sat, noon – 3am; Sun, noon – 2am
CUISINE Italian. Chef Salvatore Loi creates great sandwiches, including asparagus, brie and Parma ham, served in pizza-dough bread. They also do pasta.
CREDIT CARDS AmEx; Diners; MasterCard; Visa

Garcia & Rodrigues $$$
Avenida Ataulfo de Paiva, 1251, stores A and B, Leblon
(Between Rua Rita Ludolf and Rua Aristides Espínola)
TEL (21) 3206-4120. Sun and Mon, 8am – midnight; Tue – Thu, 8am – 12:30am; Fri and Sat, 8am – 1am
CUISINE Varied. This sophisticated culinary center serves breakfast and also has a delicatessen, wine store, bakery, and restaurant. Try the *cherne* (grouper) with potatoes.
CREDIT CARDS AmEx; Diners; MasterCard; Visa

Gero $$$
Rua Aníbal de Mendonça, 157, Ipanema
(Between Rua Barão da Torre and Rua Redentor)
TEL (21) 2239-8158. Mon – Fri, noon – 4pm and 7pm – 1am; Sat, noon – 2am; Sun, noon – midnight
CUISINE Italian. This restaurant, with its lovely ambiance, is more sophisticated than the majority of Italian restaurants in Rio. We recommend the veal dish *costeleta de vitela à milanesa*. The wine list has 60 wines.
CREDIT CARDS AmEx; Diners; MasterCard; Visa

Guimas $$
Rua José Roberto Macedo Soares, 5, stores D, E, I, F, Gávea
(On the corner of Rua dos Ottis)
TEL (21) 2259-7996. Daily, noon – 1am ALSO AT Rua Paul Redfern, 33, Ipanema TEL (21) 2529-8300
CUISINE Brazilian; French. This traditional restaurant serves dishes with a French touch, like honeyed duck with pear rice, or Brazilian dishes, such as *picadinho carioca* – cubes of fillet steak with *farofa*, fried banana, rice, beans, and egg.
CREDIT CARDS AmEx; Diners; MasterCard; Visa

Gula Gula $$
Rua Aníbal de Mendonça, 132, Ipanema
(Between Rua Visconde de Pirajá and Rua Barão da Torre)
TEL (21) 2259-3084. Sun – Thu, noon – midnight; Fri and Sat, noon – 1am ALSO AT Rua Rita Ludolf, 87, store A, Leblon TEL (21) 2294-0650; Fashion Mall: Estrada da Gávea, 889, store 224, São Conrado TEL (21) 2252-8799, 2262-7170; Avenida Ministro Ivan Lins, 270, store F, Barra da Tijuca TEL (21) 2493-2995.
CUISINE Varied. The salad and grilled meats menu is fixed, but there are daily specials for quiches and pasta. Our suggestion is grouper fillet with lemon, served with carrot and pumpkin rice.
CREDIT CARDS AmEx; Diners; MasterCard; Visa

Hipódromo $$
Praça Santos-Dumont, 108, Gávea
(Between Rua Marquês de São Vicente and Rua Jardim Botânico)
TEL (21) 2274-9720. Sun – Thu, 10am – 1am; Fri and Sat, 10am – 3am
CUISINE Meats; pizza. This is a popular local meeting point and gets very crowded, especially on Thursday and Sunday nights. Grills are served at lunchtime, and for dinner it's pizza. The *feijoada*, served on Saturdays, is a classic.
CREDIT CARDS AmEx; Diners; MasterCard; Visa

Jobi $$
Rua Ataulfo de Paiva, 1166, Leblon
(Between Rua Aristides Espínola and Rua Rainha Guilhermina)
TEL (21) 2274-0547, 2274-5055. Daily, 9am – 4am
CUISINE Portuguese; Brazilian. This is a traditional bohemian haunt. The draft beer is legendary, and the menu includes *empadas* (savory pasties), beef jerky with onions and manioc, codfish, *feijoada* and many more dishes and snacks.
CREDIT CARDS AmEx

Joe & Leo's $$
Estrada da Gávea, 899, store 203 (Fashion Mall), São Conrado
(Between Avenida Almirante Álvaro Alberto and Rua Engenheiro Amandino de Carvalho)
TEL (21) 2422-0775. Mon – Thu, noon – 10:30pm; Fri – Sun, noon – 12:30am ALSO AT Avenida das Américas, 5000, store 210, Barra da Tijuca TEL (21) 2432-4882; Avenida Ataulfo de Paiva, 270, Leblon TEL (21) 3204-9347.
CUISINE Hamburgers. Of the 15 hamburger varieties on offer, the most popular is the bravo burger, made with 350 grams (0,77 pound) of rump steak. They also serve salads, pizza and desserts.
CREDIT CARDS AmEx; Diners; MasterCard; Visa

Juice Co. $
Avenida General San Martin, 889, Leblon
(On the corner of Rua General Venâncio Flores)
TEL (21) 2294-0048. Mon – Wed, 6pm – midnight; Thu – Sun, noon – 1am
CUISINE Sandwiches; juices. The juices are creative mixes. "Popeye," for example, contains spinach, cucumber, carrot, apple, and beetroot, and "gourmet V7" has tomato, cucumber, carrot, celery, bell pepper, cabbage and beetroot.
CREDIT CARDS Diners; MasterCard; Visa

Kicê Sucos $
Avenida Nossa Senhora de Copacabana, 1033, Copacabana
(Between Rua Miguel Lemos and Rua Djalma Ulrich)
TEL (21) 2287-2141. Daily, 8am – 3am

RESTAURANTS $ up to R$25 $$ from R$26 up to R$50 $$$ from R$51 up to R$100 $$$$ above R$100

CUISINE Sandwiches; juices. The 50 types of juice and *vitaminas* (fruit with milk or yogurt) include fruits from Northeast Brazil like *cajá, mangaba*, and *cupuaçu*. They serve a wide variety of sandwiches and hamburgers.
CREDIT CARDS Not accepted

Küpper $$
Rua Cupertino Durão, 79, store B, Leblon
(Between Avenida General San Martin and Rua Ataulfo de Paiva)
TEL (21) 2512-6640. Mon – Wed, 9am – midnight; Thu – Sun, 9am – 2am
CUISINE Hotdogs. The hotdogs are the main characters in this charming restaurant. They serve two versions: traditional and *temperado* (seasoned) – served with paprika or herbs, among other seasonings. The sausage is hand-made and you can choose from French bread, milk-roll, or regular hotdog roll.
CREDIT CARDS Visa

Kurt $
Rua General Urquiza, 117, store B, Leblon
(Between Rua Bartolomeu Mitre and Rua Venâncio Flores)
TEL (21) 2294-0599, 2512-4943. Mon – Fri, 8am – 7pm; Sat, 8am – 5pm
CUISINE Sweets and cakes. This establishment has achieved success with its lightly sweetened German cakes and tarts, such as sachertorte (chocolate cake with apricot filling) and apple strudel.
CREDIT CARDS Visa

La Botticella $$$
Estrada Sorimã, 347, Barra da Tijuca
(On the corner of Avenida Flemming)
TEL (21) 2495-9340. Tue – Sat, 8pm – 1am; Sun, noon – 5:30pm
CUISINE Italian. This cozy restaurant focuses on Italian food from the Bologna region, such as mascarpone and spinach ravioli in tomato and basil sauce.
CREDIT CARDS Diners; MasterCard

La Cigale $$
Rua Aristides Espínola, 88, stores A and C, Leblon
(Between Avenida Ataulfo de Paiva and Rua Dias Ferreira)
TEL (21) 2279-4473. Mon – Fri, noon – 4pm and 7:30pm – 1am; Sat, noon – 4:30pm and 7:30pm – 1am
CUISINE Meats; French. Small and welcoming, this restaurant offers a buffet lunch and à la carte dinner. Recommended choices for main dishes include veal shin stuffed with veal thymus, shiitake mushrooms and leaks. For dessert try the crème brûlée.
CREDIT CARDS Diners; MasterCard; Visa

La Fiorentina $$
Avenida Atlântica, 458-A, Leme
(Between Rua Anchieta and Rua Aurelino Leal)
TEL (21) 2543-8395, 2543-8513. Sun – Thu, noon – 2am; Fri and Sat, noon until the last customer leaves
CUISINE Italian; varied. This cantina opened in 1957 and quickly became a haunt of artists, some of whom now have dishes named after them. The place serves salads, pasta dishes and pizzas. The wine list is short but affordable.
CREDIT CARDS AmEx; Diners; MasterCard; Visa

Laguiole $$$
Avenida Infante Dom Henrique, 85, Aterro do Flamengo
(Inside the Museu de Arte Moderna, between the Monumento aos Pracinhas and Santos-Dumont Airport)
TEL (21) 2532-0755. Mon – Fri, noon – 5pm
CUISINE Contemporary; French. This restaurant has a large dining area with minimalist décor. Among our suggestions are the grilled lamb cutlets in rosemary sauce, with mint jelly and Moroccan couscous. Their award-winning wine list has 600 vintages.
CREDIT CARDS Diners; MasterCard; Visa

Lamas $$
Rua Marquês de Abrantes, 18, Flamengo
(Between Rua Senador Vergueiro and Rua Pinheiro Machado)
TEL (21) 2556-0799. Mon – Fri, 9:30am – 3:45am; Sat, 9:30am – 4am
CUISINE Brazilian. For more than 130 years, this restaurant has been famous for its fillet steak dishes, like the classic *filé à Oswaldo Aranha* and the simple, breaded steak.
CREDIT CARDS AmEx; Diners; MasterCard; Visa

Le Pré Catelan $$$
Avenida Atlântica, 4240 (Hotel Sofitel), Copacabana
(Between Rua Joaquim Nabuco and Rua Francisco Otaviano)
TEL (21) 2525-1160. Mon – Sat, 7:30pm – 11:30pm
CUISINE French. This sophisticated restaurant serves classics such as *tournedos* Rossini (grilled fillet steak on a slice of *foie gras* in red wine, served with potatoes). The tasting menu is a good choice for anyone wanting to try the chef's inventive creations.
CREDIT CARDS AmEx; Diners; MasterCard; Visa

Maçã Café $
Rua Jardim Botânico, 585, Jardim Botânico
(On the corner of Rua J. J. Seabra)
TEL (21) 2259-8686. Daily, 11am – 11pm
CUISINE Coffee; salads; savory snacks; sandwiches. They serve delicious items such as oven baked *pastel*, quiches with salad and traditional cheesecake. Different types of coffee are served at the counter. The upper floor has a more intimate atmosphere.
CREDIT CARDS AmEx; Diners; MasterCard; Visa

Majórica $$
Rua Senador Vergueiro, 11 – 15, Flamengo
(Between Rua Paissandu and Rua Marquês de Abrantes)
TEL (21) 2205-6820. Sun – Thu, noon – midnight; Fri and Sat, noon – 1am

---

PRICES | **RESTAURANTS** | **$** up to R$25 | **$$** from R$26 up to R$50 | **$$$** from R$51 up to R$100 | **$$$$** above R$100

CUISINE Meats; barbecue; seafood. The rump steak served here is deservedly famous. Side dishes (french fries, *farofa*, salad) need to be ordered separately.
CREDIT CARDS AmEx; Diners; MasterCard; Visa

Mangue Seco $
Rua do Lavradio, 23, Lapa
(Between Rua Tiradentes and Rua do Senado)
TEL (21) 3852-1947. Mon – Sat, 11am – 1am
CUISINE Seafood; fish. This self-proclaimed number one *cachaçaria* in Rio serves seafood, mainly crab. Customers can choose from the live crabs in the tank. Live music from Friday to Sunday.
CREDIT CARDS AmEx; Diners; MasterCard; Visa

Manoel & Juaquim $
Rua Pernambuco, 384, Engenho de Dentro
(On the corner of Rua Doutor Bulhões)
TEL (21) 2592-5131. Mon – Fri, 4pm – midnight; Sat and holidays, 5pm – midnight ALSO AT Avenida Atlântica, 3806, Posto 6, Copacabana TEL (21) 2523-1128; Rua Barão da Torre, 162, Ipanema TEL (21) 2522-1863; Shopping Downtown: Avenida das Américas, 500, block 22, store 143, Barra da Tijuca TEL (21) 2492-1045.
CUISINE Meats; seafood; pizza. Here is another chain of bars that pleases locals: the menu offers generous snacks, appetizers and meat dishes. Wash down your food with the *cachaça* that bears the name of the bar.
CREDIT CARDS AmEx; Diners; MasterCard; Visa

Margutta $$$
Avenida Henrique Dumont, 62, Ipanema
(Entre Rua Ataulfo de Paiva and Rua Prudente de Morais)
TEL 2259-3718, 2259-3887. Mon – Fri, 7pm – 1am; Sat, Sun and holidays, 1pm – 1am ALSO AT Rua Graça Aranha, 1, 2nd floor, Centro TEL 2563-4091. Mon – Fri, noon – 4pm
CUISINE Italian; Mediterranean. Fish and seafood are the specialties here, for example, fish *al cartoccio* or fish with sea salt. The branch in Centro opens only for lunch (Mon – Fri, 11am – 4pm).
CREDIT CARDS AmEx; Diners; MasterCard; Visa

A Marisqueira $$
Rua Barata Ribeiro, 232, Copacabana
(Between Rua General Azevedo Pimentel and Rua Rodolfo Dantas)
TEL (21) 2547-3920. Daily, 11am – midnight
CUISINE Portuguese. This restaurant has been open for more than 50 years and is still very popular. In addition to cod dishes, it serves *caldeirada* (seafood stew) and other seafood dishes. Portuguese confections complete the meal.
CREDIT CARDS AmEx; Diners; MasterCard; Visa

Marius Crustáceos $$$$
Avenida Atlântica, 290, Leme
(On the corner of Rua Martim Afonso, beside Pedra do Leme)
TEL (21) 2104-9002. Daily, noon – midnight. Reservations are essential

CUISINE Seafood. One of the best places in Rio for seafood, though the décor is a little over the top. They offer a tasting menu. The wine list has more than 100 vintages.
CREDIT CARDS AmEx; Diners; MasterCard; Visa

Mentha $$
Rua Lauro Müller, 116, store 401, FM Hall, G3 (Shopping Rio Sul), Botafogo
(Near Praça Juliano Moreira)
TEL (21) 2543-0587, 2543-0580. Mon – Sat, 11:30am – 11:40pm; Sun, noon – 6pm
CUISINE Contemporary; varied. This restaurant has an inner dining area with an intimate atmosphere, and a more informal outside area. We suggest fish in saffron with coconut rice. They also serve grilled meats, sandwiches, snacks, salads, quiches and pasta.
CREDIT CARDS AmEx; Diners; MasterCard; Visa

Miam Miam $
Rua General Góes Monteiro, 34, Botafogo
(At the end of Rua da Passagem)
TEL (21) 2244-0125. Tue – Fri, noon – 3pm and 7:30pm – 12:30pm; Sat, 8pm – 1:30am
CUISINE Varied. This restaurant, inside a large house in Botafogo, offers furniture from the 1950s to the 1970s for sale. They serve home-style dishes with some extras, like cream of mushroom soup with pastry flakes, and traditional *picadinho* (cubes of fillet steak) with ginger rice, coriander, dried tomatoes, and mushrooms in lime butter.
CREDIT CARDS AmEx; Diners; MasterCard; Visa

Mil Frutas $
Rua J. J. Seabra, no #, Jardim Botânico
(Between Rua Borges de Medeiros and Rua Jardim Botânico)
TEL (21) 2511-2550. Mon – Thu, 10:30am – 12:30pm; Fri, 10:30am – 1am; Sat, 9:30am – 1am; Sun, 9:30am – 12:30pm ALSO AT Fashion Mall: Estrada da Gávea, 899, stall 7, São Conrado TEL (21) 3322-5417.
CUISINE Ice cream. Considered one of the best ice cream parlors in Rio, this one serves homemade fruit ices: *pitanga, jabuticaba*, tamarind, *serigüela*, cashew fruit, and many others. They also have delicious frozen cakes.
CREDIT CARDS Diners; MasterCard

Mil Frutas Café $
Rua Garcia D'Ávila, 134, store A, Ipanema
(Between Rua Barão da Torre and Rua Visconde de Pirajá)
TEL (21) 2521-1384, 2247-2148. Mon – Thu, 10:30am – midnight; Fri and Sat, 9:30am – 1:30am; Sun, 9:30am – 12:30am
CUISINE Salads; sandwiches; ice cream. Unlike other branches in the Mil Frutas chain, this tiny café in Ipanema serves coffee, soup, sandwiches, wraps and salads. They do breakfast on weekends, too. But don't forget the ice cream!
CREDIT CARDS Diners; MasterCard

RESTAURANTS $ up to R$25 $$ from R$26 up to R$50 $$$ from R$51 up to R$100 $$$$ above R$100

Milano DOC $$$
Rua Gomes Carneiro, 132, Ipanema
(Between Rua Visconde de Pirajá and Rua Bulhões Carvalho)
TEL (21) 2522-0303. Mon – Thu, 6pm – 1am; Fri – Sun and holidays, noon – 2am
CUISINE Seafood; Mediterranean; fish; pizza. What sets this place apart is that its pizza, which is made in a wood-burning oven, and its Mediterranean food and delicatessen. Despite all the variety, everything is well done. Highlights are the *pizza Milano DOC* (buffalo mozzarella and burrata cheeses, cherry tomatoes, Parma ham, arugula and slices of Grana Padano cheese), and the *peixe Milano DOC*, which consists of oven-baked fish with potatoes in white wine, rosemary, olive oil, skinned tomatoes, and garlic sauce.
CREDIT CARDS Diners; MasterCard; Visa

Mr. Lam $$$
Rua Maria Angélica, 21, Lagoa
(Between Rua Alexandre Ferreira and Rua Borges de Medeiros)
TEL (21) 2286-6661. Tue – Thu, 7pm – 12:30am; Fri and Sat, 7pm – 1am; Sun, 1pm – 7pm. Reservations recommended
CUISINE Chinese. Chef Sik Chung Lam, or simply Mr. Lam, ran the kitchen at the New York Mr. Chow for years. He now runs this restaurant that bears his own name. Try the *pato laqueado* (duck coated with Chinese vinegar and honey, served whole, accompanied by pancakes, cucumber and spring onions). They also offer a tasting menu.
CREDIT CARDS AmEx; Diners; MasterCard; Visa

Museu da Cadeira $$
Rua Martins Ferreira, 48, Botafogo
(Between Rua Capistrano de Abreu and Rua Voluntários da Pátria)
TEL (21) 2527-4044. Mon – Fri, 5pm – 1am; Sat, 6pm – 1am
CUISINE Crêpes; French. This is a pleasant combination of a restaurant, café and bookstore. Its quirky charm is captured by the collection of chairs hanging from the ceiling. The menu offers such dishes as duck breast with shiitake, shimeji and champignon mushrooms in caramelized vinegar.
CREDIT CARDS AmEx; Diners; MasterCard

Na Pressão $
Avenida das Américas, 5000, stores 119 and 120 (Shopping New York City Center), Barra da Tijuca
(Beside Barra Shopping)
TEL (21) 2432-4839. Mon – Fri, 4pm – 3am; Sat, Sun and holidays, noon – 3am ALSO AT Shopping Downtown: Avenida das Américas, 500, block 6, store 120, Barra da Tijuca TEL (21) 2493-2060; Rua Marechal Henrique Lott, 120, store 103, Barra da Tijuca TEL (21) 3325-5975
CUISINE Brazilian; snacks. The draft beer is served in chilled glass tankards, which maintains the cool temperature nicely. To accompany your drink, try *pastel, croquete do alemão* or other savory snacks.
CREDIT CARDS AmEx; Diners; MasterCard; Visa

Nam Thai $$
Rua Rainha Guilhermina, 95, store B, Leblon
(Between Avenida General San Martin and Avenida Ataulfo de Paiva)
TEL (21) 2259-2962. Mon – Fri, noon – 4pm and 7pm – 1am; Sat, noon – 1am; Sun, noon – 11pm
CUISINE Thai. They serve food from several regions of Thailand. Excellent starters, soups, noodles, meats, fish and seafood. Try the Pad Thai (rice noodles fried with shrimp) and for dessert crispy coconut cream with ginger.
CREDIT CARDS AmEx; Diners; MasterCard; Visa

Oásis $$
Rua Gonçalves Dias, 56 (mezzanine), Centro
(Between Rua do Ouvidor and Rua da Constituição)
TEL (21) 2252-5521. Mon – Fri, 11am – 4pm ALSO AT Estrada do Joá, 136, São Conrado TEL (21) 3322-3144; via Dutra, km 171.5, Dutra Highway TEL (21) 2651-2951
CUISINE Meats; barbecue. Meat is served on a *rodizio* (all you can eat) basis and is distinguished by its *picanha* (rump steak) prepared in the *gaúcho* (southern Brazil) style. They serve a variety of side dishes, for example, *pastel de catupiry* (deep-fried pastry filled with cream cheese) and manioc cakes.
CREDIT CARDS AmEx; Diners; MasterCard; Visa

Olivier Cozan $$$
Rua Vinicius de Moraes, 130, Ipanema
(Between Rua Visconde de Pirajá and Rua Barão da Torre)
TEL (21) 2247-5351/8452. Daily, noon – 1am
CUISINE French. Specialties here are the *foie gras* dishes, but there are others worth recommending, such as duck in raspberry sauce. There is also a wine store selling European and South American wines.
CREDIT CARDS AmEx; Diners; MasterCard; Visa

Olympe $$$
Rua Custódio Serrão, 62, Jardim Botânico
(Between Rua Jardim Botânico and Rua Alexandre Ferreira)
TEL (21) 2539-4542. Mon – Thu and Sat, 7:30pm – 1am; Fri, 12:30am – 4pm and 7:30pm – 1am
CUISINE French. This restaurant combines genuinely Brazilian ingredients and French cooking techniques. Try the grilled scallops with *doce de leite* (caramelized milk), and *pupunha* palm-heart salad in Madras curry sauce.
CREDIT CARDS MasterCard; Visa

Osteria Dell'Angolo $$
Rua Paul Redfern, 40, Ipanema
(On the corner of Rua Prudente de Morais, one block from Jardim de Alá canal)
TEL (21) 2259-3148. Mon – Fri, noon – 4pm and 6:30pm – 1am; Sat, noon – 1am; Sun, noon – midnight
CUISINE Italian. They serve good risottos and polenta dishes – for example, polenta with porcini mushrooms. In spring and summer they offer a special salad and cold dish menu at lunchtime.
CREDIT CARDS AmEx; Diners; MasterCard

| PRICES | RESTAURANTS | $ up to R$25 | $$ from R$26 up to R$50 | $$$ from R$51 up to R$100 | $$$$ above R$100 |

HOTELS, RESTAURANTS, AND SERVICES

Penafiel $$
Rua Senhor dos Passos, 121, Centro
(Between Rua da Alfândega and Rua Buenos Aires)
TEL (21) 2224-6870. Mon – Fri, 11am – 3:30pm
CUISINE Portuguese. The codfish cutlets come with shrimp, fried onions, and vegetables tossed in oil. The shrimp and palm-heart pasties deserve a mention.
CREDIT CARDS Diners; MasterCard; Visa

Pérgula $$$
Avenida Atlântica, 1702 (Copacabana Palace), Copacabana
(Between Rua Fernando Mendes and Rua Rodolfo Dantas)
TEL (21) 2545-8744. Daily 7am – midnight
CUISINE Brazilian; contemporary. The glass-walled dining room is right beside the pool and deck. The popular, though expensive, Sunday brunch has such delights as brie and apricot gratin tart. They serve *feijoada* on Saturdays.
CREDIT CARDS AmEx; Diners; MasterCard; Visa

Pizzaria Guanabara $
Avenida Ataulfo de Paiva, 1228, stores A and B, Leblon
(On the corner of Rua Aristides Espínola)
TEL (21) 2294-0797. Daily, 24 hours ALSO AT Avenida Armando Lombardi, 75, Barra da Tijuca TEL (21) 3153-4040
CUISINE Pizza. This restaurant serves some 30 varieties of thin-crust pizza, and you can also buy pizza by the slice at the counter. The most popular pizzas are the ones with traditional toppings, but they've got some offbeat options, too. They serve *feijoada* on Saturdays and *cozido* (meat, beef ribs and vegetables stew) on Sundays, in addition to pasta, salads, soups, and starters.
CREDIT CARDS AmEx; Diners; MasterCard; Visa

Plataforma $$$
Rua Adalberto Ferreira, 32, Leblon
(Between Rua Juquiá and Praça Cláudio Coutinho)
TEL (21) 2274-4022. Mon – Thu, noon – midnight; Fri and Sat, noon – 1am
CUISINE Meats; barbecue. We suggest rump teak with soufflé potatoes or char-grilled grouper, as well as the tasty beef flank.
CREDIT CARDS AmEx; Diners; MasterCard; Visa

Polis Sucos $
Rua Maria Quitéria, 70-A, Ipanema
(On the corner of Praça Nossa Senhora da Paz)
TEL (21) 2247-2518. Daily, 7am – 12:30am
CUISINE Juices; sandwiches. A variety of sandwiches and fresh fruit juices, including *fruta-do-conde*, are served up at the counter, where customers can stand.
CREDIT CARDS MasterCard

Porcão $$$
Rua Barão da Torre, 218, Ipanema
(Between Rua Vinicius de Moraes and Rua Farme de Amoedo)
TEL (21) 3202-9155. Mon – Thu, 11:30am – 12:30am, Fri and Sat, 11:30am – 1am; Sun 11:30am – midnight ALSO AT Avenida Infante Dom Henrique, no #, Aterro do Flamengo TEL (21) 3461-9020; Avenida Armando Lombardi, 591, Barra da Tijuca TEL (21) 3154-9255; Rua Quintino, 151, Niterói TEL (21) 3461-7080
CUISINE Meats; barbecue. An excellent meat *rodizio* (all you can eat) and very comprehensive salad buffet. This restaurant even has branches abroad.
CREDIT CARDS AmEx; Diners; MasterCard; Visa

Quadrifoglio $$
Rua J. J. Seabra, 19, Jardim Botânico
(Between Rua Lineu de Paula and Rua Jardim Botânico)
TEL (21) 2294-1433. Mon – Fri, noon – 3:30pm and 7:30pm – midnight; Sat, 7:30pm – 1am; Sun, 12:30am – 5pm
CUISINE Italian. This is one of the best Italian restaurants in the city. The dishes are inspired by the Lombardy region. Among the classics served here is *última luna* (ravioli stuffed with pears, in gorgonzola and ground peanut sauce).
CREDIT CARDS AmEx; Visa

Quinta $$$
Rua Luciano Gallet, 150, Vargem Grande
(Between Estrada Pacuí and Rua Manuel Querino)
TEL (21) 2428-1396, 2428-2568. Fri, 10pm – 5pm; Sat, Sun and holidays, 1pm – 7pm
CUISINE Brazilian; contemporary. This restaurant is on a small piece of property amid the forest, and you can often see marmosets on the veranda. One of the most popular main courses is the roast duck with fruit jelly, caramelized sweet potatoes, red cabbage with cumin, and homemade mango and apple chutneys.
CREDIT CARDS AmEx; Diners; MasterCard; Visa

Quinta da Boa Vista $$
Parque da Quinta da Boa Vista, no #, São Cristóvão
(Inside the park, opposite the zoo)
TEL (21) 2589-6551, 2589-4279. Daily, 11am – 6pm; Dinner requires reservations, except on Sat, Sun and holidays. ALSO AT Feira de São Cristóvão, in the Pavilhão de São Cristóvão
CUISINE Varied. This restaurant has been operating inside an old chapel since 1954. They serve highly praised oxtail on Tuesdays. The menu includes dishes like *caldeirada* (seafood stew), codfish and rabbit *à caçadora*.
CREDIT CARDS AmEx; Visa

Rio Minho $$
Rua do Ouvidor, 10, Centro
(Between Rua do Mercado and Avenida Alfred Agache)
TEL (21) 2509-2338. Mon – Fri, 11am – 4pm
CUISINE Seafood. This traditional Rio restaurant has been in operation since 1884. It became famous for its Leão Velloso soup, with seafood, fish and shrimp stock, corian-

| RESTAURANTS | $ up to R$25 | $$ from R$26 up to R$50 | $$$ from R$51 up to R$100 | $$$$ above R$100 |

der, and leeks. They also serve delicious savory snacks.
CREDIT CARDS AmEx; Diners; MasterCard; Visa

Rio Scenarium $
Rua do Lavradio, 20, Lapa
(Between Rua do Senado and Rua Visconde do Rio Branco)
TEL (21) 3852-5516, 2233-3239. Tue – Sat, 7pm until the last customer leaves
CUISINE Savory appetizers; varied. This restaurant functions as an antiques store during the day. At night they host live music. Try the grilled salmon fillet with tangerine sauce and pumpkin mousse (*see Nightclubs, page 229*).
CREDIT CARDS AmEx; Diners; MasterCard; Visa

Roberta Sudbrack $$$$
Rua Lineu de Paula Machado, 916, Jardim Botânico
(Between Rua Jardim Botânico and Avenida Borges de Medeiros)
TEL (21) 3874-0139. Tue – Thu, noon – 3pm and 8:30pm – 10:30pm; Fri, noon – 3pm and 9pm – midnight; Sat, 9pm – midnight. Reservations recommended
CUISINE Contemporary. Lunch is served at just two tables and a counter. On Fridays and Saturdays dinner is served at a communal table. Options change regularly.
CREDIT CARDS Not accepted

Rosita Café $
Avenida das Américas, 500, block 21, store 126 (Shopping Downtown), Barra da Tijuca
(At Avenida Afonso Arinos)
TEL (21) 3084-5202. Mon and Tue, noon – 5pm; Wed – Sat, noon until the last customer leaves; Sun, 12:30pm – 6pm
CUISINE Sandwiches; varied. Candlelit tables feature old vinyl records as placemats. Try the *gaúcho* sandwich, with fillet steak, provolone cheese and mustard sauce in ciabatta bread.
CREDIT CARDS AmEx; Diners; MasterCard; Visa

Satyricon $$$
Rua Barão da Torre, 192, Ipanema
(Between Rua Vinicius de Moraes and Rua Farme de Amoedo)
TEL (21) 2521-0627. Daily, noon until the last customer leaves
CUISINE Seafood; Italian; Mediterranean; fish. Considered a temple for fish-lovers, Satyricon serves shrimp, oysters, langoustines, *pargo* (red porgy) and lobster. Try the *misto de crustáceos* (shellfish selection).
CREDIT CARDS AmEx; Diners; MasterCard; Visa

Shenanigan's $
Avenida Armando Lombardi, 333, Barra da Tijuca
(At the corner with Rua General Ivan Raposo)
TEL (21) 2492-2798. Mon – Thu, 6pm – 2am; Fri and Sat, 6pm – 3am; Sun, 3:30pm – 2am ALSO AT Rua Visconde de Pirajá, 112-A, Ipanema TEL (21) 2267-5860
CUISINE Varied. This Irish pub serves six types of domestic and imported beer. For food, try the sampler: a selection of the house savory dishes.
CREDIT CARDS AmEx; Diners; MasterCard; Visa

Shirley $
Rua Gustavo Sampaio, 610, store A, Leme
(Between Rua Anchieta and Avenida Princesa Isabel)
TEL (21) 2542-1797, 2275-1398. Daily, noon – 1am
CUISINE Spanish. The specialty here is paella Valenciana (seafood, chicken and pork), which comes in generous portions.
CREDIT CARDS Not accepted

Simplesmente $$
Rua Paschoal Carlos Magno, 115, Santa Teresa
(Between Rua Almirante Alexandrino and Rua Monte Alegre)
TEL (21) 2221-0337. Mon – Thu, 7pm – 3am; Fri and Sat, 7pm until the last customer leaves
CUISINE Savory appetizers and snacks. Enjoy traditional snacks in a jovial, pleasant atmosphere. Spicy sausage, and strips of fillet steak with *farofa* (seasoned manioc flour), are popular. Live samba on Wednesdays.
CREDIT CARDS Not accepted

Siri Mole & Cia. $$$
Rua Francisco Otaviano, 50 (Posto 6), Copacabana
(On the corner of Rua Raul Pompéia)
TEL (21) 2267-0894. Mon, 7pm – midnight; Tue – Sun, noon – midnight ALSO AT Avenida Rio Branco, 1, Centro
TEL (21) 2233-0107
CUISINE Bahia regional. *Moqueca de siri mole* (crab stew with coconut milk) and *sinfonia de frutos do mar* (seafood "symphony") are the highlights here. On Saturday at lunchtime they serve a generous buffet with *abará* (black-eyed peas wrapped in banana leaf), *acarajé* (black-eyed pea fritters, *caruru* (shrimp with okra), *xinxim de galinha* (chicken stew) and *vatapá* (codfish and shrimp stew).
CREDIT CARDS AmEx; Diners; MasterCard; Visa

Sobrenatural $$
Rua Almirante Alexandrino, 432, Santa Teresa
(Near Largo dos Guimarães)
TEL (21) 2224-1003. Daily, noon until the last customer leaves
CUISINE Brazilian; seafood. The *moqueca de tamboril* (*tamboril* fish with shrimp sauce), *pirão* (flour-thickened sauce), or *farofa amarela* (seasoned yellow manioc flour) is highly regarded. At weekends the restaurant gets very crowded, so it's good to make reservations.
CREDIT CARDS AmEx; Diners; MasterCard; Visa

Sorvete Itália $
Avenida Henrique Dumont, 71, store C, Ipanema
(Between Avenida Ataulfo de Paiva and Rua Prudente de Morais)

| PRICES | RESTAURANTS | $ up to R$25 | $$ from R$26 up to R$50 | $$$ from R$51 up to R$100 | $$$$ above R$100 |

HOTELS, RESTAURANTS, AND SERVICES

TEL (21) 2239-1396, 3204-1920. Mon – Thu, 9am – 9pm; Fri – Sun, and holidays, 9am – 1pm ALSO AT Rua Almirante Guilhem, 317, store 320, Leblon TEL (21) 2540-9954; Avenida Nossa Senhora de Copacabana, 1033, store A, Copacabana TEL (21) 2247-0707.
CUISINE Ice cream. 50 flavors, including a diet line, sundaes and popsicles. Try mango with ginger, and tapioca.
CREDIT CARDS MasterCard; Visa

Sorvetes Chaika $
Rua Visconde de Pirajá, 321-A, Ipanema
(Between Rua Joana Angélica and Rua Vinicius de Moraes)
TEL (21) 2267-3838, 2287-8776. Daily, 9am – 1am ALSO AT Shopping Rio Sul: Rua Lauro Müller, 116, 4th floor, Botafogo TEL (21) 2275-9490, 2541-7119
CUISINE Savory snacks; ice cream. This establishment specializes in unusual flavors, like fig and Port, and lime with basil. They also serve pies, savory snacks and sandwiches.
CREDIT CARDS AmEx; Diners; MasterCard; Visa

Surf Adventures $
Avenida das Américas, 500, block 17, stores 126 and 127 (Shopping Downtown), Barra da Tijuca
(At Avenida Afonso Arinos)
TEL (21) 3982-2153. Mon – Thu, noon – midnight; Fri, noon – 2am; Sat, 6pm – 2am; Sun, 6pm – midnight
CUISINE Pizza; sandwiches; varied. They serve healthy options like vegetarian wrap (flat bread wrapped around seasoned eggplant) and others that are not so healthy, like homemade hamburgers and French fries.
CREDIT CARDS MasterCard

Sushi Leblon $$$
Rua Dias Ferreira, 256, Leblon
(On the corner of Rua Rainha Guilhermina)
TEL (21) 2512-7830. Mon – Fri, noon – 4pm and 7pm – 1:30am; Sat, noon – 1:30am; Sun, 1pm – 1:30am. Reservations recommended
CUISINE Japanese. One of the most highly regarded Japanese restaurants in the city, this place serve contemporary creations such as foie gras marinated in sweet sake and mango brunoise.
CREDIT CARDS AmEx; MasterCard; Visa

Talho Capixaba $
Avenida Ataulfo de Paiva, 1022, stores A and B, Leblon
(Between Rua General Artigas and Rua Venâncio Flores)
TEL (21) 2512-8760. Mon – Sat, 7am – 9pm; Sun, 8am – 9pm
CUISINE Breads; sandwiches. This sophisticated bakery and delicatessen offers more than 30 types of bread, with fillings that match each customer's taste. The breakfast is highly recommended.
CREDIT CARDS AmEx; Diners; MasterCard; Visa

Ten Kai $$
Rua Prudente de Morais, 1810, Ipanema
(On the corner of Rua Paul Redfern)

TEL (21) 2540-5100, 2240-5898. Mon – Fri, 7pm – 1am; Sat, 1pm – 1am; Sun, 1pm – midnight ALSO AT Rua Senador Dantas, 77, store H, Centro TEL (21) 2220-8635
CUISINE Japanese. This sushi bar sends out food with unusual ingredients like codfish and cavalinha (a type of lobster eggs). For something hot, try the grilled beef tongue.
CREDIT CARDS AmEx; Diners; MasterCard; Visa

Terzetto $$$
Rua Jangadeiros, 28, Ipanema
(On the corner of Rua Visconde de Pirajá)
TEL (21) 2247-6797. Mon – Thu, 6pm – 1am; Fri – Sun, noon – 1am
CUISINE Contemporary; Italian. They serve dishes such as papardelle with partridge ragout and white truffles, and roast duck with apple purée in calvados.
CREDIT CARDS AmEx; Diners; MasterCard; Visa

The Bakers $
Rua Santa Clara, 86-B, Copacabana
(Between Rua Barata Ribeiro and Rua Nossa Senhora de Copacabana)
TEL (21) 3209-1212. Daily, 9am – 8pm ALSO AT Rua Visconde de Pirajá, 330, Ipanema TEL (21) 3201-5050
CUISINE Sweets and cakes; sandwiches. Try the delicious sweets and cakes, charlottes and pies, for example ecstasy (chocolate cake, whipped cream and strawberries), and antiquarius (walnut cake with layers of coconut custard cream). The sandwiches are made with homemade bread.
CREDIT CARDS Visa

Tia Palmira $$$
Rua Caminho do Souza, 18, Barra de Guaratiba
(Opposite the old Ponte dos Arcos)
TEL (21) 2410-8169. Tue – Fri, 11:30am – 5pm; Sat, Sun and holidays, 11:30am – 6pm
CUISINE Seafood; fish. Locals have for years been flocking to this restaurant for its seafood and homemade flavors. The generous servings include fried shrimp, vatapá (codfish and shrimp stew), risottos and moquecas (seafood stew with coconut milk).
CREDIT CARDS AmEx; Diners; MasterCard; Visa

Torta & Cia. $$$
Estrada da Gávea, 820, São Conrado
(Between Lagoa–Barra Highway and Rua General Olímpio Mourão Filho)
TEL (21) 3322-5106. Daily, 9am – 10pm ALSO AT Rua Gilberto Cardoso, no #, store 516 (Cobal), Leblon TEL (21) 2511-5141; Rua Voluntários da Pátria, 446, store 13, Humaitá TEL (21) 2537-8484.
CUISINE Sweets and cakes. More than 30 types of cakes and some savories. The most famous is chocolate with whipped cream, covered in dark chocolate syrup.
CREDIT CARDS AmEx; Diners; MasterCard; Visa

Traiteurs de France $$$
Avenida Nossa Senhora de Copacabana, 386, stores B and C, Copacabana

| RESTAURANTS | $ up to R$25 | $$ from R$26 up to R$50 | $$$ from R$51 up to R$100 | $$$$ above R$100 |

(Between Rua República do Peru and Rua Fernando Mendes)
TEL (21) 2548-6440. Sun – Fri, noon – 4:30pm; Sat, noon – 4:30pm and 7pm – 11pm. Bakery: Mon – Sat, 10am – 8pm; Sun, 10am – 6pm **ALSO AT** Rua Marquês de São Vicente, 86, stores C and D, Gávea **TEL** (21) 2259-0408
CUISINE French; varied. Opened 18 years ago, this restaurant serves dishes like duck breast, coq au vin and mushroom risotto.
CREDIT CARDS AmEx; Diners; MasterCard; Visa

Yorubá $$
Rua Arnaldo Quintela, 94, Botafogo
(Between Rua Oliveira Fausto and Rua Assis Bueno)
TEL (21) 2541-9387. Wed – Fri, 7pm – midnight; Sat, 2pm – 11pm; Sun, noon – 6pm
CUISINE Bahia regional. Typical dishes from Bahia, in the country's northeast, are served here. Crab *moqueca* and dishes of African origin, like *ebubu fulo* (fish with coconut milk, smoked and fresh shrimp, rice and plantain purée), hit the spot.
CREDIT CARDS AmEx; Visa

Yumê $
Rua Pacheco Leão, 758, Jardim Botânico
(On the corner of Rua Abreu Fialho)
TEL (21) 3205-7322, 3205-7321. Mon, 6pm – midnight; Tue – Thu, 6pm – 1am; Fri, 6pm – 2am; Sat, noon – 2am; Sun, noon – midnight
CUISINE Japanese. The restaurant formerly known as "Miss Tanaka" continues to serve this eatery's famous dishes. Acarajapa, a spicy creation of the old owner's, consists of smoked tofu with rice noodles and shrimp. Another unusual dish is frog fondue.
CREDIT CARDS AmEx; Diners; MasterCard; Visa

Zazá Bistrô Tropical $$
Rua Joana Angélica, 40, Ipanema
(On the corner of Rua Prudente de Morais)
TEL (21) 2247-9101. Sun – Thu, 7:30pm – 12:30pm; Fri and Sat, 7:30pm – 1:30am. Open on Sunday from November to March only
CUISINE Asian, contemporary. They serve such dishes as organic chicken curry in coconut milk with oriental vegetables, lemongrass, ginger and banana. The upper floor has traditional, low-lying tables that are popular with romantic couples.
CREDIT CARDS Visa

Zuka $$$$
Rua Dias Ferreira, 233, store B, Leblon
(Opposite Sushi Leblon, on the road parallel to Avenida Ataulfo de Paiva)
TEL (21) 3205-7154. Mon, 7pm – 1am; Tue – Fri, noon – 4pm and 7pm – 1am, Sat, 1pm – 1am; Sun, 1pm – midnight
CUISINE Contemporary. The menu changes every four months. For starters try grilled octopus in Parma ham. Main dishes include *foie gras* steak with mini-pancakes, orange jelly and Grand Marnier.
CREDIT CARDS AmEx; MasterCard; Visa

SHOW VENUES

Allegro Bistrô
See Nightclubs

Bar do Tom
See Nightclubs

Café Cultural Sacrilégio
Avenida Mem de Sá, 81, Lapa
(Between Rua do Lavradio and Rua Gomes Freire)
TEL (21) 3970-1461, 2222-7345. Tue – Sat, 7pm – 3am
CAPACITY 250 (3 areas) **MUSIC** Choro; MPB; samba **CLIENTELE** Over 20; couples; families; professionals; tourists
www.sacrilegio.com.br
CREDIT CARDS AmEx; Diners; MasterCard; Visa

Cais do Oriente
See Nightclubs

Canecão
Avenida Venceslau Brás, 215, Botafogo
(Between Avenida Pasteur and Avenida Lauro Sodré)
TEL (21) 2105-2000. Box office: daily, noon – 9:20pm. Shows: Mon – Thu, 9:30pm until the last customer leaves; Fri and Sat, 10pm until the last customer leaves; Sun, 8:30pm until the last customer leaves
CAPACITY 3000 (1 area) **MUSIC** Varied **CLIENTELE** All age groups; teenagers; couples; executives; families; gays and lesbians; professionals; tourists; university students
www.canecao.com.br
CREDIT CARDS Not accepted

Carioca da Gema
See Nightclubs and Where to Eat

Centro Cultural Carioca
Rua do Teatro, 37, Centro
(Between Rua Passos and Rua Ramalho Ortigão)
TEL (21) 2252-6468. Information and reservations: Mon – Sat, 11am – 8pm. Shows: Tue and Wed, 7pm – midnight; Thu, 7pm – 1am; Fri and Sat, 8pm– 2am
CAPACITY 144 (1 area) **MUSIC** Choro; MPB; samba; samba-de-roda **CLIENTELE** Over 20; couples; executives; families; professionals; tourists; university students
www.centroculturalcarioca.com.br
CREDIT CARDS Not accepted

Céu Aberto
See Nightclubs

Circo Voador
Rua dos Arcos, no #, Lapa
(Between Rua do Lavradio and Avenida República do Paraguai)
TEL (21) 2533-0354, 2533-6179. Box office: Thu and Fri, noon – 6pm. Shows: Tue – Fri, 7pm until the last customer leaves; Sat, Sun, and holidays, 8pm until the last customer leaves
It holds events such as the short-film festival Cine-Circo. **CAPACITY** 3,000 (1 area) **MUSIC** Electronic; forró; hip hop;

| PRICES | RESTAURANTS | $ up to R$25 | $$ from R$26 up to R$50 | $$$ from R$51 up to R$100 | $$$$ above R$100 |

varied instrumental; mangue beat; MPB; pop; rap; rock; samba; varied CLIENTELE All age groups; couples; tourists; university students
www.circovoador.com.br
CREDIT CARDS Not accepted

Claro Hall
Avenida Ayrton Senna, 3000, Barra da Tijuca
(Shopping Via Parque, near Avenida Embaixador Abelardo Bueno)
TEL (21) 2156-7300. Box office: daily, noon – 8pm
CAPACITY 8450 (1 area) MUSIC Varied CLIENTELE Up to 40; teenagers; couples; executives; families; professionals; tourists; university students
www.clarohall.com.br
CREDIT CARDS AmEx; Diners; MasterCard; Visa

Clube dos Democráticos
Rua Riachuelo, 91, Lapa
(Between Avenida Gomes Freire and Rua dos Inválidos)
TEL (21) 2252-4611. Wed – Sat, 11pm – 4am; Sun, 8pm – midnight
CAPACITY 600 (1 area) MUSIC Choro; forró; pagode; samba; samba-de-roda CLIENTELE Over 20; couples; university students
CREDIT CARDS Not accepted

Comuna do Semente
See Nightclubs and Where to Eat

Drink Café
See Nightclubs

Espaço Cultural Maurice Valans
See Nightclubs

Estrela da Lapa
Avenida Mem de Sá, 69, Lapa
(Corner of Rua do Lavradio)
TEL (21) 2507-6686. Mon – Fri, 6pm until the last customer leaves; Sat, 7pm until the last customer leaves
CAPACITY 400 (3 areas) MUSIC Choro; forró; jazz; MPB; samba; samba-de-roda CLIENTELE Over 20; couples; executives; families; professionals; tourists; university students
www.estreladalapa.com.br
CREDIT CARDS Diners; MasterCard; Visa

Fundição Progresso
Rua dos Arcos, 24, Lapa
(Between Rua do Lavradio and Avenida República do Paraguai)
TEL (21) 2220-5070. Daily, 9am – 10pm. Shows: 10pm – 5am
CAPACITY 5,000 (5 areas) MUSIC Axé; electronic; forró; hip hop; varied instrumental; mangue beat; MPB; pop; rap; rock; samba; samba-rock CLIENTELE All age groups; teenagers; couples; families; gays and lesbians; tourists; university students
www.fundicao.org
CREDIT CARDS Not accepted

J. Club
See Nightclubs and Where to Eat

Mistura Fina
Avenida Borges de Medeiros, 3207, Lagoa
(Between Rua J. J. Seabra and Rua Carlos Esmeraldino)
TEL (21) 2537-2844. Mon – Fri, 6pm until the last customer leaves; Sat, noon until the last customer leaves; Sun, noon – 6pm. Shows: from 9pm
CAPACITY 180 (3 areas) MUSIC Blues; bossa nova; varied instrumental; jazz; MPB; pop CLIENTELE Over 30; couples; executives; professionals
www.misturafina.com.br
CREDIT CARDS AmEx; Diners; MasterCard

Rio Scenarium
See Nightclubs and Where to Eat

Teatro Odisséia
Avenida Mem de Sá, 66, Lapa
(Between Rua do Lavradio and Rua República do Paraguai)
TEL (21) 2224-6367. Tue – Sat, 8pm until the last customer leaves
CAPACITY 800 (3 areas) MUSIC Electronic; hip hop; MPB; pop; rock; samba-rock CLIENTELE All age groups; couples; professionals; tourists; university students; adults
www.teatroodisseia.com.br
CREDIT CARDS AmEx; Diners; MasterCard; Visa

Trapiche da Gamboa
See Nightclubs

Vinicius Piano Bar
See Nightclubs

Vivo Rio
Avenida Infante D. Henrique, 85, Flamengo
(Parque do Flamengo, next to the Museu de Arte Moderna)
TEL (21) 2169-6600 (Ingresso Fácil). Box office: Mon – Sat, noon – 10pm; Sun and holidays, noon – 8pm
CAPACITY 7,000 MUSIC Varied CLIENTELE All ages; couples; executives; families; professionals; tourists; university students
www.vivorio.com.br
CREDIT CARDS AmEx; Diners; MasterCard; Visa

NIGHTCLUBS

00
Rua Padre Leonel Franca, 240, Gávea
(Between Rua General Álcio Souto and Rua Doutor Alberto Gonçalves)
TEL (21) 2540-8041, 2540-8042. Wed – Sun, 8:30pm – 3am
Bar, open-air restaurant, and club with an undercover dance floor (see Where to Eat, page 212) MUSIC R&B; dub; electronic; hip hop; house; pop CLIENTELE Over 21; couples; executives; professionals; tourists
www.00site.com.br
CREDIT CARDS AmEx; Diners; MasterCard; Visa

HOTELS, RESTAURANTS, AND SERVICES

Allegro Bistrô
Rua Barata Ribeiro, 502-D, Copacabana
(Between Rua Anita Garibaldi and Rua Santa Clara)
TEL (21) 2548-5005. Mon – Fri, 9am – 9pm; Sat, 9am – 8pm. Shows: Mon – Fri (piano), 1pm – 5pm; Mon and Tue, 7pm – 9pm; Wed – Fri, 5pm – 9pm; Sat, noon – 8pm
MUSIC Bossa nova; choro; jazz; MPB CLIENTELE Over 20; couples; professionals; tourists
www.modernsound.com.br/bistro.asp
CREDIT CARDS AmEx; Diners; MasterCard; Visa

Bar do Tom
Rua Adalberto Ferreira, 32, Leblon
(Between Praça Cláudio Coutinho and Praça Ministro Romeiro Neto)
TEL (21) 2274-4022. Daily, 6pm – midnight
MUSIC Bossa nova; choro; MPB; samba CLIENTELE Over 40; couples; executives; families; professionals
www.plataforma.com
CREDIT CARDS AmEx; Diners; MasterCard; Visa

Bip Bip
Rua Almirante Gonçalves, 50, store D, Copacabana
(Between Rua Djalma Ulrich and Rua Sá Ferreira)
TEL (21) 2267-9696. Daily, 7pm – 1am
See Where to Eat, page 212. MUSIC Bossa nova; choro; samba CLIENTELE Over 20; professionals; tourists
CREDIT CARDS Not accepted

Cabaret Kalesa
Rua Sacadura Cabral, 61, Saúde
(Between Rua Mato Grosso and Largo São Francisco da Prainha)
TEL (21) 2516-8332. Fri and Sat, 10pm – 5am
MUSIC Electronic; MPB; samba CLIENTELE around 20 years of age; tourists; university students
www.kalesa.com.br
CREDIT CARDS AmEx; Visa

Café Cultural Sacrilégio
See Show Venues

Cais do Oriente
Rua Visconde de Itaboraí, 8, Centro
(Between Rua do Mercado and Rua Primeiro de Março)
TEL (21) 2233-2531, 2203-0178. Tue – Sat, noon – midnight; Sun and Mon, noon – 4pm
See Where to Eat, page 212. MUSIC Bossa nova; jazz CLIENTELE Over 30; couples; executives; professionals; tourists
www.caisdooriente.com.br
CREDIT CARDS AmEx; Diners; MasterCard; Visa

Carioca da Gema
Avenida Mem de Sá, 79, Lapa
(Between Rua Gomes Freire and Rua do Lavradio)
TEL (21) 2221-0043. Mon – Thu, 6pm – 1am; Fri, 6pm – 3am; Sat, 9pm – 3am
See Where to Eat, page 212. MUSIC Bossa nova; choro; MPB; samba CLIENTELE Over 20; couples; executives; families; professionals; tourists; university students
www.barcariocadagema.com.br
CREDIT CARDS Not accepted

Casa da Matriz
Rua Henrique de Novais, 107, Botafogo
(Between Rua Real Grandeza and Rua São João Batista)
TEL (21) 2266-1014. Daily, 11pm until the last customer leaves
This nightclub has a games room and exhibition space, and even hosts plays. MUSIC Electronic; hip hop; MPB; reggae; rock CLIENTELE Up to 35; professionals; tourists; university students
www.matrizonline.com.br
CREDIT CARDS Diners; MasterCard; Visa

Centro Cultural Carioca
See Show Venues

Céu Aberto
Rua do Lavradio, 170, Lapa
(Between Rua do Senado and Rua da Relação)
TEL (21) 2508-9466. Mon – Fri, 11:30am – 4pm; Thu and Fri, 11:30am – 4pm and 8pm – 2:30am; Sat, 8pm – 2:30am
MUSIC Samba CLIENTELE Over 30; couples; executives; professionals
CREDIT CARDS Diners; MasterCard; Visa

Clube dos Democráticos
See Show Venues

Comuna do Semente
Rua Joaquim Silva, 138, Lapa
(Under the Lapa Arches, near Rua Riachuelo)
TEL (21) 9781-2451. Sun – Thu, 8pm – 2am (closed Fri and Sat)
See Where to Eat, page 212. MUSIC Choro; samba; samba-de-roda CLIENTELE Over 20; professionals; tourists; university students; musicians
CREDIT CARDS Not accepted

Dama de Ferro
Rua Vinicius de Moraes, 288, Ipanema
(Between Rua Alberto de Campos and Avenida Epitácio Pessoa)
TEL (21) 2247-2330. Thu – Sun, 11pm until the last customer leaves
Hosts performances, poetry readings, and exhibitions.
MUSIC Electronic (house, tech house, techno, underground, electro and breakbeat) CLIENTELE Between 20 and 40; gays and lesbians
www.damadeferro.com.br
CREDIT CARDS MasterCard; Visa

Drink Café
Avenida Borges de Medeiros, no #, Lagoa
(In Parque dos Patins, near the Jockey Club)
TEL (21) 2239-4136. Tue – Sun, noon until the last customer leaves
Serves German cuisine. MUSIC Bossa nova; jazz; MPB; samba CLIENTELE Between 20 and 40; couples; families; professionals
www.drinkcafe.com.br
CREDIT CARDS AmEx; Diners; MasterCard; Visa

Espaço Cultural Maurice Valansi
Rua Martins Ferreira, 48, Botafogo
(Between Rua Conde de Irajá and Rua Real Grandeza)

TEL (21) 2527-4044. Mon – Fri, 5pm – 2am; Sat, 6pm – 2am
This space contains a *crêperie*, a bookstore, and a exhibition space for design, art, and photography. MUSIC Bossa nova; jazz; MPB CLIENTELE Over 30; couples; executives; professionals
CREDIT CARDS AmEx; Diners; MasterCard

Estrela da Lapa
See Show Venues

Galeria Café
Rua Teixeira de Melo, 31, stores E and F, Ipanema
(Between Rua Prudente de Morais and Rua Visconde de Pirajá)
TEL (21) 2523-8250. Wed – Sat, 10:30am until the last customer leaves; Sun, noon – 8pm
This happening café hosts a mix of entertainment and art exhibitions. MUSIC Electronic; flashback; MPB; pop; rock; samba CLIENTELE Over 30; gays and lesbians; professionals
www.galeriacafe.com.br
CREDIT CARDS AmEx; Diners; MasterCard; Visa

Guapo Loco
Rua Rainha Guilhermina, 48, Leblon
(Between Avenida Ataulfo de Paiva and Avenida General San Martin)
TEL (21) 2294-8148, 2495-2995. Mon, 7pm – midnight; Tue – Sun, 7pm until the last customer leaves ALSO AT Rua Lauro Müller, 116 (Shopping Rio Sul), Botafogo TEL (21) 2541-3726; Avenida Armando Lombardi, 493, Barra da Tijuca TEL (21) 2495-2995. Also in Niterói and Búzios.
Mexican food and drink menu. MUSIC Dance; electronic; funk; pop; rock; soul CLIENTELE Between 20 and 40; couples; professionals
www.guapoloco.com.br
CREDIT CARDS Visa

Hard Rock Café
Avenida das Américas, 700, 3rd floor, store 318 (Shopping Cittá America), Barra da Tijuca
(Next to Shopping Downtown)
TEL (21) 2132-8000. Restaurant: Mon – Sat, noon – 10pm; Sun, noon – 6pm. Nightclub: Fri and Sat, 10pm – 4am; Sun, 7pm – midnight
The large restaurant and nightclub have theme nights with a variety of musical styles. MUSIC Funk; pop; rock; samba rock CLIENTELE Up to 40; teenagers; couples; university students;
www.hardrockcafebrasil.com.br/rj
CREDIT CARDS AmEx; Diners; MasterCard; Visa

J. Club
Praia do Flamengo, 340, Flamengo
(Between Rua Cruz Lima and Rua Tucumã)
TEL (21) 2551-1278. Fri and Sat, 9:30pm until the last customer leaves
MUSIC Bossa nova; choro; jazz CLIENTELE Over 20; couples; executives; professionals
www.casajulietadeserpa.com.br
CREDIT CARDS AmEx; Diners; MasterCard; Visa

La Girl
Rua Raul Pompéia, 102, store M, Copacabana
(Between Rua Júlio de Castilho and Rua Rainha Elisabete)
TEL (21) 2247-8342. Mon, Wed and Thu, 9:30pm – 6am; Fri – Sun, 10pm – 6am
MUSIC Dance; electronic; hip hop; pop CLIENTELE Over 20; gays and lesbians
www.lagirl.com.br
CREDIT CARDS AmEx; Diners; MasterCard; Visa

Le Boy
Rua Raul Pompéia, 102, store A, Copacabana
(Between Rua Júlio de Castilho and Rua Rainha Elisabete)
TEL (21) 2513-4993. Tue – Sun, 11pm – 6am
MUSIC Electronic; flashback; pop CLIENTELE Ages 20 to 40; gays and lesbians
www.leboy.com.br
CREDIT CARDS AmEx; Diners; MasterCard; Visa

Melt
Rua Rita Ludolf, 47, Leblon
(Corner of Avenida General San Martin)
TEL (21) 2512-1662, 2249-9309. Daily, 8pm until the last customer leaves
MUSIC Electronic; flashback; house music; hip hop; MPB; pop; samba rock CLIENTELE Over 20; couples; executives; professionals
www.melt-rio.com.br
CREDIT CARDS Diners; MasterCard; Visa

Mistura Fina
See Show Venues

Nuth Lounge
Avenida Armando Lombardi, 999, Barra da Tijuca
(Between Avenida Rodolfo Amoedo and Rua Gumercindo da Silva, one block from Praça Professor Souza Araújo)
TEL (21) 3153-8595. Daily, 9pm – 5am
MUSIC Electronic; hip hop; MPB; pop; rock; samba rock CLIENTELE Over 20; couples; professionals; university students
www.nuth.com.br
CREDIT CARDS AmEx; MasterCard; Visa

Palaphita Kitch
Avenida Epitácio Pessoa, no #, kiosk 20, Lagoa
(In front of Corte do Cantagalo, near the Lagoa paddleboats)
TEL (21) 2227-0837. Mon – Sun, 6pm until the last customer leaves
With Amazon-inspired décor and cuisine, this place gets busy. MUSIC Contemporary international; MPB; pop; samba rock CLIENTELE Over 30; couples; executives; families; tourists
www.palaphitakitch.com.br
CREDIT CARDS Not accepted

Rio Scenarium
Rua do Lavradio, 20, Lapa
(Between Avenida Gomes Freire and Rua Pedro II)
TEL (21) 3147-9005, 3852-5516, 2233-3239. Tue – Fri, 6:30pm – 2am; Sat, 7:30pm – 2am

A cross between an antique store, a show venue and a restaurant (see Where to Eat, page 212). MUSIC Choro; forró; jongo; maracatu, MPB; samba CLIENTELE Over 20; couples; executives; families; professionals; tourists; university students
www.rioscenarium.com.br
CREDIT CARDS AmEx; Diners; MasterCard; Visa

Rosie's O'Gradys Pub
Avenida Atlântica, 994, store A, Leme
(Between Avenida Princesa Isabel and Rua Antônio Vieira)
TEL (21) 2543-1483. Tue – Sun, 4pm – 3am
This Irish pub is known for its good food. MUSIC Electronic; pop; rock CLIENTELE Over 30; executives; professionals; university students
CREDIT CARDS AmEx; Diners; MasterCard; Visa

Teatro Odisséia
See Show Venues

Trapiche da Gamboa
Rua Sacadura Cabral, 155, Saúde
(Between Praça Mauá and Avenida Barão de Tefé)
TEL (21) 2516-0868, 2233-9276. Tue – Thu, 6:30pm – 1am; Fri, 6:30pm – 3am; Sat, 8:30pm – 3am
A reference in Rio's samba scene. MUSIC Choro; samba CLIENTELE Over 20; couples; executives; professionals; tourists; university students
CREDIT CARDS AmEx; Diners; MasterCard; Visa

Villarino
Avenida Calógeras, 6, store B, Centro
(Between Rua Graça Aranha and Rua México)
TEL (21) 2240-1627, 2240-9634. Mon – Fri, noon – 10pm
MUSIC Bossa nova CLIENTELE Over 20; couples; executives; professionals
www.villarino.com.br
CREDIT CARDS AmEx; Diners; MasterCard; Visa

Vinicius Piano Bar
Rua Vinicius de Moraes, 39, Ipanema
(Between Rua Prudente de Morais and Rua Visconde de Pirajá)
TEL (21) 2523-4757. Restaurant: daily, 11am – 2am. Pianobar: 9pm – 2am
Varied menu. MUSIC Bossa nova CLIENTELE Over 20; couples; executives; professionals; tourists
www.viniciusbar.com.br
CREDIT CARDS AmEx; Diners; MasterCard; Visa

SHOPPING

Accessories and Jewelry

Antonio Bernardo
Rua Garcia D'Ávila, 121, Ipanema
(Between Rua Visconde de Pirajá and Rua Barão da Torre)
TEL (21) 2512-7204. Mon – Fri, 10am – 8pm; Sat, 10am – 4pm ALSO AT Rua Visconde de Pirajá, 351, store 104, Ipanema TEL (21) 2523-3192; Shopping da Gávea: Rua Marquês de São Vicente, 52, store 330, Gávea TEL (21) 2274-7796; Fashion Mall: Estrada da Gávea, 899, store 208C, São Conrado TEL (21) 3322-3113
While selling jewelry of contemporary design, this spot also has an art exhibition area.
www.antoniobernardo.com
CREDIT CARDS AmEx; Diners; MasterCard; Visa

Etra
Rua Joana Angélica, 192, store 201, Ipanema
(Between Rua Barão de Jaguaripe and Rua Nascimento Silva)
TEL (21) 3813-3124. Mon – Fri, 11am – 7pm; Sat, 10am – 2pm
Stylish accessories, produced on a small scale: approximately 550 items per season.
CREDIT CARDS Not accepted

Parceria Carioca
Rua Jardim Botânico, 728, store 108, Jardim Botânico
(Between Rua Saturnino de Brito and Rua General Garzon)
TEL (21) 2259-1437. Mon – Fri, 10am – 7pm; Sat, 10am – 2pm ALSO AT Rua Visconde de Pirajá, 351, Ipanema TEL (21) 2267-3222; Shopping da Gávea: Rua Marquês de São Vicente, 52, store 313, Gávea TEL (21) 2511-8023
Costume jewelry, cloth handbags, sandals, and home decorations.
www.parceriacarioca.com.br
CREDIT CARDS AmEx; Diners; MasterCard; Visa

Ricardo Filgueiras
Rua Visconde de Pirajá, 351, store 203, Ipanema
(Between Rua Joana Angélica and Rua Maria Quitéria)
TEL (21) 2287-1090. Mon – Fri, 10am – 7pm; Sat, 10am – 2pm
Personalized pieces in small numbers. Will deliver overseas if necessary.
CREDIT CARDS AmEx; Diners; MasterCard; Visa

Handbags and Shoes

Constança Basto
Rua Visconde de Pirajá, 371, mezzanine store 206, Ipanema
(Between Rua Maria Quitéria and Rua Joana Angélica)
TEL (21) 2247-9932. Mon – Fri, 10am – 7pm; Sat, 10am – 2pm ALSO AT Fashion Mall: Estrada da Gávea, 899, 2nd floor, São Conrado TEL (21) 2922-0355
Light, comfortable footwear, produced in satin, and alligator and snake leather, among other materials.
www.constancabasto.com
CREDIT CARDS AmEx; Diners; MasterCard; Visa

Danielle Carvalho
Rua Visconde de Pirajá, 371, store 202, Ipanema
(Between Rua Maria Quitéria and Rua Joana Angélica)
TEL (21) 2287-7607. Mon – Fri, 10am – 7pm; Sat, 10am – 2pm
Handmade handbags in fine fabrics and rustic materials, as well as costume jewelry and women's fashion.
CREDIT CARDS Visa

HOTELS, RESTAURANTS, AND SERVICES

Glorinha Paranaguá
Rua Visconde de Pirajá, 365, store 2, Ipanema
(Between Rua Maria Quitéria and Rua Joana Angélica)
TEL (21) 2522-8203, 2267-4295. Mon – Fri, 9am – 7pm; Sat, 9am – 2pm
Handbags in bamboo, cloth, leather, and crochet, as well as purses, necklaces, bracelets, and earrings. Will deliver overseas.
www.glorinhaparanagua.com.br
CREDIT CARDS AmEx; MasterCard; Visa

Louis Vuitton
Rua Gárcia D'Ávila, 114, Ipanema
(Between Rua Visconde de Pirajá and Rua Barão da Torre)
TEL (21) 2511-5839. Mon – Fri, 10am – 8pm; Sat, 10am – 4pm
Handbags, belts, purses, watches, and shoes. Also beach accessories, bikinis, and towels.
www.louisvuitton.com.br
CREDIT CARDS AmEx; Diners; MasterCard; Visa

Roberta Wright
Rua Aristides Espínola, 121, flat 202, Leblon
(Between Rua Dias Ferreira and Avenida Ataulfo de Paiva)
TEL (21) 2512-3343. Mon – Fri, 10am – 7pm; Sat, 10am – 3pm
Small stock and personalized service. Decorated sandals and pumps, and basic toe-sandals. Will ship overseas.
www.robertawright.com.br
CREDIT CARDS Not accepted

Fashion

Andrea Saletto
Rua Nascimento Silva, 244, Ipanema
(Between Rua Maria Quitéria and Rua Joana Angélica)
TEL (21) 2267-9361. Mon – Fri, 10am – 8pm; Sat, 10am – 2pm ALSO AT Fashion Mall: Estrada da Gávea, 899, São Conrado TEL (21) 3322-5435
Elegant and contemporary dresses, skirts, and blouses in imported fabrics, especially from Italy.
www.andreasaletto.com.br
CREDIT CARDS AmEx; Diners; MasterCard; Visa

Ateliê Cristina Cordeiro
Rua Garcia D'Ávila, 194, Ipanema
(Between Rua Nascimento Silva and Rua Barão de Jaguaripe)
TEL (21) 2267-7195. Mon – Fri, 10am – 8pm; Sat, 10am – 6pm
Casual and sophisticated clothes. There are hand-painted items, as well as shoes and costume jewelry.
www.cristinacordeiro.com
CREDIT CARDS AmEx; Diners; MasterCard; Visa

Ateliê Ibô
Rua Dias Ferreira, 45, store B, Leblon
(Between Rua Aristides Espínola and Avenida Ataulfo de Paiva)
TEL (21) 2540-5232. Mon – Fri, 10am – 8pm; Sat, 10am – 6pm
Stylist Isabela Capeto creates embroidery and retro patterns on trousers, dresses, and blouses. There are also mens' clothes, accessories, costume jewelry, and beachwear. Staff can speak German, English, and Italian.
www.isabelacapeto.com.br
CREDIT CARDS AmEx; Visa

Blue Man
Rua Visconde de Pirajá, 351, stores C and D, Ipanema
(Between Rua Maria Quitéria and Rua Joana Angélica)
TEL (21) 2247-4905. Mon – Fri, 9am – 8pm, Sat, 9am – 6pm
A range of daring cuts and patterns, as well as men's swimming trunks and board shorts.
www.blueman.com.br
CREDIT CARDS AmEx; Diners; MasterCard; Visa

Bumbum
Rua Visconde de Pirajá, 351
(Galeria Fórum de Ipanema), Ipanema
(Between Rua Maria Quitéria and Rua Joana Angélica)
TEL (21) 2521-3859. Mon – Fri, 9am – 8pm; Sat, 9am – 4pm
ALSO AT Shopping Rio Sul: Rua Lauro Müller, 116, 4th floor, Botafogo TEL (21) 2542-9614; Shopping Vertical: Rua Sete de Setembro, 48, 5th floor, Centro TEL (21) 2509-0224.
Bikinis in different cuts, beach bags, sandals, and other beach accessories.
www.bumbum.com.br
CREDIT CARDS AmEx; Diners; MasterCard; Visa

Carla Bokel
Rua General Urquisa, 25, apartment 101, Leblon
(Between Avenida Delfim Moreira and Avenida General San Martin)
TEL (21) 3852-2047, 2232-1000, 2274-3533. Mon – Fri, 9am – 5pm; Sat, subject to prior booking
Sophisticated and simple skirts, blouses, and dresses. The home line includes items such as cushions and table linens.
www.carlabokel.com
CREDIT CARDS Not accepted

Carlos Tufvesson
Rua Nascimento Silva, 304, Ipanema
(Between Rua Joana Angélica and Rua Maria Quitéria)
TEL (21) 2523-9200. Mon – Fri, 10am – 7pm; Sat, 10am – 2pm
Long, sensual *haute couture* dresses get modeled and tailored right on the client's body. There are also basic wardrobe items and international brands.
www.carlostufvesson.com
CREDIT CARDS AmEx; Diners; MasterCard; Visa

Casa da Alessa
Rua Nascimento Silva, 399, Ipanema
(Between Rua Garcia D'Ávila and Rua Maria Quitéria)
TEL (21) 2287-9939. Mon – Fri, 10am – 7pm; Sat, 10am – 3pm
Calico clothes, lingerie, handbags.
www.alessa.com.br
CREDIT CARDS AmEx; Diners; MasterCard; Visa

Clube Chocolate
Estrada da Gávea, 899, 2nd floor (Fashion Mall),
São Conrado
(Between Rua Golf Club and Rua Capuri)
TEL (21) 3322-3733. Mon – Sat, 10am – 10pm; Sun, noon
– 9pm; holidays, noon – 9pm
Sophisticated, modern women's fashion, as well as
books, jewelry, CDs, and things for pets. There is a sexy
shop for ladies only, where women can buy sex toys, as
well as sexy underwear, and a French restaurant.
www.estudiochocolate.com
CREDIT CARDS AmEx; Diners; MasterCard; Visa

Cristine Ban
Rua Aníbal de Mendonça, 123, store A, Ipanema
(Between Rua Visconde de Pirajá and Rua Barão
da Torre)
TEL (21) 2259-2676. Mon – Fri, 9:30am – 7:30pm; Sat,
9:30am – 2:30pm
Crocheted women's clothes, as well as handbags, purses, shoes, and costume jewelry.
CREDIT CARDS AmEx; Diners; MasterCard; Visa

Dama y Soberana
Rua Barão de Jaguaripe, 94 D, Ipanema
(Near the corner of Rua Joana Angélica)
TEL (21) 3813-0082. Mon – Fri, 10am – 8pm; Sat, 10am
– 2pm
Lívia Torres makes clothes for everyday wear and for
special occasions. She personalizes dresses and sells
costume jewelry, shoes, lingerie, and handbags.
CREDIT CARDS AmEx; Diners; MasterCard; Visa

Dona Coisa
Rua Lopes Quintas, 153, Jardim Botânico
(Between Rua Jardim Botânico and Rua Corcovado)
TEL (21) 2249-2336. Mon – Fri, 11am – 8pm; Sat, 11am
– 3pm
Sells everything from clothes to chocolates, as well as
stationery, handbags, footwear, and costume jewelry.
There is a charming café on the mezzanine.
CREDIT CARDS AmEx; Diners; MasterCard; Visa

Donna Chita
Rua Joana Angélica, 192, mezzanine store 103,
Ipanema
(Between Rua Barão de Jaguaripe and
Rua Nascimento Silva)
TEL (21) 2267-5127. Mon – Fri, 9am – 7pm; Sat, 9am – 2pm
Clothes for children up to age eight, in a range of brands.
This store produces its own shoes and jeans. Will ship
overseas if needed.
www.donachita.com.br
CREDIT CARDS AmEx; Visa

Espaço Lundgren
Avenida Vieira Souto, 234, Ipanema
(Corner of Rua Farme de Amoedo)
TEL (21) 2523-2522. Mon – Fri, 10am – 8pm; Sat, 10am
– 6pm
Sophisticated and exclusive pieces by Brazilian and international labels. A charming bar serves drinks and snacks in the back garden.
www.espacolundgren.com.br
CREDIT CARDS AmEx; Diners; MasterCard; Visa

Foch
Rua Visconde de Pirajá, 365 B, ground floor, store 10
(Galeria Fiamma), Ipanema
(In front of Praça Nossa Senhora da Paz)
TEL (21) 2521-1172. Mon – Fri, 10am – 8pm; Sat, 10am
– 4pm
Sells men's underwear – the boxer shorts are particularly popular – t-shirts, trousers, swimming trunks, and accessories, known for their comfort and irreverent designs. A big hit among the gay and lesbian crowd.
CREDIT CARDS AmEx; Diners; MasterCard; Visa
www.foch.com.br

Jujuba Dorme Bem
Rua Joana Angélica, 192, flat 203, Ipanema
(Corner of Rua Nascimento Silva)
TEL (21) 2247-8799. Mon – Fri, 10am – 7pm
Cushions, sheets, curtains, blankets, and delicate glory-box items are handmade in this studio.
www.jujubadormebem.com.br
CREDIT CARDS Not accepted

Khós
Rua Redentor, 23, 2nd floor, Ipanema
(Between Rua Maria Quitéria and Rua Joana Angélica)
TEL (21) 3813-2879. Mon – Fri, 10am – 7pm; Sat, 10am
– 2pm
This shop carries a range of brands: party dresses by
Napoleão Lacerda, romantic pieces by Daniella Martins, and sophisticated items by Carla Bockel. For kids, there are brands such as Zucca Baby and Seven.
www.khos.com.br
CREDIT CARDS AmEx; Diners; MasterCard; Visa

Leeloo
Rua Visconde de Pirajá, 547, Ipanema
(Between Avenida Henrique Dumont and Rua Aníbal
de Mendonça)
TEL (21) 2540-6389. Mon – Fri, 10am – 8pm; Sat, 10am –
7pm; holidays, 11am – 7pm
Ranges from basic wardrobe items to evening and
party clothes, as well as accessories and home decorations.
www.leeloo.com.br
CREDIT CARDS AmEx; Diners; MasterCard; Visa

Lelé da Cuca
Rua Visconde de Pirajá, 430, store B, Ipanema
(Between Rua Garcia D'Ávila and Rua Maria Quitéria)
TEL (21) 2287-5295. Mon – Fri, 9:30am – 7:30pm; Sat,
10am – 2pm
On the cutting edge of fashion, this store sells women's
fashion, footwear, and accessories.
CREDIT CARDS AmEx; Diners; MasterCard; Visa

Lenny & Cia
Rua Visconde de Pirajá, 351, stores 114 and 115,
Ipanema
(In front of Praça Nossa Senhora da Paz)

TEL (21) 2523-3796. Mon – Fri, 10am – 8pm; Sat, 10am – 3pm ALSO AT Shopping da Gávea: Rua Marquês de São Vicente, 124, Gávea TEL (21) 2259-3251; Rua Garcia D'ávila, Ipanema TEL (21) 2227-5537; Fashion Mall: Estrada da Gávea, 899, São Conrado TEL (21) 2422-3849; Shopping Rio Design Barra: Avenida das Américas, 7777, Barra da Tijuca TEL (21) 2431-0909
Bikinis and full-piece bathing suits in stylish patterns and cuts. There are also skirts, blouses, and accessories.
www.lenny.com.br
CREDIT CARDS AmEx; Diners; MasterCard; Visa

Mara Mac
Rua Visconde de Pirajá, 365, store A, Ipanema
(Between Rua Prudente de Morais and Rua Barão da Torre)
TEL (21) 2523-2340. Mon – Fri, 9am – 7pm; Sat, 9am – 3pm ALSO AT Shopping Rio Sul: Rua Lauro Müller, 116, store 331, Botafogo TEL (21) 2541-6091; Rua Ataulfo de Paiva, 270, store 212, Leblon TEL (21) 2249-5133; Shopping Rio Design Leblon: Avenida Ataulfo de Paiva, 270, Leblon TEL (21) 2431-3525.
Feminine, sensual items in fine fabrics, perfectly finished and impeccably cut. Will ship overseas.
www.maramac.com.br
CREDIT CARDS AmEx; Diners; MasterCard; Visa

Maria Bonita
Rua Vinicius de Moraes, 149, Ipanema
(Between Rua Joana Angélica and Rua Farme de Amoedo)
TEL (21) 2523-4093. Mon – Fri, 9am – 8pm; Sat, 9am – 4pm ALSO AT Fashion Mall: Estrada da Gávea, 223, 2nd floor, store 23, São Conrado TEL (21) 3322-7006; Barra Shopping: Avenida das Américas, 4666, Lagoa floor, store 140, Barra da Tijuca TEL (21) 2431-9447
Party dresses, handbags, footwear, and jewelry in classic designs. Will ship overseas if necessary.
www.mariabonita.com.br
CREDIT CARDS AmEx; Diners; MasterCard; Visa

Maria Bonita Extra
Rua Aníbal de Mendonça, 135, stores C and D, Ipanema
(Between Rua Visconde de Pirajá and Rua Barão da Torre)
TEL (21) 2540-5354. Mon – Fri, 9am – 8pm; Sat, 9am – 4pm
A sportier line by the Maria Bonita label, with items for young people. Will ship overseas.
www.mariabonitaextra.com.br
CREDIT CARDS AmEx; Diners; MasterCard; Visa

Novamente
Rua Sete de Setembro, 43, 5th floor, Centro
(Between Rua do Ouvidor and Rua São José)
TEL (21) 3852-8031. Mon – Fri, 10am – 9pm; Sat, 10am – 4pm ALSO AT Shopping Rio Design Barra: Avenida das Américas, 7777, store 154, Barra da Tijuca TEL (21) 3410-5483
This store carries Brazilian labels such as Reinaldo Lourenço, Fause Haten, and Gisele Nasser, with items ranging from jeans to party clothes, and accessories.
CREDIT CARDS AmEx; Diners; MasterCard; Visa

Nuit Nuit
Estrada da Gávea, 899, store 202, 2nd floor (Fashion Mall), São Conrado
(Between Rua Golf Club and Rua Capuri)
TEL (21) 2422-3667. Mon – Sat, 10am – 10pm; Sun, 10am – 9pm ALSO AT Rua Visconde de Pirajá, 351, store 224, Ipanema (Galeria Fórum de Ipanema) TEL (21) 2522-2601; Avenida das Américas, 7777, store 236, 2nd floor, Barra da Tijuca (Rio Design Barra) TEL (21) 2432-8204
Comfortable clothes in silk and cotton. There are robes, nightdresses, pajamas, items of lingerie, flip-flops, and travel bags.
www.nuitnuit.com.br
CREDIT CARDS AmEx; Diners; MasterCard; Visa

Osklen
Rua Maria Quitéria, 85, Ipanema
(Between Rua Joana Angélica and Rua Gárcia D'Ávila)
TEL (21) 2227-2911, 2227-2930. Mon – Fri, 9am – 8pm; Sat, 9am – 6pm; Sun, 11am – 5pm
Fun, comfortable clothes that appeal to surfers, active types, and sports enthusiasts.
www.osklen.com
CREDIT CARDS AmEx; MasterCard; Visa

Perfit
Avenida Lauro Sodré, 445, 3rd floor, store 301, part C-18 (Shopping Rio Sul), Botafogo
(Corner of Rua Lauro Müller)
TEL (21) 2275-9747. Mon – Sat, 10am – 10pm ALSO AT Fashion Mall: Estrada da Gávea, 899, 2nd floor, store 212-B, São Conrado TEL (21) 3322-0087; Barra Shopping: Avenida das Américas, 4666, Américas floor, Barra da Tijuca TEL (21) 2431-9876
The house forte is sportswear: footwear, clothes, and accessories by Nike, Puma, Ecko, and Adidas, among others.
www.perfit.com.br
CREDIT CARDS AmEx; Diners; MasterCard; Visa

Reserva
Rua Maria Quitéria, 77, store F, Ipanema
(Between Rua Visconde de Pirajá and Rua Barão da Torre)
TEL (21) 2255-3279. Mon – Fri, 9am – 6pm; Sat, 10am – 6pm; Sun, 11am – 5pm
Men's dresswear, sportswear, Bermuda shorts, and overalls. Jeans are the brand's forte.
www.reservananet.com.br
CREDIT CARDS AmEx; Diners; MasterCard; Visa

Richard's
Rua Maria Quitéria, 95, Ipanema
(Between Rua Barão da Torre and Rua Visconde de Pirajá)
TEL 2522-1245. Mon – Fri, 9am – 8pm ALSO AT Shopping Rio Sul: Rua Lauro Muller, 116, store 201, Botafogo TEL (21) 2275-8988; Rio Design Barra: Avenida das Américas, 7777, stores 249 to 245, Barra da Tijuca TEL (21) 3325-7774
T-shirts, jeans, skirts, and blouses in comfortable, modern cuts. Both the men's and women's lines are casually elegant.
www.richards.com.br
CREDIT CARDS AmEx; Diners; MasterCard; Visa

HOTELS, RESTAURANTS, AND SERVICES

Rygy
Avenida das Américas, 4666, store 126
(Barra Shopping), Barra da Tijuca
(Entrance I)
TEL (21) 2431-8949, 2431-9806. Mon – Sat, 10am – 7pm
Beach and sportswear, costume jewelry and sandals.
www.rygy.com.br
CREDIT CARDS AmEx; Diners; MasterCard; Visa

Salinas
Rua Visconde de Pirajá, 547, stores 204 and 205, Ipanema
(Between Rua Barão da Torre and Rua Visconde de Pirajá)
TEL (21) 2274-0644. Mon – Fri, 9am – 7pm; Sat, 10am – 5pm ALSO AT Shopping Rio Sul: Rua Lauro Müller, 4th floor, Botafogo TEL (21) 2275-0793; Barra Shopping: Avenida das Américas, 4666, 2nd floor, store 242-A, Barra da Tijuca TEL (21) 2431-9111; Fashion Mall: Estrada da Gávea, 899, 2nd floor, store 207-A, São Conrado TEL (21) 2422-3579
Comfort and cheery patterns are the order of the day in the bikinis, full-piece women's bathing suits, men's swimming trunks, and children's beachwear.
www.salinas-rio.com.br
CREDIT CARDS AmEx; Diners; MasterCard; Visa

Teargas
Rua Visconde de Pirajá, 444, mezzanine store 201, Ipanema
(Between Rua Prudente de Morais and Rua Barão da Torre)
TEL (21) 2267-6598. Mon – Sat, 10am – 8pm
Jeans and colorful t-shirts, with special prints, washes, and patterns. Will ship overseas if necessary.
www.teargas.com.br
CREDIT CARDS AmEx; Diners; MasterCard; Visa

Totem
Rua Visconde de Pirajá, 547, store F, Ipanema
(Between Rua Prudente de Morais and Rua Barão da Torre)
TEL (21) 2540-0661. Mon – Fri, 10am – 8pm; Sat, 10am – 6pm ALSO AT Shopping da Gávea: Rua Marquês de São Vicente, 124, 2nd floor, store 252-A, Gávea TEL (21) 2512-4151; BarraShopping: Avenida das Américas, 4666, Américas level, store 252-A, Barra da Tijuca TEL (21) 3089-1369; Shopping Downtown: Avenida das Américas, 500, block 8, store 105, Barra da Tijuca TEL (21) 2491-2930.
Trousers, shirts, skirts, blouses, and beachwear in fun colors and patterns. There is also a kids' floor in the Ipanema store, Totem Kids.
www.totempraia.com.br
CREDIT CARDS AmEx; Diners; MasterCard; Visa

Tutti Fashion
Rua Visconde de Pirajá, 282, store A, Ipanema
(Between Rua Prudente de Morais and Rua Barão da Torre)
TEL (21) 2247-1756. Mon – Fri, 9am – 8pm; Sat, 9am – 3pm ALSO AT Rua Conde Bonfim, 468, Tijuca TEL (21) 2258-6468; BarraShopping: Avenida das Américas, 4666, store 105-A, Barra da Tijuca TEL (21) 2431-8109; Nova América Outlet Shopping: Avenida Pastor Martin Luther King Junior, 126, store 406, Del Castilho TEL (21) 2581-1170
Women's clothes, including suits and leather jackets. Also carries plus-sizes.
CREDIT CARDS Diners; MasterCard; Visa

Verve
Rua Garcia D´Ávila, 149, Ipanema
(Between Rua Nascimento Silva and Rua Barão da Torre)
TEL (21) 3202-2680. Mon – Sat, 10am – 7pm ALSO AT Shopping Rio Design Leblon: Avenida Ataulfo de Paiva, 270, 3rd floor, store 301-A, Leblon TEL (21) 2274-3294; Shopping Design Barra: Avenida das Américas, 7777, 1st floor, store 137, Barra da Tijuca TEL (21) 2431-0016
Feminine, casual, and sensual lingerie. Panties, bras, pajamas, and robes in light fabrics.
www.verve.com.br
CREDIT CARDS AmEx; Diners; MasterCard; Visa

Virzi
Rua Nascimento Silva, 309, Ipanema
(Between Rua Joana Angélica and Rua Garcia D'Ávila)
TEL (21) 2267-1625. Mon – Fri, 10am – 7pm; Sat, 10am – 2pm
Classic women's clothes, handbags, shoes, skirts, dresses, and blouses.
www.virzi.com.br
CREDIT CARDS Visa

Design and Decoration

Acrilo
Rua Marquês de São Vicente, 52, store 263
(Shopping da Gávea), Gávea
(Between Rua General Rabelo and Praça Santos Dumont)
TEL (21) 2274-0649. Mon – Sat, 10am – 10pm; Sun, 3pm – 9pm
Furniture and acrylic objects created by designer Pedro Olsen Angert and ethnic furniture imported from Asia.
www.acrilo.com.br
CREDIT CARDS AmEx; Diners; MasterCard; Visa

Antique Center
Rua do Lavradio, 28, Centro
(Between Rua do Senado and Rua Tiradentes)
TEL (21) 3147-9014. Mon – Fri, 9am – 6pm; the first Saturday of each month, 9am – 6pm
The house highlight is the art deco furniture, in addition to English china, crystal, lamps, and crystal chandeliers. Will ship overseas.
CREDIT CARDS Not accepted

Area Objetos
Avenida Marquês de São Vicente, 52, store 206
(Shopping da Gávea), Gávea
(Between Rua General Rabelo and Praça Santos Dumont)

TEL (21) 3204-0770, 2294-1715. Mon – Sat, 10am – 10pm; Sun, 3pm – 9pm ALSO AT Shopping Barra Point: Avenida Armando Lombardi, 350, store 129, Barra da Tijuca TEL (21) 2492-2466
Sells handbags and costume jewelry, in addition to furniture and decorative items. Will ship overseas if necessary.
www.areaobjetos.com.br
CREDIT CARDS AmEx; Diners; MasterCard; Visa

Arquivo Contemporâneo
Rua Eduardo Pederneiras, 390, Recreio
(Between Rua Demóstenes Madureira de Pinho and Rua Professor Hermes Lima)
TEL (21) 2497-3363. Mon – Sat, 9am – 6:30pm
Personalized service and modern products signed by designers such as Sergio Rodrigues, Pedro Henrique Mendes, and Jaqueline Terpins.
www.arquivocontemporaneo.com.br
CREDIT CARDS Not accepted

Artefacto
Avenida Ayrton Senna, 2150, block K (CasaShopping), Barra da Tijuca
(Between Avenida das Américas and Avenida Luís Carlos Prestes)
TEL (21) 3325-7667. Mon, noon – 10pm; Tue – Sat, 10am – 10pm; Sun and holidays, 3pm – 9pm
Furniture in wood, steel, leather, and natural fibers. Two floors are devoted to a permanent exhibition of rooms set up by interior decorators.
www.artefacto.com.br
CREDIT CARDS AmEx; Diners; MasterCard; Visa

Bom Desenho
Rua Maria Angélica, 113, store G, Jardim Botânico
(Between Rua Jardim Botânico and Rua Alexandre Ferreira)
TEL (21) 2266-5145. Mon – Fri, 9:30am – 7pm; Sat, 9:30am – 6pm
Home decorations, objects for personal use, bath accessories and kitchen utensils, including French pots and pans by Le Creuset.
CREDIT CARDS AmEx; Diners; MasterCard; Visa

Daqui
Avenida Ataulfo de Paiva, 1174, store F, Leblon
(Between Rua Aristides Espínola and Rua Rainha Guilhermina)
TEL (21) 2529-8576. Mon – Fri, 10am – 8pm; Sat, 10am – 4pm
This store carries a mixture of fine art, folk art, and design objects, all produced in Brazil, as well as personal accessories and items for the home.
www.daquidobrasil.com.br
CREDIT CARDS AmEx; Diners; MasterCard; Visa

Design Café
Avenida Ataulfo de Paiva, 270, Leblon
(Between Rua Almirante Guilhem and Avenida Afrânio de Melo Franco)
TEL (21) 2512-8480. Mon – Sat, 10am – 10pm; Sun, 3pm – 9pm ALSO AT Shopping Design Barra: Avenida das Américas, 7777, store 121-A, Barra da Tijuca TEL (21) 2434-1511
Fun and irreverent handbags, postcards, and accessories for the home.
www.designcafe.com.br
CREDIT CARDS AmEx; Diners; MasterCard; Visa

Elle et Lui Maison
Rua Garcia D'Ávila, 124, Ipanema
(Between Rua Barão da Torre and Rua Visconde de Pirajá)
TEL (21) 2239-6749. Mon – Fri, 10am – 7pm; Sat, 10am – 2pm
Products include those made in-house and older, imported items. The furniture on display is produced to order.
CREDIT CARDS AmEx; Diners; MasterCard; Visa

Empório Beraldin
Rua Nascimento Silva, 330, Ipanema
(Between Rua Maria Quitéria and Rua Garcia D'Ávila)
TEL (21) 3206-7272. Mon – Fri, 9:30am – 7pm; Sat, 10am – 2pm
The furniture, produced in-house, is made with natural products. The shop has a special line of unique fabrics.
www.emporioberaldin.com.br
CREDIT CARDS AmEx; Diners; Visa

Fernando Jaeger
Rua Corcovado, 252, Jardim Botânico
(Between Rua Lopes Quintas and Rua Santa Heloísa)
TEL (21) 2274-6026/7115. Mon – Fri, 10am – 7pm; Sat, 10am – 2pm
These contemporary pieces are made from eco-friendly sources of wood, including wood from reforestation projects.
www.fernandojaeger.com.br
CREDIT CARDS Not accepted

Forma
Rua Farme de Amoedo, 82-A, Ipanema
(Between Rua Barão da Torre and Rua Visconde de Pirajá)
TEL (21) 2523-2949. Mon – Fri, 9am – 7pm; Sat, 9:30am – 1pm
Designer furniture for the home and office. Exclusive pieces such as armchairs by the Danish furniture manufacturer Fritz Hansen and sofas and tables by German Rolf Benz.
www.forma.com.br
CREDIT CARDS AmEx; Diners; MasterCard; Visa

Lalla Bortolini
Avenida Ayrton Senna, 2510, block H, store G (Casa Shopping), Barra da Tijuca
(Between Avenida das Américas and Avenida Luís Carlos Prestes)
TEL (21) 3325-7310. Mon, noon – 10pm; Tue – Sat, 10am – 10pm; Sun, 3pm – 9pm ALSO AT Shopping da Gávea: Rua Marquês de São Vicente, 52, stores 235 and 236, Gávea TEL (21) 2294-4046

Lalla Bortolini imports objects such as candleholders, picture frames, mirrors, china, pottery, and silverware from Europe and Asia. The crystal chandeliers are a highlight.
www.lallabortolini.com.br
CREDIT CARDS AmEx; Diners; MasterCard; Visa

Lillian Rose
Rua Visconde de Pirajá, 365, store 7, Ipanema
(Between Rua Barão da Torre and Rua Prudente de Morais)
TEL (21) 2513-4037. Mon – Fri, 10am – 7pm; Sat, 10am – 2pm
Fine leather objects for the office and a wide range of album bindings, with antioxidant paper and silk. Will ship overseas if necessary.
www.lillianrose.com.br
CREDIT CARDS Visa

Machado Antigüidades
Rua Francisco Sá, 51, stores 17 to 19, Copacabana
(Between Rua Tonelero and Rua Joseph Bloch)
TEL (21) 2235-5788. Mon – Fri, 10am – 7pm; Sat, 10am – 4pm ALSO AT Shopping dos Antiquários: Rua Siqueira Campos, 143, ground floor store 14; mezzanine store 35, 2nd floor, Copacabana TEL (21) 2547-9988, 2235-5788
This family-run antique store has over 4,000 pieces, most from the 19th century and early 20th century. Will ship overseas.
www.machadoantiguidades.com.br
CREDIT CARDS AmEx; Diners; MasterCard; Visa

Novo Ambiente
Rua Marquês de São Vicente, 52, stores 322 and 323 (Shopping da Gávea), Gávea
(Between Rua General Rabelo and Praça Santos Dumont)
TEL (21) 2239-5090. Mon – Sat, 10am – 10pm; Sun, 3pm – 9pm
For 30 years, this store has been selling designer furniture made by names such as Philippe Stark, Marco Zanuzo, Le Corbusier, and Charles Eams.
www.novoambiente.com
CREDIT CARDS Visa

Novo Desenho
Avenida Infante Dom Henrique, 85, Aterro do Flamengo
(Between Rua Jardel and Praça Pistóia)
TEL (21) 2524-2290, 2524-2291. Tue – Fri, noon – 6pm; Sat, Sun, and holidays, noon – 7pm
Inside the Museu de Arte Moderna, this shop carries pieces by celebrated professionals such as Lina Bo Bardi, Paulo Mendes da Rocha, Sergio Rodrigues, Maurício Klabin, and the Campana brothers.
www.novodesenho.com.br
CREDIT CARDS AmEx; Diners; MasterCard; Visa

Oficina Inglesa
Avenida Ataulfo de Paiva, 80 B, Leblon
(Between Rua Almirante Pereira Guimarães and Avenida Borges de Medeiros)
TEL (21) 2512-9911. Mon – Fri, 10am – 7pm; Sat, 10am – 2pm
This traditional store sells replicas of old European furniture, and also produces its own wooden pieces. Will ship overseas if necessary.
www.oficinainglesa.com.br
CREDIT CARDS Not accepted

Pé de Boi Artesanato Brasileiro
Rua Ipiranga, 55, Laranjeiras
(Between Rua Conde de Baependi and Rua Paissandu)
TEL (21) 2285-4395. Mon – Fri, 10am – 7pm; Sat, 9am – 1pm
Specializes in Brazilian arts and crafts, mostly produced in the states of Minas Gerais, Pernambuco, and Ceará. Will ship overseas.
www.pedeboi.com.br
CREDIT CARDS AmEx; Visa

Retro
Rua Siqueira Campos, 143, store 159, 2nd floor (Shopping dos Antiquários), Copacabana
(Between Rua Joseph Bloch and Rua Tonelero)
TEL (21) 2257-1310. Mon – Fri, 11am – 7pm; Sat, 10am – 4pm
The house specialty is art deco, 1950s, and 1970s furniture.
CREDIT CARDS Not accepted

Rue Jadis Antiquário
Avenida Atlântica, 4240
(Shopping Cassino Atlântico), Copacabana
(Between Avenida Rainha Elisabete da Bélgica and Rua Francisco Otaviano)
TEL (21) 2267-4346. Mon – Sat, 11am – 7pm
This elegant shop carries a collection of 18th- and 19th-century European objects and furniture.
CREDIT CARDS Not accepted

Rupee Rupee
Rua Marquês de São Vicente, 52, store 349, Gávea
(Between Rua General Rabelo and Praça Santos Dumont)
TEL (21) 2511-4151. Mon – Sat, 10am – 10pm; Sun, 3pm – 9pm ALSO AT Rio Design Leblon: Avenida Ataulfo de Paiva, 270, store 301, Leblon TEL (21) 2274-0014; Rio Design Barra: Avenida das Américas, 7777, store 233, Barra da Tijuca TEL (21) 2438-7507
English tiles, paintings, and imported furniture and objects from India are the house fortes.
CREDIT CARDS AmEx; Diners; MasterCard; Visa

Secrets de Famille
Rua Marquês de São Vicente, 52, store 173 (Shopping da Gávea), Gávea
(Between Rua General Rabelo and Praça Santos Dumont)
TEL (21) 2540-6539. Mon – Sat, 10am – 10pm
Most of the pieces here have come from Provence. There is a wide range of quality originals.
www.secretsdefamille.com.br
CREDIT CARDS AmEx; Visa

HOTELS, RESTAURANTS, AND SERVICES

Sergio Rodrigues
Rua Conde de Irajá, 63, Humaitá
(Between Rua Pinheiros Guimarães and Rua Visconde de Silva)
TEL (21) 2539-0393, 2286-8792. Mon – Fri, 9am – 6pm
In addition to reproducing famous designs, the designer Sergio Rodrigues creates new models in reforestation-grown wood. The pieces are made to order and can take up to 60 days to be ready.
www.sergiorodrigues.com.br
CREDIT CARDS Not accepted

Toque
Avenida Ataulfo de Paiva, 1015-A, Leblon
(Between Rua General Artigas and Rua General Venâncio Flores)
TEL (21) 2294-3873. Mon – Fri, 9am – 7pm; Sat, 10am – 2pm
This store carries a mixture of domestic items and bed and table linens, as well as furniture produced to order in-house.
www.toqueobjetos.com.br
CREDIT CARDS AmEx; Visa

Shopping Centers

Barra Garden Shopping
Avenida das Américas, 3255, Barra da Tijuca
TEL (21) 2136-9191

BarraShopping
Avenida das Américas, 4666, Barra da Tijuca
TEL (21) 3089-1050

Botafogo Praia Shopping
Praia de Botafogo, 400, Botafogo
TEL (21) 3171-9559

CasaShopping
Avenida Ayrton Senna, 2150, Barra da Tijuca
TEL (21) 2429-8000

Center Iguatemi Rio
Rua Barão de São Francisco, 236, Vila Isabel
TEL (21) 2577-8777

Città América
Avenida das Américas, 700, Barra da Tijuca
TEL (21) 2132-7777

Downtown
Avenida das Américas, 500, Barra da Tijuca
TEL (21) 2494-7072

Fashion Mall
Estrada da Gávea, 899, São Conrado
TEL (21) 2111-4444

Gávea Trade Center
Rua Marquês de São Vicente, 124, Gávea
TEL (21) 2239-7640

New York City Center
Avenida das Américas, 5000, Barra da Tijuca
TEL (21) 2432-4980

Nova América Outlet
Avenida Pastor Martin Luther King Jr., 126, Del Castilho
TEL (21) 3083-1000

Rio Design Barra
Avenida das Américas, 7777, Barra da Tijuca
TEL (21) 2430-3024

Rio Design Leblon
Avenida Ataulfo de Paiva, 270, Leblon
TEL (21) 2430-3024

Rio Plaza Shopping
Rua General Severiano, 97, Botafogo
TEL (21) 2542-5693

Rio Sul Shopping Center
Rua Lauro Müller, 116, Botafogo
TEL (21) 3527-7000

Shopping da Gávea
Rua Marquês de São Vicente, 52, Gávea
TEL (21) 2294-1096

Shopping Leblon
Avenida Afrânio de Melo Franco, 290, Leblon
TEL (21) 2540-7341

Shopping Tijuca
Avenida Maracanã, 987, Tijuca
TEL (21) 2176-6031

Via Parque Shopping
Avenida Ayrton Senna, 3000, Barra da Tijuca
TEL (21) 2421-9222

SERVICES

AVLRJ – Associação de Vôo Livre do Rio de Janeiro
Avenida Professor Mendes de Moraes, no #, Praia do Pepino, São Conrado
TEL (21) 3322-4176. Hang gliding and paragliding.
www.avlrj.com.br

Be a Local
TEL (21) 9643-0366, 7816-9581. *Favela* tours, and shuttle services to funk dances and to soccer games at Maracanã Stadium. www.bealocal.com

Bike Lazer
Rua Visconde de Pirajá, 135, store B, Ipanema
TEL (21) 2521-2686. Mon – Fri, 9am – 7:30pm; Sat, 9am – 2pm. Outings and bike rental.

Hotels, Restaurants, and Services

Carioca Tropical Tour Operator
Avenida Nossa Senhora de Copacabana, 534, mezzanine store 304, Copacabana
TEL (21) 2547-6327. Mon – Fri, 9am – 6pm. Visits to samba schools.

Centro de Escalada Limite Vertical
Rua Bambina, 141 (around the back), Botafogo
TEL (21) 2527-4938, 9343-8972. Daily, 5pm – 11pm. Climbing. www.trilhasdorio.com.br/limite

Cia. da Escalada
Rua Valparaíso, 81, apartment 401, Tijuca
TEL (21) 2567-7105, 9393-5060. Daily, 9am – 6pm. Climbing courses. www.guiadaurca.com/companhia

Cruzeiro Táxi-Aéreo
Avenida Ayrton Senna, 2541, hangar 11, Jacarepaguá Airport
TEL (21) 3325-6500, 9808-2828. Mon – Fri, 8am – 5pm. Panoramic helicopter flights. www.cruzeirotaxiaereo.com.br

Escola de Surf Rico de Souza
Avenida Sernambetiba, in front of Posto 4
TEL (21) 2438-1692. Tue and Thu, 9:30am – 11:30am and 3pm – 5pm; Sat and Sun, 9:30am – 11:30am. Surf school. www.ricosurf.com.br

Favela Tour
Estrada das Canoas, 722, block 2, apartments 124 and 125, São Conrado
TEL (21) 3322-2727, 9989-0074, 9772-1133. Daily, 8am – 10pm. *Favela* tours that provide informative context on Brazil's social conditions. www.favelatour.com.br

Frajola Kitesurf School (K-08)
Avenida Sernambetiba (Avenida do Pepê), kiosk 8, in front of 1070, Barra da Tijuca
TEL (21) 2494-4869, 8747-1548. Daily, 8am – 8pm. Kitesurfing school. www.k08.com.br

Helisight
Avenida Borges de Medeiros, no #, City Council Helipad
TEL (21) 2511-2141, 2542-7895. Daily, 9am – 6pm. Panoramic helicopter flights. www.helisight.com.br

Jeep Tour
Rua João Ricardo, 24, São Cristóvão
TEL (21) 2108-5800. Mon – Fri, 10am – 2pm (bookings can be made daily, 7am – 7pm). Jeep tour through Rio's forests.
www.jeeptour.com.br

KS Naish – Kitecenter
Avenida Armando Lombardi, 663, Barra da Tijuca
TEL (21) 2495-7815, 8111-5600, 9935-6247. Daily, 6am – 11pm; Sat, 8am – 2pm and 5pm – 8pm; Sun, 9am – 2pm. Kitesurfing and windsurfing school. www.ks.es.br

Paulinho Dollabela
Praia de Ipanema, in front of Rua Maria Quitéria
TEL (21) 2259-2320, 9814-9702. Daily, 8am – 10am (group classes). Other times are available, if booked in advance. Surfing lessons on Ipanema Beach.

Pedro Müller
Avenida Sernambetiba, between Posto 5 and Posto 6, in front of #4000, Barra da Tijuca
TEL (21) 2428-2271, 8121-8641. Tue and Thu, 7am, 8:30am and 3:30pm; Sat and Sun, 7am, 8:30am and 10am. Surfing lessons. www.escolapedromuller.com.br

Recreio Open Sports
Praia do Recreio, between Posto 11 and Posto 12
TEL (21) 9922-9584. Mon, Wed, Fri, Sat, and Sun, 9am – 11am and 1pm – 5pm. Surfing lessons on Recreio Beach. www.recreioopen.com.br

Rio Hiking
Rua Coelho Neto, 70, flat 401, Laranjeiras
TEL (21) 2552-9204, 9721-0594. Daily, no set times. Hiking, climbing, rafting, ocean kayaking, surfing lessons, hang-gliding, cycling, horse-riding, bird-watching, parachuting. www.riohiking.com.br

Rio Kite Surf School
Avenida Sernambetiba (Avenida do Pepê), kiosk 7, Barra da Tijuca
TEL (21) 9893-6475. Daily, 10am – 9pm. Surfing and kitesurfing lessons, boat ride through the islands, diving, and hiking trails near Pedra da Gávea.

Rio Wind
Avenida Prefeito Dulcídio Cardoso, 400, Barra da Tijuca
TEL (21) 2438-2273, 9106-1045. Windsurfing school. www.riowind.com.br

Skydive Rio
Avenida Ayrton Senna, 2541, Barra da Tijuca (at Jacarepaguá Airport, in front of the tower)
TEL (21) 3410-4599, 7845-7119. Daily, 8:30am – 6pm. Parachuting. www.skydiveriodejaneiro.com

Sottomare
Marina da Glória, store 16, Glória
TEL (21) 2245-9525, 2245-9577. Mon, 2pm – 6pm; Tue – Fri, 9am – 6pm; Sat, 8am – 4pm. Diving with guides in the Cagarras Islands.

Trilharte
Rua Almirante Tamandaré, 77, flat 01, Flamengo
TEL (21) 2225-2426, 2205-0654. Mon – Fri, 9am – 6pm. Photography courses, photographic outings, hikes, abseiling, ocean kayaking. www.trilharte.com.br

Trilhas do Rio
Rua Francisca Sales, 645, Jacarepaguá
TEL (21) 2424-5455, 9207-1360. Mon – Fri, 9am – 6pm. Guided hikes and other adventure activities.
www.trilhasdorio.com.br

PRICES	HOTELS (couple)	$ up to R$150	$$ from R$151 up to R$300	$$$ from R$301 up to R$500	$$$$ above R$500

NITERÓI

AREA CODE 21 **INHABITANTS** 474,046 **DISTANCE** Rio de Janeiro 11 mi **ACCESS** From Rio de Janeiro, over the Rio–Niterói Bridge www.niteroiturismo.com.br

WHERE TO STAY

Tio Sam Hotel & Fitness $$
Rua Álvaro Caetano, 908, Camboinhas
(In front of Rua Cinqüenta e Dois)
TEL (21) 2619-9500 **FAX** (21) 2619-9521
This establishment is part of a sports and leisure complex. There is a play park for children with inflatable toys, a mini go-cart track, and a swimming pool with rides (guests have a discount). The restaurant serves international and Brazilian cuisine. **ACCOMMODATIONS** 83 rooms, with air-conditioning; Internet access (broadband); bathroom; safe; DVD (in the suites); mini bar; Jacuzzi tub (in the suites); hairdryer; telephone; pay TV. **FACILITIES AND SERVICES** bar; parking; restaurant; play park; swimming pool; heated pool; tennis court; convention room; games room; sauna; business center; organized recreational activities for children; pool service; 24-hour room service; transport to the beach and a nearby shopping center on weekends.
www.tiosam.com.br
CREDIT CARDS AmEx; Diners; MasterCard; Visa

WHERE TO EAT

Bar Devassa $
Avenida Quintino Bocaiúva, 185, Praia de São Francisco
(Corner of Rua Aimorés)
TEL (21) 2611-1006. Mon – Thu, 5pm – 1am; Fri, 5pm until the last client leaves; Sat and Sun, noon until the last client leaves
CUISINE Varied. This sea-front bar serves traditionally made *chope* (draft beer). To accompany your beer, try *frigideira de Niterói* (onion cubes, parsley, melted mozzarella, and crispy manioc). From Sunday to Tuesday there is a *rodízio* (all you can eat) of appetizers and savory snacks.
CREDIT CARDS Diners; MasterCard; Visa

Caneco Gelado do Mário $$
Rua Visconde de Uruguai, 288, store 5, Centro
(Between Rua São Pedro and Rua Colonel Gomes Machado)
TEL (21) 2620-6787. Mon – Fri, 9am – 4am; Sat, 9am – 7pm
CUISINE Seafood, fish, Portuguese. Mário, a native of Portugal, has been running this restaurant for 37 years. He offers a traditional menu, and the *moquecas* (seafood stew), which serve three people, deserve special consideration.
CREDIT CARDS Not accepted

Família Paludo $$
Avenida Quintino Bocaiúva, 251, São Francisco
(Between Rua Tapuias and Rua Aimorés)
TEL (21) 2715-3205. Daily, 11:30am until the last customer leaves
CUISINE Varied. Choose between the buffet or à la carte. One of the menu highlights is *polvo paludo* (squid, octopus, shrimp, buttered onions, and broccoli). The affiliated, more sophisticated Paludo Gourmet restaurant is next door.
CREDIT CARDS AmEx; Diners; MasterCard; Visa

Luiz Fogão $$
Rua Tenente Aviador Carneiro Filho (formerly Rua 60), block 57, lot 6, Cafubá-Piratininga
(Between Rua Doutor Heleno de Gregório and Rua Deputado José Luiz Erthal)
TEL (21) 2709-7130, 9101-6714. Mon – Sun, noon – until the last customer leaves
CUISINE Meats; seafood. The owner serves his food on the veranda of his own home. Enjoy such dishes as shrimp risotto and breaded octopus laced with garlic.
CREDIT CARDS Not accepted

Torninha $$
Rua Nóbrega, 199, Icaraí
(Between Rua Maris e Barros and Rua Cinco de Julho)
TEL (21) 2714-2750, 2714-5596. Tue – Thu and Sun, noon – midnight; Fri, noon – 12:30am; Sat, noon – 1am
CUISINE Italian. This tiny restaurant serves such dishes as seafood risotto, with langoustine, fish, octopus, shrimp, and two cheeses: mascarpone and Grana Padano.
CREDIT CARDS Diners, MasterCard, Visa

SERVICES

Neltur – Niterói Empresa de Lazer e Turismo
Estrada Leopoldo Fróes, 773, São Francisco
TEL (21) 2710-2727, 0800-2827755. Daily, 9am – 6pm. Tourist information.

Estação Barcas S/A
Praça Araribóia, 6, Centro
TEL (21) 2620-6756, 4004-3113 (Telebarcas). Regular boats (24 hours) and catamarans (Mon – Fri, 7am – 10am and 5pm – 9pm) to Rio de Janeiro. It takes 20 minutes to cross by regular boat and 8 by catamaran.

Rodoviária Roberto Silveira
Avenida Feliciano Sodré, no #, Centro
TEL (21) 2620-8847. Interstate bus lines, especially to São Paulo, Bahia and Espírito Santo.

Terminal Hidroviário Charitas
Avenida Quintino Bocaiúva, no #, Charitas
TEL (21) 2711-2235. Mon – Fri, 7am – 8pm. Catamarans to Praça Quinze, in Rio, run every 15 minutes. The crossing takes 15 minutes.

Terminal Rodoviário João Goulart
Avenida Visconde do Rio Branco, no #, Centro
TEL (21) 2719-1515, 2719-1673, 2621-0156. Municipal bus lines and buses to Rio and other destinations in the Baixada Fluminense region.

RESTAURANTS $ up to R$25 $$ from R$26 up to R$50 $$$ from R$51 up to R$100 $$$$ above R$100

Useful Information

AREA CODE 21
INHABITANTS 6,136,700
DISTANCES São Paulo 429 km (267 mi), Belo Horizonte 434 km (270 mi), Vitória 521 km (324 mi), Brasília 1,148 km (713 mi)
ROUTES INTO RIO From São Paulo, BR-116 (Rodovia Presidente Dutra). From Belo Horizonte and Brasília, BR-040 (Rodovia Washington Luís). From Vitória, BR-101.
www.rio.rj.gov.br; www.riodejaneiro-turismo.com.br

Tourist Information

Alô Rio
Phone information service in Portuguese, English, and Spanish
TEL (21) 2542-8080, 0800-2850555 (toll-free number)

Centro de Atendimento ao Turista
Avenida Princesa Isabel, 183, Copacabana
TEL (21) 2541-7522, 2542-8004
Mon – Fri, 9am – 6pm

Riotur
Rua da Assembléia, 10, 9th floor, Centro
TEL (21) 2217-7575
Mon – Fri, 9am – 6pm

Aeroporto Internacional do Rio de Janeiro/Galeão (Antônio Carlos Jobim)
Terminal 1, blue sector (international) –
TEL (21) 3398-4077
Terminal 1, green sector (domestic) –
TEL (21) 3398-3034
Terminal 2, international sector – TEL (21) 3398-2245
Terminal 2, domestic sector – TEL (21) 3398-2246

Rodoviária Novo Rio (Bus Station) Information Booth
Arrivals – TEL (21) 3213-1800, extension 397

Airports

The city of Rio de Janeiro has three airports. The **Rio de Janeiro International Airport (Antônio Carlos Jobim)**, on Ilha do Governador, 12 miles from Centro (Downtown Rio), services domestic and international flights. **Santos-Dumont**, in Centro, has flights coming from and going to Congonhas Airport, in São Paulo (air shuttle), and regional flights to the state of Minas Gerais and the Lagos region. **Jacarepaguá Airport**, in Barra da Tijuca, 19 miles from Centro, receives regional and interstate flights. It also offers air taxi, panoramic flights, and parachuting services, as well as flying lessons. Shuttles run between Santos-Dumont Airport and the International Airport every half hour from 5:30am – 1am.

Rio de Janeiro International Airport (Antônio Carlos Jobim)
Avenida Vinte de Janeiro, no #, Ilha do Governador (12 miles from Centro)
TEL (21) 3398-5050
FAX (21) 3393-2288

Santos-Dumont Airport
Praça Senador Salgado Filho, no #, Centro (half a mile from Centro)
TEL (21) 3814-7070/7246
FAX (21) 2533-2218

Jacarepaguá Airport
Avenida Ayrton Senna, 2541, Barra da Tijuca (19 miles from Centro)
TEL (21) 2432-7070
FAX (21) 2432-7040

Airlines

BRA – Avenida Rio Branco, 85, 9th floor, Centro
TEL (21) 3213-3233; www.voebra.com.br

Gol – Avenida Vinte de Janeiro, no #, Ilha do Governador (International Airport)
TEL (21) 3398-5136, 3398-5132, 0300-7892121; www.voegol.com.br

Ocean Air
Rio de Janeiro International Airport – Avenida Vinte de Janeiro, no #, Ilha do Governador
TEL (21) 3398-4648
Santos-Dumont Airport – Praça Senador Salgado Filho, no #, Centro
TEL (21) 3814-7329, 4004-4040, 0300-7898160; www.oceanair.com.br

TAM – Avenida Rio Branco, 242, Centro
TEL (21) 3212-9300, 4002-5700; www.tam.com.br

Varig
Rio de Janeiro International Airport – Avenida Vinte de Janeiro, no #, Ilha do Governador, terminal 2, no tel.
Santos-Dumont Airport – Praça Senador Salgado Filho, no #, Centro
TEL (21) 3814-7318, 4003-7000; www.varig.com.br

Air Taxi Services

Jacarepaguá Airport
Nacional Aerotáxi – TEL (21) 3325-5742; www.natnep.com.br
Riana – TEL (21) 3325-0510, 3325-7929; www.riana.com.br

Santos-Dumont Airport
Aeroleo – TEL (21) 2210-2434; www.aeroleo.com.br
Cruzeiro – TEL (21) 2532-6056; www.cruzeirotaxiaereo.com.br
DS – TEL (21) 3150-3737; www.dsair.com.br
Líder – TEL (21) 2517-7400; www.lideraviacao.com.br

Useful Information

Transportation to and from the City

Gol, the budget airline, provides passengers with a free shuttle service between Rio de Janeiro International Airport and Jacarepaguá Airport. The company Real Auto Ônibus operates an air-conditioned bus service known as the *frescão*. The buses leave Santos-Dumont Airport and go to the International Airport or the Terminal Rodoviário Alvorada (bus station), in Barra da Tijuca. The *frescão* passes through various neighborhoods, following the Linha Vermelha (Red Line) and the Linha Amarela (Yellow Line). In addition to carrying visitors to and from the airports, it can be used to get from one city neighborhood to another, although, on account of the comfort provided by the A/C, the fare is a little higher than it is for standard buses.

Bus Stations

Terminal Rodoviário Alvorada
Municipal lines and buses to the International Airport
Avenida Ayrton Senna, no #, Barra da Tijuca, no tel.

Terminal Rodoviário Américo Fontenelle
Buses to other towns in the Baixada Fluminense region, such as Nova Iguaçu, Magé, and Ana Clara
Rua Barão de São Félix, 165, (Central do Brasil), Centro
TEL (21) 2299-2572

Terminal Rodoviário Mariano Procópio
Buses to municipalities in Greater Rio, such as Nilópolis, Nova Iguaçu, Mesquita, and the Baixada Fluminense region
Praça Mauá, 5, Centro
TEL (21) 2299-2025

Terminal Rodoviário Menezes Cortes
Municipal lines and buses to other towns in the Baixada Fluminense region to the Lagos region, and other nearby cities, such as Teresópolis and Petrópolis
Rua São José, 35, Castelo
TEL (21) 2544-6667

Terminal Rodoviário Novo Rio
Avenida Francisco Bicalho, 1, Santo Cristo
TEL (21) 3213-1800, 2213-3818 (Cruzeiro do Norte), 2263-9471 (Pluma)

Taxis

Most taxis are painted yellow with a blue stripe; taxis companies number the body of their vehicles. Company-run cabs tend to be safer than independent operators, so opt for the former when you have a choice. Major taxi companies include:

TELEBLON – TEL (21) 2512-5547
JB TÁXI – TEL (21) 2178-4000, 2501-3026
TRANSCOOTOUR – TEL (21) 2590-2220, 2590-2300
TRANSCOOPASS – TEL (21) 2560-4888

Metro

Rio has two metro lines, which are integrated with several bus lines. The metro runs from 5am to midnight, Monday through Saturday, and from 7am to 11pm on Sundays and public holidays. The following metro stations offer bus connections.
Information, tel. 0800-5951111.

Line 1
- Siqueira Campos
- Cardeal Arcoverde
- Botafogo
  Flamengo
- Largo do Machado
  Catete
  Glória
- Carioca
  Cinelândia
  Uruguaiana
  Presidente Vargas
  Central
  Praça Onze
- Estácio
  Afonso Pena
- São Francisco Xavier
- Saens Peña

Line 2
- Estácio
  São Cristovão
  Maracanã
  Triagem
  Maria da Graça
- Del Castilho
  Inhaúma
  Engenho da Rainha
  Thomaz Coelho
  Vicente de Carvalho
  Irajá
  Colégio
  Coelho Neto
  Acari/F. Botafogo
  Eng. Rubens Paiva
  Pavuna

Buses and Vans

Buses and vans are both common methods of transport, but they should be avoided in outlying areas for safety reasons. Some shopping centers offer tourists a free shuttle service to and from hotels. There are also air-conditioned *frescão* buses that run along the beachfront every 30 minutes; these charge slightly higher fares than regular buses. Regular buses run daily from 4am to 11pm. Frescão buses run daily from around 5am to around 11:30pm.
Information, tel. 0800-2828664

Boats

Boats are the best way to reach certain locations near the capital, including Niterói, Ribeira, Paquetá, Ilha Grande, Mangaratiba, and Angra dos Reis. They run non-stop, including Saturdays, Sundays, and holidays.
Information, tel. (21) 4004-3113.

Car Rental

To rent a car in Rio, one must be over 21 years of age, show his or her passaport, have had a driver's license for at least two years, and pay with a credit card. To avoid unpleasant surprises, inquire about extra fees, including the cost of car insurance.

Avis
0800-7252847, (11) 2155-2847 (in São Paulo)
International Airport – TEL (21) 3398-5060
Santos-Dumont Airport – TEL (21) 3814-7378
www.avis.com.br

Hertz
0800-7017300, (11) 4336-7300 (in São Paulo)
International Airport – TEL (21) 3398-4421

Santos-Dumont Airport – TEL (21) 2262-0612
www.hertz.com.br

Localiza
0800-9792000
International Airport – TEL (21) 3398-5489
Santos-Dumont Airport – TEL (21) 2220-5455
www.localiza.com.br

Mobility
0800-160525, (11) 5561-7771 (in São Paulo)
www.mobility.com.br

Parking Cards

The streets of Rio de Janeiro have a parking system called *Rio-rotativo*, which allows parking on public thoroughfares, for a fee. Whenever parking, you have to buy a parking card, fill in the time you arrived, and place it on the dashboard where it can be seen by parking inspectors. The cards are sold only by operators in grey vests who circulate through the areas where the *Rio-rotativo* system is in force. These streets are signposted. In most cases, parking must be paid for from 7am to 7pm, Monday to Friday, and on weekends from 7am to 3pm. Cards are available for either two or four hours or the entire day. You can use a single card to park as many times and in as many places as you wish, as long as the card remains valid.
TEL (21) 2539-2022, 2226-5566; www.rio.rj.gov.br/smtr

Restaurants

Some of Rio's traditional restaurants are pretty relaxed and allow customers to enter without a shirt on or even in bathing suits. There are, however, places where this informality will never be allowed. Starting on page 212, we describe the gist of each establishment. Please note that bars and taverns operate on a first-come, first-serve basis. Another common – and paradoxical – fact about Rio is that busy restaurants only accept reservations at times when they are not busy. This being the case, we recommend trying to get to popular restaurants as early as possible at conventional meal times (which go from 1pm – 3pm). Another option is to place your name on the wait list and go for a quick walk. This can be especially rewarding in interesting neighborhoods like Ipanema and Leblon – but don't be gone too long, or you'll lose your place in the queue.

Safety

While it may be among the world's most beautiful cities, Rio is not among its safest. While the *favelas* (shantytowns) are deservedly most notorious, virtually all areas of the city experience their fair share of petty and violent crime. Apart from exercising common sense, here are some suggestions on how to stay safe.
In the streets: Wear informal clothes whenever possible. Avoid flaunting valuables such as expensive jewelry. Be careful about carrying cameras and laptops, and leave them in your hotel whenever practical. Stay clear of poorly lit, deserted streets, especially at night. Keep a firm hold on backpacks and handbags, and wear them across the front of your body if you can. Men should avoid putting wallets in their back pockets, and all travelers should keep important items, such as passports and plane tickets, in concealed pouches underneath their clothing. Split up your money among several different pockets so that you aren't left penniless if a pickpocket strikes.
In the hotel: Keep valuables such as passports and plane tickets in a hotel safe; many hotel rooms have a private safe in each room. Don't allow into your room employees who offer services you haven't requested.
At ATM machines: Look for ATMs located in supermarkets, shopping centers and other busy, well-policed places. Do not accept help from strangers.
In the car: Always drive around with your windows rolled up and doors locked. Don't leave wallets, cell phones, and handbags in plain view. Even in busy areas, avoid sitting in a parked car talking. Don't offer strangers a lift, and don't accept rides from strangers either.
In public transport: Before you get on, set aside the money you need to pay the fare so you don't have to open your wallet in public. Avoid train cars that contain few passengers. In empty buses, sit near the driver. When carrying handbags, backpacks, and briefcases, always try to keep them in front of your body.

Tourist Police

Rio has a police station that specializes in helping foreign tourists. (See **Deat**, below.) For further information, visit the site www.policiacivil.rj.gov.br.

Deat – Delegacia de Atendimento ao Turista (Tourist Police)
Rua Humberto de Campos, 315, Leblon
TEL (21) 3399-7170

Dairj – Military police post at Rio de Janeiro International Airport
Terminal 1, blue sector, 2nd floor
TEL (21) 3398-4150

Health

Rio's high temperatures dictate that travelers take particular care with their health. Sunscreen, light clothes, and plenty of fluids are essential in combating the effects of the intense heat. Minimize exposure to the sun between 10am and 4pm. On hot days, opt for light foods and be aware that not all beachside restaurants are hygienic. For hikes in parks or forested areas, use insect repellent as a precaution against diseases such as dengue fever and yellow fever.

Major Private Hospitals

Hospital Copa D'Or
Rua Figueiredo de Magalhães, 875, Copacabana, TEL (21) 2545-3600
www.copador.com.br

Hospital Barra D'Or
Avenida Ayrton Senna, 2541, Barra da Tijuca, TEL (21) 2430-3600
www.barrador.com.br

USEFUL INFORMATION

Hospital Quinta D'Or
Rua Almirante Baltazar, 435, São Cristóvão, in front of Parque Quinta da Boa Vista, TEL (21) 3461-3600
www.quintador.com.br

Clínica São Vicente
Rua João Borges, 204, Gávea, TEL (21) 2529-4422
www.clinicasaovicente.com.br

Hospital Samaritano
Rua Bambina, 98, Botafogo, TEL (21) 2537-9722
www.hsamaritano.com.br

Major Public Hospitals

Hospital Municipal do Andaraí
Rua Leopoldo, 280, Andaraí, TEL (21) 2575-7000

Hospital Municipal Lourenço Jorge
Avenida Ayrton Senna, 2000, Barra da Tijuca, TEL (21) 3111-4600

Hospital Municipal Sousa Aguiar
Praça da República, 111, Centro, TEL (21) 3111-2732

Hospital Municipal Miguel Couto
Rua Bartolomeu Mitre, 1108 (main entrance), and Rua Mário Ribeiro, 117, Gávea, TEL (21) 3111 3600

Hospital Municipal Paulino Weerneck
Estrada da Cacuia, 745, Ilha do Governador, TEL (21) 3111-7701

Climate

Summer (December to March) days in Rio de Janeiro are sunny, with occasional afternoon showers. The average high temperature is around 35ºC (95ºF) and the average low is 24ºC (75ºF). Temperatures drop in winter (June to September): the average high is around 21ºC (70ºF) and the low is around 15ºC (59ºF).

Local Public Holidays

JANUARY – Rio de Janeiro worships its patron saint, St. Sebastian, on January 20, which is also recognized as the city's birthday

APRIL – Saint George's Day (April 23)

Major Events

JANUARY
New Year's Eve/Copacabana Beach – one of the most famous places in the world to see in the New Year
1st Edition of Fashion Rio (autumn/winter collection) – Rio's main fashion show, at Marina da Glória (exact date varies)

FEBRUARY/MARCH
Carnival (date varies)

MARCH
Volvo Ocean Race/Rio Stopover Mar – The longest ocean regatta, this race covers a course more than 30,000 miles long (date of stopover varies)

MAY
Rio Boat Show – Latin America's largest nautical show (first half of the month)

JUNE
2nd Edition of Fashion Rio (spring/summer collection) – Rio de Janeiro's most important fashion event, at Marina da Glória (date varies)

JULY
Parada do Orgulho GLBT – Gays, lesbians, bisexuals, and transsexuals meet on Avenida Atlântica for the annual gay pride parade (early July; sometimes late June)
Anima Mundi – Festival of Brazilian and international animation films and videos (date varies)

AUGUST
Degusta Rio – An event that brings together chefs, restaurateurs, and bar owners to discuss Brazil's gastronomic culture (date varies)

SEPTEMBER
Bienal do Livro – One of the country's largest book fairs (date varies)
Festival do Rio (International Film Festival) – Feature-length and short films hit screens in several cinemas around town (end of month)

NOVEMBER
Oi Noites Cariocas – Shows by Brazil's major singers and bands, put on over a four-month period on Morro da Urca (November to February, dates vary)

Ticket Sales

Ingresso Rápido – TEL (21) 2169-6000
www.ingressorapido.com.br

Ticketmaster – TEL 0300-7896846
www.ticketmaster.com.br

Ticketronics – TEL (21) 2542-4010
www.ticketronics.net

Emergency Telephone Numbers

Emergency and assistance services have consistent telephone numbers throughout Brazil. Calls to nearly all of the numbers below are free from any public phone.

AMBULANCE – 192
FIRE BRIGADE – 193
DEFESA CIVIL (Civil Defense) – 199
DETRAN (State Traffic Department) – 154
IBAMA (Brazilian Institute for the Environment and Renewable Natural Resources) – 152
CIVIL POLICE – 147
FEDERAL POLICE – 194
MILITARY POLICE – 190
STATE HIGHWAY PATROL – 3399-4857 (this is not a free call from public phones)
FEDERAL HIGHWAY PATROL – 191
PROCON (Consumer Affairs) – 151
VIGILÂNCIA SANITÁRIA (Sanitary Board) – 150

Useful Information

CONSULATES IN RIO DE JANEIRO

ARGENTINA
Tel: (21) 2553-1646

AUSTRIA
Tel: (21) 2102-0020

BELGIUM
Tel: (21) 2543-8558
www.diplobel.org

BOLIVIA
Tel: (21) 2552-5490

BULGARIA
Tel: (21) 2532-3912
www.bulgariario.org.br

CANADA
Tel: (21) 2543-3004
www.canada.org.br

CHILE
Tel: (21) 2552-5349

COSTA RICA
Tel: (21) 2522-8833, 2267-9513

FRANCE
Tel: (21) 3974-6699

GERMANY
Tel: (21) 2554-0004
www.alemanha.org.br/riodejaneiro

ICELAND
Tel: (21) 2285-1795

ITALY
Tel: (21) 2282-1315
www.conrio.org.br

JAPAN
Tel: (21) 3461-9595
www.rio.br.emb-japan.go.jp

MALTA
Tel: (21) 2533-7274

MEXICO
Tel: (21) 3262-3200
www.mexico.org.br

PARAGUAY
Tel: (21) 2553-2294

PORTUGAL
Tel: (21) 2544-2444, 2544-2523
www.consuladorj.org.br

SPAIN
Tel: (21) 2543-3200

SWITZERLAND
Tel: (21) 2221-1867

TURKEY
Tel: (21) 2551-4673, 2553-5716

UKRAINE
Tel: (21) 2542-1704

UNITED KINGDOM
Tel: (21) 2555-9600
www.gra-bretanha.org.br

UNITED STATES
Tel: (21) 2292-7117
www.consuladoseua-rio.org.br

URUGUAY
Tel: (21) 2553-6015, 2553-6030

VENEZUELA
Tel: (21) 2554-6134, 2554-5955
www.consuven.com.br

EMBASSIES IN BRASÍLIA

Algeria
Tel: (61) 3248-4039
Fax: (61) 3248-4691
Angola
www.angola.org.br
Tel: (61) 3248-4489
Fax: (61) 3248-1567
Argentina
www.embarg.org.br
Tel: (61) 3364-7600
Fax: (61) 3364-7666
Australia
www.brazil.embassy.gov.au
Tel: (61) 3226-3111
Fax: (61) 3226-1112
Austria
www.austria.org.br
Tel: (61) 3443-3111
Fax: (61) 3443-5233
Belgium
www.belgica.org.br
Tel: (61) 3443-1133
Fax: (61) 3443-1219
Bolivia
Tel: (61) 3366-3432
Fax: (61) 3366-3136
Bulgaria
Tel: (61) 3223-6193, 3223-9849
Fax: (61) 3323-3285
Cameroon
www.embcameroun.org.br
Tel: (61) 3248-2400
Fax: (61) 3248-0443
Canada
www.dfait-maeci.gc.ca/brazil
Tel: (61) 3424-5400
Fax: (61) 3424-5490
Cape Verde
Tel: (61) 3364-3472

Fax: (61) 3364-4059
Chile
www.eta.com.br/chile
Tel: (61) 2103-5151
Fax: (61) 3322-0714
China
www.embchina.org.br
Tel: (61) 3346-4436
Fax: (61) 3346-3299
Colombia
www.embcol.org.br
Tel: (61) 3226-8997
Fax: (61) 3224-4732
Costa Rica
Tel: (61) 3328-2219/3328-2485
Fax: (61) 3328-2243
Croatia
Tel: (61) 3248-0610
Fax: (61) 3248-1708
Cuba
www.embaixadacuba.org.br
Tel: (61) 3248-4710, 3248-4130
Fax: (61) 3248-6778
Czech Republic
www.mzv.cz/brasilia
Tel: (61) 3242-7785, 3242-7905
Fax: (61) 3242-7833
Democratic Republic of Congo
Tel: (61) 3365-4822, 3365-4823
Fax: (61) 3365-4822
Denmark
Tel: (61) 3445-3443
Fax: (61) 3445-3509
Dominican Republic
Tel: (61) 3248-1405
Fax: (61) 3364-3214
Ecuador
www.embequador.org.br
Tel: (61) 3248-5360

Fax: (61) 3248-5560
Egypt
www.opengate.com.br/embegito
Tel: (61) 3323-8800
Fax: (61) 3323-1039
El Salvador
Tel: (61) 3364-4141
Fax: (61) 3364-2459
Finland
www.finlandia.org.br
Tel: (61) 3443-7151
Fax: (61) 3443-3315
France
www.ambafrance.org.br
Tel: (61) 3312-9100
Fax: (61) 3312-9108
Gabon
Tel: (61) 3248-3536, 3248-3533
Fax: (61) 3248-2241
Germany
www.alemanha.org.br
Tel: (61) 3442-7000
Fax: (61) 3443-7508
Ghana
Tel: (61) 3248-6047, 3248-6049
Fax: (61) 3248-7913
Greece
www.emb-grecia.org.br
Tel: (61) 3443-6573
Fax: (61) 3443-6902
Guatemala
Tel: (61) 3365-1908, 3365-1909
Fax: (61) 3365-1906
Guyana
Tel: (61) 3248-0874
Fax: (61) 3248-0886
Haiti
Tel: (61) 3248-6860, 3248-1337
Fax: (61) 3248-7472

Useful Information

Honduras
Tel: (61) 3366-4082
Fax: (61) 3366-4618
Hungary
www.hungria.org.br
Tel: (61) 3443-0822
Fax: (61) 3443-3434
India
www.indianembassy.org.br
Tel: (61) 3364-4195, 3248-4006
Fax: (61) 3248-7849
Indonesia
www.indonesia-brasil.org.br
Tel: (61) 3443-8800
Fax: (61) 3443-6732
Iran
www.webiran.org.br
Tel: (61) 3242-5733
Fax: (61) 3244-9640
Iraq
Tel: (61) 3346-2822
Fax: (61) 3346-7442
Ireland
Tel: (61) 3248-8800
Fax: (61) 3248-8816
Israel
brasilia.mfa.gov.il
Tel: (61) 2105-0500
Fax: (61) 2105-0555
Italy
www.embitalia.org.br
Tel: (61) 3442-9900
Fax: (61) 3443-1231
Japan
www.japao.org.br
Tel: (61) 3442-4200
Fax: (61) 3242-0738
Jordan
Tel: (61) 3248-5407, 3248-5414
Fax: (61) 3248-1698
Kuwait
www.embaixadadokuwait.org.br
Tel: (61) 3213-2333
Fax: (61) 3248-0969
Lebanon
www.libano.org.br
Tel: (61) 3443-3808
Fax: (61) 3443-8574
Libya
Tel: (61) 3248-6710, 3248-6716
Fax: (61) 3248-0598
Malaysia
Tel: (61) 3248-5008, 3248-6215
Fax: (61) 3248-6307
Malta
Tel: (61) 3272-0402
Fax: (61) 3347-4940
Mexico
www.mexico.org.br
Tel: (61) 3244-1011
Fax: (61) 3244-1755
Morocco
Tel: (61) 3321-4487
Fax: (61) 3321-0745
Mozambique
Tel: (61) 3248-4222, 3248-5319
Fax: (61) 3248-3917
Namibia
Tel: (61) 3248-7621
Fax: (61) 3248-7135
Netherlands
www.embaixada-holanda.org.br
Tel: (61) 3321-4769
Fax: (61) 3321-1518

New Zealand
Tel: (61) 3248-9900
Fax: (61) 3248-9916
Nicaragua
Tel: (61) 3248-1115, 3248-7902
Fax: (61) 3248-1120
Nigeria
Tel: (61) 3226-1717, 3226-1870
Fax: (61) 3226-5192
North Korea
Tel: (61) 3367-1940
Fax: (61) 3367-3177
Norway
www.noruega.org.br
Tel: (61) 3443-8720
Fax: (61) 3443-2942
Pakistan
Tel: (61) 3364-1632
Fax: (61) 3248-0246
Panama
Tel: (61) 3248-7309
Fax: (61) 3248-2834
Paraguay
Tel: (61) 3242-3732
Fax: (61) 3242-4605
Peru
www.embperu.org.br
Tel: (61) 3242-9933, 3242-9435
Fax: (61) 3244-9344
Philippines
Tel: (61) 3224-8694
Fax: (61) 3226-7411
Poland
www.polonia.org.br
Tel: (61) 3212-8000
Fax: (61) 3242-8543
Portugal
www.embaixadadeportugal.org.br
Tel: (61) 3032-9600
Fax: (61) 3032-9642
Romania
www.romenia.org.br
Tel: (61) 3226-0746
Fax: (61) 3226-6629
Russia
www.brazil.mid.ru
Tel: (61) 3223-3094, 3223-4094
Fax: (61) 3226-7319
Saudi Arabia
Tel: (61) 3248-3525, 3248-2201
Fax: (61) 3248-1142
Senegal
Tel: (61) 3223-6110, 3321-5866
Fax: (61) 3322-7822
Serbia and Montenegro
Tel: (61) 3223-7272
Fax: (61) 3223-8462
Slovakia
Tel: (61) 3443-1263
Fax: (61) 3443-1267
South Africa
www.africadosulemb.org.br
Tel: (61) 3312-9500
Fax: (61) 3322-8491
South Korea
www.korea.net
Tel: (61) 3321-2500, 3321-2506
Fax: (61) 3321-2508
Spain
Tel: (61) 3244-2776, 3244-2023, 3244-2145
Fax: (61) 3242-1781

Sri Lanka
Tel:(61) 3248-2701
Fax:(61) 3364-5430
Syria
Tel: (61) 3226-1260, 3226-0970
Fax: (61) 3223-2595
Sudan
www.sudanbrasilia.org
Tel: (61) 3248-4834, 3248-4835
Fax: (61) 3248-4833
Suriname
Tel: (61) 3248-3595, 3248-6706
Fax: (61) 3248-3791
Sweden
Tel: (61) 3442-5200
Fax: (61) 3443-1187
Switzerland
www.eda.admin.ch/brasilia_emb
Tel: (61) 3443-5500
Fax: (61) 3443-5711
Thailand
www.thaiembassy.org/brasilia
Tel: (61) 3224-6943, 3224-6849
Fax: (61) 3223-7502
Trinidad and Tobago
Tel: (61) 3365-1132, 3365-3466
Fax: (61) 3365-1733
Tunisia
Tel: (61) 3248-7277, 3248-7366
Fax: (61) 3248-7355
Turkey
www.turquia.org.br
Tel: (61) 3242-4563
Fax: (61) 3244-4257
Ukraine
Tel: (61) 3365-1457
Fax: (61) 3365- 2127
United Arab Emirates
www.uae.org.br
Tel: (61) 3248-0717, 3248-0591
Fax: (61) 3248-7543
United Kingdom
www.uk.org.br
Tel: (61) 3329-2300
Fax: (61) 3329-2369
United States
www.embaixada-americana.org.br
Tel: (61) 3312-7000
Fax: (61) 3312-7676
Uruguay
www.emburuguai.org.br
Tel: (61) 3322-1200
Fax: (61) 3322-6534
Vatican
Tel: (61) 3223-0794
Fax: (61) 3224-9365
Venezuela
Tel: (61) 3322-1011, 3322-9324
Fax: (61) 3226-5633
Vietnam
Tel: (61) 3364-5876, 3364-0694
Fax: (61) 3364-5836
Zimbabwe
Tel: (61) 3365-4801, 3365-4802
Fax: (61) 3365-4803

Additional information

MINISTRY OF FOREIGN RELATIONS
www.mre.gov.br
Tel: (61) 3411-6161, 3411-6456

Acknowledgments

Alexandre Leonardo Ristoff, André Cintra, André Ribeiro, Antonio Moreira Salles, Beatriz Fonseca Corrêa do Lago, Beatriz Radunsky, Branca Moreira Salles, Bruno Rodrigues, Bruno Trachez do Couto, Carolina Spinola Montenegro, Catarina Malan, Claudia Guerra, Claudia Melli, Claudia Paes Leme, Claudia Witte, Cristiano Mascaro, Dante Calligaris, Demosthenes Madureira de Pinho Neto, Denise Werneck, Eduardo Barros, Egeu Laus, Elisabeth di Cavalcanti Veiga, Fernando Costa Barros, Flávia Martinez Rodrigues, Francisca Izabel Pereira da Silva Teixeira, Gabriel Werneck, Gabriela Einloft, Gustavo Badauí, Henrique Guerreiro, Hiro Kozaka, Jader José de Sant'Anna, Janete Bolite Frant, Kati Almeida Braga, Leonel Kaz, Manoel Damasceno dos Santos, Marcelo Spinola Montenegro, Marcia Paula Migliacci, Marcio Andrade Schettini, Marcos Caetano, Marcos Spinola Montenegro, Maria Cristina Falcão, Maria Helena Carneiro da Cunha, Mariana Hermeto, Martha Vasconcellos, Max Perlingeiro, Paulo Celso Pereira, Paulo Vieira, Pedro Moreira Salles, Pedro Pamplona, Pedro Stephan, Raquel Brandão, Raul Figueiredo, Renata Salgado, Ricardo Furtado, Roberto Carneiro de Mendonça, Rui Alvim, Sergio Bressane, Sílvio Braga, Terezinha Cruz, Thomaz Souto Corrêa, and Tomaz Soares Filho.

We would like to thank the following institutions:

Capivara Editora, Gabinete de Arte Raquel Arnaud, Instituto Moreira Salles, and Videofilmes

Credits

PHOTOGRAPHS

Al Hamdan/F. Bueno, page 52
Antonio Bernardo/Publicity, 133 (rings)
Arquivo Sítio Burle Marx/Iphan, 194
Carlos Moraes/Agência O Dia, 35
Circo Voador Publicity, 55
Copacabana Palace Publicity, 108
Cristiano Mascaro, 20, 23, 28, 30, 31, 32, 33, 34, 38, 43, 50, 56, 62, 72, 76, 158, 200
Cristiano Mascaro/Publicity, 167
Eduardo Alonso/Publicity, 162
Eduardo Costa, 18, 21, 36, 40, 41, 42, 44 (masks), 46, 47, 57, 64, 71, 73, 82, 83, 112, 113, 114, 160, 204 (Comuna do Semente)
Flávia Anselmo/Publicity, 173
Gerson Rego/Publicity, 212
Kadu Niemeyer/Publicity, 177
Luis Calazans Luz/Publicity, 190
Luiz Viola/Publicity, 67 (soup)
Mama Ruisa Publicity, 68, 204
Marcos Sá Correa/Associação de Amigos do Jardim Botânico, 156
Pedro Oswaldo Cruz/Publicity, 39
Planetário Publicity, 166
Renata Mello/Pulsar Imagens, 29
Ricardo Azoury/Pulsar Imagens, 9 (beach promenade), 54, 58, 121, 137, 173, 174, 196, 198
Ricardo Fasanello/Strana/Editora Abril, 8 (Christ statue)
Riotur, 44 (parade), 78, 98
Rudy Huhold/Devassa Publicity, 84
Selmy Yassuda/Publicity, 59
Sérgio Carvalho, 7, 63, 65, 66, 67 (sweets), 70, 74, 80, 85, 88, 90, 93, 94, 95, 96, 102, 103, 106, 109, 110, 115, 117, 123, 126, 128, 129, 130, 131, 132, 133 (Reserva), 134, 135, 136, 140, 144, 146, 147, 148, 149, 150, 159, 161, 165, 178, 180, 181, 183, 185, 188, 189, 192, 193, 204 (Livraria Beco, Tia Palmira)
Severino Silva/Agência O Dia, 122
Solange A. Barreira, 120
Vicente de Mello/Publicity, 154

MAPS AND ILLUSTRATIONS

Alex Silva, 10, 49, 75, 81, 89, 97, 155, 163, 175, 202
Luiz Fernando Martini, 17, 25, 27, 37, 45, 53, 61, 69, 86, 101, 104, 119, 124, 139, 142, 151, 152, 169, 170, 179, 182, 186, 191, 197

Every effort was made to contact the copyright holders for the images reproduced in this guide. For further information, please write to: fotografia@bei.com.br.